# Feminist Perspectives on Land Law



*Feminist Perspectives on Land Law* draws upon the diverse disciplinary fields of law, anthropology and geography to open up perspectives that go beyond the usually narrow topography and cartography of land law. Addressing an unorthodox variety of sites where questions of women's access and rights to land are raised, this book includes chapters on shopping malls, ancient monuments, nature reserves and housing estates, as well as a consideration of the more conventional location for feminist debate in this area, the family home. The gendered analysis of land use and ownership that is pursued here focuses not only on England and Wales, but also reaches out to Botswana, Papua New Guinea and the Muslim world. And it is in exploring such new terrain, in conjunction with old pathways, that *Feminist Perspectives on Land Law* constitutes an original and critical approach to the intersection between law and land.

**Hilary Lim** is a Principal Lecturer at the School of Law, University of East London.

**Anne Bottomley** is a Senior Lecturer in Law at the University of Kent.

# Feminist Perspectives on Land Law

# Feminist Perspectives on Land Law

Edited by Hilary Lim
and Anne Bottomley

Routledge
Taylor & Francis Group
LONDON AND NEW YORK

First published 2007
by Routledge
2 Park Square, Milton Park, Abingdon, Oxon, OX14 4RN

Simultaneously published in the USA and Canada
by Routledge
605 Third Avenue, New York, NY 10017

*Routledge is an imprint of the Taylor & Francis Group, an informa business*



Typeset in Times New Roman by
RefineCatch Limited, Bungay, Suffolk



*British Library Cataloguing in Publication Data*
A catalogue record for this book is available from the British Library

*Library of Congress Cataloging-in-Publication Data*
A catalog record for this book has been requested

ISBN13: 978–1–85941–806–2 (hbk)
ISBN13: 978–0–415–42033–4 (pbk)

# Contents

# Contributors

**Rosemary Auchmuty** is a Reader in Law at the University of Westminster and Associate Director of the AHRC Centre for Law, Gender and Sexuality. She has also contributed to the Feminist Perspectives volumes on Equity and Trusts and on Contract.

**Anne Bottomley** is a senior lecturer at Kent Law School. She has published in the areas of feminist theory, land and trusts and is currently writing a book with Nathan Moore entitled *Cities, Cinema and Control*. She is on the editorial board of *Feminist Legal Studies* and she was overall editor, with Sally Sheldon, of the Feminist Perspectives series for Cavendish Publishing.

**Helen Carr** is a solicitor and a lecturer at Kent Law School who specialises in housing law. Her recent publications include 'Someone to watch over me. Making supported housing work' 14(3) *Social and Legal Studies* 387–408. Forthcoming is 'Labelling: Constructing definitions of anti-social behaviour' in John Flint (ed.) *Housing, Urban Governance and Anti-Social Behaviour: Principles, Policy and Practice* (Bristol: Policy Press) (with Dave Cowan).

**Melissa Demian** received her PhD from the University of Cambridge and is now a Lecturer in Social Anthropology at the University of Kent. She has published on the subjects of child adoption, legal pluralism, dispute settlement and property theory in Papua New Guinea.

**Sue Elworthy** spent her childhood in Africa. She graduated as a mature student from the Faculty of Law, Warwick University. She has written extensively on environmental issues and has taught law in a number of legal institutions. She is presently at King's College London.

**Penny English** is a Senior Lecturer in Law and member of the Centre for Legal Research at Middlesex University. Her research interests concern the intersection of law with archaeology and heritage, which derives from having studied both academic disciplines and having worked in field archaeology for a number of years.

**Margaret Greenfields** is a Senior Lecturer in Social Policy at Buckinghamshire Chilterns University College. She is co-author (with Colin Clark) of a key text – *Here to Stay: The Gypsies and Travellers of Britain* (University of Hertfordshire Press, 2006) (4th edition) – and has worked with diverse Gypsy and Traveller communities for over 20 years. Most recently she has undertaken Needs Assessments with Robert Home and is module leader on the United Kingdom's only Master's level course on Gypsy and Traveller public health.

**Anne Griffiths** is a Professor in the School of Law at the University of Edinburgh University. Her major research interests include anthropology of law, comparative and family law, gender culture and rights. Her recent publications include *Remaking Law in Africa: Transnationalism, Persons and Rights* (Centre for African Studies, University of Edinburgh: 2004), co-edited with J. Murison and K. King and 'Using Ethnography as a Tool in Legal Research: An Anthropological Perspective' in *Theory and Method in Socio-Legal Research* (Oxford: Hart Publishing, 2005), co-edited by R. Banaker and M. Travers.

**Robert Home** is Professor of Land Management, Law School, Anglia Ruskin University. His research interests are in land and management, both in the United Kingdom and Third World, on which he has published widely. His most recent book is on land titling in Africa and the Caribbean. He is currently undertaking Gypsy and Traveller Accommodation Assessments for local authorities in three counties in England.

**Hilary Lim** teaches at the University of East London. Her research interests are in the fields of trusts, child law and Islamic law. She was co-editor with Robert Home of a collection entitled *Demystifying the Mystery of Capital: Land Tenure and Poverty in Africa and the Caribbean* (London: Cavendish Publishing, 2004) with Robert Home.

**Siraj Sait** is a Senior Lecturer in Law at the University of East London and until recently was a Legal Officer, Land Tenure Section, Shelter Branch, UN HABITAT. His expertise lies in the areas of human rights and development, as well as immigration and asylum laws, Islam and the Middle East. He is co-author with Hilary Lim of *Land, Law and Islam* (London: Zed Books, 2006)

**Rosy Thornton** is a Lecturer in Law at the University of Cambridge. She is a Bye Fellow of Emmanuel College, having previously been a Fellow of New Hall. Her areas of research and teaching include property, trusts and housing law. She co-founded Cambridge's Women and Law course in 1991.

**Simone Wong** is a Senior Lecturer in Law at the University of Kent. Her particular research interests include cohabitation and equitable doctrines, especially in relation to home-sharing. Her latest publications include:

'Property regimes for Home-sharers: the Civil Partnership Bill and Some Antipodean Models' (2004) in the *Journal of Social Welfare and Family Law*; 'Trust(s) and Intention in Resolving Disputes over the Shared Home' (2004) in the *Northern Ireland Legal Quarterly*; and 'The Human Rights Act 1998 and the Shared Home: Issues for Cohabitants' (2005) in the *Journal of Social Welfare and Family Law*.

# Acknowledgements

The authors have received considerable support in putting together this collection and would particularly like to thank Beverley Brown for her belief in this project from the outset, as well as all the contributors. Fiona Fairweather, Patricia Berwick and Sharon Senner at the University of East London provided institutional and practical help. We would also like to thank Clarissa Augustinus, Kate Green, Catherine Hobby, Ambreena Manji, Belinda Meteyard, Elizabeth Stokes, Marilyn Strathern and Ann Varley who at various times and different ways gave us encouragement, scholarly advice, insightful comments and friendship. Our thanks also go to everyone at Cavendish Publishing, Glasshouse Press and Routledge, but especially Colin Perrin for his patient understanding over a long period of time. We owe a special debt of gratitude to Chneah, in London, and Nathan and Bea, as well as Dean and Charlie, in Cambridge. Finally, we would like to dedicate this volume to our mothers, Barbara Bottomley and Pat Robinson, who would have appreciated the endeavour.

# Acknowledgements

# Table of cases

# Table of statutes

**Australian legislation**



**Botswanan legislation**

# Table of statutory instruments

Chapter 1

# Feminist perambulations

## Taking the law for a walk in land[1]

*Anne Bottomley and Hilary Lim*

Time and space, the dimensions through which we inhabit our world, are crucial to any attempt to make (give) shape to our sense of the world. Lefebvre (1991, 2004) and de Certeau (1989) write of the need to walk to know a place: not merely the topology of place in terms of tracing a path through the physical environment, but to become sensitive to the time and rhythm of place, constitutive of, as well as constituted by, the 'everyday lives' (Lefebvre 1971) of people.[2] This deeper geography of place, a fleshy map of the many intersections between the physical environment and the inhabitation of it, grounded and embodied in the everyday movement of people, is the primary impetus for our 'feminist perambulation',[3] for taking 'the law' for a walk 'in land': an expression through which we attempt an articulation of our concern, as feminists working in the subject area named 'land law', to re-embed 'land law' into the 'everyday', the 'space that claws and gnaws at us' (Foucault 1986: 23). As Blomley (1994: 76) describes: 'the essence of law is always understood as disembodied rather than formed in material and historical conditions' and for Berman also (1983) this 'dis-embedding' has characterised the traditions of legal scholarship. Thus to 'take the law for a walk' back into the everyday of land is the focus of both this chapter and our collection.

But two caveats have to be entered even at this stage of introducing our perambulation. First, this is not intended as a walk around 'everyday life' which then moves into a critique of the extent to which 'law' adequately, or not, meets the needs and expectations of 'ordinary people' (especially, but by no means exclusively, women), important though this has been to feminist work. Such a form of walking presumes a 'reality' to material conditions and pursues a form of legal critique which can do no more than require of law that it meets the needs exposed from an examination of that 'reality'. This form of walking in the everyday makes too many presumptions of the relationship between 'law' and its 'context', in which law is portrayed as little more than a tool to meet social needs, rather than being constitutive, not only of those conditions, but also of the ways in which we perceive of, and analyse, them. Therefore we must guard against any presumption of the kind of dualism encountered in critiques founded on a representation/reality approach. Second, we are interested in a form of walking which allows us to open (our) perspective beyond 'law' as it maps the terrain of 'everyday lives', by bringing into our vision acts of 'the mappings of law', specifically its scholarly depiction as 'Land Law'.[4] In this way we are able to consider the extent to which these acts of mapping construct and restrict our potential for walking.

Feminist geographers have been at the forefront of moving into explorations of terrain beyond the orthodox topography of their subject. Rose (1993), for instance, (drawing from Bondi and Domosh 1992), sought a move away from the stance of geographers as 'detached explorers', with their distant, disembodied envisioning of the world, which renders unseen or unimportant 'women and everyday spaces' (the title of her second chapter). Although it may satisfy institutional criteria and institutional imperatives of what is held to be good geographic scholarship, this approach (necessarily) fails to provide maps which allow for a more nuanced and detailed account of everyday life or which would (again necessarily) bring onto the map the figure of the 'explorer' to disrupt his privileged construction as external to, removed from, the process of constructing the 'object of study'. Rose not only challenges the 'gaze' of the 'scholar/explorer' (which she links to masculinist pleasures), but also questions the extent to which this configuration of a perspective from the 'outside' and 'above' is actually able to 'see', let alone 'encounter', in terms of a 'deeper' or 'embodied' geography.

An 'embodied geography' insists upon the need to return to the physicality of place, and 'people' in it within the dimensions of time as well as (and therefore) space. It also insists upon the need to recognise that any interpretive act, any act of mapping, requires examination in and of itself. In the traditional mapping practices of legal scholarship, as we shall examine later, 'distance' and 'height' is manifested in ever increasing abstractions which remove the 'scholar/explorer' even from the practices of law itself, let alone its impacts on the messiness of 'everyday lives' (Bottomley 1996, Lim 1996). An 'embodied geography' of our terrain therefore requires that we try to break through the constraints of traditional acts of mapping which presume to define our 'object of study' and place us as no more and no less than the distanced 'scholar/explorer'. In this sense, there is a doubled effect: not only do we seek to re-embed law in the everyday, but also ourselves. Hence to take the law for a walk is, at the same time being, ourselves, taken for a walk. As Klee (quoted in Kudielka 2002: 53) wrote of being taken for a walk by the line he drew, as the line meandered over the page and opened up new possibilities to him, so our walking of law is not a form of walking in direct lines towards things we can already see, but rather a perambulation through which, within which, we are open to new encounters. This form of walking is an embodied process of seeking to think differently rather than being caught within the sediments of the past. We hope to create a process through which we may more freely explore the potential for alternative acts of mapping, which are rather more informative and malleable in terms of encountering the 'everyday' of our present, and our potential for futures.

## To begin, modestly and with lightness of foot

de Souza Santos (1987) pointed out the extent to which the process of (orthodox) cartography distorts 'reality' on the ground. Maps are projections which filter out those details which are determined to be unimportant for technical reasons, such as the requirement to be flat and the need for scale. They are also inscribed with the ideology of the cartographer. For de Souza Santos 'the relations law entertains with social reality are similar to those between maps and social reality'. He continues: 'Indeed laws are maps; written laws are cartographic maps; customary informal laws are mental maps' (1987: 282), with striking resemblances between law's distortions and processes of projection, to those carried out in this form of cartography. de Souza Santos points to colonial and post-colonial practices which affect cartographic constructions, of which the gross deflation of the whole size of the African continent in maps produced under British imperialism is an obvious example. Similar questions are raised about law: What practices did/do 'we', from a western perspective, deploy in deciding what would be/is recognised as law? What violence was/is done to societies and communities upon which western-style law was/is imposed, or whose legal regimes were/are reinterpreted through western legal concepts and techniques? Such questioning does enable a focus on the characteristics of law 'as we know it', as well as re-opening complex questions concerning the relations between legal and socio-cultural systems. It begins to open the way for walking with a fresh lightness of foot and a readiness to act on the moment in choosing our way.

Defining through law, access to, and control over, property, especially 'land' as a fundamental economic resource, has been, and is, a contested site of particular significance. In recent years there have been attempts by indigenous peoples to 'reclaim' territory, with all the difficulties of representing and protecting use rights (often held collectively) through the vector of western law (Belgrave 2007). Attempts to impose 'rational' systematised property relations upon land, introducing cadastral and land titling systems, with the aim of liberating its economic potential to generate capital, highlights the privileging in western law of individuated, private property holding focused on 'ownership' and formal legal systems to encourage land markets (de Soto 2001). Through the related patterns of economic and legal globalisation, locally differentiated but increasingly closely enmeshed, 'land' and 'law' as 'Land Law' is presented as transcending juridical boundaries. These patterns require that we very carefully delineate the juridical map within which we operate or from which we move.

Bringing into account post-colonial struggles over land and law is an important element in destabilising westernised presumptions about both the heritage and the future(s) of Land Law. We mean this in two ways: not only are we challenged to think more carefully about 'maps' which presume the benefits of westernised Land Law systems, especially when they are presented as the necessary culmination of 'development', but also that such work enables us to interrogate our own heritage and the constraints which have been imposed upon us by the prevalent hegemony of the 'ownership model' and private property (Blomley 2004). In fact, we could think of such a 'return' to an examination of our own condition as a necessary 'obligation' placed upon us by acts of mapping which refuse an encounter with the 'maker of the map'. As so well argued by Dewsbury and Thrift (2005: 101), this form of travel is not about the 'importing of (arti)fact, it is not one that charts places. Rather it presents . . . encounters' and in this 'foreignness subjects us; it makes subjects out of us through the way in which we counter-actualise the encounters we have with the other, the strange, the unique and the elsewhere and the not known. In this space we experience without interpreting, thus we experiment, moulding what we did know with that which is hitherto unknown to us.' In Strathern's words (1988: 16), when writing about the uses of ethnography as a tool in research: 'the intention is not an ontological statement to the effect that there exists a type of social life based on premises in an inverse relation to our own. Rather, it is to utilize the language which belongs to our own in order to create a contrast internal to it.'

At the same time we must seek to guard against becoming intellectual nomads, taking seriously the critique that movement can be sometimes no more than 'slipperiness', 'a flight *from* philosophical responsibility rather than a flight toward *anywhere*' (Dorn 1998: 185). Therefore we construct for ourselves two 'compass points' to keep ourselves sufficiently grounded and with some direction. First, we aim to keep contact with a material topography, the land, on which our travelling takes place. Again, to repeat, it is not that we offer 'land' as an unmediated 'real', but rather that it gives us a sufficient 'material grounding' for walking. Second, our feminism continues to require of us that we address the materiality of women's condition: in this case in relation to the resource of land. Again, this is no more than a sufficient 'material grounding', but it is one that gives us a sense of purpose and direction, a place from which we can begin to walk. (When in doubt, sidestep, even cultivate some elusiveness, guard always against escape into pure metaphor or worse colonialist and post-colonialist myths of nomadism.)

Both this travelling and a 'return' must be undertaken modestly. The theorists with which we work, and our own feminist practices, insist upon 'walking' as a series of small incursions into the terrain, from which we might be able to draw lines, explore intersections between these lines, realise that some lines turn back on themselves or follow paths already well trodden. To walk is to look up from the path and glimpse things we did not expect, pause for a moment's reflection to catch up with the present moment, receptive to beginnings in movement all around, to recall half-remembered old trails, see horizons open and mirages fade, with endings and beginnings, chaos and order, endlessly present. In other words, we have to take a certain level of risk, walking without the certainty of 'sticking to' established paths on established maps, even sometimes cherishing and passing through derelict spaces (Massumi 1992: 103–4). Such incursions are acts which disturb, disrupt and unsettle rather than mimic heroic feats of exploration, seeking the revelation of entire, newly discovered, terrains. When Daniels (1993: 8) writes in his work on landscape, that his 'intention is not iconoclastic, to smash the aesthetic surface of landscape images, to describe some deeper, more authentic world of social relations', but rather to 'render their meanings more mutable and ambiguous' and to 'emphasise fluency rather than fixity', he could also have been describing our intentions for this project.

Therefore whilst writers such as de Souza Santos graphically and usefully describe the 'distortions' of imposing westernised maps, including legal ones, onto other territories, we need to be clear, following Daniels, this is not to suggest that, as a general proposition, our task is to create maps which are more faithful to 'reality'. We have to guard against any suggestion that maps are no more than representations of 'a real-world beyond map', to be judged by their congruency with 'the real'. The question is the extent to which certain forms of mapping constitute forms of 'reality' and enable or inhibit our ability to envision the fuller, complex messy plenitude of our 'everyday lives'. Because no form of mapping can be finally complete – in the things that slip and seep through, that do not fit and insist upon becoming visible, we operate often, and necessarily so, as if there is a 'real' behind the map. The danger lies in envisioning this 'real' as an all-encompassing, absolute, complete and fully formed landscape simply waiting to be revealed (Pottage 2001). In this sense, rather than 'distorting', maps push and pull 'reality' into certain shapes and forms. We can share with Rose and de Souza Santos a critique of the effects of orthodox cartographies, and seek, with Deleuze and Guatarri (1998) different forms of mapping beyond 'mere tracing'. However, we do not do this in order to better represent a 'reality' but to be able to open ourselves to the new, the unexpected and the disruptive, to the plural potentials of our many 'realities'.

The motif of walking is a statement of engagement with cartography itself which can begin to open up terrain. Our perambulation, our form of wandering, is therefore one of 'walking purposefully' – it is an exploration which seeks other ways of encountering and imagining our world and our potentials. Our feminism offers a starting point. We can begin by looking for the fleeting appearances of the figure of W/woman (or women), sometimes found in places we would not expect to encounter her. From these moments of visibility we can begin to consider what might be drawn from these encounters in terms of, for instance, parallel lines or intersections of similarity. Our 'modest engagement' through walking does not presume to use an abstract map of gender relations, but rather seeks to tease out the relevance, or even the possibility, of such a map. We expect, as a result of our walking, to 'know more' of the constellation of conditions which impact on women's access to the resource of 'land'. But this form of mapping is not for making generalised statements about 'the condition of women', or seeking 'causes' and 'origins'. It is not about finding answers and insisting on the 'right' programmes for reform. It does no more than raise questions, possibilities and potentials. Refusing the comforts of the old maps, which have so beguiled and constrained us, involves a modest subversive exploration motivated by the hope of, the need for, opportunities for new encounters.

## The collection, this chapter

When we first (many years ago) considered the possibility of this collection, we had to consider our terms of reference. Should this be a collection about 'land' or 'property'? Should we refrain from reproducing such a distinction derived from our legal tradition which, in the 'everyday', is perhaps not so sharply 'lived' as it is 'understood' by legal scholars? Would the extraction of 'land' from a wider mesh of property relations be to lose its 'place' within 'everyday lives'? However, the distinction has the merit of delineating certain 'forms' of property: those defined as 'land' and those sets of legal relations which are not 'land' *per se* but touch it so closely that we can think of them as 'part' of 'the law relating to land'. As we shall see later this is by no means an adequate or settled account of the vexed question of exactly what 'land law' is, but it serves for now to differentiate 'land law' from a more generalised account of 'property' in law.

'Property' does not, within our legal tradition, hold together as a legal construct.[5] It is no more than a term for an amalgam of rules which coalesce around certain types of objects or activities which gain some focus and status from the use, or importation, of a 'property' label (Murphy *et al.* 2004). It offers, in fact, a rather interesting series of examples of finding routes by which to assert and defend claims over use, exploitation of, and economic returns from, objects or activities which, within our cultural traditions and political heritage, are given greatest strength if they can be thought and presented as 'property rights'. This is essentially pragmatic, but it is rendered problematic when it is called to account with a demand for a definition 'of' property in law. Within our scholastic tradition, defining a subject area such as 'property law' is achieved through a process of identifying a 'core principle' which stabilises and legitimates the area of law as an internally coherent and externally differentiated site. However, as Worthington (2000: 655) laments in her casebook on personal property:

> At the end of all the readings in this book it is necessary to ask what is really meant by the word property? Is it simply a label which the law attaches to achieve a desired end? Is it a word which describes a unified concept, or does it have different meanings in different contexts?

Having introduced a selection of reading exploring these issues, she goes on to say that 'attempts to find positive answers tend to add uncertainty rather than remove it'. Gray (1991: 252) argued that 'few other legal notions operate such gross or systematic deception' as property, which he described as 'a vacant concept . . . oddly enough rather like thin air'. However, to refrain from this pursuit would be to accept that there is nothing more to the object of study than a collection of rules, lacking the internal coherence and carefully defined boundaries that a 'core principle' would guarantee. Even worse, the object of study, on close inspection, might be revealed as uneven and messy, marked by pragmatic compromises forged from struggle and opportunistic use of law for an outcome, rather than the smooth and comfortable application of established principles to new situations. The multiple operations of random forces do not match the expected reflection of the law in the coherent and rational Empire of the Same.

Gray later expressed eloquently the thwarted desire from within the scholastic tradition to 'find' and capture property, beyond and behind the law, in other places such as philosophy, as just as surely 'the pursuit of an illusion'. He famously wrote:

> With private property, as with so many illusions, we are easily beguiled into the error of fantastic projection upon the beautiful, artless object we think we see. We are seduced into believing that we have found an objective reality which embodies our intuitions and needs. But then, just as the notion seems reassuringly three-dimensional, the phantom figure dances way through our fingers and dissolves into a formless void.
>
> (Gray 1991: 252)

We could, of course, through an examination of the many appearances in law of a figure named property, or perhaps more correctly the many tracings inscribing 'property' onto sets of practices, pursue an investigation into the strength of the seductive call (the 'siren call', to echo Smart 1989: 25) of the illusion. We might even begin to open up to examination the importance of the very elusiveness of the figure: in not only keeping open a pursuit which keeps property scholars engaged in such a compelling search, but at the very same time provides the all important shadow (the seeming depth) to what might otherwise be revealed as a far too pragmatic intersection of forces. Rather than lamenting that absent presence, we should turn not to examine the 'failure' of the positivist promise of an essence but rather directly engage with the power, the affect, such a pursuit of such a promise has had.

The absence of a 'magnetic core' in law elicits a shift in the search for a 'grounding principle' in 'law' into that grey borderland where 'jurisprudence' and 'philosophy' meet. Here there are quick turns, towards politico-philosophical justifications for the ownership of private property (primarily Locke 1964) or towards explanations of the inter-relationship between 'object' and 'subject', that is 'what' can be owned and 'who' can own (primarily Hegel 1975), to try and ground 'property relations'. Together these trajectories have proven to have such force in constructing our 'idea' of property that they seem unassailable. It is as if the domain they have made possible has allowed the idea of property to come into being. Indeed, when placed within the context of a lineal pattern of development 'into' this fully formed 'property idea' (as in the export of it to developing countries), the power of the idea draws not only upon a form of 'naturalisation' (it 'seems' so obvious that this is what property is about) but also upon the presumption that this is the most sophisticated form of property thinking, enabling the necessary development of commodification and market economies. Thus 'property' as constituted within this configuration trumps all other possible ways of thinking about property. 'Property' becomes constrained into a pattern of private ownership and exchange. Within this pattern, property is presumed to carry the characteristic of 'absolute dominium': the ability to control and alienate at will being the imprimatur of 'ownership'. And yet, whether this is sustainable as a philosophical trope or not, we know that it is not, has not and cannot be sustained in law (Gordon 1996, Gray and Gray 1998, Pottage 1994, 1995, 1998).

Further, although a concentration on the ownership of private property has certainly had the effect of suppressing other forms of holding and using land, both of a collective nature and in terms of recognising use value, it has not been able to completely eradicate either the memory and practices of, or demands for, other 'property practices' (Blomley 2004, Gray and Gray 1998, Rose 1994). The major constraint on recognising and thinking through other 'property practices' has come about, we would argue, not so much because of 'law' but because of the forging of a link between 'law' and a particular pattern of politico-philosophical thinking. To break this chain, or at least to weaken it, would enable a consideration of potentials within law.

Yet so much 'theory work' on 'property' remains caught within, and continues to invest in, this paradigm as if axiomatic rather than open to critique. Thus such feminist work as that of Radin (1993, 1996) continues to constrain itself within the trope of 'ownership' as a strategy for empowerment, without considering the potential of alternative 'property practices'. Whilst Radin argues that this is no more than a strategic move addressed to finding a place within the dominant paradigm of ownership, she necessarily reinforces the idea that it is, in reality, the only, or best, form of using 'property thinking'. This is also true of the seeming intransigence of the object/subject distinction – which continues to try and confine property practices into a duality which, again, draws strength from the linkage made between specific patterns within philosophical thinking and 'law'. The potential made visible by a de-coupling movement is lost. As Pottage (2004) argues so forcefully, if the operation of such a duality was ever actually possible in law, sustaining it now is certainly impossible as we, and the law, engage with such issues as 'body parts' and genetic material. Yet, adherence to the presumed operation of the object/

subject duality still marks, and inhibits, much contemporary scholarship, including feminist work (Davies and Naffine, 2001: 201). Thus most 'property theory' manifested in the contemporary academy seems, to us, to remain overburdened by, and layered into, restrictive philosophical mapping practices. Rarely are the conventions of the 'private ownership model' or the distinction between object/subject challenged. 'Law' is read as mapped from and within these tropes, despite the difficulties of maintaining them and without confronting, recognising, the limits this places upon our thinking and therefore upon a fuller engagement with emerging or potential 'property practices' in law (Pottage 2004).

If, on the one hand, 'property' in law offers no definitional core and, on the other hand, when linked with 'property theory', settles like sediment into a restrictive account of ownership of objects, then we do not find it useful, for our purposes here, to pursue this figure of property. It is rather as if we are placed at a cross roads and offered either a pathway which will link places through little more than a similar term and over thin ground, or a pathway which is (already) signposted back to the past with little prospect of a new view. We recognise that we could try and bend these pathways, crossing between and through them, rather than following the well trodden paths. In doing so (especially helped by the maps of scholars who have already refused to be constrained to the paths), we could seek to examine the many 'whys' and 'hows' and 'with what effects' the utilisation of the 'property label' has in law through the refusal of either a map which seeks essence and 'core' as its defining feature, or a map which continues to deploy the symmetries of a landscape of theory divided into public/private, object/subject and so on and on. But that would have been a different project and one which would have cost us the loss of a focus on 'land'.

However, we could argue, that such a spotlight on 'land' is not merely a turning away from a broader investigation of 'property', but rather provides an alternative form of engagement with 'property' by insisting on a strategy of embodiment and embedding. 'Property', in this account, needs to be examined through micro-strategies focused on specific sites and the constellation of practices within those sites. 'Land' is such a site, through which we can encounter the many ways in which the figure of property is given shape and form. In the everyday, the practices of property, within a set of sites linked through no more and no less than an idea of 'land use' in its many variables, we can begin to re-engage with 'property' not as an elusive lady but rather as what we have made, or could make, of 'her' in all her many, plural, aspects. Thus a different form of mapping, refusing mere tracings, constructed through a particular form of walking, in law, is our attempt to rethink/re-engage with that slippery terrain formed somewhere between, and inside of, land and law and property.

So – we begin with land and law. From that configuration we permit a combination of choice and chance to guide us to the figure of W/woman in different land/law scenarios and our perambulation within and through this collection has begun. We will visit a number of sites, each with a different guide, and from these outings we might start to sketch a map of parallel lines and intersections.

When we received the chapters for the collection, we found, teased out from them, patterns and repeating themes which by their persistent presence intrigue us. It becomes clear from these chapters that women's access to property/land is predicated upon, and mediated through, a complex pattern of socio-economic factors in which familial relations remain central. Further, it is more often the use value of property/land rather than ownership claims which are significant. And, as we track through our different encounters, we find significant gender issues beyond the well trodden site of the home which require that we, again, refuse any simple division between public and private law. However, we have chosen not to reflect upon these patterns in this chapter. To follow the common practice of outlining the chapters in an introduction and drawing out from them our own 'readings' of them, would be to constrain our own methodology of walking maps into existence. Not only does leaving open any mapping exercise at this stage most appropriately represent our own encounter with the material, we hope also that it will more readily allow the reader to develop their own engagement with the text(s). To borrow from Nast and Pile (1998: 15) 'like pick up sticks, many lines could be chosen, juxtaposed, or heaped upon one another'. Our role then, in this chapter, is not to provide an introduction which might be to fore-call or foreclose these potential encounters with a route map. It is rather to explore why it is that an orthodox map of Land Law would place many of these sites 'off map', dangerous places and experience very great difficulty in including them within the traditional mapping exercise. In this sense we are willing to say, with Rose (1993), that seeking the figure of W/woman becomes an exercise in gendering the orthodoxies of our subject as masculinist, in that the mapping practices they uphold are inimical to the feminist project of a more inclusive, open, scholarship which can address potentials for futures rather than constantly re-inscribing the past.[6]

## The cartography of Land Law

We turn then to examining our own heritage: the cartography of Land Law as it appears in the academy, sustained by a plethora of textbooks of ever-increasing thickness and weight, articles and journals, practised in the handing down of a tradition from one generation to the next, through Land Law courses which are compulsory for every student of law in this country.[7] These courses derived their origin, primarily, from a concern to address client-need for future practitioners and thus concentrate on those aspects of the market in land which we associate with private property ownership and conveyance. However, attempts to transmute them into truly scholastic enterprises worthy of study in universities, insisted that a study of such practices could only be accomplished by setting them within a frame of 'Land Law' which underpinned the pragmatic practicalities of the conveyancing process. This was accomplished through a doubled effect of presenting 'law' as a set of rational and coherently established principles, which had emerged over a long period of time. Thus at one and the same time Land Law was given legitimacy derived from long duration, but was taken out of a time frame by a focus on the establishment, with the help of legal scholarship, of an internally coherent doctrinal map. Land Law came into being within the academy. Torn from its origins in the dimensions of space and time, it became embedded into a set of scholastic practices which, whilst seemingly predicated within space and time, was actually concerned with leaving both behind in order to establish a 'place' within the academy (Bottomley 1996, Lim 1996).

The heritage of these scholastic forms derives, at least in part, from an era when academic law struggled to establish its legitimacy, in the latter half of the nineteenth century. Sugarman (1991) has documented how legal scholars laid claim to a 'special body of expertise'. They emphasised that while law may appear disorderly, it is in fact cohesive due to its grounding 'upon relatively few general principles' which the scholar 'was in a unique position to tease out' (Sugarman 1991: 38). The most obvious product of the 'naming and claiming' being the textbooks of the 'core law' subjects, with their 'celebration of law as general principles', 'organised in numbered paragraphs or as codes subdivided into numbered rules' (Sugarman 1991: 39). These same forms were (super)imposed as part of the colonial encounter, with the codification of legal norms, such as those of Islamic law, both by and for imperial officials and as an 'imperial archive', into the medium of a familiar text (Lim 2001). The image of law evoked by these scholarly forms is that of 'a proudly erect tree' (Massumi 1988: xii), with its branches regularly pruned and its foliage carefully clipped by the trained gardener.

Contemporary scholars true to this heritage, continue to try and display the integrity of their chosen subject area, to produce the textbooks and to rationalise their area of work into discrete areas around 'core characteristics'. Here an interesting elision takes form. These 'core characteristics' are those which, the reader is told, are 'present' in the law, yet to maintain them often requires acts of separation and suppression. These acts serve to maintain the illusion that the textbook is no more than a record of the law and that the law is capable of being rendered into such discrete patterns. Take the simple example of easements, rights held by a property owner over another's land, for instance a right of way. These rights are defined, now by statute, as 'land' (we shall return to this later) sutured to the ownership of the property and passing with it on sale. The classical rendition of the characteristics of an easement (that is 'when' a practice can be recognised and enforced as embodying this form) are cited in the textbooks of Land Law as derived from *Re Ellenborough Park* [1956] Ch 131. However, a reading of the case reveals that bringing these attributes into a definitive list was the action of a textbook writer, Cheshire, although given legal authority in the judgment.

Why turn to Cheshire and not earlier case law to extrapolate the decision? Pressing the case further reveals that previous case law was ambiguous, reflecting as it did pragmatic and plural conveyancing practices in which rights were inscribed in legal documents without sharply delineating the 'character' of the right. Cheshire, who took a major part in the design for codification of land law in the 1920s, was firmly implicated in 'modernising' land law, which required an exercise in precision, a level of certainty about 'which' legal form was being brought into land and what particular 'drawer' it would occupy in the statutory chest. These patterns of clarification and formalisation can be viewed as no more than what was required for the better functioning of an emergent market in land: but the important point here is the process by which the 'core characteristics' became naturalised: from textbook into law and then back into 'text of law'.

The mutual roles of judge and academic in mapping a level of coherence and certainty onto the plural practices of the practitioner may certainly serve to enhance and sustain the conveyancer's role. However, the conveyancer will continue to respond pragmatically, selecting and deploying legal forms as appropriate for a client's needs, sometimes creating new blends when no suitable device is available. This is particularly the case in relation to easements understood as only one form of establishing rights and responsibilities between neighbouring land owners. In practice, the inter-relationship between 'easements' and 'covenants', which builds and sustains a network of obligations, requires that we move between and often through them: blending and bending them to our purpose. But their distinctive origins and 'core' (one is 'land', the other no more than a 'contract in land'), and the consequent differences required for the construction and implementation of them, still require that they are presented as 'separate' species in their own chapters of the text.

Cheshire's role in describing the characteristics of easements became the starting point for a section of the map of Land Law. Not only were the pragmatic issues of the conveyancer 'lost in the middle', but also as far as possible each entity is rendered coherent to itself, with the focus on the characteristics of each legal mode rather than its effects. Descriptions of 'characteristics' quickly become acts of definition and more interconnected accounts of the ways in which seemingly disparate parts are mutually constitutive are excluded. An examination of how cases deal with and develop the doctrinal fabric becomes an exercise in the extent to which they build upon, ignore or subvert 'core principles'. This internal stabilisation of the subject area through the effect of classification also operates to detract from the porous nature of the subject boundaries, mapping an assertion of coherence onto much more complex phenomena.

One instance in this area being the call for an end to what many now see as the unwieldy, and no longer useful, distinction between easements and covenants in land and their replacement with an integrated 'land obligation'. There are examples of textbook writers who, at least on a surface reading, bring together easements and covenants, seeking to address an 'irrational' division. Sparkes (2003: 713), who perhaps more than any other textbook writer celebrates what he regards as the ever increasing rationality of Land Law, describes the lack of development of land obligations as 'an astounding defect in our law' and as being 'a category of rights needed to regulate the legal relationship of neighbours'. At one level this is simply interesting in that it breaks through not only the presumed differences of 'core', but also calls into account the distinction between 'easement' constructed as 'land' and 'covenant' constructed as a 'contract in land'. Sparkes is, in effect, refusing to maintain a slippage between 'land' and 'contracts', which reveals the porous nature of the subject as historically constituted. Land Law is not a hermetically sealed site. It is dependent upon inter-relations with other legal forms and practices: most obviously contracts and equity. However, the appeal to the rationality of the need for a more cohesive category to 'regulate the legal relationships between neighbours', is at the same time an assertion of the need for a more modern form of internally coherent Land Law. This insists that easements and covenants are merged into one account within one site, thus enabling a continued movement towards an ever more complete and contained rationality. What is lost in this 'flattening out' of differences is a more difficult, but perhaps more fruitful, exploration that confronts not only their inter-relationship but also what those differences reveal of the construction of Land Law.

## On boundaries

As Waddams (2003) has so ably and concisely argued, attempts to divide private law into watertight compartments is always a fraught act of mapping which requires heroic feats of delving down from the abstract heights to find and preserve an underpinning 'core principle'. One problem for the academic seeking to maintain the overarching coherence of Land Law is the need to establish its basic 'legal principle' capable of being contrasted and compared with those in other areas of law. Yet Land Law hangs together as no more than a set of practices associated with the holding and use of land from which it is difficult to extrapolate basic principles. We can turn to statutory definitions of 'land'[8] as forming one focus but it is all too obvious that the borders between 'land' as a legal construct and the practices associated with it cross subject boundaries. The simple fact is that the subject area is a hybrid; born out of contracts and equity, but continually destabilised by both as they remain directly implicated in land law's development (much more than mere traces of history). Further, the subject area is increasingly governed by statutory forms constituted within their own imperatives (especially in relation to registration), which again detracts from a jurisprudential grounding for the subject area (Pottage 1995).

It requires very partial accounts of history to suppress those difficult times when either the absence of 'a core', or the presence of a mixed jurisprudence, is all too obvious (Gordon 1996, Waddams 2003). Just as it requires keeping 'registration' on the margins, as if no more than a gloss on an established text, rather than engaging with the radical redrawing of 'land law' through new sets of requirements. Sometimes a destabilising paradox cannot be easily slipped into the text as 'belonging' to one area or another. However, such a threat to the coherent and boundaried nature of the subject must be dealt with, the tree pruned and the fortress defended. A recent example of this, which will be examined more closely later in this chapter, is the outcry from some academics in response to the House of Lords judgment in *Oxley v Hiscock* [2004] EWCA Civ 546; [2004] 3 All ER 703. It is claimed that that an error was made in treating implied trusts (as within the domain of property) and proprietary estoppel (as within the terrain of equitable remedies) as if they were congruent with one another, or even worse, the same thing (Thompson 2004, Hudson 2005). Academics sometimes police the integrity of the area so industriously that they are in a position to tell a judge that he is, in principle, wrong (Thompson 2004). The 'scholar/explorer' does not merely describe, but also prescribes. Not only do such acts of mapping suppress and render invisible crucial 'unevenness' or 'breaches in the wall', they also inhibit our potential understandings of developments in law.

Such cartographies are connected to a more general aversion to randomness, contingency and coincidence found amongst orthodox lawyers and legal theorists. A focus on localised acts of mapping doctrine extrapolated from the judgments in cases, into the carefully classified detail of the law in the textbook requires continued and careful pruning. Indeed displaying such skill has frequently been the hallmark of the successful scholar. As Goodrich (1986: 209) wrote: 'lawyers have always been indecently zealous to reduce behaviour to rules, and, in constructing the abstract world of the doctrine and science of law, have tended to be forgetful both of the irrationality and chance embedded in social life as well as the instability and change intrinsic to human purpose and human personality'. Whilst many legal scholars would readily agree that, around the edges, the law may be contingent, they (and the law) are nevertheless sustained by adherence to fixed and hard certainties. Consequently, loosely constructed situations, or simple contingencies, become burdened with coherence. Many tactics are employed in attempts to sustain a rational account. For instance, middle order 'justifications' lying behind doctrinal 'lines of authority', are debated by legal scholars in terms of which is the most 'satisfactory'. Are testamentary secret trusts upheld because equity will not allow a statute to be used as an engine of fraud, or because they are not really testamentary trusts at all? In relation to constructive trusts, does 'the search for principle' continue? Often extrapolations of doctrine from judgments 'leave behind' the clear policy elements folded within them and avoid an examination of a particular historical conjuncture, which might have 'explained' more clearly (and coherently!) the grounds for the decision. This is even more crucial as a mode of operation when the decision has subsequently become embedded into a line of authority (as in, for example, *Saunders v Vautier* (1841) Beav 115). The garden is kept neat and the trees clipped to perfection. (So much may happen with/in a case or a rule or a right, we may tell its past and its future in multiple ways, but too often its record is no more than an ex post facto, seemingly inevitable, linear journey towards what is actually a footnote but has consumed the fullness of the text itself.)

The defence of the borders and suppression of that which is contingent, follows the scholar into the constructed 'reality' of doctrinal analysis. Such journeys are well documented (Bottomley 1996) and one example here will suffice. The concept of 'touch and concern the land' is used as foundational in the law of leases, as well as easements and restrictive covenants, to determine the extent of, (and to create), liability in relation to land which is owned by or shared with another person. In leasehold law, this concept is used to decide whether a first tenant may wander off and escape her history, her original contractual liability, and whether a new landlord or tenant is to be bound by a promise made by others. The phrase is said to originate in *Spencer's Case* (1583) 5 Co Rep 16a and a vast number of land cases go through here. It became the event of *Pattison v Mayor of Congleton* (1808) 103 ER 725, a fairly cobwebbed 'touch and concern' case but one which religiously appears in the texts. Here the lessor (the town council) imposed a covenant in the lease of a silk mill to the effect that the mill should only employ workers certificated as resident within the parish. The promise was breached by the lessee – effectively, he was employing migrant labour. The town council had imposed the covenant to prevent 'foreign poor' entering the town; once resident, they might necessitate a rise in local taxes which would not only increase the costs of the mill itself and render the lessee less able to pay the rent, but would also reduce the value of the lessor's reversion. Although the meaning of 'touch and concern' is defined to include any effect on the value of the leased land or on the lessor's reversion, it was held that this covenant did *not* 'affect the value of the land demised'.

Was this decision because of the 'true' interpretation of 'touch and concern', or was it because of national policy in relation to localities erecting boundaries preventing the free movement of workers? Were parish councils – the year after the abolition of the British slave trade and in war-time – to be allowed to control local immigration at the expense of other parishes? What combination of forces brought this case on war-time poor law policy within the law of leases, into the category of 'cases on touch and concern', so that it must be followed by 'like cases'? What throws of the dice made 'touch and concern' itself a ground of land law? And what throws of the dice brought the Landlord and Tenant (Covenants) Act 1995 which abolished 'touch and concern' for new landlords and tenants? A case can be like a dead leaf hanging on a tree, but is also a fish darting in water, or a bird flying between the branches. However, these multiple operations of random forces do not match the expected reflection of law in the fixed aerial photographs and must be suppressed.

We might think of this 'cartographer' of law as one who is constantly engaged in protecting their territory; stabilising the 'fortress-core' and defending their boundaries against attacks and incursions, both locally and regionally. Sometimes he turns adventurer and looks to territories that seem ill-defended as potential sites to extend the terrain of his map. Is Land Law too narrowly defined in the modern world of complex property relations? Is 'property' not better thought of as a branch of obligations and, indeed, are not obligations better thought of as branches of an overarching arboreal law of restitution? Such questioning is, of course, properly part of a scholarly examination of subject areas: but, in practice, this often becomes a battle over the territory of borderlands and investments in defending fortress-core. The development (the huge growth) of areas of 'law which does not fit' may be rendered invisible within and to scholarship, unexamined and unexplored. In such cases as, for instance, 'anti-social behaviour law', a hybrid which is neither simply in the civil realm nor simply in the criminal realm and defies traditional categorisation, emerging practices of law are left to create a 'new' place in the margins largely ignored by the mainstream academy (Bottomley and Moore 2007).

'Grounding principles' are inscribed upon the law retrospectively and the boundaries of legal subject areas are, and always have been, porous. It is the job of the academic to make what sense can be wrought from the complex 'everyday' of the law. However, what must be guarded against are the acts of mapping which transmute into cartographies of no more than 'mere tracings', banal repetitions designed to satisfy, empower and consolidate the academically defined territory, rather than enhance a more forward and outward-looking pattern of scholarship.

Potentially enabling futures may be curtailed by the presence and utilisation of texts, even in the courts of law, which continue to emphasise traditional features, to gain comfort from the reassertion of orthodoxies, rather than take the risks and disturbance from considering innovations. We have already discussed one aspect of 'land law' which reveals the porous nature of the boundary between 'land' and 'contracts'. Such 'incursions' are often developed as 'creative linkages' which allow for movement, they are pragmatic and enabling in the instant case. They are made possible by traces of history and blurrings in jurisprudence which lie fallow, no more than shadows of possibilities, until brought into play when offering a hook upon which to hang a new route map required for movement forward. But, for the scholar/explorer the task is to make 'sense' of these incursions, by re-embedding them within the existing maps, enforcing order in the face of potential chaos and defusing the unsettling nature of boundary blur.

One of the hardest tasks in land law in this country comes from the intersection between common law and equity, in the area of the map labelled 'trusts'. Here the territory is hard to defend against the destabilising aspects of equity in its remedial modes. A response in the recent past was imperialist incursions from the (then) vibrantly expansive restitutionary approach (Birks 1985, Jones and Goff 2002), intent on redrawing maps of both common law and equity, but challenged by academics successively defending their terrain, providing key secondary texts which would be deployed in the courts. However, this incursion is not the particular concern of this chapter, rather we return to the case of *Oxley v Hiscock* which permits a focus upon a further defence against disorder in land law.

## Defending fortress-land (an outpost of fortress property)

The judgment in *Oxley v Hiscock* disrupted the smooth surface of land law. Its suggestion that beneficial interests acquired (recognised) through the jurisprudence of the imputed trust could be equally theorised through estoppel principles challenged the presentation of the two concepts as discrete juridical forms. In their history the imputed trust has been treated and understood within 'land law' as a property right, while estoppel is essentially an equitable remedy. The distinction has been important for feminists, since in the jurisprudence of land law a property right, a claim to a thing 'itself' is not limited by orthodox contractual doctrine and is potentially enforceable against third parties. Forged on the middle ground of contracts and equity, the property right gives rise to a stronger claim, more than simply compensation for its loss. We intend briefly to track the case law recognising 'property right held through trust' to demonstrate not only its hybrid nature but also the simple fact that recognising rights for (usually) women in circumstances where the home was held in another's name required a claim carrying property status. A property right can trump countervailing claims, principally that 'ownership' vested in the person 'holding title to land'.

One objective of the modernising 1925 legislation was to provide sufficient certainty and formality to enhance the market in land. As a consequence, holding a trust interest in land was deemed to be no more than a money interest, as opposed to a property interest capable of binding third parties. Lord Denning in *Bull v Bull* [1955] 1 QB 234 held that it could also be an interest giving the right to live in the land itself. The 'owner' (the person who held title) could not exclude the person claiming the trust benefit. Eventually, through a series of steps and creative interpretation of the legislation, this right to occupy land derived from a money right took on the characteristics of a property right 'in land', which would later be confirmed as being 'more than a money right' by new legislation.[9] The claims of (mostly) women to these rights in land held by their partners were concerned not only with having their interest recognised and protected in law, but also with the proportion of their claim upon the home vis-à-vis the title holder or in some cases third parties. Traditionally the extent of the claim was a matter of tracking economic investment in the form of direct financial contributions, raising some disquiet amongst feminists. Again a creative judiciary found ways of decoupling proportions of ownership from reliance on an economic account to the detriment of many women, providing an assault upon the fortress of 'land law'. It led to mainstream academic criticism of (some of the) judges for the old offence of importing a lack of certainty, particularly into an area of law which demands high levels of certainty, and worse that it had been achieved through the construction of a 'fiction' of common intention.

The judicial enterprise of recognising social justice imperatives and circumventing case law which impeded the development of a more responsive body of rules did not merely require a 'move away' from privileging certainty. Creative decision making also allowed for a progressive seepage of factors recognising social 'reality', including 'why' a woman might not have been able to accumulate wealth into 'land law'. And the latest judicial manoeuvre, in *Oxley v Hiscock*, suggests that the decision about the proportions in which the beneficial interests in land are held is better decided by deploying the jurisprudence of estoppel rather than the 'fiction of common intention'. Thus, there is the opening of another possibility, that the principles of estoppel might also be used to raise the claim itself. And so law always becomes, it flies, swims and walks: 'It is not a question of any special place on earth, nor of any given moment in history, but rather of a model that is ceaselessly set up and that collapses, of a process that ceaselessly extends itself, breaks off and starts again' (Deleuze and Guattari 1988: 20). It is not surprising that the decision in *Oxley v Hiscock* provoked an outcry from some orthodox academic land lawyers for confusing an area of law which requires certainty and for conflating a traditionally remedial principle – estoppel – derived from equitable principles addressed to limitations in contract law with a 'property right'. However, the vehemence of some authors such as Thompson, the reaction, as well as the willingness to challenge the judiciary and their role as producers of law, was less predictable and worthy of consideration.

The traditionalists are countered by other established authors, who for the sake of convenience we will term as 'more progressive' thinkers, who have an essentially pragmatic approach to the decision as an enabling move (Battersby 2005, Dixon 2005). Theirs is broadly an argument that one area – estoppel – has now developed to the extent that it might be usefully deployed in a related area and that it has begun, anyway, to be deployed in certain circumstances such that it can carry some features of property-in-land. In other words this approach is not wedded to a belief that 'property-in-land' holds 'core characteristics' which must be policed, but recognises that it is no more than an effect, brought about by a constellation of features being grafted onto a set of practices, constituted by out-come rather than by adherence to fundamental principles 'properly' applied. Academic authors necessarily and understandably spend much of their time helping to locate shifts in judicial thinking, including any possible impacts in future cases (Watt 2003: 40). However, to be constantly concerned with policing orthodoxies is to be necessarily blinded to the pragmatic movements of judges who respond to new situations, by blending and bending forms, and leaning on the rules, to allow for a responsive approach to new problems or situations.

Like conveyancers, judges do not operate in compartmentalised segments of law and neither are they over-concerned with doctrinal or conceptual purity when they can envision other ways of moving forward (Watt 2003: 40). To take another much more prosaic example, the rule concerning certainty in leases which was, in the texts, unquestionably certain but became retrospectively uncertain with the case of *Prudential Assurance Co Ltd v London Residuary Body* [1992] 3 WLR 279 (HL). The case expresses a meeting of forces, including the force of the rule that a lease must be a 'term of years absolute',[10] a rule which is said to define the essence of a lease as enjoyment of land for a fixed duration with a predetermined beginning and end. However, it is clear in *Prudential* that several kinds of lease are possible, in this case a lease 'from year to year', and other cases show that alternative labels may also be attached, such as contractual and estoppel licences, which can have similar effects to a lease. The law may state the essence of the lease, but what the judges actually do with the rule is to enable parties to enter and give effect to their negotiations. And there are other such examples in leases, as for instance in *Bruton v London and Quadrant Housing Trust* [2001] 1 AC 406, where a 'personal lease' was found by creatively deploying contracts to enable the 'tenant' to take advantage of an implied repairing lease where 'land law' had effectively placed a block on finding a route forward.

It is one thing to attempt to situate these developments in judicial thinking and try to fore-call what judges will say, or not say, in future cases. This is what academics do. However, it is quite another thing to critique the judiciary in the courts of authority as being 'wrong' on the law, or an area of law. We turn again, then, to consider why some 'traditional' thinkers have responded in such a way to *Oxley v Hiscock*. What is at stake appears to us to be twofold: first, the effort expended in 'maintaining' a coherence to property-in-land is exposed; and second, the general concern with the 'lack of certainty and formality' in an area in which the economics of the market are challenged by social imperatives according to which other factors are sufficiently significant to demand recognition in law. Put crudely, attempts within 'Land Law' to engage with the messy consequences of gender relations and home use/ownership disrupt and render problematic assertions that property-in-land is expressive of an internally stable and rational account of 'land as law'.

It is not, of course, that the law of the 'family home' is the only area which disturbs the familiar and the reassuring, but it is often the most persistent and most problematic for more 'traditional' thinkers. It is no surprise that they, as much as any feminist author who views land law and land lawyers as unresponsive to women's needs, wholeheartedly support suggestions for the expulsion of such troublesome subjects to a different (more marginal) area of law. Family law is regarded as the most suitable repository by commentators from a range of perspectives. However, such an act of exclusion would not finally stabilise 'property in land'. We have suggested that rather as, by tradition, 'ownership in land' is no more than a bundle of divisible rights and claims, so 'property in land' is no more than a bundle of sticks. It is a constellation of forces which, if the bundle is sufficiently weighty, may give the effect of 'property in land', a sum greater than its parts. This effect draws upon other discursive practices for the 'final touch'. Primarily it utilises 'common sense', what Gray (1991: 252) called 'intuition', but there is also as suggested already an attempt to derive support from a philosophical grounding, with reference to a 'core principle', to search beyond land, beyond property-in-land, delving into that most abstract and erudite of scholastic fields to seek property.

Gray's (1991: 252) description of the beguiling and illusive figure of private property which seduces scholars of land law, in part because of the need for an objective foundation or core principle to provide at least the appearance of a coherent field of study, is one to which we have already referred. Attempts are made to map property as 'something' which can be rendered into 'ownership' arising in, or from, a claim to be able to exclude others from the use of that 'thing'. Either there is a focus on the 'thing' itself as holding certain properties which make it reducible to property or, instead, on the relational patterns (between subjects in relation to objects) which render the 'thing' property by excluding others claims to use it.[11] The pursuit of this 'illusive lady' serves to fend off the realisation that 'land law' is merely a collection of rules, although at the moment of capture, as Gray suggests, the figure dissolves.

However, we would say that she has value in and of herself, in that her virtue lies in her floating and shifting form, to be, if you like, something we all 'know' because of her very irreducibility. This is not to deny that within our western tradition she has become enmeshed in certain patterns, especially as the recognition of those patterns might help us to free her, if and when she seems useful to us. But the rendition of 'her' as a very particular type of 'object', limits an account of her to those western traditions, or at least privileges them as 'authoritative guides' to what she should be or how she should be 'properly dressed'. It also inhibits potential for attempts at thinking 'property' as no more and no less than a way to organise access to, and use of, limited resources (as part of an array of legal forms and cultural practices).

## The 'scholar/explorer' in the tree

The features of traditional Land Law scholarship we could, following Rose, characterise as essentially 'masculinist'. Such a portrayal is possible with respect to the pleasures derived from battles over the authenticity of legal doctrine and the 'proper' terrain of the subject. The method used in, and patterns of, the constant struggle to defend the integrity of the territory, also exhibit 'masculinist' tones. These consist of repeated references to increasingly abstract 'core' principles as 'present', but often it is the strength of the assertion rather than the relevance or rationality of the principles which is notable. Waddams (2003) points out that at the level of legal doctrine and in the everyday of legal practice, continued attempts to stabilise sharp distinctions between private law subjects inhibit a fuller account of law as it crosses subject boundaries, which is capable of exposing those boundaries as porous and questioning the seeming stability of 'core principles'. In short, conventional academics are involved in acts of reification distancing them from the 'everyday', in order to maintain their traditional role and practices. As Rose (1993) indicates, although in the context of her own discipline, this necessitates standing outside and above the messiness of 'law' to assert over it an orderly regime which is made available to the scholar/explorers because of their distanced perspective on law-out-there. Their 'everyday' closeness to the acts of mapping which allows them to 'find'/construct the underlying patterns of core principles that seem more immediate than the untidy, chaotic and often pragmatic operations of law.

The descriptions of law from 'scholar/explorers' are presented as both normative and prescriptive. Normative in the sense that the values of certainty and coherence are valued above all else, and prescriptive in that judgment of the 'law-out-there' is in terms of whether or not it matches the prescribed standard. This becomes particularly problematic when, again as Rose (1993) points out, the presence of the academics themselves, their practices and perspectives, within this picture are unacknowledged. Unlike geographers, the legal 'scholar/explorer' is in a paradoxical position. He can see and take pleasure, a *particular* pleasure, in those instances when as an individual he has a direct impact on the subject, the law-out-there. When an academic article is cited in judgment, it operates as a major reinforcement of the writer's position as not just a mere commentator on the law but as part of 'the law' itself.[12] We can expand Rose's analysis by recognising not only the masculinist pleasures of holding such authority, but also the masculinist way in which these articles are written and received as dispassionate accounts of law. When an account is out of line with what has been argued in the courts it can be presented as a better account of law, or even true law, as opposed to a description imbued with the values of the authors. Paradoxically then, the legal 'scholar/explorer' becomes the repository of 'real' law, trumping the law of the courts and, sometimes, with his descriptions being utilised as maps to guide the judiciary back onto the correct path. There are a small number of signed paths and where they divide 'we' must take either this one or that one, in a continuing sequence of limited choices, safeguarded against the mutability of chance and contingency.

It may well be that it is the disorderly, 'off-route' cases that offer more enabling maps for those who 'come to law' looking for small, progressive incursions into an otherwise unfriendly landscape, within and in between the frontiers of law. However, drowned in doctrinal detail and countering any threat to the borders of the subject area as a scholarly enterprise, the legal 'scholar/explorer' avoids and excludes potentially destabilising 'realities'. Anything pertaining to the family is problematic, not least because 'family law' approaches are soft, pliable and fail to offer clear-cut rules (Smart 1989: 15, Bottomley and Roche 1988: 95–96). The border with 'family matters' in trusts and estoppel is strongly policed amid constant reminders of the need for clarity, matched with dire warnings about the dangers of discretion and of taking into account broad social factors when making rules or applying them. It is as if this particularly leaky border must be sealed and resealed against the potential of fluidity and threat of pollution. So much has been marginalised and excluded that it is no wonder that feminists have tended to look to equity (rather than trusts within Land Law) or family law as sites holding more potential in meeting women's needs. Others have gone further off-map into the more malleable and possibly more attractive terrain of environment and housing. 'Evacuating' the area of Land Law serves, incidentally, the ongoing process of 'securing' Land Law's borders and keeping out potentially disruptive public law elements. It is as if the subject has been emptied of so much of its potential, left like a pattern of dry bones in a desert for the remaining 'scholar/explorers' to pick over.

To map the evidence of the way in which the masculinist pleasures found in the traditional rendition of Land Law inhibit the potential of the subject area and foreclose a deeper geography of embodiment is a task beyond the limited space offered in this chapter. However, we argued earlier that despite its intractability, there has been no lack of investment in presenting Land Law as a coherent subject area, a set of doctrinal instances expressing adherence to a set of core elements rendered visible through carefully constructed historical accounts. The pattern expressed in this form of construction, to borrow from Deleuze (1995: 146), is that of a tree: 'an arborescent process' with hierarchically arranged branches and roots – a tree of knowledge. Vertically imaged Land Law emanates from a central core, rather than a splintered horizontal network of related practices. The pattern is set for the legal 'scholar/explorer' 'in the tree', although it requires heroic acts of reification to sustain. He needs not only to deliver a rational and internally coherent account of the law, but also to record his skill in being able to find/construct the account.[13] We would argue that for legal 'scholar/explorers' in land two strategies mark their acts of mapping: excessive concentration on doctrinal detail; and an awkward and ambiguous relationship with land registration which is clumsily grafted onto Land Law.

Registration may be on the map, but it remains confined to Land Law's margins. Strangely, the most seemingly bureaucratic aspect of land and law is pushed into the outer realms of the terrain where the more informal rights such as those derived from estoppel also dwell. What the state guarantee of land title and related interests in land recognises and upholds is those aspects of land use which hold an economic value and are significant to the market in land. Thus it is those things which encourage the market which are portrayed in the account of 'land' as Land Law. The reconstitution of the subject through registration cannot be ignored, but what this signified for many scholars was that Land Law was essentially dominated by conveyancing, the product and practices of the market place, a collection of rules concerned with the exchange of land. Land Law becomes the study of statutes and the practices of registration, mere training for conveyancers.[14] Ironically perhaps, as the law relating to the exchange of land is, therefore, slipping away from the land lawyer, the response of the legal 'scholar/explorer' is to become even more fixated on the doctrinal heritage of the subject. Faced with a terrain of regulation through registration, which offers little of value to the scholar, the struggle goes on to embed Land Law into a jurisprudence of principles and the courts' response to novel situations not covered by statutes, as if by keeping this body still alive the reality that the subject is actually, rapidly, contracting, can be suppressed. There is an effort and energy, but essential futility to this which is not unlike that of early twentieth century white colonial explorers who stalked across African deserts seeking to make their mark and give their names to sand dunes and fossil trees (Ondaatje 1993).

## Law, land

Land Law derives the specificity of its terrain from its focus on the land conveyance, the market and definitions of 'real property' and 'land'. An orthodox history of 'how we got here', which predominates in the Land Law of the classroom and the textbook, helps to give shape and form to this terrain. However, many histories of the complex relations between people, law and the land which did not 'succeed' or 'survive' are simply, perhaps understandably, written out and forgotten, with only the traces of the losses, compromises and resilience of the less powerful who fought to protect their few rights. It could be said that this exclusion is a matter only for historians, but we would argue that it should also be of importance to lawyers and academics. These other histories remind us that land is a limited and contested resource. Law as a social construct privileges those who have been able to assert their economic and social power, embedding that privilege within authoritarian legal discourse; but the power of law is not a simple one-way, all-enveloping, relation and that discourse remains 'incomplete' and is resisted. Not only must it respond to the demands made upon it by the socially and economically powerful, but also it can never, within its own rhetoric be finally closed to attempts made to use it by the less powerful.

Matsuda (1987: 323) argued two decades ago for the 'irrational position' of simultaneously having faith in the law – 'having a right to participate equally in society with any other person' – and at the same time suspending that faith – 'rights are whatever people in power say they are'. Similarly, de Souza Santos (1995: 348) argued that the twin pillars of law are emancipation and regulation. Sometimes the proponents of the counter discourse may force the law to live up to its own rhetoric, although it may be difficult to predict when such an occurrence will arise. Here the question is the extent to which inscribing law in the academy as a set of practices in a particular form inhibits any potential in keeping open, or opening, progressive potentials which might enable the less powerful to resist dispossession or assert claims which protect fragile access to land. Without overemphasising its importance, the academy is a component in drawing and maintaining acts of mapping which are more open to disruption. However, to achieve this is to accept that maps might need to be uneven and disorderly, allowing for lines which extend beyond and over neat boundaries, which may or may not indicate new terrain, let alone be capable of mapping as 'territory' in any conventional sense.

The loss of the rural commons and informal rights in law provide two examples of what has been written out of history, although remaining of immediate significance today. Traces of the demise of customary rights of access to land can still be found in the public law protection of common lands. The residues and recollections of the loss of informal rights in law with the sharpening focus on 'ownership' are more difficult to detect, particularly as we move ever more deeply into a fully registered system. Folk memories of the commons are now almost obliterated by time and the shift to urban patterns of living, with access to land now seen principally as concerned with recreation rather than having any economic or political dimension (other than the protection of 'their' land by the landowners). It is difficult to recover the much more overtly politicised notion of what it means to lose rights of entry to, and use of, an economic resource held by a community for the community benefit, an important mechanism by which the value and interdependency of 'community' was inscribed in and through the landscape of everyday practices (Home 2007 forthcoming, Guadagni 2002). The general trajectory towards the triumph of the individual property owner and the parallel dispossession of those whose claims to their plots were informal or customary, defined not only the use of land but also the lens through which 'law' redefined land. However, the triumph of 'possessive individualism' is still not quite complete, as evidenced by the attempt in the Land Registration Act 2002 to 'tidy up' adverse possession, marginalise and suppress the traces of disruptive histories.[15] And, paradoxically, within a logic required by a focus on the register, certain informal rights under s116 of the same Act, particularly estoppel rights, are elevated to a new status.[16]

Tracking and bringing into account these shadows reminds us that the history of private property is not one of 'natural origins' but one of political struggle (Charlesworth 2007 forthcoming). Those struggles continue today, most obviously in the examples of indigenous peoples asserting their rights to land from which they were dispossessed. While communal/customary claims can all too often only be reasserted by translation into forms that can be understood within the capitalist market place (Belgrave 2007), what is important is the extent to which some of those struggles, for example in Scotland centred around the provisions of the Scottish Land Reform Act 2003, are now focused on the means by which rights can be achieved through the assertion of a 'collective holding' (Sellar 2003, Bryden and Geisler 2004). In Africa and South America, informal land tenure systems and a network of informal rights and practices within kin groups have resurfaced to contest the hegemony of western models of registration of title (Durand-Lasserve and Royston 2002, Home and Lim 2004).

This is not simply a rural issue, since the urban and peri-urban 'squatter settlements' are being progressively 'regularised' or 'legalised' (Fernandes and Varley 1998, Payne 2002). Some are being accredited with the new status of formal ownership, within the frame of private property rights, but it is a process which involves new acts of dispossession and creates new 'outsiders'. Allowing a land market to develop may benefit lending agencies and already wealthy property owners, rather more than enfranchising new owners of private property. The loss of informal practices and enclosure of land raises important issues for feminists with respect to its impact on women's access to land, to which we will return. The patterns developed from the colonial and post-colonial imposition of 'received' western law and legal mechanisms overlaying pre-existing legal relations in developing jurisdictions creates conflicts and confusions, not least about legitimacy, which can have devastating consequences for ordinary people in their everyday lives. They serve also to highlight the very partiality of western legal systems, including that in England and Wales, and the extent to which it not only upholds a regime of private property ownership but inhibits the development of more communal or hybrid means of holding and using land.

It is not surprising to us that there has been a recent resurgence in this country in an interest in holding and using land beyond the confinements of individuated property ownership patterns. It is not only that some, albeit few, individuals wish to purposefully find more communal ways of living and wish that communality to be expressed in law, it is also the pressure on land as a resource and the financial cost of individual units of land as homes has led to the recognition that new forms of joint tenure are preferable to trying to purchase ever smaller scraps of 'land' for individual use. However, the means by which this is achieved through a legal framework focused on individuated property ownership is unwieldy and property academics (with the notable exception of Gray and Gray) have made little attempt to find new facilitative means to accomplish satisfactory forms to hold land more communally or jointly. This is not only to the detriment of those who seek to break the dominant mould, but also to a fuller academic account of 'land law'.

Informal rights and the extent to which they can and should be brought into the 'formal' legal system and emerging communal, joint or hybrid land holding mechanisms are barely visible on the margins of an orthodox map of 'land law'. As Rose describes and analyses in relation to geography, it is on these margins that issues of gender are clearly visible. For instance, it has long been recognised that developments in communal patterns of land use may well benefit women in making possible, through shared space, the breaking down of domestic isolation, the distribution through the community of domestic tasks and childcare, through providing economies of scale and 'blending' the 'public'/'private' spheres. In bringing 'the margins' into account we necessarily challenge a map which has kept them so far from sight. These margins are disruptive because they do not focus on 'land law' as about the private ownership of land and formal rights in land ownership and use. If we reflect back too, for a moment, on our reference to 'loss of rural commons', we might now consider also what some commentators have identified as 'the new enclosures' and 'the loss of urban commons', both in our own jurisdiction and others (Robins 1993, Marcuse 1995). Again, few 'scholar/explorers' in 'Land Law' have spent much time, if any, on these legal trends, despite the importance of the dispossession of land from common use through the burgeoning of exclusive often gated or 'secured' enclaves designed to protect some (new) city inhabitants from 'others'. Their insistence on the core principles of the subject area renders this terrain to be 'off-site'. Once, as feminists, we begin to examine the margins and challenge the paucity of traditional mapping, we render visible this dangerous terrain which not only exposes and challenges 'the law', but equally exposes and challenges the practices of 'mapping law' still dominant within the academy.

To begin walking, then, our contingent map will be one which seeks 'land', taking the risk of the unexpected, even if only as a glimpse from the corner of the eye and refusing the constraints of Land Law. In order to walk, we need to unfold the old map of Land Law with its deeply ingrained creases, refolding its seemingly continuous surface (Pottage 1994: 384) in new ways, in new terrains, making visible the potentials of other multi-dimensional maps, the splinters of possibilities, beyond 'mere tracings'.

## Women and everyday places

> But you may say, we asked you to speak about women and fiction – what has that got to do with a room of one's own?
>
> (Woolf 2000: 3)[17]

When Virginia Woolf was asked to give a lecture to women undergraduates in Cambridge, she wrote in the 1927 essay which became its record, that she had found it impossible to decide how to weave a simple linkage between 'women' and 'fiction'. She writes of the encounter, when moments assemble in the present, constellations of infinite forces, of our past thoughts and yours in the present, even perhaps the meetings of old cases in new texts. As she contemplated the possible permutations for her lecture by the River Cam:

> Thought . . . had let its line down into the stream. It swayed, minute after minute, hither and thither, among the reflections and the weeds, letting the water lift it and sink it until – you know the little tug – the sudden conglomeration of an idea at the end of one's line: and then the cautious hauling it in, and the careful laying of it out.
>
> (Woolf 2000: 7)[18]

There was an infinite number of possible becomings, like birds flying through the air, or fish glinting silver in the water, so she continued:

> how small, how insignificant this thought of mine looked . . . But however small it was, it had, nevertheless the mysterious property of its kind – put back into the mind, it became at once very exciting and important, and as it darted and sank . . . set up such a wash and tumult of ideas that it was impossible to sit still. It was thus that I found myself walking with extreme rapidity across a grass plot. Instantly a man's figure rose to intercept me.
>
> (2000: 7)

Her 'small thought', which she told the 'starved but valiant young women' (2000: xix) of Girton, was of the importance to anyone wanting to write of having their own space, by which she meant not only a physical space but also mental space ('freedom of mind'), space to find and give expression to what is 'true'.[19] This is not the place to explore the extent to which Woolf's essay meets the rigours of a 'feminist' critique. It is simply our contention here that her essay importantly recognises the material constraints which impact upon the production of writing – a point with much resonance for those of us writing as feminist scholars in the academy attempting to think the law 'as we know it' differently.

In a similar way to that experienced by Woolf, placing together 'feminism', 'land' and 'law' offers many possible permutations, but it must begin with the material conditions which impact on women's access to land that in turn impacts on women's everyday lives. Woolf famously argued for 'a room of one's own', but within her essay reflects also on access to semi-public space. The 'man's figure who rose to intercept' her was a servant charged with ensuring that only faculty could walk on the grass in the courts of the college, limiting the many others, which significantly at that time included all women, to the paths which bordered them. And for Woolf, we think, there is a further image at play here. The courts are boundaried only by the paths, not by any fence or barrier. It is all too easy to trespass onto them if you do not recognise the conventions or are not thinking too carefully about where you are walking.

Woolf in her essay was explicitly and implicitly challenging the conventions and restrictions of a social order which privileged men, although perhaps we should add that it privileged white men drawn from particular social and economic classes. To make that challenge she needed to trespass – just as through her novels she wrote into existence new narrative patterns, playing with time/space and refusing distinctions between descriptions of 'reality out there' and what was being experienced (thought) through each encounter. And so, modestly, our feminist perambulation must also be, indeed can only be, an act of trespass.

## Notes

1 Our title plays with Paul Klee's description of a line 'going for a walk' in his explorations into the construction, and evocation, of movement and rhythm within his art (Kudielka 2002). Klee's work is used in Dewsbury and Thrift (2005: 89) when, considering the effect of a Deleuzean approach on the study of space and the practices of geography, they begin to explore thinking space as a 'moving concept', an 'imminent spatiality'. This sense of movement – of becoming ungrounded from, and of unsettling, what has become sedimented into terrains of 'naturalness', 'inevitability', 'common sense' and 'good scholarship' is the vector through which our chapter begins to take form. We walk 'in' land, as a recognition that 'land', as much as 'law', is a construct that, as with the geographers 'space', we should think of as a 'moving concept'. However, whilst this chapter has been influenced by this pattern of thinking, we do not here pursue 'this line' as far as it clearly could be walked. Rather, we have folded this chapter into another form of walking which recognises our feminist materiality, and in this sense we were tempted to talk of walking 'on' land to invoke a corporality which we find so significantly lacking in most contemporary scholarship in our field.

2 See Lechte (1995), Part Six of Borden, Miles and Hall (2000). We would draw attention to the work of Iain Borden (Bartlett School of Architecture, UCL), the films of Claire Denis and the instillations of Francis Alys (2004) as particularly pertinent examples of finding patterns for exploring, through the practices of diverse forms of representation, what we have called the 'deeper geography of place'. See also Careri (2002).

3 The use of the term 'perambulation' might recall for some readers the city walking of London ramblers for their visual pleasure (Rendell 1996) or later Parisian 'flaneurs' in the tradition of Baudelaire *et al.* (Wilson 1995), or even the expeditions of white Victorian lady travellers (Domosh and Seager 2001: 143–146), but it should be clear from our chapter that we intend much more than an encounter with the 'everyday' as spectacle to which we are no more than witnesses and recorders.

4 We have attempted throughout this text to distinguish between 'Land Law', by which we mean the supposedly tightly boundaried and relatively fixed 'subject' which predominates in mainstream textbooks and the classroom, and 'land law', as a more open, fluid and dynamic constellation of multiple relations between land and law. The possibilities of the latter are seen in some academic texts, such as Gray and Gray (2005), or glimpsed in the work of academics including Dixon (2005) and Battersby (2005), but we would seek to move further along the trajectory.

5 Attempts have been made (on a regular basis) to deploy the Roman law distinction between rights *in rem* and rights *in personam*: whilst this duality has been deployed in specific instances with some success, to try to establish and maintain such a

distinction as fundamental in common law has proven impossible as a map of distinctive and impenetrable 'oppositions'. However, reference to the typology can sometimes be useful when trying to tease out the complex interrelations and patterns of development in specific sites, for instance in trusts and estoppel (Bottomley 2001, 2006).

6 This is not to suggest that the chapters in this book were placed alongside one another in a random manner. It would be disingenuous to suggest that our own appreciation of particular recurrent themes did not cause us to see a number of possible 'walks' through the collection. Some chapters were also 'slipped between' between obvious pairings and groupings in order to cut across conventional 'tracings' enabling (we hope) readers to walk in ways we have not even begun to envisage.

7 Land law is a 'core' subject for students who wish to use their degrees to qualify for exemption from the first stage of professional examinations. Many courses now present themselves as 'property courses', but in our experience they remain primarily concerned with 'Land Law'.

8 Law of Property Act 1925, s 205(1)(ix); Land Registration Act 2002, s 132.

9 Two important steps in the process were the cases of *Williams & Glyns Bank v Boland* [1981] AC 487 and *City of London Building Society v Flegg* [1988] AC 54, which were concerned with the nature of the beneficiary's interest under s 70(1)(g) of the Land Registration Act 1925. The Trusts of Land and Appointment of Trustees Act 1996, s 3, replaced the trust for sale and the full operation of the doctrine of conversion which had rendered beneficial rights as only money rights, with a 'trust of land'. However, it maintained one element of the doctrine of conversion in still allowing the beneficial interest to be 'overreached'.

10 Law of Property Act 1925, ss 1(1)(b), 205(1)(xxvii); Land Registration Act 2002, s 132(1)

11 There is, of course, an impact from such approaches, not only upon seemingly progressive claims to extend 'property' use to enhance visibility and value (Radin 1993, 1996), but also on feminist work which remains fixed on object/subject relations with reference to 'subjectivity' or what Radin and others have called self-hood. As if the ability to 'own' more will somehow build and sustain 'self' – a curiously nineteenth-century fixation in the modern world.

12 We had originally written here 'influencing the law', but that would be to retain the model of the 'scholar/explorer' as outsider. What we want to convey is that to maintain a sharp distinction between law-out-there and academy is often as tenuous as other binary constructions.

13 'Precedent, principle, policy, and pragmatism are blended subtly in the mind of the judge. Nevertheless, the task of students in this, as indeed in any area of law, [is] to attempt to discern the true basis of decisions and to distil from the subtle blend the fractions of precedent, principles, policy, and pragmatism in the purest form they can. It is the task of the textbook writer to help in this distillation process . . . We will discover that decisions that seem to be unprecedented and to make no principled sense can sometimes make sense' (Watt 2003: 40).

14 Sparkes perhaps more than other textbook writers embraces registration and the imperatives of conveyancing, with an opening chapter on it, in which he makes the grand claim that 'land was made to be registered' (2003: 1). He likens registration to the grey squirrel which has placed the red squirrel (unregistered land) on the endangered list. However, even here the 'graft' of registration onto the Land Law tree appears to us to be clearly visible and incomplete, an intruder upon well-established terrain. His second chapter is a more conventional tour of 'land' and 'law', including what he describes as the 'Informal not-land' and 'Land and

not-land borderline' (2003: 15–20), as well as the traditional 'land or property' debate.

15 See Part 9 and Sched 6 of the Land Registration Act 2002.

16 Section 116 of the Land Registration Act 2002 addresses the status of an estoppel interest, which is to be treated as a proprietary right capable of binding third party purchasers of the registered land.

17 Our decision to include Virginia Woolf's essay is primarily for its content, but more broadly it is also a gesture of recognition of the importance given to her work by Deleuze and Guattari (for example 1987: esp. 276–28 and 1994). 'To be fully a part of the crowd and at the same time completely outside it, removed from it: to be on the edge, to take a walk like Virginia Woolf' (Deleuze and Guattari 1987: 29). 'Virginia Woolf's walk through the crowd, among the taxis. Taking a walk is a haecceity' (Deleuze and Guattari 1987: 263).

18 'Time is the time of change – not localised change but the change of transition and the transitory . . . the River is the symbol in which reality and dream are one and which is without form . . . Time – the time of the narrative, flowing, uninterrupted slow, full of surprises and sighs, strife and silence, rich, monotonous and varied . . . The history of a single day includes the history of the world . . . its source unrevealed, is symbolished over and over again in womanhood and in the river' Lefebvre writing of Bloom's perambulations in Dublin in James Joyce's *Ulysses* (Lefebvre 1971: 4). As with Deleuze and Guattari (above) the multiple sense of duration is important here. See further Johnson (2000) on Woolf and Joyce 'walking in the city'.

19 This is not the place to explore the extent to which Woolf's essay meets the rigours of 'a' 'feminist' critique or to ponder on the seeming coldness of her diary entry: it is simply our contention here that her essay importantly recognises the material constraints which impact upon the production of writing – a point with much resonance for those of us writing 'as feminist scholars' in the academy. In this sense we think her reference to 'freedom of mind', as the circumstances which allow us to explore in writing what is important to us, is particularly pertinent.

Chapter 2

# National nature reserves

## Nature as other confined

*Sue Elworthy*

### Introduction

In this essay I explore some of the cultural underpinnings that are embedded in the designation of land in Britain as national nature reserves, with a focus on the Huxley Report (1947), published during the period of reconstruction following the Second World War. As a legal strategy, designation, or zoning of areas, has been the backbone of British nature conservation law and has been more influential than might be realised. After the 1940s, Sir Julian Huxley, who proposed the nature reserves in Britain, was the first chairman of the United Nations Educational, Scientific and Cultural Organisation and the Duke of Edinburgh was the head of the World Wildlife Fund, so the British approach to nature conservation was exported and became the pattern for much international and European Union law. The suggestion here is that this strategy, to set aside places for 'nature', is symptomatic of a deep malaise which sees and experiences 'nature' as 'other'. Consequently, it is ambiguous and flawed as a technique for protection. I do not propose an alternative blueprint because, pragmatically, very often species are protected better inside the areas than they would be without the designations. It might be thought that after nearly half a century the system is now probably so entrenched as to be beyond dismantling, but I am not sure about this: national nature reserves come into being from public law which is still vulnerable to private property interests. My purpose, rather, is to look at some of the ambiguities inherent in it. I offer a feminist perspective on the allocation of land for nature reserves as a contribution to the subject of using law for nature conservation rather than as a total refutation of designation of land as a strategy. I also want to express my admiration for Sir Julian Huxley, whose achievements were monumental, and admit that I rather enjoy his 'man of action' style. Is it contradictory to recognise a rampant masculine approach, and critique it as such, and to admire the energy that seizes an opportunity, argues a case forcefully and gets things done? The masculinity I discuss is situated here in the 1940s: the Second World War and the post-war reconstruction period.

## Background: a post-war legislative legacy

The Labour government after the Second World War enacted extensive legislation to re-order life in Britain, much of it based on reports that had been prepared during the war. With hindsight we might judge these reports as contradictory in that sometimes they foresaw the need for radical change after the fighting had stopped, and sometimes they assumed that peace would bring a return to the old settled ways. Their legacy, in the physical shape of the land we live in now and our assumptions about the proper places for activities, is a good reason to return to them. There were three items of legislation in particular that were concerned with arrangements for land use and that have determined the character and function of the land in the half-century since they were enacted: the Agriculture Act 1947, the Town and Country Planning Act 1947 and the National Parks and Access to the Countryside Act 1949.

The first, the Agriculture Act 1947, was not concerned with nature conservation at all but is central to understanding the countryside we have now and the place of 'nature' within it. The Act was strongly influenced by the Scott Report (1942) which argued that after the war a prosperous farming industry would be essential. The Government had assured farmers there would be no return to relying on imported food. Free trade in food had been the consistent policy since the repeal of the Corn Laws in the 1870s until the Agricultural Marketing Act 1931 replaced it with a policy of protection, apart from a brief period from 1920–1 when the Corn Production Act 1917 attempted to stimulate farmers to produce more home grown food by supporting grain prices. Although the Corn Production Act 1917 had been an emergency measure related to the First World War, its repeal became known to farmers as 'The Great Betrayal', because severe agricultural depression in Britain followed the return to free trade in food. In the 1940s, with such recent experience of near starvation during another war, as a result of the loss of Atlantic shipping convoys, and more crucially a lack of money to pay for imported food, it was essential to continue the wartime policy to maximise agricultural production.

With hindsight, the most significant measure was s 11(2) of the Agriculture Act 1947, which set out rules of good husbandry. At the time, this section merely put wartime regulations on a new statutory footing, but the rules became central to farming culture. This was achieved by 'carrots', in the form of generous price supports and grants, as well as 'sticks' by appointing Country Agricultural Executive Committees to ensure the rules of good husbandry were followed. If they were not, the Committee had coercive powers. Under the rules, permanent pasture was to be properly mown or grazed and 'maintained in a good state of cultivation and fertility'. The manner in which arable land was being cropped was to be such as to maintain that land 'clean' and in a 'good state of cultivation and fertility'. If livestock was kept, the unit was to be 'properly stocked'. The County Committees kept a close eye on the farmers in their areas to make sure the rules were being followed. Between the enactment of the Agricultural Act 1947 and its repeal in 1958, under a Conservative administration, five thousand farmers were placed under supervision orders and four hundred were dispossessed (Lowe 1986). Despite the repeal of the powers in 1958, the rules of good husbandry have been referred to in legislation for farming ever since. The rules are usually incorporated into agricultural tenancy agreements so that tenants may be served with a Certificate of Bad Husbandry should they fail to abide by them. These rules form the basis of highly intensive industrial agriculture, heavily dependent on agrochemicals and huge machinery, which has become known as 'conventional farming'. This has proved to be disastrous for wild animals, wild plants and, especially, for insects and the birds that feed on them.

The second Act to organised land use after the Second World War was the Town and Country Planning Act 1947. This Act ensured that development was to be controlled and no urban development could take place without planning permission. Crucially, agriculture and forestry were exempted from development control, including agricultural buildings and the intensification of use which could otherwise constitute development under the Act. Instead, in the countryside there has grown up an elaborate system of designation of areas of land, often overlapping (Ross and Stockdale 1996). This Act separated urban and rural land use fundamentally, reserving the rural for commercial agriculture and commercial forestry. In particular, the Town and Country Planning Act 1947 was intended to control 'shackery'. It prohibited the pre-war attempts by people who lived in the towns to have a weekend place in the country by converting disused railway carriages, building makeshift huts and setting up smallholdings. This influx of poor people from the cities to the country horrified the landowning class, which viewed it as disorderly urban sprawl and as blight on the idealised countryside of the Scott Report (Elworthy and Holder 1997). The countryside was to be for farming, to be productive and above all to look tidy and well cared for. Overgrown hedges and scruffy pastures spelt pre-war depression; not, as they would today, biodiversity:

> In large part the beauties of Britain are man-made. Left to themselves the fields would quickly revert to thickets of shrub and brambles interrupted by bogs choked with reeds and rushes. The British countryside to-day owes its characteristic features to the fact that it has been used – in other words it has been farmed. The countryside cannot be 'preserved' (though its particular value to the nation can be); it must be farmed if it is to retain those features which give it distinctive charm and character.
>
> (Scott Report 1942)

The third Act to organise the use of land was the National Parks and Access to the Countryside Act 1949. This Act was a response to the demand in the 1930s from the urban industrial workers for access to land for recreation. What is striking now is how very modest the Ramblers' Association's demands were: just to be allowed to go for walks across moorland, while enjoying some fresh air and sunshine away from the smoky cities. Equally striking is just how adamant the landowners were that walkers would disturb the grouse on the moors. Even now, walkers are only reluctantly tolerated by most landowners, many of whom seem to the latter to be close to vermin. After rallies and demonstrations by thousands of people in Derbyshire and the historic mass trespass of Kinder Scout in 1932, after which five protesters were imprisoned, it was clear that any post-war settlement must accommodate the demand for townspeople to walk in the country (Coates 1995: 69). The Ministry of Town and Country Planning set up the Wildlife Conservation Special Committee, chaired by the biologist Julian Huxley, and the Scottish Wild Life Conservation Committee, chaired by Professor James Ritchie, to consider setting up national parks. Huxley seized the chance to have some space allocated for nature conservation. The National Parks and Access to the Countryside Act 1949 also provided for the state to either buy or lease land to be set apart as national nature reserves. In this Act lie also the origins of the system of Sites of Special Scientific Interest, on which all subsequent nature conservation law rested until the Countryside and Rights of Way Act 2000 transposed the UN Convention on Biological Diversity 1992 into domestic law.

Creating areas where 'nature' will be protected probably reinforced the thrust of the Agriculture Act 1947 to maximise production and normalised the view that modern, progressive farmers should fight with natural forces to grow food for the country, should overcome 'nature' rather than working with it, or at least alongside species other than those cultivated or husbanded for the market. The Town and Country Planning Act 1947 left farmers free to get on with their 'good husbandry', as it was now defined by the rules in the Agriculture Act 1947. One thinks again of the great report writers of the Second World War, as the bombs fell around them and London burned, imagining a sunlit upland, a country of peace and order. Here was a chance for a new beginning. Initial scarcity would be overcome and eventually there would be plenty and wellbeing for all. The nation would prosper.

## Designation for 'nature'

As a strategy for control, designation or zoning has a long colonial history. The British Empire was a patchwork of designations of land with an elaborate system of reserves for diverse peoples; governance by 'divide and rule' entrenched differences with the result that many parts of the world have had to live with the consequences ever since. For example, South Africa's system of apartheid was built on solid British foundations. Zoning for game conservation, in order to protect the game and give it land to roam, would have followed it quite naturally in the colonial bureaucracy from designating tribal reserves. After the International Conference of Wildlife in 1933, a national parks system was set up in Kenya to protect game from people. The settlers were clearing wild animals from land they were turning into cattle ranches, the 'white hunters' were killing game excessively on their safaris, and also Africans were hunting for the pot, for sport and to trade ivory and skins (Steinhart 1989). These game reserves themselves, of course, are the descendants of the royal forests in England, established by the Normans, where land was reserved for the King's hunting parties.

I suggest there are similarities between delineating areas of land for 'nature' and marking out domestic space as the proper place for women. The Beveridge Report, also written during 1942, was in many ways as conservative as the Scott Report. Scott imagined away the wholesale ploughing up of ancient pastures to feed a wartime population, which was proceeding as the report was being produced, and wrote of the farmers and foresters as 'unconsciously the nation's landscape gardeners' (Scott 1942: para 160). In a similar fashion, Beveridge assumed the millions of married women working in factories and on farms to help the war effort would go back to their kitchens after the war. Married women were to access the new welfare state through their husbands' national insurance. They would play their part in reconstructing society doing 'work which is vital though unpaid, without which the nation could not continue' (Beveridge 1942: 49).

An obvious but still fundamental point is that any designation immediately creates the class of all that is not designated. If the designation is for the protection of what is inside the delineation, then all that remains outside becomes more vulnerable to the forces operating there. Here I remember the Contagious Diseases Acts from 1864 to 1886 which controlled prostitution in naval and military districts. In those districts any woman could be arrested on suspicion of being a common prostitute and unless she could prove she was not, would be registered as such and medically examined on a regular basis (O'Donovan 1985: 100). The division of women into the chaste, the domesticated, and the unchaste, those outside, most certainly rendered the undomesticated more vulnerable to police attention and fixed the identity of prostitute, by criminalisation, on many girls who would otherwise have merely offered sexual services to the fighting men of the Empire as a transitional stage in their working lives. And the division between the private sphere of the household and the public sphere does not protect women from male violence. I do not want to stretch this analogy to the absurd and suggest that dedicated wardens of our nature reserves are in reality frequently persecuting the animals and birds and pulling up protected plants, but I do think that it holds for the increased vulnerability of species outside the reserves. From the late 1940s the whole administrative apparatus of nature conservation was focused on the national nature reserves and the sites of special scientific interest. This continued until 1990, when the Countryside Survey started to log wildlife and flora on ordinary farmland. By this time the ravages of modern industrial agriculture had reduced many populations drastically (Barr 1993).

The division into public and private spheres in the case of national nature reserves and the surrounding country is contradictory and at first sight seems to be the reverse of the domestic demarcation for women. The nature reserves are administered by the state, with the land outside in private ownership and under private control. Any participation in a scheme for conservation, such as the environmentally sensitive areas scheme, is on a voluntary basis. When this scheme was first established the state compensated farmers for the extra profits they might have made if they had farmed the land intensively. The Countryside Stewardship schemes are also voluntary and farmers are paid by the state directly for their extra work, which it is understood by both sides to the agreement is only done as a public benefit and as a service to the 'townies'. The wider countryside is, in effect, a jealously guarded private sphere (Cooper 1999) where the farmer is free to exploit the land to the limit and other species live there on sufferance. The right of the landowner to use his land as he pleases is, paradoxically, reinforced by the ownership of much land by conservation charities such as the Royal Society for the Protection of Birds, who find ownership of land the most effective way to protect birds. If the land is, in formal terms, in public ownership, the rights of the public body are not the same as for a private property owner, again reinforcing the countryside as a private sphere. In *R v Somerset County Council ex p Fewings* [1995] 3 All ER 20, where the council attempted to ban hunting on its land, the courts held that local government's rights as property owner depended on the statute under which the land was held. In this case Somerset Council had acted *ultra vires* (Cooper 1999: 117).

Davina Cooper has shown how the rural is analogous to the domestic and is perceived as bearing and reproducing national identity (Cooper 1999: 122). The Scott Report (1942: para 160) was explicit on this point:

> We regard the countryside as the heritage of the whole nation and, furthermore, we consider that the citizens of this country are the custodians of a heritage they share with all those of British descent and that it is a duty incumbent upon the nation to take proper care of that which it holds in trust.

Indeed the countryside, or rather the rural scene, could be said to have constituted a national identity. Elizabeth Helsinger tells us that Constable himself saw his paintings of rural scenes as portable icons, 'movable household gods to accompany the displaced rural bourgeois and his family to the city (or to the colonies), where they might help to reconstitute his household by blessing it with distinctively English presiding presences' (1997: 27). The landscapes of England, both representations and in actuality, with their 'naturalness' of asymmetry, apparently unpruned trees and roads following contours could be contrasted with the rigidities of French constructed landscapes, particularly Versailles. This 'naturalness' could mean 'liberty' to the British, meaning the liberties of constitutional monarchy and the freedoms of the common law. The countryside, as landscape, was central to the construction of national consciousness. And, after a war against the Nazis, how important as a 'heritage' of the nation, indeed of all those of 'British descent', the countryside would continue to be. The ironies embedded here are deep indeed. During the 1940s, the period in which I situate my perspective, my own father was planting trees on savannah land in colonial Kenya quite self-consciously in order to create a landscape as close to Constable's rural scenes as he could. The freedoms of the common law most certainly did not apply to the common people of Kenya then, but he never doubted that creating a 'rural scene' that was recognisably English was to bring a blessing to East Africa. Along with building bridges, roads and railway lines, changing the land to resemble a Constable rural scene was to civilise a wild land, to bring it into proper shape, to give it 'character'. Ant hills were broken down, the antelope were fenced out and windbreaks of trees were planted. Ayrshire cattle were imported to cross-breed with the native cattle. The results were impressive and when I visited our farm in 1996 my family thought it looked just like Devon.

## The Huxley Report

I now turn to the arguments in the Huxley Report (1947) for setting land aside for national nature reserves. The first argument is the 'heritage' one – the sites to be selected were 'both ancient monuments and living museums'; but conservation was not to be a passive exercise, protecting nature against something. Rather, this 'negative attitude' was to be replaced with an 'active policy' to advance pure knowledge and to apply that knowledge for the greater benefit of man. In sites of scientific education a better appreciation of nature could be fostered to 'invigorate and refresh the mind'. The sites would become outdoor classrooms for training students, amongst whom would be the recruits to the Biological Service it was proposed to set up (Huxley 1947: 12). There are issues for feminists here.

### *A past history of land*

In the Huxley Report (1947) the first argument for the establishment of nature reserves makes a radical assertion. 'Nature' is appropriated as culture, there being 'but a narrow gap' between the custody of ancient monuments, museums for the preservation of objects of artistic, scientific and cultural value and the proposed nature reserves. The report claims the reserves would be 'a living embodiment of the past history of the land'. But the sites selected were where there were the least traces of human activity, where the land was 'for one reason or another beyond the margins of economic development' (Huxley 1947: 13). The 'past history' that the sites would illustrate is so distant as to be before humans had made an appreciable difference, where the marks of the last ice age can be discerned easily and the 'boney structure' of the land is evident: 'the forms and dispositions of the rocks . . . the shapes of the valleys and summits, the flow of the streams, the cliffs and dunes and flats of the past' (Huxley 1947: 12). The gap between these examples of rock formations and sand dunes and ancient monuments such as iron age forts seems to me far from narrow, denying the very meaning of culture as that which is cultivated, tilled, worked upon. The reserves were selected for their wildness, for their 'naturalness', for their lack of the marks of people. This is a pre-history of the land. Hedges, in contrast, do tell a history of the land, of ancient paths to hill forts, of forest remnants, of Celtic field borders and, of course, of enclosures (Holder 1999).

Certainly an appreciation of landscape is enhanced enormously by some understanding of geology, but there is much to unpick in 'wildness' and especially in protecting wild spaces, in protecting wild 'nature' (Heller 1993). At one level wildness, or wilderness, is where the household is not. From this perspective wilderness is another place, a place for putting aside, for reaching for a spiritual plane above the mundane world. Our culture has deep roots in wilderness, from the Biblical Old Testament prophets, Jesus in the wilderness, to the modern deep ecologists' thinking like glaciers and being like mountains, saving the planet, our Mother Earth. Generally wilderness has been where there are no women, or at least it is far from the settled, tilled, worked upon places where women will be. Today one finds as many women as men walking the wild hills, and many men in the kitchen, but perhaps women too, go to the hills to escape the constraints and responsibilities of the household.

### *The need for educational facilities*

The national nature reserves were to serve two important educational functions. The first was as outdoor classrooms. Students need to be trained, and field trips to the reserves would enhance their understanding of the principles they had been taught in the lecture rooms. Without field trips, teaching 'tends to become warped and lifeless' (Huxley 1947: 13). In the Huxley Report there is much emphasis placed on the aesthetic importance of the reserves in fostering a general public opinion:

> The true appreciation of scenery rests in part upon, and is certainly enhanced by, some understanding of what may be likened to its boney structure – the forms and dispositions of the rocks and the variety of landscape which these induce, the shapes of the valleys and summits, the flow of the streams, the cliffs and dunes and flats of the past, and all the rich

> verdure with which they are clothed. These are things which can invigorate and refresh the mind. The more widely the appreciation can be diffused, the sounder will be the mental and physical health of the nation and the safer will become the places where these pleasures are to be enjoyed.
>
> (Huxley 1947: 12).

This is wilderness transcendentalism. It is a celebration of supposedly 'virgin' country, of land that is not obviously 'husbanded', made to bear fruit by cultivation. It is difficult not to feel that the minds that are to be 'invigorated and refreshed' by contemplating cliffs and summits will be in male bodies, healthily sweaty from the climb to the top; the mental equivalent of the boarding school cold shower after a good game of rugby in the rain. This brings together the attitude to nature of the Romantics, in particular Wordsworth, finding spiritual refreshment in contemplation of unspoilt landscape, and the attitude that sees land as 'an invigorating obstacle course' (Smout 1990: 25). Here there is an engagement with the land, but it is almost consumerist: the hill-walkers who 'bag' Munros, the peaks over 3,000 ft in Scotland, surely have healthy minds in healthy bodies. It is a view that is content with surfaces, with a superficial quick look at the land before the gaze is turned inward and the serious task of spiritual purification is undertaken. But in Britain there is virtually no land which has been untouched by humans (Bennet 1996). The open character of our uplands is the result of forest clearance by Neolithic farmers and continuous grazing since. Aerial archaeology has shown field patterns everywhere. Any summer, coachloads of tourists will head north from Inverness, most believing they will see one of Europe's few remaining 'wildernesses', but some will be returning Gaels from the outer islands or from overseas come to see the land of the Clearances. They will look for the faint remains of their ancestors' fields. Some understanding of glacial formation may enhance an appreciation of scenery, but a reading of landscape that includes human history must lead to a richer understanding and a deeper culture (Rackham 1986).

### *Woman as nature*

In the post-war settlement of the 1940s the Beveridge Report firmly zoned married women in the domestic sphere again, and the Huxley Report zoned nature into the national nature reserves. Both were once again constructed as 'other'; women domesticated (retamed, reclaimed, after their wartime spent as workers); nature as 'wild' but also confined. The central theme of defining both women and nature as 'others', separate from the world of action, of production and exchange, is played out. In both demarcations for these 'others', reproduction is the assigned purpose; children and cultural reproduction for women, wild species reproduction for nature so that the 'representative samples' can be studied.

I want to look a little here at the connections between wild nature and women. This theme has been central in western culture, worked and reworked in every medium of cultural reproduction. The woman portrayed most often in western art has, of course, been the Virgin Mary, and the tensions inherent in the contradiction of the twin ideals of the virgin mother have informed our art for 2,000 years (Warner 1976). The body of Mary, as a sealed vessel who gave birth with neither penetration nor labour, was used to symbolise purity and spirituality in contrast to the leakiness of mortal women's natural bodies; in this iconography the only acceptable fluid is milk, life-giving milk and the comfort of the breast. But for 400 years this has not been the art of Britain, where the dominant religion has been Protestant Christianity: in Marina Warner's words 'a sombre-suited masculine world . . . altogether too much like a gentleman's club to which the ladies are only admitted on special days' (Warner 1976: 338). Women priests are now changing this but they face the overwhelming masculinity of a Protestantism without any female focus. And why are they called 'women priests', rather than 'priestesses'? Perhaps because 'priestess' is too suggestive of heathen nature cults. The cult of romantic love from the troubadours on depicted an ideal woman, disembodied and remote. The ideal love is unconsummated and the lady needs the protection of her knight from all manner of dragons. These images recur again and again in modern deep ecology where nature is idealised (Sale 1985). The suffragettes struggled with the weight of representations of women's physicality, their potential fecundity presupposing their unfitness for anything beyond reproduction. Their campaign had to be visible, and highly visible, to claim a space in the public sphere. The figure of the female warrior, especially Joan of Arc, actively pure and spiritual with her straight boyish body clothed in armour, was used in campaign posters and possessions to counter the opponents' portrayal of the suffragettes as hysterical, hysteria being so closely associated with women's menstruation (Betterton 1966). Occasionally fecundity has been celebrated, as in Reynold's painting 'Three Ladies Decorating A Herm of Hymen' (1773), now in the Tate Gallery, where the three Montgomery sisters celebrating the marriage of one of them hang garlands of flowers, the flowers signifying nature and fecundity. And some feminists have been positive about women's identification with nature, aligning men's supposed separation from both women and nature as instances of the false dichotomies of patriarchy (Griffin 1978).

### A constructive scientific policy

The Huxley Report stressed that what was needed was a constructive scientific policy, rather than 'the merely passive idea implied in the word conservation . . . to protect something *against* something else' (1947: 12). Its conclusions were not based on this 'negative attitude' but on 'a positive need for reserves of varying types because they are required in pursuit of an active policy – a policy which will make the best use of the nation's heritage not only for the advancement of pure knowledge . . . but for the application of that knowledge for the greater benefit of man' (Huxley 1947: 12). So, nature was to be zoned into national nature reserves and studied. This is an extreme expression of a deep-seated anthropocentrism that sees nature as totally separate from people, as a resource to be exploited or at best harnessed. Here is articulated the Enlightenment certainty that rests on the Baconian creed that the laws of nature are first quite knowable and second that they can and should be for man's benefit (Holder 2000). This seems to me a very western masculine approach to the pursuit and application of knowledge. It is a male gaze that seeks to capture the other, in this case to study it and then to use it. I suggest it is both instrumental and voyeuristic. We have here the core Enlightenment rationality. Nature is all that is wild and savage. Civilised man's role is to subdue, tame and dominate nature, by ordering it in a rational scientific way, and then use it to develop technology. Thus nature reserves would be places first to observe and then to classify (Foucault 2002).

Ordering was to be the first part of the project. How we describe the world is how we live in it; naming is the first domination: 'And out of the ground the Lord God formed every beast of the field, and every fowl of the air; and brought them unto Adam to see what he would call them: and whatsoever Adam called every living creature, that was the name thereof' (Genesis, Chapter II, verse 19). Today's lists of species, annexes that run to pages and pages at the end of European directives, international treaties and domestic regulations are a defining characteristic of nature conservation law.

Richard Leakey tells us that Huxley even suggested that the ordering and naming should classify humans entirely separately from the rest of the world of nature: 'Non-human animals, plants and all other organisms are classified in various kingdoms of their own, each in company with many species. In Huxley's view, humans would be the sole occupants of their own biological kingdom', because they were evolving by the new method of cultural transmission (Leakey and Lewin 1998: 81). Since then Jane Goodall's work with gorillas has eroded the boundary between humans and apes who also use tools, have a culture and are self-aware. They may even have language (Leakey and Lewin 1998: 82).

Designating areas as 'representative samples', geologically, which contain specified species, implies a view of 'nature' as essentially static. The half-century since the first national nature reserves were designated has proved this not to be so. In comparison with the situation outside the reserves, 'nature' inside them has flourished and an apparent paradox is that protection has in some cases come near to destroying the very features for which the site was first selected as successful species have overrun the available area. To keep the reserves as they are takes an enormous effort of management and intervention. However, in many places it has proved impossible to manage 'nature' successfully in the sites, as the outside world has impinged with acid deposits from the air and water over-enriched from agricultural fertilisers.

The work in the nature reserves was to be carried out by a 'Biological Service'. Again this must be placed in its historical context. It is no surprise that in 1947, so soon after a war, there should be an almost military call for its formation. Under the National Parks and Access to the Countryside Act 1949 this became the Nature Conservancy. Later, under the Environmental Protection Act 1990 this body would be split into English Nature, Scottish Natural Heritage, the Countryside Council for Wales and the Joint Nature Conservation Committee with representatives from other bodies and from Northern Ireland. It is not that I want to suggest any maleness in this approach during the 1940s. Masculinities are also historically specific (Connell 1995). Here is a man who wants to get on with his important work: scientific studies, research and experiments to provide the data upon which 'a practical and active policy' are to be based. So who are these national nature reserves for? I want to give the last word to Julian Huxley: 'For instance, there is the natural history bent. Many boys, often with poor mechanical ability, have a passion for Nature. When this is combined with a strong collecting instinct, it may produce the systematic zoologist or botanist; when not so combined it is likely to give the world the general biologist or geologist. Charles Darwin had a very strong collecting instinct, combined with a deep love of Nature' (Huxley 1934: 215–16). 'Science is not the disembodied sort of activity that some people would make out, engaged on the abstract task of pursuing universal truth, but a social function intimately linked up with human history and human destiny. And the sooner scientists as a body realise this and organise their activities on that basis, the better both for science and for society' (Huxley 1934: 279).

## Conclusion

The post-Second World War reconstruction project was given effect through extensive legislation to reorder life in Britain. How the land was used was central. The creation of national nature reserves on land that was 'beyond the margin of economic development' was a fairly effective way to protect the rare and the beautiful and to provide 'outdoor classrooms' for scientific study, but was quite inadequate to safeguard the common song birds and wild flowers against the thrust of the rules of good husbandry laid out in the Agriculture Act 1947 with the Common Agricultural Policy of the European Union superimposed to maximise agricultural production. The farmers have been the guardians of the countryside that now, indeed, seems close to the 'factory floor' as they often call it. The 'nation' is poorer.

Chapter 3

# Ancient monuments of national importance

## Symbols of whose past?

*Penny English*

### Introduction

The evidence of the past surrounds us; the physical environment which makes up the rural landscape, as much as obviously man-made townscape, is the result of the past activities that have shaped them. Although the totality of the environment is the result of the accumulation of human activity over time, certain elements stand out, both physically and in social consciousness, as monuments to the past history of the land. These have gained the attribute of historical significance which makes them publicly valued. Not all the material remains of the past are perceived in the same way. Some places where the past use of the land is clearly evident are regarded as not important but simply as derelict or blighted land, brownfield sites ripe for redevelopment. Others are considered to be places of historical or archaeological significance, preserved from future decay or destruction. The visible remains of the past may be preserved, destroyed or allowed to decay as a consequence of decisions about what is worth publicly remembering. Some of these are identified in law as being of national importance, as part of a 'national heritage'. Ancient monuments and historic buildings which have been designated in this way have thereby been identified as representing the nation's cultural and social identity in a very tangible way, forming physical markers of its history on and in the ground. They take on a political and symbolic role in the present as part of the telling and retelling of the nation's story. These decisions are culturally determined, subject both to the deliberate pursuit of political considerations in the present and the unconscious projection of modern social roles and relationships of power onto the past. Approaching from a feminist perspective the process which decides the nature of the public vision of the past, represented by the ancient monuments which have been chosen for protection, highlights the political nature of such decisions.

Particularly significant ancient monuments may be singled out for recognition as monuments of national importance. Ancient monuments can include anything from a prehistoric stone circle to a modern house, from buried archaeological sites to substantial standing buildings. Indeed, under the definition of monument in the Ancient Monuments and Archaeological Areas Act 1979, they need neither be ancient nor monumental. When such places are identified as of national importance, the legal rights of the owner are affected. This acknowledges that because of their connection with the past, the public has an interest in them sufficient to override certain private property rights. In England and Wales, designation of places as 'scheduled ancient monuments' does not change their legal status as private property, but it does enable the law to place restrictions on the absolute rights of the landowner. They have become, in some limited sense at least, public property. Having attained this status, it then becomes relevant to question the basis for determining which monuments should be included in this category.

Archaeological heritage management, the policy and associated legislation of protecting, preserving and conserving sites and monuments, is more than a set of procedures and rules. Rather than being a purely neutral and technical process, it is an intensely political activity, intertwined with identity politics because of the link with the way heritage is used to symbolise group and individual identity at national, local and ethnic levels. Since political power in the present determines how history is told, alternative versions of the past such as those of minority or other subordinate groups may be either actively discounted or passively rendered invisible. Those pasts may risk being invisible in a very real sense if the selection process concentrates on the conservation and preservation of monuments and buildings which represent a particular vision of the past. The choice of which places are protected for the present and future (and how these are interpreted and presented) cannot therefore be viewed uncritically: 'the traditional subaltern roles and positions of women, working-class communities and migrant and ethnic communities in the present can be reinforced or challenged by providing uncritical interpretations' (Smith 2004: 7).

The law concerning the protection of the historic environment in the UK is complex. There are currently different regimes which apply to ancient monuments and historic buildings. The former may be scheduled ancient monuments under the Ancient Monuments and Archaeological Areas Act 1979, while the latter may be listed buildings falling within the Planning (Listed Buildings and Conservation Areas) Act 1990. As well as these mechanisms to protect individual sites or buildings, the historic environment is taken into consideration in planning decisions.[1] Planning law is increasingly important as the mechanism for protecting places of archaeological significance, since only a small minority of monuments are individually protected as scheduled ancient monuments. The Government plans to simplify this web of provisions and has embarked on a process of revision which will remove the distinctions between the protection for ancient monuments and historic buildings, merging them into a single register. Some changes have already been made while others will require primary legislation. A White Paper was expected in 2006, and the Government announced its intention to include new legislation in the 2006–7 parliamentary session.

## Ascribing significance

The focus of attention here is on one of the existing categories, that of ancient monuments which are scheduled under the Ancient Monuments and Archaeological Areas Act 1979.[2] This means that they have been identified as having a significance which marks them out as being of 'national importance'. This attribution of significance is crucial. It is the process which identifies those places deemed to be of sufficient importance that they should be protected by law in the public interest. The criteria on which these decisions are based can never be wholly objective or purely technical, but will always be a product of socially and politically situated assumptions and priorities.

Nevertheless, decisions have to be made about which parts of the cultural heritage should be preserved, since it would be neither feasible nor desirable to retain everything. The remains of the past undergo a process of significance evaluation. This distinguishes, formally or informally, those parts of the past which are worthy of being remembered and those which are to be discarded. Not all the monuments which are now protected by law have always been treasured in the public consciousness. Many have been allowed to decay and their materials have been reused for new buildings, before a later generation has decided that they are of such value that they should be preserved.[3] Significance is therefore not a constant: 'objects or places may be considered important at one time and "not worth bothering about" at others' (Ucko 1990: xiii). Other parts of the past may be deliberately erased for political reasons.[4] What is clear is that the value of archaeological and historic sites and monuments is a socially determined variable. Besides changing over time, no one single value equates to significance. The result is a 'cacophony of voices' (Warren 1989: 1), each expressing different values. It is too simple to say that it is the 'public interest' which is being represented:

> Value is not inherent in any cultural items or properties received from the past . . . Value is learned about or discovered in these phenomena by humans, and this depends on the particular cultural, intellectual, historical, and psychological frames of reference held by the particular individuals or groups involved.
>
> (Lipe 1984: 2)

From a feminist perspective, if the values underlying the archaeological interpretations which form the basis of significance evaluation include gendered assumptions, this will bring the selection process into question.

## Development of archaeological legislation

The current legislation, and the ways in which significance is determined, need to be viewed in the context of their own history. The framework for the public determination of significance was established within the development of archaeology as a discipline and the parallel introduction of legislation concerning the archaeological heritage. The degree of interest shown in the remains of the past, and the specific focus of that interest, is very much a product of its own age. Although systematic study of the past began in Europe in the seventeenth century, it was not until the nineteenth century that archaeology emerged as a scientific discipline. Prior to that, interest in the past was largely an aristocratic pursuit taking the form of antiquarianism, which had the classical past of Greece and Rome as its main interest.[5] The focus of the discipline of archaeology was different. It was primarily interested in prehistory rather than classical antiquity, and Darwin's work on evolution was pivotal to the development of a scientific approach to the study and classification of the material culture of the past.

The basis for the understanding of prehistory was therefore developing within the broader intellectual framework of the age as part of part of a wider evolutionary metanarrative, linked to ideas of social progress (Walsh 1992: 9). Archaeology was becoming a professional activity rather than an aristocratic pursuit, moving out of the private domain and into the public arena. At the same time, archaeology became closely involved with contemporary political developments. The emergence of archaeology and of legislation to protect ancient monuments cannot be divorced from the rise of the nation-state in Europe. The imagined community (Anderson 1991) of the nation needed a past to legitimise its political existence, and by projecting the nation back into the distant past, and linking it to a distinct cultural or ethnic group in history, it was possible to demonstrate the continuity of the nation as an entity. Archaeology was able to provide the physical evidence of cultural continuity through the study of prehistoric sites and remains, whereby the political boundaries of the present could be portrayed as natural and enduring. These prehistoric monuments then became symbols of that nation and its history, helping to reinforce its existence in the present. A distinct place, then, is being established for archaeology within the public sphere, within the positivist and evolutionary scientific discourse of the age and with the emerging professional class. At the same time it has close links with the formation of national identity and the consolidation of political power within the state. Legislation to protect and preserve the monuments which archaeology had now established as belonging to the national past was then a logical step. This relationship of archaeology to the construction of identity, particularly national identity, has been a prominent theme in recent archaeological writing (see, for example, Graves-Brown and Gamble 1996, Diaz-Andreu and Champion 1996, Jones 1996, Kohl and Fawcett 1995).

The current legislation to protect ancient monuments is based on the system established by the earliest legislation in England to be concerned with ancient monuments, the Ancient Monuments Protection Act 1882. That Act did not have an easy passage through Parliament. For a decade Sir John Lubbock (later Lord Avebury), a leading archaeologist and prehistorian and a close friend of Darwin, annually but unsuccessfully introduced his Private Member's Bill in Parliament. Influenced by the system in place in Denmark, he proposed the setting up of a National Monuments Commission to look after ancient monuments, which would be able to acquire monuments by agreement, or compulsorily where an owner wished to destroy a monument. His Bill was consistently opposed in Parliament because it was seen as encroaching on private property rights.[6] The opposition to Lubbock's Bill had its roots in the major social and economic transformation which was taking place in England in the nineteenth century. The landed aristocracy had long been the dominant political power, but this was changing. The landowning class, the lobby that most vociferously opposed the ancient monuments legislation, was increasingly under threat from the rising and increasingly prosperous professional and middle classes. As Carman puts it: 'The dispute over preservation was ultimately less to do with the relative merits and demerits of the protection to be afforded to ancient monuments by the law on one hand and private owners on the other, than simple and rather brute power politics' (Carman 1996: 87).

Eventually a compromise Bill was introduced by George Shaw-Lefevre which was passed. The resulting Act was less effective than the one which had first been envisaged by Lubbock, since it did not include any element of compulsion (Saunders 1983: 11, Baldwin Brown 1905: 7, Murray 1989, and Chippindale 1983). It did not, unlike some other European jurisdictions, provide for monuments to automatically become state property. Its achievement, however, was to put in place the framework for the present legislation, despite achieving comparatively little in itself. It established a schedule, or list, of sites, which consisted originally of some 50 prehistoric monuments. 'Monument' was not defined as a term, nor were the grounds for inclusion on the schedule. This was to be a matter for the professional judgment of the Inspector of Ancient Monuments. The schedule remains the backbone of the legislation in force today. Subsequently the 1882 Act came to be recognised as the first step in 'rolling back the landowner's absolute right to treat his property, and any historical relics that might lie on or under it, as he wishes, and towards the building of that apparatus of planning and control that now constrains him' (Chippindale 1983: 1).

The schedule established by the 1882 legislation comprised only prehistoric monuments. This concern with a limited class of monuments is significant because this indicates the extent to which the profession of archaeology was setting the agenda for decisions about what was of national significance. Prehistory was the central concern of professional archaeologists and it was this profession, through the office of the Inspector of Ancient Monuments, that was becoming the arbiter of what was of national importance. It was from the new middle class, operating within an expanding public sphere, that professionals including the prehistoric archaeologists came. Archaeology was born at a time when women had very limited visibility in the public sphere and 'the public sphere was exactly what interested Victorian men as well as those Scandinavian men then involved in forming archaeology as a tool in the process of nation-building' (Dommasnes 1998: 337). Archaeology (and predominantly male archaeologists) had a central role in creating a national identity, and this was predominantly a male identity.

## Theoretical archaeology

Archaeological data, the sites and monuments and the information derived from them have to be interpreted to give them meaning. The theoretical basis for interpretation has undergone several changes of direction since the late nineteenth century. Most recently, since the 1980s, there has been a significant shift in the direction taken by archaeological theory which has implications for the way the material culture of the past is interpreted. The current approaches are termed 'postprocessual' or 'cognitive'.[7] Prior to this, archaeological theory had been dominated by 'processual' archaeology. This had itself been in reaction to the earlier culture-historical approach which had interpreted the archaeological record in order to establish the history of specific peoples based on the association of material assemblages with distinct cultural groups (Trigger 1995: 269). From the 1960s, the 'new archaeology', or processualism, dominated. This sought to base its methodology in positivism, in timeless neutral objectivity. Despite attempting to ally itself with the hard sciences by identifying the processes operating within societies in order to come to generally applicable models, this notion of objectivity in archaeological interpretation has now largely been rejected as false by postprocessual theory. This theoretical shift away from an easy acceptance of a positivist view of knowledge is not one specific to archaeology alone. Feminist research in other disciplines has shown that scientific knowledge is constructed and dependent on context:

> Philosophers of science have demonstrated that there are no disembedded facts. The data used result from the questions asked and the theories held. Facts are not 'out there' waiting to be discovered . . . The idea that science is value-free, objective, and uninfluenced by its cultural milieu has been thoroughly debunked . . . Scientists are fooling themselves with the chimera of objectivity.
>
> (Nelson 2004: 24)

While processual archaeology sought a unified theory, since the 1980s the emphasis has been on recognition of the positioned and subjective nature of archaeological interpretation. The result has been a diversity of approaches within archaeological theory including distinct strands such as post-structuralist, hermeneutic and feminist. The processual view of individuals as passive reflectors of the forces in the environment has been challenged by a developing concern with agency (see, for example, Dobres and Robb 2000). More importantly, as a consequence of the rejection of the possibility of objective interpretation, archaeology has come to be viewed as in inherently and inevitably political enterprise rather than neutral and detached. The archaeologist, far from objectively observing facts and piecing them together as an accurate picture of the past, is an active agent in the construction of a past 'thought expedient for, or dictated by, present interests' (Wylie 1998: 64). Central to this awareness of subjectivity is a critical epistemology which asks whose interests are being served by a particular interpretation of the past: 'Statements about the past are seen as ideological, either supporting the interests of the dominant, or underpinning the resistance of subordinate groups. The relationships between archaeological knowledge and power are examined, and processes of legitimation exposed' (Hodder 2002: 79).This was particularly evident in the context of indigenous peoples' pasts when in the 1980s and 1990s alternative voices began to be heard, but is equally applicable to other identities, such as class, ethnicity – or gender (Gathercole and Lowenthal 1994, Shennan 1994, and Layton 1989).

Archeological accounts of the past cannot, though, be pure fiction. The physical evidence cannot wholly be discounted in writing the story of the past, but some degree of balance has to be sought:

> Where feminist initiatives in *archaeology* are concerned, the encompassing philosophical problem at issue is . . . how we can conceptualise scientific enquiry so that we recognise, without contradiction *both* that knowledge is constructed and bears the marks of its makers, *and* that it is constrained, to a greater or lesser degree, by conditions that we confront as external 'realities' not of our own making.
>
> (Wylie 1998: 67)

Nevertheless, despite the acceptance that there are limits to the extent to which all interpretations of the past can be equally valid, the authenticity of a single scientific and professional body of knowledge has clearly been challenged by opening up the possibility of a plurality of interpretations 'suited to different purposes, needs, desires' (Shanks and Hodder 1995: 5). Without the existence of a single interpretation of archaeological evidence, the justification for a single, professionally-based mechanism for determining the significance of sites and monuments loses its theoretical foundation. 'National heritage' becomes a term without substance. Indeed, the idea of a single national identity itself begins to lose its pre-eminence in the context of the present if identities are themselves multi-layered and dynamic (Franck 1999) and at least partially self-determined; 'the names we give to the different ways we are positioned by, and position ourselves within, the narratives of the past' (Hall 1990: 225).

## Gender archaeology

Within this rejection of positivist processual archaeology and the recognition of the situated and political nature of archaeological interpretation, that it is 'a socially organised, historically contingent context that interacts with and thoroughly conditions the data it is designed to collect' (Gero 1996: 251), a specific focus on gender has evolved. The development of a reflective post-processual archaeology set new agendas for archaeology. In particular, the exposure of the relationship of nationalism to archaeology led to further scrutiny. As Wright (1996: 2) suggests: 'For feminist scholars, this has raised the question "If there is a nationalist bias, then are there other socially informed biases?" '

Feminism played an important part in its development, especially the feminist critiques of science which identified scientific discourse as gendered, privileging a particular way of thinking:

> the dominant categories of cultural experience (white male, middle class) and as such the scientific veneration of objectivity and neutrality have come to be associated with (white middle class) masculinity, as opposed to alternative modes of knowledge that might seek, for instance, intimate knowledge – nuanced, even unique understanding of phenomena.
>
> (Gero 1996: 265)

Women archaeologists had been present from the earliest days of archaeology, although archaeology remained a largely male-gendered profession (and the 'Indiana Jones' stereotype of the archaeologist as intrepid male adventurer still persists). Some feminist influence is evident from the 1970s, especially in Scandinavia (Sørensen 2000: 20–4), but this early feminist archaeology tended to be obscure and marginal, disseminated as grey literature rather than mainstream publications (Nelson 2004: 26). It was relatively late (compared with other disciplines) that the ideas of feminism gained respectability in archaeology, and it is not until the 1980s that a specifically feminist archaeology becomes visible. Conkey (1993: 3) suggests the reason for this late development may be that feminist theory has had less impact in areas 'anchored in positivist epistemologies'. The landmark publication in the emergence of feminist archaeology was a paper by Conkey and Spector in 1984. This was followed in 1991 by the classic *Engendering Archaeology* edited by Gero and Conkey, since when there has been a wealth of publications under the heading 'gender archaeology'.

The earliest phase of the feminist critique of archaeology focused on documenting the absence of women in archaeology. There were two strands to this: firstly, the male domination of the practice of archaeology and secondly, the androcentric bias in the interpretation of material cultures of the past. The problem was more deep-seated than simply a question of the number of women involved in the discipline. Gender assumptions and stereotypes 'pervade conventional approaches, whether applied by men or by women' (Hays-Gilpin and Whitely 1998: 6). That pervasive culture meant interpretations of the past were based on the ascription of higher prestige to the characteristics associated with men, and assumptions were made about the activities undertaken by men and women. Conkey and Spector argued persuasively in their 1984 paper that archaeology was using these gender stereotypes uncritically, despite the claims of the discipline to scientific objectivity: 'Archaeologists, consciously or not, are propagating culturally particular ideas about gender in their interpretations and reconstructions of the past. This aspect of archaeological interpretation not only undermines the plausibility of our reconstructions of the past but also has serious political and educational implications' (Conkey and Spector 1984: 12). Their paper did more than analyse the uncritical assumptions beneath this use of stereotypical beliefs about behaviour. It challenged the function of archaeology in contemporary society, particularly the way it reinforces values, especially those concerning gender roles and the 'pervasive and emotionally charged' public/private dichotomy (McGaw 1996: 69).

The consequence for archaeological interpretation is that rigid division of labour along sexual lines is projected onto past societies, artefacts are interpreted in terms of stereotypical activities and hierarchies of value placed on different activities. Lower value is ascribed to those activities assigned to women than for those activities believed to have been performed by men. The first stage of feminist archaeology, which engaged in revealing embedded androcentrism, led on to a second stage which sought to remedy the absence, trivialisation and marginalisation of women in interpretations of the past. The sometimes unsatisfactory nature of this has been described as a process of 'add women and stir' (Engelstad 2004: 40). The engendering of archaeology is not as simple and straightforward as merely 'finding the women' in the past (Conkey 1993: 3), but this will 'entail much more profound reassessment of orienting theoretical and epistemological presuppositions than had been anticipated' (Wylie 1999: 39). As Sørensen (1996: 52) puts it, there is a need to *think* gender into archaeology, not just *find* gender. The mere *presence* of women should not be the sole aim. So for example, in rethinking bronze age metal-working, 'knowing that both women and men were present, we should aim to explore and understand how the organisation of these various productive technologies affected both men and women and their relationship' (Sørensen 196: 59), producing a far more nuanced understanding of social relationships in the past.

More recent work has indeed shifted the focus towards 'making gender visible rather than making women visible' (Engelstad 2004: 41). Engendering archaeology then becomes a much more complex task:

> Being able to 'assign' certain activities or material culture to males and/or females is not *the* goal; it is not an end nor is it *the* means . . . gender attribution is not even a necessary stage in the process whereby we engender the past, although it *is* certainly and inextricably part of the enquiry.
>
> (Gero and Conkey 1991: 11)

An examination of gender relations rather than gender roles broadens the scope of the enquiry, and leads to an examination of other power relations in society. It embraces a greater plurality of approaches together with an emphasis on difference and the individual construction of meaning. Gender cannot be viewed as an entirely separate, isolated consideration, limited to differences between men's and women's roles, but is 'intertwined and inseparable' from other socially constructed categories such as race and class (Delle 2000: xii). Conkey uses the term 'intersectionality' to describe this; that is 'hierarchies of gender, race, economic class, sexuality, nationality, and so forth, are intersected' (2005: 12).

Although interest in gender developed out of feminism, the relationship is now being pushed into the background. The focus is on gender as a category alongside other major analytical categories, which challenges the 'embedded assumption that it (gender archaeology) should produce a radical and distinctly different feminist past. This view has been necessary for gender archaeology to find a voice, but it has been burdensome and it should now be replaced by more complex agendas' (Sørensen 2000: 4). Viewing archaeological interpretation from a gendered perspective therefore not only ensures that women emerge from the shadows, but leads to a radical shift in the understanding of social relationships in the past. It also opens the way for a different, and more active, engagement with heritage in the present, one which also resonates with recent thinking in geography.

## Feminist historical geography

Ancient monuments are part of the land, fixed points not just in history but also in space. The issues for historical geography are similar to those for archaeology, since both are concerned with the intersection between place, time and society. In parallel with feminist archaeology, a distinctive feminist historical geography has been developing (Morin and Berg 1999) and a similar acknowledgment has been made of the marginalisation or absence of women from the histories that geographers were writing. Geographical knowledge and historical perspectives are as bound up with politics and power as is archaeology. As Doreen Massey puts it: 'challenging certain of the ways in which space and place are currently conceptualised implies, also, indeed necessitates, challenging the currently dominant form of gender definitions and gender relations' (1994: 2).

Space is increasingly seen as a relational concept, not a static one. The spatial, the temporal and the social are all constituted by their interactions with each other. The interconnectedness of these elements has been explored for example by Lefebvre (1991) and Soja (1989). Places are both concrete and products of the mind, made up 'of buildings, field systems, roads and railways as well as myths and legends, statues and ceremonies that link people to a place' (McDowell 1997: 2). Identities are constituted through places, by the social interaction of the individual with locations, a process which takes place within the context of time. The intangible and complex web of social relations which is the concern of gender archaeology is anchored in tangible places, not only in individual iconic monuments but in an active relationship with the locality as a whole. The result is 'a view of space opposed to that which sees it as a flat, immobilised surface, as stasis' (Massey 1994: 4–5). This is precisely what the legal definition of places as monuments of national significance does. In identifying individual places for protection, it attempts to fix their meaning, to create 'a view of place as bounded . . . a site of authenticity, as singular, fixed and unproblematic in identity.' It takes them out of both place and time and fossilises the past by its emphasis on the monumental.

In a modern multicultural world of multiple identities, where social relationships are never static but fluid and contested, it becomes more important to acknowledge that these individual identities are constantly being created out of the interrelationships between place, time and society. The implications for the legal framework for protecting the cultural heritage are clear. This is a feminist issue, but also more than simple a matter of taking gender into account. Ultimately, it is about democratic processes and the place within them for subordinate voices.

## Ancient Monuments and Archaeological Areas Act 1979

As has been noted above, the establishment of the Ancient Monuments Protection Act in 1882 ensured that the professional archaeologist was at the forefront in determining the way in which sites and monuments are selected for legal protection as scheduled ancient monuments, and therefore as in some sense public property. Archaeological theory may have accepted that interpretations of the past are complex, subjective and multiple, but this does not necessarily transfer to the practice of managing the historic environment. If alternative voices, minority, feminist or others cannot be heard, then the assumption of some of the attributions of ownership by the state of such property may even serve to exclude the public, or sections of it as 'State intervention is not inherently more public – more democratic, more empowering' (Robbins 1993: xv).

The Ancient Monuments and Archaeological Areas Act 1979, direct successor to the 1882 legislation, is the current framework within which such decisions are made in England. The position is similar in Wales, but significantly different provisions apply in Scotland and Northern Ireland. The Department for Culture, Media and Sport has overall responsibility for the historic environment. In fulfilling this role with respect to ancient monuments, the Secretary of State is advised by the Historic Buildings and Monuments Commission (more commonly known as English Heritage), a body which was formed by the National Heritage Act 1983. This is an independent body, although most of its funding comes from the Government. A key function of the Secretary of State under the Ancient Monuments and Archaeological Areas Act 1979 is the scheduling of monuments as it requires the Secretary of State to keep a schedule of monuments of national importance (s 1(1)). Although proposals for scheduling can come from private individuals, conservation bodies or local authorities, the Secretary of State must consult English Heritage (s 1(2)) before making a decision, and it is ultimately the Secretary of State who has responsibility for deciding which sites are of national importance. The Secretary of State has the power to include in the schedule any monument which appears to be of national importance. This is the only statutory criterion for inclusion on the list (s 1(3)). The Secretary of State may also exclude any monument from the schedule or amend an entry. There is no statutory definition of national importance, although there are eight non-statutory criteria which relate to the selection of a representative sample of monuments.[8] One of the key proposals for reform to the legislation is to change the role of the Secretary of State. If these changes are enacted, primary responsibility will in future lie with English Heritage, and the role of the Secretary of State will be concerned more with overall policy than decisions about individual sites.

The current legislation therefore retains the original concept of scheduling as the means to protect monuments of national importance. Of the several categories of monument recognised by the Act, scheduled monuments are the most important, since they are the ones which are protected from alteration or destruction. That scheduling serves to preserve monuments is based on the requirement that such sites can only have work carried out on them after formal permission (scheduled monument consent) has been granted. The requirement to obtain permission to carry out works from the Secretary of State (s 2(1)) restricts the owner's freedom to alter or destroy the monument on his or her land. Before consent is given, a public local inquiry must be held, or the applicant given the opportunity of an informal hearing (see Pugh-Smith and Samuels 1996: 28 and Cookson 2000: 98). There is no formal right of appeal, though the decision may be capable of challenge by way of judicial review. Scheduling does not automatically affect the ownership of the site, nor does it provide for access by the public. The Secretary of State does, however, have the power to acquire ancient monuments compulsorily or by agreement or gift (Ancient Monuments and Archaeological Areas Act 1979, s 61). English Heritage or a local authority may also acquire monuments (s 11). In addition the Secretary of State, English Heritage and local authorities can also become guardians of an ancient monument, which means that they have responsibility for maintaining and managing the monument without affecting ownership.

By the 1980s, the number of monuments included on the schedule had increased significantly from the original 50 prehistoric monuments to around 13,000 monuments. Its scope had been extended by the Ancient Monuments Protection Act 1900 to include monuments from later periods as well as prehistoric monuments. Despite this growth, it was recognised that the schedule was inadequate as it represented only a small fraction, perhaps 2 per cent, of the total number of archaeological sites in the country (Darvill, Saunders and Startin 1987). As a result the Monuments Protection Programme was initiated in 1986 to speed up the rate at which sites are added to the list. The purpose underlying the scheme was to ensure the preservation of a representative sample of sites:

> The procedures are framed to enable the case for preservation to be justified on the most objective basis possible. It is one thing to convince fellow archaeologists of the arguments behind the selection process, we must also convince the general public of the validity of our judgments.
>
> (Darvill, Saunders and Startin 1987: 403)

Clearly, then, priority is given to an assessment of the value of a site in terms of an objective, professionally-determined significance. Viewed from outside professional heritage management, this may be seen as both narrow and exclusive, privileging the interests of the profession above the public interest. In attempting to preserve rational and objective sample, the theoretical basis seems to be rooted in processual archaeology, rather than the complex, nuanced and multiple interpretations of the past suggested by postprocessual theory.

## Determining 'national importance'

The Department for Media Culture and Sport was previously known as the Department for National Heritage. The name may have changed,[9] but the idea that there is an identifiable 'national heritage' has not disappeared. There is an underlying assumption that 'national' importance represents a social consensus of what is significant. If archaeological theory accepts that there are multiple ways of interpreting the past, there can be no objectively determined, single view of what is of public importance. The public fractures into multiple publics, but if each of these publics constitutes their identity with reference to the past, then each needs to be able to influence the decisions about the parts of the past which have their survival protected by the law.

Even if a site does appear to the Secretary of State to be of national importance, there is no obligation for it to be included on the schedule. The Secretary of State has broad discretion both when deciding whether remains are of national importance, and if so, whether to schedule them. There is limited statutory right of challenge which applies to the granting of scheduled monument consent, but not to the scheduling itself. The proposed reforms will remedy this by adding a statutory right of appeal, but this will be limited to appeal by the owners of the property. Currently, decisions other than the granting of scheduled monument consent may only be challenged by judicial review. These depend on the rules regarding the establishment of standing, of having 'sufficient interest in the matter to which the application relates' (Supreme Court Act 1981 s 31(3)). This came into prominent notice in the Rose Theatre case.[10] The sixteenth-century Rose Theatre, one of Shakespeare's theatres in London, was discovered during the course of redevelopment. A campaign was mounted to save the site because it was considered to be of national significance, but despite agreement that the site was indeed of national importance, the Secretary of State declined to schedule it. Campaigners formed the Rose Theatre Trust Company and then took legal proceedings by way of judicial review with the aim of compelling the Secretary of State to schedule the site. Schiemann J considered the extent of the Secretary of State's discretion in deciding whether or not to schedule and decided that even if a site is of national importance, this does not give rise to a requirement or presumption that it should be scheduled. Furthermore, the Secretary of State was entitled to take into account additional factors, as he did in this case, not least financial considerations.

## Decision making

Although the decision whether or not to schedule lies with the Secretary of State, the rationale for decisions is based on archaeological significance, with the consequence that 'archaeology, as a privileged form of expertise, occupies a role in the governance and regulation of identity' (Smith 2004: 3). Through the role English Heritage plays as the advisory body guiding government decisions, professional archaeology has an active and central part in determining which places are scheduled and therefore in the way heritage is used to project (or marginalise) identities and groups. 'Such a centralised process, placed in the hands of an unelected body, results in the creation and maintenance of a heritage which, by its very nature, is constituted anti-democratically, and thus represents the past of a favoured fragment of society' (Walsh 1992: 79). By being the state-authorised arbiter of what is significant, the potential for groups to use the heritage as the focal point for their identity and sense of belonging and location is circumscribed. There is an additional problem here. There is a disjunction between contemporary trends in archaeological theory, which do recognise the multivocal and contingent nature of versions of the past, and the theoretical basis of archaeological management decision making.

This theme is explored by Laurajane Smith (1993, 1994, and 2004), who highlights the distance between the highly politicised postprocessual archaeology and the practicalities of heritage management, which is where archaeology is most directly engaged with politics. She writes largely from the perspective of the Australian experience, where the issues of Aboriginal heritage and identity have come under intense political scrutiny. In the context of indigenous peoples' rights to their cultural heritage, it is very clear that where there are disputes over the management and meaning of heritage, what is at stake is the control of identity. However, as Smith observes, 'it operates nonetheless . . . in disputes over the meaning of such things as class, gender, or ethnic or other social, cultural and historical identities' (Smith 2004: 195–6). Postprocessual archaeologists, in accepting the political nature of archaeology as a means to forge identity, recognise the need for a democratic dialogue in order to determine the significance of sites. If this is to have practical reality the mechanism for determining significance, and thereby giving legal recognition to those sites selected, has also to be rooted in democratic discourse.

As archaeological theory has become more and more abstract, 'where abstruse and self-indulgent post-modernist rhetoric thrashes about in search of a referent' (Smith 1994: 301), it has become detached from the practical management of the archaeological resource. The legislation is founded on a rational, positivist archaeological framework. The scientific values and principles of processualism therefore underpin decisions made about what should be identified as worthy of protection, in the interests of stewardship 'an objective and cumulative model of archaeological knowledge . . . whereby archaeology primarily serves posterity by building up a resource of information about the past for future scholars' (Merriman 2002: 558). These values themselves developed when archaeology was predominantly a male profession, and dominated by the values of scientific rationality, itself highly gendered.

Smith links this predominance of processualism to the particular time when archaeology was developing its place within heritage management: 'ideas about archaeological "significance" developed in the same timespan of the 1970s and 1980s as processual theory . . . it was the discourse of archaeological significance that explicitly facilitated the development of archaeology as a technology of government' (Smith 2004: 103). At the time archaeology was establishing itself as a systematic, scientific profession, there was also established a body of legislation which effectively legitimised and institutionalised the profession. The concept of archaeological resource management serving to protect an objective, scientific body of evidence was consistent with the establishment of bureaucratic state structures. The converse was also true: incorporation within state institutions aided archaeology, since it helped to legitimise the 'new archaeology' as a rational scientific discipline. The consequence has been that 'a processual archaeological science has been integrated and institutionalised into state discourses about heritage, its authority frames archaeological interpretations, practice and theory within heritage management' (Smith 1994: 303).

If the archaeological determination of significance is valued above other interest groups, and that archaeological discourse is itself gendered, then the feminist point of view (or that of any subordinate group) is devalued to the point of invisibility. Archaeological theory accepts that knowledge about the past is subjective, multiple, contingent and dynamic. Decision making which takes place in a public sphere in the classical mould, based on outdated assumptions is ill-suited to the recognition of such a diversity of viewpoints. This is particularly difficult when the dominant view is entrenched in both the discourse and the institutions. History has been marked by male experience and male status, its fixed points in time are wars and political events (Gilchrist 1999: 79). History of the nation, especially a nation in the Western enlightenment context, is connected with dynamism, change and progress which is precisely those values which are deemed male. History itself is male, linked to highly gendered concepts: 'History, Progress, Civilization, Science, Politics and Reason, portentous things with capital letters' (Massey 1991: 73). Castles, those most obvious of the ancient monuments surviving in the English landscape, have been studied predominantly from the military perspective, despite having clear domestic functions as well. This bias has 'led to the personification of the castle as a purely masculine domain' (Gilchrist 1999: 109); 'archaeologists and social historians have eulogised the male domain of the castle, reeking of sweat, testosterone and horses' (1999: 121).

## Negotiating meaning

The idea of 'public archaeology' highlights that it is not just the archaeological community which has an interest in archaeology: 'Active contestation over the significance of archaeological sites in different parts of the world has forced professional archaeologists to recognise that there are constituencies wider than their own with very definite and different views about the past and what should be done with it in the present' (Merriman 2002: 544). Two examples from the UK of contested sites, where the articulation of alternative sets of values and subordinate voices were central, are Seahenge and Stonehenge. At Seahenge, a wooden Bronze Age monument on a beach in Norfolk, the debate concerned the decision by English Heritage to remove the monument (in order to study and conserve the timbers), rather than leave it in place. Although making its decision in the public interest, acting as steward of a threatened resource as the monument would be destroyed by the sea, there was no uniform public view. A number of publics existed, not all of whom were in agreement with the evaluation of English Heritage which put recording archaeological information as the highest priority, above a perceived spiritual value in the place. What was clear from the dispute was that the existing system for decision making concerning ancient monuments fails to take account of multiple viewpoints, and in such situations fails to represent a clear consensus of what is the public interest. The situation at Stonehenge is somewhat different. It has always been recognised as significant (it was one of the prehistoric monuments on the original schedule), but has been the site of long-standing disputes over access to the site for solstice celebrations (Chippindale *et al.* 1990, Bender 1993, 1998). Compromises have now been reached, but it has been a long and painful road. The underlying problem was similar to that at Seahenge: the differing significance the site has for diverse groups of people, and the impossibility of identifying a single public and a single set of meanings for the place.

The current framework for decision making concerning ancient monuments appears to rest on the philosophical basis that there is a single public sphere (Habermas 1962), which is where consensus concerning the public good is reached. That this model is a possibility has been questioned, suggesting that there was never a single public sphere and that it always excluded groups from the debate on the grounds of class and gender (Fraser 1993, Robbins 1993). This provides a convincing model for the process of determining which monuments form part of the national heritage. The debate takes place within what is itself an interest group rather than a genuine public sphere. It is a place where the expert is privileged, since discussion is based on rational argument, a 'culturally biased conception of discussion that tends to silence or devalue some people or groups' (Young 1996: 120) The values of the (male-biased) scientific archaeology are institutionalised:

> The professional elite decides on the basis of its knowledge, claims and interests, what is important in the past and then recovers or preserves it. After subsequent interpretation the public is told that this is its past. This sets up and perpetuates a total disjunction between the professionals who produce the past and the public who are firmly placed in the role of passive consumers and in the end are alienated from it.
>
> (Tilley 1989: 107)

Debate needs to become truly public and democratic if the multifaceted identities of the present, including the feminist view of the past is to be heard. Rather than a single public interest, there is a need for 'multivocality and an arena where "subaltern counterpublics" provide a parallel discursive arena for the circulation of counterdiscourses' (Fraser 1993: 15). Mouffe (1996) argues that creating a proliferation of public spaces is a positive move, preferable to the tendency to relegate difference to the private sphere. Pluralism is not something to erase but 'constitutive at the conceptual level of the very nature of modern democracy' (Mouffe 1996: 246). 'To negate the ineradicable character of antagonism and aim at a universal rational consensus – this is the real threat to democracy' (Mouffe 1996: 248). A 'radical and plural democracy rejects the very possibility of a non-exclusive public sphere of rational argument where a non-coercive consensus could be attained' and in doing so, ensures that democracy is alive. Interpretation of the past, like democratic engagement, is never static, but 'heritage is a moment or point of negotiation over the value and meaning of the past, individual and collective memories and their roles in the present' (Smith 2006).

## Reform

A major process of review of heritage legislation is currently being undertaken by the Government, which began in 2000. From the outset, it has been clear that the model for the future is for greater inclusiveness and transparency: The word heritage to some signifies a selective, exclusive definition, suggesting that only those things validated by officialdom are significant. In reviewing policies for the whole historic environment, by contrast, we will aim to help all communities to define and value what is important to them (English Heritage, 2000). English Heritage accepted that there can be no single meaning attached to the historic environment:

> It is many-faceted, relying on an engagement with physical remains but also emotional and aesthetic responses and on the power of memory, history and association. People have radically different views about the historic environment. It is contested territory: something to be argued about and debated, not simply accepted as a given passed down from above or by our predecessors.
>
> (English Heritage 2000: 5)

The result of the initial consultation exercise and the associated working groups was published as *Power of Place* at the end of 2000. The recommendations included giving higher priority to consultation and participation. There is a very welcome shift in emphasis towards thinking in terms of locality, treating the historic environment as an integrated whole rather than as monuments and sites in isolation, divorced from their context, 'By breaking the mould that assumes society should only value a few places and things that experts have judged important, it offers an inherently more inclusive approach in which the views of local people can make a greater contribution' (Cumberpatch 2001).

The DCMS consultation paper *Protecting our historic environment: Making the system work better* followed in 2003. Its major concerns were the needs for simplification, openness, flexibility and rigour, picking up the same theme of public engagement:

> to ensure that we have a respected means of deciding what needs protecting which reflects not only the knowledge of experts but also the values of our diverse communities. . . .
>
> (2003: 2)

In 2004 a summary of the responses to this was published as *Review of Heritage Protection: The Way Forward* (DCMS, 2004a). Again the same key ideas were reiterated. It aims to produce a system which is transparent, inclusive, effective and sustainable and central to social, environmental and economic agendas at local and community as well as national level.

The main change planned is that there will be a unified register, bringing together within a single 'Register of Historic Sites and Buildings of England' scheduled monuments, listed buildings, and registered parks, gardens and battlefields (DCMS 2004a). English Heritage, rather than the Secretary of State, is to have statutory responsibility for designating at a national level, although the Secretary of State will retain a power to call in exceptional cases for a decision. English Heritage will be responsible for national designation, working within nationally agreed and published criteria. The Government will put on statute an overarching definition of historic assets and there will be a set of strictly technical criteria for each category of asset which will be non-statutory. In this respect, there is little change from the present. The main reforms have shifted more towards improving the efficiency and effectiveness of the current system, increasing its clarity and accountability (DCMS 2004b) rather than producing a radical new way of looking at the historic environment. The theoretical basis for designation will be very similar to that currently in place. The tangible and monumental elements of heritage remain dominant. In determining a 'public value' for the heritage, it is 'established value', 'that on which everybody agrees' and which is embodied in the listing and scheduling system, which is central (Jowell 2006). There is 'an absence of a serious critical unpacking of naturalised ways of seeing the heritage', or of incorporation of an understanding that 'meaning is not in things but in their contextual interaction' (Waterton 2006).

There is certainly more scope for public consultation in the proposals, and there will also be a statutory right of appeal for owners on decisions to designate or not designate a site. Pilots of the new system have been set in place, and in announcing these Simon Thurley, Chief Executive of English Heritage, described them as heralding a new era for the management of the historic environment 'in which there will be less distinction between the regulator and the regulated', part of a complete culture shift 'from its generally passive, reactive and often adversarial form towards an approach that is positive, collaborative and strategic' (English Heritage 2004). The themes of inclusivity, dialogue and open, democratic decision making are recurrent ones in discussion of the heritage: 'Negotiation, communication, facilitation, information, analysis: this is what those leading the field are becoming good at. This is working towards democracy in action' (CPRE *et al.* 2004: 3).

Recently the Secretary of State, Tessa Jowell, in *Better Places to Live* (DCMS 2005: 12), suggested that the Government is aware of the need for radical reform:

> The heritage world . . . has been debating questions of the values of heritage ever since it began its work some 150 years ago. Heritage is always a creation of the present: an act of ascribing present-day values to aspects of our inheritance from the past. It is therefore entirely subjective, forever evolving as attitudes and opinions change. But values are not shared equally among people or across time, and sometimes clash. Government and heritage organisations intervene both by encouraging people to express these values, and by establishing frameworks and procedures to balance competing priorities. . . . I am firmly committed to moving towards a more democratic system, and one that empowers people.

However, it can be questioned whether this is genuinely more democratic or empowering if in practice this reinforces the authorised view of what constitutes significance: 'experts would share their knowledge with the public and facilitate people making more of their own informed judgments' (Jowell 2006). This is some considerable distance from genuine empowerment, if the process is based on educating the public, rather than a negotiation based on different ways of valuing and conceptualising the heritage. The public consultation on the future of the historic environment has continued, with the Parliamentary Culture, Media and Sport Committee enquiry into the heritage sector announced in November 2005 entitled 'Protecting, preserving and making accessible our nation's heritage'.[11] It sought evidence on a number of issues, including the priorities for the forthcoming Heritage White Paper and the remit and effectiveness of English Heritage and other organisations.

Despite this very welcome emphasis on inclusion and diversity, there are problems with the extent to which this is truly a radical departure from the current system. Concern is expressed that the heritage needs to involve all sectors of society (as part of the overall social inclusion agenda), but this focuses issues of class, race and ethnicity. The challenge for the future remains the need to recognise that different identity groups claim ownership in a different past or pasts, which may find expression in intangible rather than monumental heritage, and to translate this into cultural heritage management. This is never static, but 'heritage is a moment or point of negotiation over the value and meaning of the past, individual and collective memories and their roles in the present' (Smith 2006). Gender archaeology may be considered as a significant strand in postprocessual archaeological theory, but 'a sense of marginality lingers' (Sørensen 2000: 3) and its potential has not been fully realised (Baker 2000: 56–7). It is absent from the political agenda for the heritage. This is despite the fact that there is a recognition that gender cannot be separated from class, race and ethnicity, and that 'archaeological research concerned with gender necessitates as well a concern with other aspects of social inequality' (Scott 1994: 13). The reverse is also true. A concern with social and racial inclusion necessitates a concern with gender if there is to be a genuinely inclusive heritage.

## Notes

1 Planning Policy Guidance (PPG) 16 *Archaeology and Planning*, 1990 sets out how archaeological considerations are to be taken in account on planning decisions. http://www.odpm.gov.uk/index.asp?id=1144057 (site accessed 02/05/2006).
2 This applies to England and Wales. The law has some significant differences in Northern Ireland and Scotland.
3 Thompson (1979) develops this cycle of changing value into a 'rubbish theory'.
4 A very clear illustration of political motives underlying the selection of the significant elements of the past can be found in the debate which surrounded the history content of the National Curriculum in England and Wales. While advocating a fact-based history, what was being promoted by the Government was a particular version of the national identity (Crawford 1995, Lee 1994, and Coulby and Jones 1995).
5 Daniel (1967) and Daniel (1981) recount the history of archaeology.
6 Examples of the sentiments expressed in Parliament are quoted by Baldwin Brown (1905: 153), Chippindale (1983: 13), Murray (1989: 62), and Kennett (1970: 30).
7 Whitley (1998) provides an overview of these approaches.
8 Contained in Annex 4 to Planning Policy Guidance Note 16 *Archaeology and Planning* (PPG16), they are period, rarity, documentation, group value, survival/condition, frailty/vulnerability, diversity and potential.
9 Secretary of State for Culture, Media and Sport Order 1997, SI 1997/1744. The Department of National Heritage was itself formed in 1992 (art 2(1) the Transfer of Functions (National Heritage) Order (SI 1992/1311) by putting together activities from several departments, including the heritage division of the Department of the Environment.
10 *R v Secretary of State for the Environment ex p Rose Theatre Trust Co* [1990] 1 All ER 745.
11 The written evidence is now available http://www.publications.parliament.uk/pa/cm/cmcumeds.htm (site accessed 20/04/06).

Chapter 4

# A trip to the mall

## Revisiting the public/private divide[1]

*Anne Bottomley*

### Introduction

We continually utilise a division between 'public' and private' and, all too often, that 'division' is thought of in terms of a 'divide' which we can clearly differentiate. Much Anglo-European feminist work in the twentieth century was focused on a critique of this 'divide', characterised, as it tended to be, as a division between the 'private sphere' of the domestic environment and the 'public sphere' of, in particular, paid employment and the processes of political decision making. The focus of this work was derived, in great part, from a perceived need to counteract the strength of a nineteenth-century heritage which continually reasserted and reproduced the division. However much nineteenth-century economic and social practice actually allowed for, and in some cases required, the participation of women in the public sphere, especially in relation to low-paid employment, the prevalent ideology was one which associated women's role, and the fulfilment of feminine ideals, with the home and designated the 'public sphere' as essentially 'masculine'. This gendered account of division was folded into one of the key tenets of liberalism: that the state must respect the privacy of the domestic sphere.

We could characterise feminist critiques of the 'divide' as clustered around three major foci – one, that the domestic sphere was not a benevolent place around which the state should draw a boundary of non-intervention; two, that women had a right, as much as men, to access the benefits and privileges of the 'public sphere'; and, three, that the seeming division between public and private was, anyway, in practice far more problematic than the dominant narrative allowed for and that therefore it was important to examine why so much effort had been invested in building and maintaining it.

Of course, the presentation of mutually exclusive 'public' and 'private' domains characterised other discursive forms – not least that of property. We work in Land Law within a frame which takes its focus from a presumption, so embedded that it is rarely directly examined, that 'private property' embodies the characteristics of 'property' as we understand it. Thus ownership of an asset, defining the rights of use of that asset including the right to dispose of it, is the dominant way in which we have to come to think of the idea of 'property'. Blomley (2004) characterises this 'ownership model' as one which dominates our thinking to the exclusion of all other forms of 'holding' rights in the use of property – especially, rights of a collective nature. Further, the idea of 'ownership' conveys a sense of 'absolutism' which itself embodies and reinforces a narrative of individual hegemony (the 'boundaried subject') – and it is no coincidence that private property, the development of the market, liberalism and arguments against state intervention into the 'private sphere' (not only of 'the family' but also of 'the individual'), meld together. The domination of this model of property is such that it takes a major leap of faith to try and break out of it and think differently. Not only our own heritage, but also two contemporary developments reinforce the primacy of the model. The first is the export of it to developing countries as the necessary model for economic development and social progress, and the second is the pattern of 'privatisation' of assets once held by public bodies for the 'benefit of the community'. In this sense we seem to be witnessing the final, and necessary, triumph of 'possessive individualism' made flesh and stone in 'private property'.[2]

However, other scholarship invites us to think more carefully about the seeming hegemony of this approach – history reveals the paucity of an account in law which assumes 'absolutism' in and of private property (Gordon 1996), anthropology reveals not only the practices of other forms but also requires of us a more careful account of the models we employ when speaking of property (Pottage 2004), contemporary politics provides numerous accounts of other potentials struggling against the dominant model (Blomley 2004) and it is open to us, as lawyers and legal scholars, to 'think' the intellectual resources we have in order to promote alternative patterns of 'property' practices (for example, Rose 1994, Gray and Gray 1998, 2005).

This chapter requires us to 'think differently' about property: because although it must begin within the shadow of 'private property', it attempts to make visible a notion of 'public property'. As we shall see this idea cannot be rendered, in our jurisprudence, as equivalent to the 'ownership model', and so must find another route to a 'place in the sun'. But, I shall argue, in finding that route we will encounter difficulties with holding, anyway, to an absolutist model of private property. It will destabilise, at one crucial level, an attempt to hold to a descriptive divide between 'private' and 'public' property.

What marks such an investigation as specifically feminist? There are two aspects which I think of as derived from the practices of feminist scholarship. The first is to return to feminist concerns with access to the 'public sphere', in this case with access to urban public space. The second is to revisit the critique of the seeming simplicity of a divide between public and private spheres. These two aspects are brought together in this chapter through an argument that feminist work in law needs to be much more sharply attuned to the development of new patterns of governance which reconfigure the interrelationship between 'private' and 'public': in which, to put it very simply, what is presented as 'private' now crucially carries the practices of control and regulation which were once more visibly aligned with and within the 'public sphere'. Being able to render this visible requires that we make a break from a focus on the 'private sphere', which has marked both legal scholarship and feminist work on property law. In terms of legal scholarship, this has meant that we have few tools, at least as yet, to fully investigate the 'public sphere' of property. In terms of feminist scholarship, an understandable concentration on access to the resource of private property has marginalised other forms of property use or thinking.[3] Brought together these trajectories have resulted in a domination of 'ownership' thinking in our work and a failure to engage with the importance of either protecting the 'use' value of property or of thinking more carefully about what a 'public sphere' in property might involve.

This chapter takes its shape from the increasing concern, in this country, with the privatisation of urban public space. Both in our scholarship and in our jurisprudence, we have somewhat lagged behind North American work which located this as an issue in the last decades of the twentieth century.[4] 'Privatisation of urban public space' carries, within its term, a number of significantly different but closely related issues, as we shall discover later in this chapter. However, what needs to be clarified from the beginning is that this is not limited to the privatisation of once publicly held assets, although this is important, it is also a function of changes in building practices and urban design. In other words, it is as much about 'how' public space is produced, as about the withdrawal of an already existing asset. Further, I shall argue that the idea of public space is not found in a legal definition, but rather in sets of practices which construct 'public space' through design and use: thus, in many instances it is not a question of legal 'ownership' which is significant, but rather 'how' space is used.

Linking all these aspects together is the figure of 'the mall'. I use the term 'figure' to indicate that my use of 'the mall' is not only a reference to a design process, of retail and leisure units enclosed within gated streets and squares, but also to an argument that 'the mall' has been the carrier of a significant shift in our attitudes towards the use of, our expectations of, public space. 'The mall' can be deployed to represent, both practically and symbolically, the collapse of any rendition of a simple divide between 'public' and 'private' space. The North American experience, both in terms of planning history and jurisprudence, is very different from our own: we can draw useful parallels but not a congruent mapping exercise. In our terms, the figure of 'the mall' might be more usefully rendered as an enclosed 'shopping centre', but I have chosen to keep the term 'mall' as it encapsulates the characteristics of those of our shopping centres, like the Metro Centre or Bluewater or Swansgate or The Galleries (all of which are used in this chapter), which I want to concentrate on, and it carries us through into the broader, and I would argue more significant, aspects of those trends within our urban centres which requires of us a much more focused and nuanced concern with the 'privatisation of public space' than has hitherto been visible.

## The idea of public space

The term 'urban public space' conveys a particular characteristic: that it is, somehow, open to general public use. We could suggest, for the moment, that it is made up of sites to which the public have a presumed right of reasonable access. In other words, such space is not subject to the rules and practices we associate with private property, in particular the right of the owner of such property to exclude us from it. (It is interesting how quickly we slip into looking to private property in order to try to define what we mean by 'public space'. It is also interesting how often the term 'space' is employed here, as if it is no more than what has not been taken as 'private place'.) 'Urban public space', however, in these terms might be thought of as little more than the infrastructure, the streets and squares, between private sites. But this would be to ignore important practices of urban living: we more than traverse such space in order to access private sites, we share the amenities of these spaces as places to wander, relax, meet and so on. Streets are more than highways: they are the very fabric of urban living. Further, places designed for public use take on certain characteristics: whether green parks or concrete squares, we presume rights of use, even if we also accept that certain places might be closed at night or that we are subject to rules (bylaws) regulating the use of that space. Over such public space we tend to presume there is some form of benevolent public authority regulating and protecting the public use of a public asset, but we rarely directly consider it.

It is an indication of our focus on private property and ownership that the little statutory authority and case material relevant to the use of urban public space is rarely covered in textbooks or Land Law courses. Gray and Gray (2005: 288) provide the most notable exception. They argue that 'it is now broadly agreed in England that there exists a critical distinction between the legal position of the private landowner and that of a land-owning public authority', in that a public authority's power to 'exclude or evict persons from their premises is nowadays limited by public law standards of reasonableness and fairness'. First, note that there is an element here of assertion – the Grays (as we shall see later) have been concerned to proactively promote and protect the use of urban public space. Second, the difficulty with so sharply distinguishing between public and private ownership (which they are aware of, but which serves them well in how they later develop their argument), is that it not only obscures the fact that much public space has always been privately owned,[5] but also that it might be privatised by the public body through sale or lease.

But let us, for the moment, return to 'use' rather than issues of 'ownership'. Carried within the idea of 'urban public space' are a number of assumptions.

Firstly, that 'the public' shares a use, and expectation, of these sites in patterns of sufficient similarity that their practices and sense of use-rights can meld or cohere into 'a public'. In other words, it is not simply that individual members of the public share rights of use, but rather that they 'share use' *per se*. Folded into this assumption is a suggestion that there is 'a public benefit' in such sites, which supports and sustains the very notion of 'a public sphere'. When we press at the idea of public urban space, we find not only concerns with access and recreational use, but also an interest in the facilitation of a 'public sensitivity', whether expressed in terms of 'community' or, in urban history, 'a civic polity'. Deeply engrained into our expectations of public urban space is, or has been, a set of practices associated with politics and the democratic process. It was, and still to some extent is, on our streets and in our squares that we meet to organise, support or protest against, the decisions of government. From this perspective it is not only access to streets and squares which is important, but specifically access to significant sites, often ones which symbolically represent government or are centrally located. In this sense, even in big cities, we still seek the equivalent of the 'market square' or 'urban commons' which formed the privileged sites of civic protest in our history. Further, the 'market square' or 'urban commons' were the traditional sites in which the full plurality of urban activities crossed and met. Sometimes and in part recreational user, sometimes and in part retail user, sometimes and in part civic and political user (either by authority or against authority): they were the focus for a full account of 'urban activity'. But this rendition of history too quickly becomes an account of a lost 'urban idyll', which too easily suppresses the extent to which the use of urban public space is contested.

It has been argued, by many, that attentiveness to preserving, or building, a 'public domain' is crucial to a strong social, and therefore political, environment.[6] However, there are major theoretical and political differences between those who support such a position and the policy implications they draw from it. Possibly the strongest contemporary trend is derived from the work of 'communitarians' concerned with the regeneration of the idea and practices of 'community' as a necessary counterbalance in a society which has become predicated on individualism resulting in a breakdown of social values and concerns. Their influence is visible, for instance, in the architectural and urban planning practices associated with 'New Urbanism' in which the provision of public space has been a major feature.[7] 'New Urbanism' arose from a particular concern with building practices associated with 'suburbanism', constructing swathes of housing with little provision for public space and facilities and, especially, lacking the focus of 'town centres'. For them, a lack of such provision in the built environment radically curtails the potential development of a community ethos.

However, both 'communitarianism' and 'New Urbanism' have been strongly critiqued as predicated on a particular image of 'community' which is conservative (in the sense, in particular, of nostalgia for a 'lost past' of community spirit), conformist and antithetical to a more plural account of diversity inclusive of 'others' whose lifestyles may be very different from our own and, indeed, ones which we may find difficult to deal with (Berka 2004). In other words, the concern expressed by many thinkers, including feminists such as Young (1991), has been that 'community' can too often be utilised to mean 'similar-to-us' and therefore composed only of ones we choose to live with, and that this ethic begins to dominate the construction of so-called 'public' sites. Obviously, building communities of choice and similarity tend to be a privilege of those who have the economic power to build, or buy into, such communities, excluding those who do not fit either through economic power or the utilisation of legal forms which reproduce and reinforce the exclusion of 'others' (Duncan and Duncan 2004).

There is one thread within the 'New Urbanism' movement which is rather more sensitive to matters of privilege than might seem from some of their own building practices. An early concern within their literature was not only with 'suburbanisation', but also with the building of gated communities and shopping malls: both of which were seen as exclusionary building practices. What they argued for, in preference, was 'open' housing developments with 'open' shopping streets built around 'town centres' providing amenities other than retail outlets and including open (public) spaces.[8] However, and particularly visible in 'New Urbanism' activities focused on regeneration programmes in inner city districts (involving both housing programmes and the upgrading of public amenities), there is often a sense that 'regeneration' is fuelled by a concern to 'clean up' the inner city through a process which many critics identify as 'gentrification' with a consequent impact on increasing the use of inner city space for those with wealth, to the cost of the greater number who lack wealth or power and whose presence is only tolerated if they conform (in their lifestyles) to the new *modus vivendi* of 'city living'. 'Regeneration' is based, within this perspective, on making the inner city environment attractive not only in terms of the services provided, but also on an overall 'effect' of pleasure, convenience, comfort and safety, the factors which led many to seek an escape from the inner city when they fled to the suburbs, as well as constraining the development and use of public space.

What becomes clear as we begin to look at the wealth of literature on the provision and use of public space, is that it is a highly contested idea which has to be approached with some caution: it is all too easy to slip into a rhetoric of the importance of a 'public domain' for the promotion of social and community values without recognising that the values promoted may be of a very specific, and not necessarily progressive, nature. It also becomes clear that the provision and use of public space will vary considerably between different urban forms (from villages through small market towns to cities and 'urban villages' or neighbourhoods) – and within each urban form the idea of 'public' will also vary considerably based on where the space is located, what kind of space it is and under what circumstances it is used by which groups of people.

In other words, the very idea of 'public space' covers a wide range of spaces and the use of them – the more we push at the concept and try to find definitions of it, the more slippery it becomes to hold onto (Blomley 2004). But the amount of literature utilising it suggests that the idea does hold an important value and, as I shall suggest, it is as much in the loss of public space as in any attempt to define in the abstract what we mean by it, that we begin to get a sense of the importance of that value and can begin to map the features we might want to associate with, and defend in, the idea of 'urban public space'.

In this chapter I approach the idea of public space obliquely – if we begin with a distinction between public and private space, in which we 'know' that certain space is 'private', once we turn to try and define 'public space' through this trajectory, we are left with little more than some idea of spaces to which we have 'open access' as members of 'the public'. This account can become too quickly negative in two ways, first, we presume a 'right' of access because it has not been denied to us and, second, it does not convey any sense of 'why' certain spaces take on a 'public character'. 'Public space', I would argue, is an idea composed of a number of elements which coalesce around 'perception' and 'use practices' (Sarai 2001, 2002). 'Perception' includes elements related to building practices and architecture. New Urbanists are right in suggesting that 'open' space is more likely to be perceived of as 'public' than enclosed spaces. But New Urbanists are wrong if they think that the simple provision of open spaces is enough to make them 'public', because the other essential element is that the space becomes inhabited by the public through 'use'. In this sense the most important aspect of 'perception' is that practices of 'public use' marks space as 'open to the public'.[9] However, to this we need to add the third element: 'the public'. As with 'community' the idea of 'the public' has been subject to criticism and some have resorted to referring to 'many publics' (Fraser 1993) as indicating that to maintain an idea of 'a' public is to still seek the kind of consensual, conformist (and inherently conservative) idyll that is represented in communitarian politics.

In this chapter it will become clear that I follow Young's concern of holding to an idea of 'the public' as 'being amongst strangers', a recognition that our social composition is made up of a diverse range of social actors all of whom hold, with me/us, a right to share in the 'common good' of public space and that it is in public space that we encounter (however uncomfortably) these strangers. Using Young's 'being amongst strangers', or Michelman's use of 'civic sociability' (Michelman 1997), emphasises that the value of public space lies in open access to all, as not only a 'common good' but also as the place in which we encounter the many others who form part of our polity.

Inscribing onto public space the idea of 'civic commons' is one attempt to assert and profile open access to public space as an important political as well as social value, which is fundamentally more challenging than an evocation of 'community use'. However, even references to 'civic commons' can carry value judgments which we may wish to unpack and critique. To use the term 'civic', as also in 'civic sociability', may pull us back to a communitarian presumption that we are still searching for a 'consensual community' of responsible individuals who are fully playing their part as respectable members of 'the community' committed to the existing apparatus of (democratic) governance. 'Commons', however, carries more radical ideas of places which do not easily 'fit' into dominant political structures: they can be places of disorder and dissent which are unsettling to the establishment. I mean this in two ways. First, that they may provide the space (literally and figuratively) for active political dissent and second, rather differently, they may represent (literally and figuratively) activities viewed by the establishment as irresponsible and disorderly. This makes what I prefer to think of as 'urban commons', much more politically and socially challenging than the communitarian focus on public space to enhance an inclusive 'community' ethos. 'Sociability' is pushed to the extreme when we face the challenge of a much more plural account of society. The idea that 'all' have a right to share in the 'common good' of public space and that to pursue this as a basic social value is to, necessarily, rethink political trends imbued with either the privileging of private space, or the presumption that the use of public space is a 'community' value only to be granted to those who 'deserve' it.

However, 'using' public space in everyday life is predicated on issues of class, gender, age, ethnic identity and such crucial factors as responsibility for children, both in how such space is utilised (what presumptions we make of how we might use it) and whether the use of it by some constrains the use of it by others. Recognising this has been fundamental to feminist work in this area which has argued that women (all women, but some more so than others) are still constrained in their use of public space, particularly due to issues concerning their (or their children's) safety but also concerned with their ease of use, their sense of being 'comfortable' in public spaces (Duncan 1996, Watson 2002).

This chapter draws on the trajectory of women's use of public space through the specific context of changes in the architecture, planning and management of our urban centres as they undergo 'regeneration' programmes. I shall argue that we can begin to excavate and confront more sharply many of the issues involved in attempting to define and sustain a public domain within the built environment by looking, firstly, at the practices associated with the construction and use of shopping malls and shopping centres and, subsequently, the planning practices associated with 'New Urbanism' in the move away from the enclosed and gated environment of the mall towards more 'open' urban planning as evidenced in contemporary regeneration programmes. From this perspective, I shall argue that there is a major problem with feminist work focused on enhancing women's access to public space when it does not take into account how this concern feeds into, and from, an agenda which is increasingly contracting public space in the sense of constricting and constraining access to it.

## Public space: enclosure

One of the histories which is rarely referred to in contemporary property law courses, focused as they are on the ownership of private property, is the period of enclosure of rural land, which not only removed many of the agricultural labouring classes from their fields, their commons and their homes but also excluded them (apart from limited rights over footpaths) from access to large tracts of land enclosed for the recreational and agricultural use of the land-owning classes. The inheritors of this dispossession (if we can think of it in this way!) have clawed back some of this loss in the increased protection of the public use of footpaths (and what little remains of the commons) and the relatively recent historical victory of the 'right to roam' over some of the rural land from which they/we had been excluded. In modern terms this process of dispossession (which directly impacted on specific individuals who lost their, often customary, rights as well as effecting 'the public' community) could well be thought of as a process of 'privatisation'.

Since the early 1980s the centres of many English towns and cities have also undergone a process of enclosure and privatisation, leading to some commentators referring to the modern process of urban dispossession as equivalent to the loss of rural commons by referring to 'the loss of urban commons'. But, whereas the rural poor were all too aware of their dispossession, entailing as it often did loss of land and livelihood, this later process of urban dispossession has occurred relatively unnoticed and uncontested.

The process of urban enclosure and privatisation in this country has to be understood within a pattern of changes in the ways in which we build and use our urban centres. Increasingly what was once a pattern of mixed use (to shop, to meet people, to promenade, to pursue civic and political activities, to celebrate fairs and festivals and so on) in the heart of such centres (a market square or open central public space surrounded by civic buildings), became disaggregated in the twentieth century (encouraged both by market forces and the relatively new activity of urban planning) into specific activities in designated sites. A general trajectory was to come to regard urban centres as primarily places of retail, rather than broader, civic, activity. We could think of this pattern as 'emptying' the public, civic centre and replacing it with a much narrower focus on consumption, particularly retail consumption. This paralleled the way in which 'New Towns'[10] were being built in the post-war period (from the 1950s), with town centres built around linked shopping precincts in which the retail outlets tended to dominate the built landscape, rather than buildings (or open spaces) which spoke of civic involvement.

The 'New Town' movement is important to understand as indicative of a generation of planners and policy makers developing new urban patterns not only in terms of housing supply, but also in constructing a broader concept of 'urban' living.[11] Of course, to generalise is dangerous: 'New Towns' were built over a period of nearly 40 years and involved different urban planners with rather different agendas; further, many of them were grafted onto existing villages or small market towns: but all 'New Towns' were significant in that they offered the opportunity to build a new 'town centre' and all of them took as their focus a pedestrianised network of retail outlets (incorporating some civic services), often taking the form of covered malls and internal squares. Pre-existing towns and cities mimicked this development in pedestrianising, and often covering, existing street networks, enclosing them and branding them as 'malls' or 'shopping centres'. It was not simply that the architecture of 'New Towns' had become a blueprint for such developments, which can also be viewed as an extension of the use of arcades and covered markets which had been popular in earlier centuries, but the difference now was that such developments were encouraged, planned and financed by public bodies as part of an overall urban plan, rather than being dependent upon the initiatives of private developers. In the immediate post-war period such regeneration initiatives were often necessitated by the consequences of war damage, but later the impetus (and model) arose primarily from a concern that existing urban centres were caught in a spiral of economic decline as shoppers, increasingly with access to cars, became enamoured both with visiting 'New Town' shopping centres and, even more so, out-of-town (privately developed) shopping centres which offered not only a wide choice, but moreover a choice to be made within the comfort of an enclosed, comfortable and 'stylish' modern environment.

Although the pattern of out-of-town centres in this country tended to develop from large single retail units into 'shopping centres', we can draw a useful parallel with the development in the United States of shopping malls and retail centres. Malls in the States were developed initially as part of the extensive process of 'suburbanisation', made possible by cheap land, cheap cars and cheap 'gas', which required the provision of retail services in a context in which there was little or no 'centre'. Developed by private investors rather than a public authority, malls offered retail services within the comfort of an enclosed space, facilitated by heating and air-conditioning, and, like department stores before them, the possibility of controlling access and use by the provision of door keepers, or floor walkers, to not only aid the customer but also keep out or remove those who were unwelcome. Malls developed into enclosed environments of pleasure and the pattern was set. Investors, merchants and consumers realised, as they had done with department stores, that an enclosed and controlled environment was the most productive way to pursue the development of the pleasures of leisure-shopping. The development, in this country, of enclosed out-of-town shopping centres was, in great part, inspired by the American experience. And so also, both directly and indirectly, was the creation of covered and enclosed precincts in the newly built centres of the 'New Towns', as well as the process of enclosure in existing urban centres.

'Enclosure' can mean simply to build within, or to create, an enclosed space: but it can also mean to close off what was once 'public' space, in the sense that space which was once open to public access becomes enclosed and gated. The idea of 'enclosure of urban commons' refers specifically to the latter: it marks the significance of losing the right of public access to open spaces within an urban setting or to routes which formed our street network (and those buildings accessed through this network). Shops once linked by public highways (on which we have a right to reasonable user), become 'malled' zones controlled by the developers of the 'malls'. The loss of public rights of access (in other words the loss of 'street rights') in these circumstances is the result of two developments. The first is that 'old' urban centres are 'regenerated', primarily by private investment in partnership with local authorities, resulting in the areas now malled (often called 'arcades') and newly enclosed 'shopping centres' being privatised by the granting of long leases on the sites to the developers. The second is that the 'New Town' centres, built with public investment, have also been privatised and assets which were planned, built and financed by a public authority have now been sold to private agencies (either freehold or on long lease) as part of the winding down of the 'New Towns' programme. Thus we can talk of a doubled movement of enclosure and privatisation in urban centres which mirrors, both architecturally and legally, out-of-town shopping centres. This doubled movement fuelled the 'emptying' of 'civic' centres by transmuting them, increasingly, into little more than 'centres of consumption'. Areas once inhabited as public space become enclosed and restricted to public access not only in terms of 'street loss', but also in terms of the loss of what had been designed, or used, as 'public squares' equivalent to 'town squares', that is as places used for a range of civic/community activities.

Milton Keynes, for instance, included within its covered centre not only malls but also squares designed for civic/community uses by the public, intended to encourage the use of the city centre for a wide range of activities not limited to traditional shopping hours. Later morphed through privatisation into an enclosed and gated shopping centre, not only was pedestrian access through the centre restricted to shopping hours, but also the use of the squares for civic/community use, even within shopping hours, was sidelined. It ceased to be a 'town centre', as had been envisaged by the original planners, and became no more than a 'shopping centre' for the city and the surrounding district.[12] However, what we should note here is that although the 'loss' was considerable and the subject of some criticism by informed commentators, it was primarily a 'loss' of the potential to inhabit the 'town centre' as public space rather than a radical sense of actual loss experienced by the inhabitants of Milton Keynes which was at issue. Milton Keynes, as with many other 'New Towns', actually exemplified not only the 'move' from civic centres to centres of consumption, but also how difficult it is, in practice, to 'design' space which becomes inhabited as fully 'public' space used for a wide range of activities. It is not simply a question of 'access' to space, but also the 'perception' of space as open to a range of public activities, and therefore used in such a way, which is important. Enclosed and/or covered environments simply seem to be less 'open' in this sense to 'public' inhabitation.

## Public space and women's place

Feminist work on public space has long emphasised the gendered nature of our movement through, and encounters in, public places (for example Duncan 1996, McDowell 1999, Wilson 1991, Watson 2002). Women's experience of being 'in public' varies radically depending on cultural, religious and class expectations either in terms of the groupings they themselves belong to, or in encountering in public space responses from those who hold certain attitudes as to how women should 'appear' (in particular how they should dress) or act 'in public'. But the theme which underpins all aspects of a concern with women-in-public is that of woman as sexual object (see especially Wilson 1991). Whether figured as a concern with woman as potential victim, or of woman as potential (and therefore predatory) temptress, women have been, and I would argue to a great extent remain, caught in a complex problematic relation to public space. On the one hand, one set of variables cluster around the assemblage of our own characteristics as individual actors, and how we handle and present these variables: how visible do we make crucial aspects of 'ourselves' and what messages do we convey in the clothes we wear and the ways in which we act? On the other hand, there is a cluster of variables which differentiate different types of public spaces and how we use them: how open or enclosed they are, what time of day or night it is, what functions the space carries as part of its geography and what groupings tend, if any, to dominate these spaces?

Travelling and waiting in public places without a male escort seemed, again and again, to be portrayed as activities of vulnerability for women (that is 'respectable women') in the late nineteenth and early twentieth century. They mark, of course, not only changes in technologies of scale and pace, but also the simple fact that more women were moving into and through these public spaces. The changing geography of urban, especially city, spaces threw up new questions about women moving through, and using, public space. Parks, museums and art galleries, places of genteel recreation and self-improvement, were enclosed and semi-enclosed spaces which could be serviced (patrolled) by attendants and could therefore be deemed to be 'safe'. Cafes and restaurants, as with theatres and concert halls, were places which could be differentiated between those requiring a male escort, or those requiring one for certain events or at certain times of the day, and those in which women were able to meet together as women or even to visit on their own. These spatial and temporal divisions marked places which could be used by women without provoking concern – as long as they were respectably dressed and using them at the right hours. They all shared the characteristics of being to some extent 'enclosed', serviced in some way and physically marked as spaces separate from fully 'public' space and the 'general public' (people, strangers, men). They also shared two other characteristics: They were either only open to those who could afford them or could afford the leisure to use them (in other words 'respectable' women who came from a limited socio-economic class), and they were 'functional' in that there was always a purpose attached to the use of the facilities. What this left were two aspects of danger and difficulty: women traversing public highways and other routes in order to access these facilities and women, even more problematically, simply wandering (or loitering!) in public places for pleasure without a specific purpose, focus or destination (Wilson 1991).

## Shopping and being 'in public'

Feminist historians (and others) of the nineteenth and twentieth centuries have tracked the large-scale development of shopping from a functional activity to one that became imbued with the consumerist pleasures of recreation and leisure (for example, Rappaport 2000). As our society became wealthy enough to afford time and money in the pursuit of pleasure, so, for women in particular (and for certain categories of men) shopping, both in terms of actually purchasing and in terms of the more generalised activity of enjoying the pleasures of visiting retail outlets, developed into a pursuit far outstripping the visit for the purchase of necessaries. Feminist critics would correctly point to the extent to which women have been targeted by advertising and have been the focus of the ways in which retail activities have been packaged for consumer consumption. They might also point out that, within the traditional roles and spheres allocated to women, the pursuit of shopping has been, and remains, one of the 'authorised' activities for women in a society which is still riven by gender divisions. However, whatever conditions have given rise to, and sustain, this phenomenon, women and leisure-shopping have become intrinsically linked. In the history of modern and contemporary shopping what is interesting, for this chapter, is the extent to which the topography of shopping has changed and the extent to which these changes have inscribed within them a 'feminine' aspect.

A great deal of work has been done on the development of topographies of retailing – from the open (often 'street' but also 'square') market through the bazaar to the development of the department store in the late nineteenth century (Shields 1992). It is well established that this development fed very directly from, and into, concerns with respectable women shopping in 'public places' (McDowell 1999). To place as much as possible for sale under one roof not only encouraged women into a retail environment, but also encouraged them to stay for some time in a place which was exciting and relaxing as well as safe, comfortable and hospitable. A place to shop and a place to eat, to be on one's own or to meet friends, a place in which one could effectively go from one shopping experience to another (through different departments) without having to be on a street travelling from one shop to another. A place where one could wander, safely, seemingly with purpose but without the need to always make a purchase. A place to spend time, as much as a place to shop. A 'pleasure dome', encouraged by retailers, and supported by men who would not want to spend much time there themselves but were perfectly happy that their wives and daughters did (Nead 2000, Rappaport 1996, 2000). A controlled space – open to all, but welcoming only to those who had the money to spend, or at least looked as if they did. A place for respectable women to be engaged in respectable activities – consumption and (respectable) display.

The story of the department store on the high street is now, however, one of decline.[13] It has been replaced by the equally compelling story of the malled shopping centre – whether built out-of-town by private investment, or developed within existing town centres through the doubled process of enclosure and privatisation. Just as was once the case with department stores, these are places where activities can be highly controlled, and are designed to offer zones of safety and comfort in contrast to being 'on the open street'. The major function in their design is to encourage people (especially women) not only to visit them, but to spend extensive periods of time within their precincts in order to spend their money either on purchases or within the cafes, restaurants and other recreational facilities. They provide, through carefully designed internal architecture features, places in which one can promenade, rest and feel rested sitting by water or under internal arboretums. The scale, lighting and the furnishings (especially the use of marble!) all create a relatively peaceful backdrop against which to pursue leisure in what otherwise might, because of the concentration of crowds and facilities, become too chaotic, noisy and claustrophobic. It is all a beautifully constructed and finely balanced environment of measured excitement and leisured time.

These purpose-built enclosed zones were initially constructed externally like fortresses: high blank walls, few windows and few portals for entrance, one such example being the Gateshead Metro Centre. Internally, once over the threshold and 'inside', the 'external' in these sites was referenced by overhead light from glassed domes or the use of internal trees and greenery, but this was not a form of building which turned outwards in any real sense. There were rarely places to sit outside, whether on roof-terraces or even more rarely in transitional zones of, for instance, cafes at ground level, offering seating in the open air as well as inside. This was a highly controlled environment; both in terms of entering it and in terms of what happens (or does not) internally. These zones of pleasure and safety replaced the problematic open street or market: where inclement weather, unruly crowds or the nuisances of anti-social behaviour (including graffiti and litter) threaten the untrammelled pleasures of leisure-shopping.

Such spaces form a play between the illusion of public space (that is a space into which the public are invited, indeed encouraged, to enter and use at leisure) and the reality of it being a highly controlled and regulated private environment. Entering the portals of the mall is to enter into a zone of organised and controlled activity – the trick from the controller's point of view is to regulate the consumers' awareness of the level of control: a few carefully placed (that is highly visible) security guards suggest safety from the point of view of the consumer, what is much less visible is the real motor of control, the use of CCTV cameras watching everything and everyone in the precincts, linking security guards to the focus of operations, the room from which the controllers watch and interpret the environment and then instruct and direct the personnel on the ground. Such a fine balance is addressed to a concern to make the consumer/visitor feel secure, but not to the extent of feeling too observed and controlled. As with the organisation of the retail units, the display of the goods and the internal organisation of the shops, which we as consumers prefer to be deluded into thinking is all organised for our convenience rather than to entice us to shop and spend, most of us do not want to think beyond our enjoyment of the pleasures of the space to consider the technologies of control which inform and control our activities within that space.

## Shopping and being 'in private'

The out-of-town developments (designed, financed and run by private developers) in an important sense 'set the stage', not only in establishing standards of comfort and safety which any in-town development then has to match in order to attract custom, but also in constructing a model through which users of the centres came to accept certain presumptions – most notably that these are essentially private spaces to which access is determined by the owners and operators and in which a level of surveillance, as an aspect of comfort and safety, is necessary. They are, in effect, zones of private space to which 'public access' is determined by one factor alone: is this person, or category of persons, one whom the owners of the centres wish to encourage into that place? 'The public' becomes differentiated into the welcome and the unwelcome and extensive regulation (including exclusion) of the unwelcome is easily justified by an appeal to the need to provide for the safety and comfort of the welcome.

In May 2005 Bluewater, one of the largest out-of-town retail and leisure complexes in the UK, announced through the publication of a 'Code of Conduct' a zero tolerance approach to anti-social behaviour to ensure 'that Bluewater is a safe and pleasant environment for our guests'.[14] Any anti-social behaviour, including swearing or the wearing of clothing which obscures the face (unless for religious purposes), will result in automatic exclusion from the centre. The use of the term 'guests' suggests an almost domestic environment: an implicit parallel being drawn between the ways in which we expect guests to act in our own homes and the use of a shopping centre. 'Safety' and 'a pleasant environment' are brought together through a focus on the needs of 'guests', resulting in a list of unacceptable behaviour which becomes fused with those activities of a more traditionally 'criminal' nature (most obviously shop lifting), radically extending the potential for intervention and exclusion. The wearing of 'hoodies' (the dress practice particularly targeted by the code of conduct) has become a problem for CCTV surveillance technologies, which rely on being able to photograph faces and run face recognition programmes in order to target individuals deemed to be unwelcome as soon as they enter the complex. Wearing a 'hoody' has also come to be regarded as indicative of a 'person' (young man) who is likely to engage in anti-social behaviour. Thus under the rubric of a concern with 'anti-social behaviour', and carrying the implication that 'guests' might experience fear when faced with a wearer of such a garment, Bluewater is able to rationalise their need for full face exposure, as well as having clear grounds for the exclusion of individuals who wear such garments without having to wait for them to actually engage in any activity which might be deemed to be anti-social.

What is illustrated in Bluewater's 'Code of Conduct' is the extent to which owners and operators of private shopping centres have brought together the issues of safety and comfort for those they wish to encourage into their enclosed environments, with the advantages which accrue to them in designing and operating a heavily controlled environment. Extending control beyond the 'traditional' concerns with criminal activities to the regulation of nuisances (anti-social behaviour) mirrors and extends the wider pattern of an increased use of anti-social behaviour measures by government. What is interesting, however, in this case is that 'private' authorities are not only utilising the rhetoric of anti-social behaviour, but also operating so as to normalise the extensive regulation of it through the publication of a written 'code'. Kent police welcomed the initiative: 'the code will allow staff and police officers to work together in maintaining the quality of experience for guests',[15] as did Prime Minister Blair, in his first press briefing following his re-election (when profiling anti-social behaviour as a major target for his third term in office).

Wolpole, writing on the Gateshead Metro Centre, concludes that:

> . . . this is an architecturally structured private world. And this, quite consciously, is what Hall [the developer] and his business colleagues see as a model for a future 'orderly society': the poor, the infirm, the unemployed without money, are to be excluded from this consumer paradise.
>
> (Wolpole 1991: 141)

This 'architecturally structured private world', reinforced by the rights of private property owners to control their private property, might well have provided an important pattern, a process of normalisation, for accepting such levels of regulation in other architecturally 'enclosed' spaces. But, when such spaces were once clearly marked as public space, then we confront questions about the use of public space in a rather different light and it becomes part of a concern about enclosure and privatisation of once open (in both senses of the word) urban space.

Wellingborough's 'Swansgate Centre' was part of a redevelopment programme in which an existing urban centre was remodelled under the 'New Towns' programme. Incorporating an existing street pattern into an enclosed and covered space (of c. 12 acres) of primarily retail units, with some public services, it continued to be used by members of the public as an access route through the town centre. Publicly planned and financed it was subsequently, under the central government programme of privatising 'New Town' assets, leased to a private property company. A group of young black men, who had taken to 'hanging out' in the centre, much as they would have done in an open square but with the benefit of protection from inclement weather, were regarded by the centre's security staff as disorderly and undesirable. After a number of verbal warnings, they were excluded (by written letter) from access to the centre, for life. This draconian action not only prohibited them from 'hanging out' in the centre, but also excluded them from the use of the services and employment opportunities in the centre. They were, effectively, banned, for life, from their local town centre: not by a court order or by a public authority, but by a private decision-making process, without benefit of due process. They took their case to court and, in the court of first instance, the judge found in their favour: the process of their banning had been without good cause and due process and to be banned for life was not a proportional response to their behaviour. At the Court of Appeal, however, judgment was given for the property owner on the simple ground that all that was being exercised was the right of a private property owner to exclude at will.[16] When asked to take into consideration the fact that the centre had been constructed by public finance from land which had once been open to the public, and subsequently become enclosed and privatised, the Court's response was that the local authority, when negotiating the lease, could have insisted on clauses allowing reasonable public access or could have taken the precaution of registering the covered and enclosed malls as public footpaths, and had failed to do either. An appeal to the European Court of Human Rights was refused on the grounds that no rights under the Convention had been infringed: specifically that a right to assemble did not include a right to gather together for pleasure.[17]

Washington (Tyne and Wear) was designed and built as a 'New Town' around a central hub which took the form of a covered centre (of c. 50 acres), given the grandiose name of 'The Galleries', designed as a shopping complex with related leisure activities and some civic amenities. Again, having been planned and financed by a public authority, in 1987 it was sold to a private developer as part of the privatisation programme. In 1998, as part of a campaign to try and save the only open green space in the area, a group of local individuals decided to collect signatures on a petition to be handed to the local council. In a gesture reminiscent of 'civic politics', they went to 'The Galleries', as not only a place frequented by large numbers of people and therefore good for collecting signatures but also, and this is clear from evidence they gave in court, as the 'town centre' in which they could make their concerns public. Finding that they needed permission to collect signatures within 'The Galleries' from the owners, they applied and were refused on the grounds that it was the owner's policy not to allow political activities within the centre. Already well politicised by their campaign to save the green space, they decided to legally challenge their exclusion from campaigning in 'their' town centre. Given the Court of Appeal judgment discussed above, it was clear that the trajectory for such an action was an appeal to the European Court. In 2003, their case was heard on the basis that their rights to freedom of assembly had been denied as a result of the failure of the public authorities to protect their rights on the privatisation of once public assets (Arts 10, 11 and 13).[18] Although the majority of the Court did not accept their argument (based primarily on the evidence that the protestors could have gone elsewhere to collect signatures and therefore had not lost their rights of assembly), in a robust and important minority judgment Judge Maruste squarely faced the issue of privatisation of public land (and other public assets) and the consequent loss of civic rights. He argued that to divide the geography of the law into a binary of 'public' and 'private' space does not reflect the increasing blur in urban planning between public/private space both in terms of how it is designed for use, and how it is inhabited. Judge Maruste employed the civil law term 'forum publicum' to indicate that he believed that there were certain types of property that could not, by their design or use, be designated as simply 'private' because of their ownership and that they should be subject to a different regime of rights.[19]

It is not only enclosed urban space which has become subject to rights of exclusion arising from privatisation. In 1987, for instance, the open town centre of Basingstoke (also the product of 'New Town' development), largely owned by the Prudential Assurance Company,[20] was the subject of press headlines when the local Women's Institute was refused permission to set up a charity stall by the company, who deemed the activities to be potentially detrimental to local businesses (Wolpole 1991: 142). A letter to the *Guardian* newspaper the following year asked:

> The Prudential has taken upon itself to deny access to anyone it chooses to see as 'undesirable'. This extends to any individual or group seen to be unacceptable by its private security forces . . . Just what does 'citizenship' mean in a privatised town?
>
> (Bianchini and Schwengel 1991: 220)

It does seem that the realisation that an 'open' centre was now privatised and subject to the rights of the owner to exclude 'undesirables', was more of a 'shock' to citizens than exclusion from enclosed zones. And yet, objections to the process of privatisation remain generally muted: perhaps not only because of its low visibility, unless and until one becomes subject to exclusion, but also because it is so closely tied in with the twinned benefits of enhanced 'comfort and safety' which mark the regeneration programmes of our urban centres.

Further, in the contemporary urban landscape the 'boundaries' between privately owned and regulated space and 'open' public space is increasingly blurred both through changes in building practices and through changes in the technologies of control and regulation.

## 'The mall goes under cover'[21]

We can track related architectural developments in the changing topographies of both 'the mall' as shopping centre and within broader patterns in urban regeneration programmes. In terms of enclosed shopping centres, there is now a clear turn towards the 'outside' and an increasing blurring between internal and external space. Not only do many centres, for instance Bluewater, now include outdoor leisure activities (climbing walls, boating etc) on their periphery, but also cafes and restaurants (especially of the more upmarket variety) now often turn 'outwards', with seating provided on external terraces. The increased use of mobile walls (which can be drawn up or aside) and glass enhance the sense that 'inside' and 'outside' are now brought together through more porous boundary practices. 'Fortress building' of clearly defined internal space with little external profile is no longer fashionable. In this sense malls and shopping centres, although still formed around a core of internal space and still concerned to provide the comfort and security of a covered and enclosed environment, are reproducing the trend back towards 'open streets and squares' within urban centres.

Under contemporary schemes to 'regenerate' urban centres, private investors are still being brought in through offers of enclosure and privatisation, but increasingly in partnerships with local authorities in which swathes of urban planning now integrate 'public' space with space placed under the ownership and control of private agencies. The regeneration of one retail area of Liverpool is a prime example of the new pattern. The Grosvenor Estate is the principal investor in the regeneration programme known as the 'Paradise Road Development', covering 43 acres.[22] The development plan for this area moves away from enclosed and covered malls and takes up the now far more fashionable urban planning of open spaces, pedestrianised streets and themed 'quarters'. Walking and sitting at leisure 'in the open air' is currently the central motif for regeneration of urban centres: the use of greenery, water and public art now seen as an investment to create a sense of pleasurable open space. Physical barriers and sharply defined boundaries are eschewed and, in preference, a sense of movement and ease-of-access is sought to establish a kind of urban pleasure garden. Covered areas increasingly use glass and 'open walls' to increase the sense of space and being 'outside'. What makes this emerging pattern possible is not only a change in architectural fashion, in great part inspired by 'New Urbanism', but also the willingness of such large players as the Grosvenor Estate to invest in a new model of public–private partnership which blurs the simple division of public/private space in terms of 'control' through 'ownership'.

This pattern removes any distinctive physical boundaries between public/private space and replaces it with a partnership between public and private agencies[23] in controlling the use of the urban environment. This is, in large part, made possible by changes in the technology and regulation of 'public' space. Not only is open, public space now as extensively covered by CCTV as enclosed, private space, but the extensive use of anti-social behaviour orders and dispersal zones to regulate nuisance (within the broader pattern of an environmental agenda focused on 'Cleaner, Safer and Greener Communities'[24]) means that the agendas of private and public authorities in extensive regulation of urban (and related) space have converged, as have the technologies for their achievement. As both Bianchini and Schwengel (1991) and Crawford (1999, 2001) make clear, movement through and between 'public' and 'private' space is now no longer a question of clear physical or legal boundaries but rather, in Crawford's words: 'we appear to slip seamlessly from one . . . "bubble" of governance to the next' (Crawford 1999: 84). Thus even in relation to those spaces so clearly marked as 'private property' in their design and history, for instance 'Bluewater', partnership between the agencies of regulation across the public/private divide make the division, in terms of control over access to the site, one which increasingly is not limited to the rights of the 'private property owner' to exclude, but is forged through the common concerns and closely related practices of the regulatory agencies working together. When the Kent police and Tony Blair welcomed the initiative, it was not simply to 'welcome' it for the specific site of Bluewater, but as a pattern they wished to encourage in other environments, not only those under 'private' control but also those of a more overtly 'public' nature, thus enhancing the 'partnership' between public and private agencies in the overall concern to regulate anti-social behaviour.

It remains the case that we should be concerned about the impact of enclosure and privatisation of urban centres, but in an important way, concentrating on this issue now misses the point. In either public urban space or private shopping centre, we are now subject to very similar technologies of regulation. Trying to keep the idea of public/private as separate spheres in this context is increasingly difficult and, indeed, can blind us to the convergence of the two (as Crawford's work, in particular, so extensively and carefully describes). We cannot simply argue against privatisation as an issue of public access when, at the very same time, our streets and open spaces are increasingly regulated and citizens whose behaviour is deemed problematic are excluded from them. As 'nuisance' becomes less and less tolerated and more and more thought of as 'anti-social behaviour', it hardly matters whether it is a public authority or a private body who are the agents of regulation.

## The malling of public space

The 'malling of public space' is generally associated with the physical process of enclosure and privatisation. But, at another level, and as has been implied in much of the discussion so far, we can also think of it in terms of a psycho-cultural geography.[25] 'Malling' has developed into a construction of worlds-within-worlds in which the 'inside world' of pleasure, comfort and safety has become the leitmotif of the way in which we approach, and what we expect of, the 'outside' (Zukin 1991). As shopping has become a more leisure-based activity and centres have to keep themselves attractive to consumers with access to retailing through the internet, so the pleasures and excitements of related leisure activities have become the new consumption focus. Packaging enclosed spaces 'thematically', especially referencing 'tourist destinations' or pastimes associated with 'glamour' or 'excitement', and providing leisure activities which would not normally be available locally or out-of-season (ski slopes in Milton Keynes and pleasure domes enclosing tropical beaches in English forests!), all now construct spaces which bring the 'outside' into the comfort and safety of the 'inside'. Malls are now part of a network of 'theme parks' which not only incorporate sanitised geographical and historical versions of the world, but spill out into the 'outside' reconfiguring the 'outside' into the patterns of comfort and safety made familiar 'inside' (Urry 2002, Buchanan 2006). Disney has not only rebuilt sections of downtown Los Angeles to make them more palatable consumer paradises (Davis 1998), but has moved on to build a New Urbanist dream town[26] and to be seriously considered as a suitable vehicle for 'saving' and regenerating Venice.

As malls are now more fashionably built to an 'open' plan, so also is the 'content' of mall lifestyles leaching from the enclosed environment into public space (as in the Liverpool development). Reconfiguring public space in this manner is not simply about a consumerist ethos dominating the environment, it is also about the expectations of 'the public' being reconfigured as well. If comfort and safety are the foci of the mall, and the exclusion of all undesirable and disorderly conduct a necessity to ensure comfort and safety, then so also should public space meet these criteria.

This links into what I think of as the creeping 'domestication' of public space. When Bluewater used the term 'guests' and the Kent police referred to the 'quality of experience' (they could also have been talking about 'lifestyle'), they were echoing a phenomenon which constructs our 'public lives' as an extension of the rights and expectations we have of how we lead our lives in our own private space. Expectations of safety and comfort extend into a refusal to deal with difficulties or anomalies which unsettle us. Hirst (1989) referred to this level of intolerance for strangeness and disruption as 'a suburban mentality' and, drawing on Cooper's work (2004) on nuisance, we could call it 'a domestic mentality'.[27] Neither of these terms are innocent of gender, both the domestic and the suburban settings have been seen, traditionally, as spheres of feminine influence (Berka 2004). If we add to the domestic and the suburban, the figure of the 'woman who shops', whether once in a department store or now in a mall, then we bring together a powerfully gendered combination. The 'domestic' is carried by the 'woman who shops' into an environment constructed with, one could say, the 'suburban' mentality of pursuing respectable pleasures in comfort and safety.[28] Specifically for Hirst and Cooper, this leads to an increasing unwillingness to accept aspects of disorder or nuisance which are experienced as unsettling: even to the extent that the possibility of such disturbances is problematic. Thus not only in malls are such possibilities guarded against for 'the comfort of our guests', but equally public space is increasingly subject to governance for the comfort of 'the public'. Hazel Blears, when asked what anti-social behaviour actually 'means', answered 'it is whatever the victim says it is'[29] and the most recent legislative extension in this field (the introduction of 'dispersal zones') requires nothing more than the possibility of behaviour of an anti-social nature for individuals or groups to be subject to 'dispersal' from the zone (Anti Social Behaviour Act 2003, s 4).

The 'domestication' of public space can be linked to the practices and effects of malling as a regulatory technique. What makes it so powerful is that it meets the expectations of an 'ordered' public. It feeds from and into a wish for well-ordered public space akin to the experience of a privately ordered world. It is as if the authenticity of what we 'have a right to expect' is set through a lens of 'domestic' comforts, rather than an acknowledgment of the more discomforting 'being amongst strangers', requiring degrees of tolerance and risk.

We could think of malls as exemplifying Foucault's 'heterotopias', places seemingly 'outside' which carry within them the possibility, the development of practices, which may reconfigure the 'inside' (Hetherington 1997). Of course, such a seeming duality as inside/outside is as problematic as private/public and was only, I would argue, for Foucault a way of 'thinking', of modelling, sites of potential and change. It might be better, perhaps, to think in terms of Deleuze's image of 'folding' surfaces into each other in which inside/outside and public/private are intensities of practice and modalities of place, rather than oppositional points (Deleuze 1992). What seems useful, however, is to 'image' the mall as a site which allowed for the development of regimes of control over movement in 'public places' – from which seeped technologies of control which now meet, fold into, similar technologies of control in all public space. This pattern matches Foucault's description of 'governance' post-Panopticon (1980, 2002, 2003), and Deleuze's (1995) account of 'regimes of control' post-sovereign state. In addition, Donzelot (1997) specifically addresses ways in which aspects of 'the private' can be used to develop and extend 'regimes of control': both as a carrier of values and as the mode through which we discipline each other into the virtues of order and respectability (Bottomley and Moore 2007). Linking these themes together we can say that the 'domestication' of public space has been a major vehicle for the development of what is, effectively, the loss (or potential) of 'urban commons' replacing it (or its potential) with a self-disciplining and ordered public, and that the 'mall' has played both a real and a symbolic role in this dispossession.

Some have argued, understandably, that such a dispossession can never be complete: human agency displays creativity in the many ways in which it can continue to inhabit place and resist being overwhelmed by practices of normalisation (Morris 1993). Marion Crawford focuses on 'the margins' of public/private space as still being 'open' to inhabitation through a plethora of informal activities (M Crawford 1999). Such work is concerned to caution against being overwhelmed by a focus on 'regimes of control', which might ignore or downplay the power of resistance and resilience as well as the 'incompleteness', in the sense of final closure, of such regimes. But equally, such work makes clear that the overall affect of dispossession, as well as the patterns of regulation associated with it, are the context within which 'resistance', or features of 'resilience', take form.[30]

What is important is that such authors continue to be concerned with the 'ordinary' and the 'everyday' as not necessarily working to 'the script' and in Morris's case being concerned, in particular, with how 'ordinary people', in their 'everyday' experiences, inhabit 'place' in ways which may not be as obvious as they seem to 'others' (whether academic researchers or figures of authority). However, other research suggests that the mall experience is of such an order that 'resistance' to it is both muted and transformed into little more than a 'politics of inclusion'. Auge (1995) and others have written of such 'spaces' as malls as 'non-places', that is 'spaces' which are not only 'uninhabitable' as 'places', but also play a part in 'desensitising' us to the very idea of 'inhabitation' (Jameson 1991, Zukin 1991). In other words, we only move through malls within clearly defined roles which have been set for us, as leisure-consumers, and cannot inscribe into these spaces patterns of inhabitation which evoke other roles or practices, for example citizen/activist or undisciplined/layabout. As we move through, are moved through, such spaces we neither gather sensation/experience/memory which builds expressive identity, nor are we able to leave sensation/experience/memory in the environment for others to gather and build on: not only is 'being amongst strangers' lost, but we also lose 'ourselves in relation to place'. As the mall experience becomes our world experience, so we carry into and through 'the world' little more than our knowledge of ourselves as leisure-consumers and our politics can become little more than our right to be part of, to share the privileges of, the leisure-consumer society, in which we are as comfortable and as safe as if we were 'at home'.

## Women in public space: a feminist perspective?

The Women's Design Service, following a three-year funding grant from government, provided an agenda to encourage the use of public space by women in safety and comfort. Placed within the context of the work of the Deputy Prime Minister's Office which, at that point in time, was responsible for urban regeneration programmes linked to providing 'cleaner, safer, greener communities' through the use of anti-social behaviour orders etc, these proposals took on a rather interesting gloss: 'Britain's streets are to be made more "female friendly" as part of plans by John Prescott's department to civilise city centres.'[31] The figure of 'vulnerable women' used as further confirmation of the need to act against all forms of anti-social behaviour, matched with the figure of 'women as civiliser' brought out of the nineteenth-century closet, combines into a powerful political rhetorical tool. From the need to 'protect' women as (potential) victims by the provision of greater surveillance, through to encouraging (respectable) women to use urban centres through such 'initiatives' as the provision of women-only spaces such as restrooms with hairdryers and good mirrors: the proposals of the WDS dovetail neatly with a political agenda of recasting urban centres as places of comfort and safety for leisure-consumption.[32]

Without wanting to dismiss the importance of 'safety' for women in public places, and whilst acknowledging that women remain subjected to the constraints of women-as-sexual-object, the limitations of remaining within this trope as 'the' feminist focus should be all too obvious.[33] Not only is an acknowledgment of how a focus on safety and comfort can play into the dominant theme of 'ordering' public space required, but also we need to think more carefully about how 'the feminine' may be ordering the 'feminist agenda'. Reading the 'women in planning' literature, I am struck by how much it is focused on either woman as victim or woman as mother, and whilst I recognise and welcome the very pragmatic approach taken by many women planners in terms of a concern to create environment which are 'gender-inclusive' (that is, as open, in practice, to women as much as to men), I am concerned that the figure of woman deployed through many of their recommendations is very conventional. Greed (1994) for instance, in her summation of her proposals for 'a caring city', in which 'safety is prioritised', calls for the closer integration of domestic responsibilities with employment and presents the use of public space as no more than a recreational margin between the two.[34] She gives, as 'the third important element' for woman-focused planning, the need for convenience in shopping. It is clear that from within this 'gender-inclusive' form of planning, concerns about how the figure of woman might be used to carry domestic virtues into public space, to the potential exclusion of not only the 'unsafe' but also the disorderly or disruptive (for instance, young black men from a shopping centre), is not an issue. Greed uses as a subtitle to her book 'Creating Gendered Realities', but a perspective which does not take into account broader patterns in the planning and architecture of contemporary governance misses the extent to which a 'women's agenda' might feed very directly into an agenda of 'exclusion', a harsh reality which we cannot afford to ignore.

## Public/private: a divide?

My argument that 'regimes of control' utilise public/private partnerships in patterns of regulation which transcend a continued focus on the privatisation of urban public space should not, however, be read as implying that we, as legal scholars, should not use the tools available to us to resist the pattern of dispossession incurred through privatisation. Neither should we ignore the wider implications it carries for our ideas of 'property' and public/private thinking.

Blomley (2004) argues that fully appreciating the idea of 'public space', and being able to recognise and defend the many practices associated with it, has been constrained by a focus on 'the ownership model'. This has a number of consequences, not least of which is an inability to even 'think' public space as 'property' in that it so often fails to conform to an ownership model. Consequently, it is also difficult to 'think' rights in relation to the use of such land if they are not carried by and within the 'ownership model'. Hence, we can easily conceive of the right to exclude, but cannot find within the same discourse a countervailing 'right of public access'. At this level, the decision of our courts to uphold the right to exclude seems all too simple and obvious.

However, the assertion of the rights of the private property owner as 'absolutist' in character, is not unchallenged.[35] As Judge Maruste so strongly argued in his dissenting judgment in *Appleby and Others v United Kingdom* (2003) 37 EHRR 38, especially with reference to the privatisation of once public assets, to continue to divide the world into public and private property domains does not adequately reflect the reality of modern urban living. In *Porter v Commissioner of Police for the Metropolis* [1999] All ER (D) 1129, very clear and direct statements were made in the Court of Appeal (albeit *obiter*) calling into doubt the claim that privately owned premises used by 'the public' could be, or remain, subject to the same rights and privileges of 'private property' ownership.[36]

Gray and Gray (2005: 291–3) argue that these breaches in the wall around private property ownership are indicative of a trend towards treating 'quasi-public space' in this country as (potentially) subject to the principles governing land held by public authorities (that is as subject to public law rules). They are only able to argue this with some force by beginning in the public sphere, bringing fully into account the little jurisprudence there is in relation to land held by public authorities and using it as strongly as possible. This is an important (and too rare) example of three factors: first, not only including such material in a standard text and thereby raising its profile in the academy, but also, second, in reversing the usual move from private to public to allow them to argue 'out' from public law and thereby, third, to help 'prepare the way' for a time in court when a judge may have both the opportunity and the will to establish the jurisprudential potential of the argument.

There are other significant clues to be found in the cases which suggest that the primacy of the ownership model is not as unassailable as it might seem when read in a rather different register. In *CIN Properties v Rawlins* [1995] 2 EGLR 130, reference was made to the failure of the local authority to impose conditions on the leaseholders to protect reasonable public access, or to use their ability to register the malls as public footpaths. Pinkstone (2005) directly addresses this as a strategy for keeping open reasonable access, and we could extend this into an examination of the extent to which local authorities can, and have, used planning applications as a vehicle through which to impose conditions relating to the provision (and upkeep) of public space, as well as protecting reasonable public access. Of course, market forces, as well as political will, are a major factor in determining how far any public authority can succeed in laying down such conditions, but in circumstances in which developers are pursuing a major economic investment there have been many examples of their willingness to provide new physical infrastructures to the benefit of the local community and, with sufficient political pressure, there is no reason why public access should not also be part of the agenda of any relevant planning application. What this means is that regulation over the use of any privately owned development is not to be 'read' simply at the level of formal rights, particularly the 'right to exclude'.

Underlying all these stratagems it is not so much a concern with ownership, but rather with the 'use' of what has come to be thought of as 'quasi-public space'. In American jurisprudence, this term has been deployed in relation to spaces which are privately owned but designed for public use, in an effort to determine and defend rights of use of such spaces.[37] Using the idea of 'quasi-public space' highlights the extent to which so much or our urban topography now falls under this 'category', as well the significance of 'use' value rather than 'ownership'. Thus, in using the term we do not need to limit ourselves to issues of privatisation or privately owned space, we can deploy it to cover all urban public spaces and places of a particular character. In this sense, through 'use' we can radically destabilise the ownership model.

It also allows us to connect back to the theme of 'partnership' between public/private bodies as central to emerging patterns of governance. Thus, in the example, given above, of negotiations over leases and planning applications, it might seem as if public authorities and private bodies are set in opposition to each other, whereas a better model to convey the interaction between them is one of 'partnership'. However, it is in the shared concern of the regulation of conduct (anti-social behaviour) that the interests of both public and private agencies converge.

Under the 'control model' of governance, public agencies increasingly devolve 'policing' (in its broadest sense) to private bodies as part of their responsibilities (rather than simply privileges) in relation to 'their' control over 'their' property.[38] In this sense 'quasi-public space' takes on a rather different resonance – we could deploy it to characterise space which is privately owned (but subject to a potential set of claims about reasonable 'public use'), which forms part of a network between public/private agencies resulting in a continuum of 'control'.

As I have argued in this chapter, the present trend towards architectural practices of 'flow' and 'openness' are both made possible by, and require and facilitate, this process of networking which transcends a simple division between the operation of 'private rights' and public space. Therefore, to concentrate on the effects of private ownership, is not only to ignore the constraints increasingly placed upon public use of public space, but also to ignore the significance of the inter-relationship between public and private bodies and their shared concerns with control over use. In fact, we could begin to think of all public space, irrespective of ownership, as increasingly subject to a 'quasi-public' regime, in that our rights of access to it are increasingly subject to control. In particular, the increasing use of 'zones', under both anti-terrorism legislation and anti-social behaviour provisions, in which the police have been given extensive powers to exclude individuals or disperse groups, is creating a topography of quasi-public space for those who are deemed to be suspicious or a potential nuisance.

I have suggested that the mall operated as a kind of 'hinge' between 'public' and 'private' space, an historical and geographical 'threshold' between the two terrains, the first 'quasi-public' space.[39] So often using a division such as that of public/private leads us to not only try and allocate (in this case) space into each category, but also leads to a focus on 'boundaries' and, at best, a questioning of where the boundary lies or the extent to which the boundary is sealed or porous. I think that an exploration of the use of the idea of 'quasi-public' space suggests the paucity of being held into such a figure and that, whilst we might still find it useful to deploy public/private distinctions in some contexts, what I seek to do here is to focus on the idea of a 'threshold' rather than 'boundary' and to suggest that in using 'threshold' we can think of quasi-public space as an increasingly expansive terrain which folds together public/private space.

Borden (2000: 21) writes of boundaries in the postmodern city emerging as a 'thick edge', which are 'ultimately zones of social negotiation'. In this sense 'thresholds' are a 'thick edge', which act not only as intersections, but also as sites which are 'zones of social negotiation'. Thus quasi-public space, such as a mall, is a 'thick edge' within which and through which we carry practices and expectations of both a 'public' and 'private' providence. By this I mean that the space is not merely defined as 'quasi-public' through its design, purpose or legal definition, but through our 'sense' of what it means to be 'in public' and our sense of 'our rights' to be there as a mode of habit or use. Borden (2000: 21) describes threshold signals which 'combine to create a time-space in which the visitors check themselves, validating their identity against that suggested as normative by the city architecture; as a result, everyone assumes a normative identity and behaviour and becomes a cast-member in the Disney movie of the postmodern city'. In this sense, the mall operated as a threshold through which the norms of domesticity and the suburban mentality (comfort, safety, conformity) were carried into quasi-public space and then outward and, most importantly, carried by 'us'.

Of course, Borden's account suggests that 'we' have little choice but to become 'cast-members' – the passive recipients of the pleasures of consumption, tutored all too well in our role through the vector of world-in-mall. But we can read this not so much as a 'description' of a necessary present/future, as much as a 'warning' against passive collusion with such a corrosive pattern. In this sense, Borden might be read as signalling two important issues. First, that it is important to recognise the potential in 'ourselves' for resistance to (and resilience within the face of) the hegemonic pattern of public space constructed in such a limited way, denying the risks of discomfort, insecurity and lack of conformity – to risk instead 'being amongst strangers'. Second, to recognise that 'public' is most importantly a 'way of being', a network of practices and expectations, which 'we' carry in relation to 'others' as 'a polity'. In other words, it is dependant upon our commitment to a political-social practice, and a spatial practice, which holds some form of 'common good' as a value in itself and which necessarily recognises the rights of the marginalised and dispossessed.

Thus we can draw a distinction, although perhaps not too sharply, between public space as embodying and carrying the exercise of power and patterns of governance through control, and public space constructed through the performance of 'counter publics' in 'counter commons', alternative patterns and practices which, in certain space/time configurations crystallise into modes of resistance (Blomley 2004). This is very different to the communitarian appeal to 'community' and to the building, or preservation, of public space as enhancing 'community' and 'civic spirit'. As Blomley demonstrates in his work, groups which come together to claim 'public rights of use' to space (especially when faced with its loss), are as likely to be resisting public authorities as much as private developers. And it is through their assertion of what is valuable to them as 'rights', and the activities which they engage in to protect these rights, that 'community', for them, is forged in their sense of communality through collective action. However, what Blomley is also highlighting is that such a sense of public space as 'communal' (through shared use) and as a 'community asset', is a trope which has a long history and which, despite the dominance of 'the ownership model', is still one regularly drawn upon by people in their everyday lives as much as by political activists.[40] The simple fact is that we, as lawyers, have failed to fully engage with this, focused as we are on private property and ownership. We have generally failed to construct adequate legal tools to protect and enhance public 'use' rights, let alone a concept of ownership vested in such an amorphous thing as 'community' or 'public', or, even more so, to rethink what we mean by 'ownership'. The limitations attributed by us to a notion of 'property in land', illustrates our own continued enchantment with/by the traditions of 'Land Law', and hence our passivity in the face of contemporary challenges in relation to urban land use.

It is as if our own world-in-a-mall has been the orthodox Land Law textbook which has tutored us, too well, to limit ourselves to 'private land law' and so to the continued usage, or presumption, of a public/private divide which blinds us to the emergence of new patterns of governance and new roles for law, as well as new potentials.

## Notes

1 With especial thanks to Nathan Moore and Hilary Lim.
2 Historical work on the development of 'the private sphere' as an aspect of the 'the construction of privacy', the 'long moment' of the arrival of 'the individual', again reinforces linkages between the domains of 'personhood' and 'property'. (See Aries and Duby's series 'The History of Private Life', especially Vols. IV and V.) A moment which, it is argued, is still being played through in, for instance the predominance of 'identity politics' in the early twenty-first century (Bauman 2001).
3 For one example of the attempt to problematise the public/private divide in feminist scholarship in land law, see Green and Lim (2001). The implication of the argument made there, and here, is that feminist work in this area has tended to 'begin' in the private sphere, making it difficult to approach work on the 'public sphere', let alone to destabilise the divide.
4 To list the substantive literature covering this material would take up too much space, but see Gray and Gray (1999a and b, 2005) for an introduction and Michelman (1997).
5 In Cambridge a part of one pathway which forms a side to the market square (the central town square) is owned by one of the colleges. The boundary of the college land is marked by a thin brass line in the pavement.
6 Habermas's account of the emergence of a 'public sphere' (a site of open discussion and exchange) between civil society and the state, and its later loss by incorporation into state practices, remains an important thread in many attempts to account for the need for a 'public domain' as conducive to a strong 'political environment'. See Hetherington (1997) for a critique of this position, which I share. However, what is important is that it refuses a conflation between 'public domain' and 'state practices'.
7 The 'New Urbanism' movement is located in the United States, but is increasingly referenced in this country. See Talen (2005) for an introduction to 'New Urbanism' and Beuka (2004) for a sustained critique. Visit the New Urbanism' website: http://www.newurbanism.org.
8 For a 'progressive' reading of New Urbanism, see Frug (1999).
9 Further, 'public space' changes in both its form and in the uses made of it, through different social practices, by a range of social actors. These 'uses' may be constrained or enhanced by the design of public space for particular purposes. Equally, how space is 'inhabited' by public use, is dependant upon what sections of the public want of public space and how capable they are, or imaginative, in 'bending' public space to their needs and wishes. Bringing together the design of public space with the everyday practices of the public in their use of it, raises issues

of the extent to which the 'inhabitation' of public space is feasible beyond the 'planning' of authorities.

10 'New Towns' are a specific category of urban units planned, financed and built by government as 'development corporations' under the New Towns Act 1946. The Commission for New Towns, formed in 1959, took over the assets of development corporations once a New Town had been established. Since the 1981 New Towns Act this role has become one of the disposal of such assets by privatisation. The Commission is now part of 'English Partnership' (along with the Urban Regeneration Agency) (Hall and Ward 1998).

11 A major influence on the development of the town planning profession and on the planning of 'New Towns' was the Garden City movement, which succeeded in building two 'garden cities' (Letchworth and Welwyn), both of which had suffered from dependency on private investment. Welwyn became designated as a 'New Town', a move made primarily in order to share in the benefits of public financing, which subsequently resulted in its assets being privatised. Letchworth's assets (never subject to 'New Town' legislation) are now held by the 'Letchworth Garden City Heritage Foundation', incorporated as a charitable Industrial and Provident Society (Miller 2002).

12 Llewllyn-Davies (the socialist designer of the Milton Keynes Centre) specifically addressed the issue of provision of civic space, akin to a town square, in the design of the centre (Osborn and Whittick 1977). It is interesting to note that the first designer of shopping malls in the US, the European Victor Gruen, also included spaces for 'civic activities' (see http://cpn.org/topics/community/malltown.html). Their purposes were overcome by market, property and architectural forces, all of which militated against such space being 'owned' by 'the public'.

13 The relocation of department stores into shopping centres has been crucial to the success of such centres, as well as offering a new site for department stores. Shopping centres and large malls in this country are formed from 'anchors' of well known department store names, around which smaller retail units form 'street profiles'. Those department stores which remain 'on the high street' have often been morphed into 'bazaars' composed of 'brand-name' concessions. The floor plan of such developments tends to keep them 'open' rather than as a series of semi-enclosed sites: thus the 'feel' of them is very different to the operation of the more enclosed units in malled spaces. A good example of this, in London, is Selfridges.

14 The quote is taken from the press statement (Bluewater Sets Standards) issued through the Bluewater website, http://bluewater.co.uk. Similar codes have been used in malls in the United States: Desert Ridge (Arizona), for example, includes within its list of forbidden activities 'non-commercial expressive activity' and 'excessive staring'. See Blum (2006).

15 Again quoted in the press statement on the Bluewater website.

16 *CIN Properties v Rawlins* [1995] 2 EGLR 130.

17 *Mark Anderson and Others v United Kingdom* (1998) EHRR CD 172. No appeal could be based on 'freedom of movement', as the UK has not ratified the relevant convention.

18 *Appleby v United Kingdom* (2003) 37 EHRR 38.

19 If *Appleby* had been successful, it would only have served to support the distinction between 'purposeful' civic activities (as covered by a 'right to assemble') and the rights, or needs, of those who simply wish to inhabit public space for pleasure, to loiter or to find a place to try and rest when cold, hungry and homeless. As the Grays (Gray and Gray 1999a, 1999b) have pointed out, the people who most need access to 'urban commons' are those who have least, but it is these groups

who find themselves excluded from enclosed centres, whether private *ab initio* or subsequently privatised.

20 They are now the owners of 'The Galleries' in Washington, Tyne and Wear.

21 This quote is taken from the title of an article dealing with developments in the US: 'The Mall Goes Under Cover: It Now Looks Like a Shopping Street' (Blum 2006).

22 See http://www.liverpoolpdsa.co.uk. In 1995 this website featured a quote from the Deputy Prime Minister linking the planning design features to 'New Urbanism'.

23 It should also be noted that one of the primary investors in such development is pension funds – including the university lecturer's pension fund.

24 See http://www.cleanersafergreener.gov.uk.

25 See Voyce (2005) for a parallel argument to mine, but drawn from the traditions of a focus on neo-liberalism and the market (and with a rather different 'take' on property.)

26 'Celebration' in Florida. Visit http://www.clebrationfl.com/.

27 For a focus on the development of 'comfort' as a key trope, see Sennett (1994).

28 Critics of New Urbanism argue that their planning schemes evoke a 'small town mentality' (Bueka 2004), which we might associate with the kind of mentality which Hirst (from a UK perspective) calls 'suburban'. Differences in cultural geography require some care with the use of such terms, especially when drawing parallels between them – but I would argue that behind both lie similar images of a community conforming to shared expectations and lifestyles. Scale (small), pace (slow, predictable rhythms) and settlement (sedentary) suggest an inclusive conformity and hence the comfort and safety of the 'known' nuanced by the additional attractions of mutual respect for property and privacy.

29 Quoted by the director of Liberty, Shami Chakrabarti, in a lecture given at the British Institute for Human Rights (10 January 2006) entitled 'Asbomania'.

30 I have drawn a distinction between 'resistance' and 'resilience' as the first, although more commonly used, implies a conscious act of opposition, whereas the latter connotes a more 'everyday' continuity of habit and inhabitation through use practices of a mundane nature. I should also recognise the argument that 'open' spaces, especially in cities, still carry 'counter practices' of a more oppositional or disorderly nature, in that they become sites for expressive activities, such as skateboarding, music or entertainment. This displays resilience, as well as often very imaginative 'bending' of public sites. Such activities are often tolerated by the authorities when they add to the picture of a 'vibrant' street life (especially if attractive to visitors or tourists).

31 *The Sunday Times*, 21 August 2005. The article mentions Demos ('a think tank close to the Labour party') working on similar issues: 'It's women-friendly suggestions include crèches in nightclubs, giving women priority for taxis . . . a range of toiletries in public conveniences, separate areas for women on trains and buses, and citing hairdryers and chargers for mobile phones in public lavatories.' The WDS organised a national conference in November 2005 entitled 'Women's Safety in Our Cities' and participated in a London Women and Planning Forum Seminar held in February 2006, entitled 'Public Space in the City'.

32 We can presume that the 'female friendly' city centre is not one focused on the figure of the young woman who drinks and parties as much as her male counterpart on a Friday night! On the 'threat' of disorderly and dangerous women in an urban setting, see Wilson (1991).

33 A similar concern is expressed by Wilson (1991: 10): 'recent feminist contributions to the discussion of urban problems have tended to restrict themselves narrowly to issues of safety, welfare and protection. This is a mistake, since it recreates the traditional paternalism of most town planning.'

34 This tallies, I think, with the Demos publication on public space (Tims and Mean 2005) which uses pictures of women with children to emphasise recreational user, as if this is 'the' most important element of public space. Perhaps it is not too surprising that, in 2006, Demos launched an initiative (an 'action plan' headed by Mean) to reinvigorate 'suburban living'. Their press statement was headlined 'New Suburbia: needs to be nurtured'. See http://www.demos.co.uk.

35 It should also be remembered that the portrayal of private property rights as so 'settled' in law, especially in relation to such issues as the right to exclude, is at odds with a more nuanced and sophisticated account of both historical and contemporary legal patterns (Gordon 1996, Gray and Gray 1998).

36 Recall, also, the decision in the court of first instance in *CIN Properties v Rawlins* (1995) 2 EGLR 130.

37 A review of the fragility of the American jurisprudence protecting public rights in 'quasi-public space' is found in Coffin (2000).

38 As Gray and Gray point out (2005: 291) the right to exclude at will is now of much less significance in quasi-public space in this country, given the introduction of anti-social behaviour legislation which covers all property to which the public have access 'as of right . . . or by virtue of express or implied licence' (Anti Social Behaviour Act 2003, s 36).

39 I do not mean this literally in terms of time – to claim it as the 'first' in such a sense would be open to dispute! But I do think that it can be thought of symbolically as 'the first', given the concentration in this 'space' of the characteristics which I have examined in this chapter.

40 I have tended to be critical when issues of the use of urban public space have focused on recreational activities, as if this is something of a diversion from (or lessening of) a fuller account of 'civic life'. However, it may be important to rethink this and to recognise that much contemporary activism, patterns of 'resistance' and 'resilience', are focused around public space in terms of recreational user – especially around such issues as allotments and green spaces and the use of public squares for informal entertainments and gatherings of a social or cultural nature. This may now form the vector carrying the potential of 'counter commons', requiring a shift of focus from seeking the civic in urban centres towards a range of practices on 'the periphery'.

Chapter 5

# Scapegoating and the legal landscape

## Homeless women and the law

*Rosy Thornton*

### Introduction

> How do we explain to the young couple, who want to wait for a home before they start a family, that they cannot be re-housed ahead of the unmarried teenager expecting her first, probably unplanned, child? . . . What signal about family responsibility does that send out?[1]

Ever since homeless people were given a statutory right to accommodation in 1977, debate over the allocation of public sector housing in Britain has been permeated by the image of the pregnant teenage girl of popular mythology, who uses the legislation to 'jump the housing queue'. During the passage through Parliament of the Housing (Homeless Persons) Bill, in 1977, which for the first time placed duties upon local housing authorities to find homes for the homeless, Conservative backbench MPs warned of the many 'scrimshankers and scroungers'[2] who, they feared, would manipulate the newly established rights in order to obtain unmerited priority for council accommodation. Pressure from this lobby led to the insertion in the Bill of the 'intentional homelessness' provisions. These limited the local authority's duty for those who are deemed homeless as a result of their own deliberate conduct to short-term accommodation and 'advice and assistance'.[3]

Despite the inclusion in the law of this apparent safeguard, popular belief in the prevalence of queue-jumping continued to hold sway in many quarters, and by the early 1990s the myth had taken firm root in government circles. Sir George Young's speech to the Conservative Party Conference in 1993 brought the issue to the top of the political agenda, and set in motion changes to the law, in the form of the Housing Act 1996, removing the entitlement of any homeless household to permanent accommodation. Subsequently, through the Homelessness Act 2002 the Labour Government abolished the specific time limit upon assistance for the homeless by amendment of the Housing Act 1996 to its current form. However, the legislation retains the structure of a two-tier system of entry into public sector housing, with the homelessness route in Part VII of the Act being characterised by less choice and greater uncertainty, almost invariably involving a spell in temporary accommodation. Young single mothers may have been pushed from centre-stage by asylum-seekers and paedophiles as the main targets for popular opprobrium in the first decade of the twenty-first century, but the stereotype persists in many quarters, and the long-term effects both of the queue-jumping myth and of the changes in the legislative landscape which it provoked, are still being felt by homeless people.

Has the homeless persons legislation in fact provided an easy short-cut to cheap, secure housing for feckless teenage mothers? Tracing the development of the law through the punitive changes effected in 1996 to the partial restoration of rights in 2002, this chapter will examine how the legislation has impacted and continues to impact upon women who find themselves in situations of urgent housing need.

## Of good and bad mothers

Carol Smart (1996) has argued that motherhood is a social construct rather than a natural condition. She has shown how the institution of motherhood is built upon and perpetuates expectations about 'proper' mothering, against which women's conduct is continually judged. Her contention is that these 'dominant normative constraints . . . create certain categories of mothers as bad or inadequate because they are perceived to fail to live up to the ideals of motherhood that are imposed through legal and public policies' (Smart 1996: 39). Single mothers, and particularly those who have never married, have been especially demonised. The Good Mother should be married to her children's father, should provide a secure home for them, and should act selflessly, always putting her children's needs before her own. The woman who is bringing up a child alone, who is reliant upon the state for support, is seen to fall below the expected standards of motherhood, to be a Bad Mother.

In the 1990s vilification of single mothers, by policy makers and in the media, reached an acute pitch. Sasha Roseneil and Kirk Mann (1996) have branded 1993 in particular as 'The Year of the Lone Mother'.[4] Moral fears about the decline of the family and a desire to see a return to 'family values', together with political concern about the increasing cost of welfare benefits, combined to create an atmosphere in which teenage mothers became scapegoats for many of the problems in society: for juvenile crime, the dependency culture, and the perceived development of an excluded underclass. As Roseneil and Mann (1996: 192) have shown, 'the discourse about the underclass that developed in 1993 dichotomised women along age-old lines: good women who do the right thing, get married and then have children, versus bad women, who have children, don't get married and depend on state benefits.' Welsh Secretary John Redwood spoke out against women who become pregnant 'with no apparent intention of even trying marriage or a stable relationship with the father of the child'.[5] The broadsheets as well as the tabloid newspapers took up the hue and cry against single mothers,[6] and a BBC television *Panorama* programme 'Babies on Benefit', screened in 1994, brought the matter to the forefront of public attention.

In the housing context, concern was focused upon the fear that young lone mothers would gain unwarranted priority for scarce council accommodation, at the expense of more deserving families. The myth of the teenage girl who gets pregnant in order to leapfrog the housing waiting list held wide sway in the mid-1990s. It was propagated not only by Government ministers such as Sir George Young, but also by some within the housing profession. The Director of Housing at the Conservative flagship London Borough of Wandsworth, Richard Sheppard, was quoted in the press in 1993 as saying: 'There is increasing dissatisfaction among young couples on the waiting list who are being usurped by young single mums who can go to the head of the queue by virtue of their homeless status.'[7]

It was directly out of this climate of moral panic that the Housing Act 1996 was born (Cowan and Fionda 1994). The beliefs and attitudes exemplified by Sir George Young's 1993 Conference speech were reflected in the Green Paper which was issued in 1994 (DoE 1994). Here the homelessness legislation was described as 'a fast track' into a council tenancy (DoE 1994: para 1.1), and as being 'the more attractive way into subsidised housing for those wishing to be re-housed' (DoE 1994: para 2.7). The Green Paper was resonant with the language of traditional family values. In contrast with those irresponsible and greedy enough to take the 'quick route' (DoE 1994: para 2.8) of a homelessness application, the image that was presented of those on the waiting list was inevitably that of a family with two (married) parents. The Government's stated moral assumption was that 'establishing a home – particularly as a place in which to raise a family – is a matter for which married couples want to feel personally responsible' (DoE 1994: para 1.2), and their stated aim was 'to ensure that subsidised housing is equally available to all who genuinely need it, particularly couples seeking to establish a good home in which to start and raise a family' (DoE 1994: para 3.1). The Green Paper was followed in 1995 by a White Paper setting out the Government's proposals for legislative change. Entitled *Our Future Homes: Opportunity, Choice, Responsibility* (DoE 1995), the White Paper was again strong in asserting a particular model of responsible parenting. Its stated policy aim was to ensure that council housing allocation schemes 'should balance specific housing needs against the need to support married couples who take a responsible attitude to family life, so that tomorrow's generation grows up in a stable home environment' (1995: 36). To be on the housing waiting list was to be responsible, a Good Mother; by implication, therefore, to find oneself in the acute housing need which meets the statutory definition of homelessness was equated with irresponsibility.

## Exploding the myth

Section 175 of the Housing Act 1996 defines a person as homeless if 'he[8] has no accommodation available for his occupation', whether by virtue of a proprietary interest in it, an order of court, an express or implied licence to occupy, or a statutory or common law right to do so. The accommodation must be available not only to the homeless person but also to other people who normally reside or might reasonably be expected to reside with her;[9] it must also be reasonable for her to continue to occupy that accommodation.[10]

Priority need for accommodation is established where the applicant falls either within one of the paragraphs of s 189(1) of the Act, or one of the categories recently added by order of the Secretary of State.[11] As well as those who are vulnerable as a result of old age, mental or physical illness or disability or 'other special reason',[12] or in consequence of an institutional background[13] or of having fled their accommodation due to violence,[14] persons who are homeless as a result of an emergency such as a fire or flood,[15] 16- and 17-year-olds,[16] and those aged under 21 who have recently been in care,[17] the section designates as priority categories pregnant women,[18] and persons 'with whom dependent children reside or might reasonably be expected to reside'.[19] Clearly the definition is of assistance to large numbers of women who are pregnant or have children, and indeed these two categories account for the great majority of those homeless and in priority need. Statistics indicate that of homeless households accepted by local authorities in England as being in priority need, over half contain dependent children and a further 12 per cent include a pregnant woman.[20] However, it is not and has never been the case that the legislation gives single mothers priority over two-parent families; married couples with dependent children, or who are expecting their first child, are equally covered by s 189 of the 1996 Act.[21]

Research conducted in the early 1990s, when rhetoric targeted at 'queue-jumping' lone mothers was at its most vitriolic, paints a very different picture from that put forward by Government Ministers. A survey undertaken by the Institute of Housing (1993) found that only between a quarter and a half of households accepted as homeless by local authorities were single parents. Similarly, of the statutorily homeless housed by housing associations in 1992/93, only 37 per cent were lone parents, while 51 per cent were two-parent families or childless adults.[22] Moreover, a substantial proportion of those on general council and housing association needs registers at this time were also single parents (a reflection of the relative poverty and difficulty in finding accommodation experienced by those bringing up children on their own). Department of the Environment research shows that of those households securing tenancies via council waiting lists in 1991, 24 per cent consisted of one adult with a child or children (Prescott-Clarke, Clemens and Park 1994: table 5.17). Such data undermines any simplistic representation of the homeless as single mothers and those on waiting lists as married couples. Indeed, the homeless and waiting list applicants were frequently the very same people. Research carried out by Shelter (1994) revealed that on average 59 per cent of households accepted as homeless by local authorities were already registered on the housing waiting list; as a Department of the Environment (1992) report concluded, 'in many local authorities, those who are homeless are simply people on the waiting list with nowhere to wait'. Both married and unmarried mothers were registering their need for accommodation, but those on their own were just more often reaching the crisis point of statutory homelessness before being allocated a tenancy. The relatively small difference in the average waiting time before the grant of a council tenancy, which was according to Prescott-Clarke, Clemens and Park (1994: 95) 0.7 years for homeless persons compared with 1.2 years for those on the general waiting list, would seem to be little more than an indication of the more urgent housing needs of the former group.

Even amongst those homeless applicants who were single parents, very few in fact fitted the stereotype of the irresponsible teenage mother. Most of this group consisted of older women, divorced or separated; the Institute of Housing (1993) survey referred to earlier found that only between 2 and 14 per cent of homeless applicants were unmarried teenagers with children. Current statistics[23] suggest that this is still the case today. Of the homeless households accepted by local authorities in England as being in priority need in 2005, 23 per cent were homeless because parents were no longer able or willing to accommodate them. This category is likely to cover most never-married young single parents, but they will by no means account for all or even most of the 23 per cent figure, which will also include many other people and situations, such as vulnerable youngsters without children. By comparison, 20 per cent of accepted households were homeless as a result of the breakdown of a relationship with a partner, representing a large number of (mainly) older lone parents who are far from fitting the popular stereotype. This figure exposes as false the characterisation of homeless single parents as Bad Mothers who start a family before securing a home in which to raise it, or even as a means to obtaining such a home. Rather, it tells a story of women who will frequently have been raising a family for many years in settled accommodation, before losing it through the personal and financial upheaval of relationship breakdown. Nor can it be maintained that these women are too ready to leave the marital home without good reason in order to seek council assistance; over recent years the statistics have consistently shown that approximately two-thirds of those homeless as a result of relationship breakdown have been escaping from domestic violence.

At the same time, a closer analysis of households registered on general council housing lists in the 1990s does little to support the picture which was presented by the Conservative Government, of married couples patiently waiting for a tenancy before having children. Only one in three households on council waiting lists in 1991 consisted of two or more adults and no children

(Prescott-Clarke, Clemens and Park 1994: table 4.12) (a category which would in any case include not only young childless couples but also, for example, older couples whose families had grown up and left home). Of those waiting list applicants interviewed in a Government survey, a mere 3 per cent gave their wish to start a family as their reason for seeking accommodation (Prescott-Clarke, Clemens and Park 1994: table 4.26).

More recent research also gives the lie both to the notion that single parents are predominantly young women who have never been married, and that they enjoy privileged access to housing resources. A major survey by the Policy Studies Institute (Marsh, McKay and Stephenson 2001) for the Department of Social Security, conducted in 1999, found that the average age of all lone parents was 35, that only 23 per cent had never cohabited or been married, and that, far from the popular image of the irresponsible mother with a clutch of illegitimate children, the majority had only one child. The Census similarly revealed that only 7.4 per cent of the 2,360,000 lone parents in England and Wales were aged 24 or under, compared with 70.3 per cent aged 35 or over and 31.2 per cent aged 50 or over[24] – hardly in line with the stereotype. Rowlingson and MacKay (2002: 203–8) have shown how, far from enjoying any advantaged status by reason of priority housing rights, single parents tend to be clustered in poor quality housing, often in over-crowded conditions, amounting in some areas of the country to 'ghettoisation'.

The queue-jumping myth of the mid-1990s rested upon the assumption that acceptance as homeless and in priority need would give absolute preference for the offer of a council tenancy, ahead of those on the general waiting list. Again, however, research conducted during this period shows that this was very far from being so. The local housing authority's statutory duty towards the priority homeless under the law as it then stood was to 'secure that suitable accommodation becomes available for [their] occupation'.[25] This duty could be performed not only through the provision of a council house or flat, but by securing instead that suitable accommodation be obtained 'from some other person'.[26] The Shelter (1994) survey found that 95 per cent of authorities were using nominations to housing associations as a means to the discharge of their duty in some instances, and almost one-third were finding accommodation for homeless persons in the private sector. The suggestion that the homeless were taking all the available council housing and squeezing out waiting list applicants was demonstrably untrue; Department of the Environment statistics showed that of 255,872 lettings made by local authorities in 1992/93, only 39 per cent went to the statutorily homeless.[27] Many housing authorities operated a quota system, keeping a fixed percentage of lettings for homeless persons, for transfers, and for allocation from the general waiting list.[28] Others operated a more flexible, *ad hoc* system, or determined priority between homeless and other applicants through a points scheme, but not one authority responding to Government research in 1994 reported giving homeless households automatic priority access to all their accommodation as it became available (Prescott-Clarke, Clemens and Park 1994). Similarly, a major study of housing allocation practices commissioned by the Department of the Environment, Transport and the Regions and published in 2001 observed that prior to the 1996 Housing Act, in the majority of local authorities 'homeless households were already integrated within allocations priorities, rather than representing an "exceptional category" with overwhelming priority, as some of the Act's backers seemed to assume' (Pawson *et al.* 2001: 57).

Nor is it easy to agree with the suggestion in the 1994 Green Paper that the homeless persons legislation ever represented an 'attractive' way into council housing. Apart from the obvious trauma of homelessness itself, applicants for accommodation via this route were frequently faced with punitive attitudes and policies in terms of allocation. Shelter's (1994) study recorded 13 per cent of housing authorities as operating a strict policy of making only one offer of accommodation to the homeless in discharge of their statutory duty, while waiting list applicants would be offered some choice over their future home; only 5 per cent of authorities reported routinely making more than one offer to homeless people. Institute of Housing (1990: table 5.7) research discovered that a significant number of councils had a policy of offering 'difficult-to-let' properties to those being housed under the homelessness legislation. Such practices would tend to mean that the homeless received the lowest quality housing on the least popular estates. At the same time, allocation policies concerning household type and size of accommodation impacted adversely upon single parents. In later research the Institute of Housing (1993) found that 20 per cent of lone parents were given the tenancy of a flat or maisonette rather than a house, compared with less than 10 per cent of two-parent families; over one-third of local authorities would not offer two- or three-bedroomed properties to lone parents. The interaction of these two forms of discrimination was effective to ensure that homeless single parents tended to receive, and become concentrated in, the least desirable council housing. The more recent picture is very similar. The DETR survey of allocations recorded far lower percentages of local authorities routinely offering homeless applicants on the Housing Register the chance to specify area preferences and preferred property types than was the case with non-homeless applicants (Pawson *et al.* 2001: figure 2.3 and table 2.14). Where preferences were elicited, the eventual offers made were also much less likely to accord with stated choices in the case of homeless applicants (Pawson *et al.* 2001: tables 2.13 and 2.15). 'One-offer-only' policies for homeless applicants on the Housing Register were now being operated by three-quarters of local councils, compared with 21 per cent restricting non-homeless applicants to a single offer of accommodation (Pawson *et al.* 2001: table 2.17).[29]

Moreover it was by no means always the case, even before the 1996 changes to the legislation, that homeless applicants were placed straight into a permanent home by their local authority. Shelter's (1994) survey found local councils placing the statutory homeless in a variety of temporary accommodation, including not only refuges, hostels and short-term private sector housing, but also highly unsuitable hotel accommodation; no fewer than 78 per cent of respondent authorities admitted to using bed and breakfast rooms for homeless people. The legislation provides explicitly for interim accommodation to be provided for a homeless person pending a decision on her case[30], but Shelter's report shows that in a substantial number of areas homeless families were spending periods in excess of six months in bed and breakfast hotels, clearly longer than the time required for inquiries into their circumstances to be completed. In most cases the length of time before the offer of a permanent home was a simple factor of the lack of a sufficient stream of available tenancies, but there is evidence that some authorities may have expected homeless households to spend time in temporary accommodation before being rehoused as a punitive or deterrent measure.[31]

The inappropriateness of bed and breakfast accommodation, in particular, for homeless families has long been well documented (Conway and Kemp 1985, Conway 1988, HVA&GMSC 1988, Power, White and Youdall 1996, Vostanis and Cumella 1999). Hotel rooms are usually cramped, lack adequate facilities for the hygienic preparation and consumption of food, may constitute a fire hazard when filled with household possessions, and make study difficult and individual privacy impossible; they are generally highly detrimental to health, safety and education, and destructive of family life.[32] Since 2002, Government guidelines made it clear that local authorities were to use bed and breakfast accommodation for homeless families only as a last resort and for the minimum period possible.[33] At that time bed and breakfasts were commonly used to accommodate the homeless; at the end of December 2002, for example, over 12,600 homeless households in England were living in hotel rooms, having been placed there by their local housing authority,[34] many of them having been there for some considerable period of time.[35] Growing concern about the situation led to the creation in October 2001 of a Bed and Breakfast Unit with the task of reducing the use of hotel accommodation for the homeless, subsequently subsumed within the new Homelessness Directorate. In March 2002 the then Secretary of State Stephen Byers gave an undertaking that by March 2004 no homeless family with children would have to remain in bed and breakfast for more than six weeks; a consultation paper was issued by the Homelessness Directorate in May 2003[36] seeking views as to how this target might be achieved and proposing delegated legislation to bring local authorities' statutory duties into line with the new policy. The result was the Homelessness (Suitability of Accommodation) (England) Order 2003 SI 3326/2003 under which, with effect from 1 April 2004 and subject to certain limited exceptions, bed and breakfast accommodation is only to be regarded as suitable for homeless households including dependent children or a pregnant woman in emergencies, and only for a maximum of six weeks. Although the numbers of families placed in bed and breakfast has been substantially reduced in consequence, reliance upon it nevertheless remains commonplace, at least in the short term. A National Audit Office (2005) report found that there were still 1,370 homeless families with children living in bed and breakfast hotels in September 2004, of which 167 had been there for longer than the six-week maximum. When faced with the prospect of raising their children in a hotel room – and in the past, at least, this may have been for many months – it seems unlikely that large numbers of single mothers ever realistically viewed the homelessness legislation as an easy route into a council flat.

One commonly encountered strand of the folklore surrounding homeless teenage mothers is the belief that girls deliberately become pregnant as a means to obtaining council accommodation. In his speech to the Conservative Party Conference in 1992, Peter Lilley, then Secretary of State for Social Security, condemned 'young mothers who get pregnant just to jump the housing list'.[37] This archetype of the Bad Mother, the teenager who would embark upon parenthood without proper consideration of the responsibilities involved and for the entirely selfish motive of getting away from the parental home and into independent housing, gained a firm hold upon the popular imagination. Anecdotal evidence of young women who were alleged to have acted in this way could always be found, even by those who were less judgmental and more sympathetic to the circumstances of those in question. In a House of Lords debate on homelessness in the 1980s, for example, Liberal peer Lord Kilmarnock reported being told by social workers that '9 out of 10 of the girls leaving council care aged 18 . . . get pregnant within a year, largely because that is the only means of getting somewhere to live. Pregnancy becomes a passport to accommodation.'[38]

It is of course likely that there are some teenage girls for whom the opportunities are so restricted, and the chances of securing employment yielding an income sufficient to secure independent accommodation so negligible, that such housing and social security entitlements as ensue from having a child may indeed be one motivation behind the decision to have a baby. It is sobering to reflect that for many of these young women the reality may prove to be very different from the dream. To claim that a child was conceived as a route into housing may appear an attractive rationalisation, perhaps in some cases even to the mother herself. However, to isolate one single consideration as explaining such a complex and important decision must be an oversimplification of the many emotional, psychological, social and economic factors which play a part in the making of our life choices. Moreover, formal research has always failed to uncover significant evidence of pregnancies engineered in order to jump the housing queue. The Institute of Housing's (1993) investigation into the alleged phenomenon concluded that 'it was rare for unmarried teenage girls to present themselves for rehousing, and the correlation between having a child and seeking a local authority home was at best tenuous.' Sociological studies conducted in the late 1990s produced similar results. Rowlingson and McKay (1998) found that only after becoming pregnant did single women usually begin to consider the question of their rights to housing and other state benefits, while Allen and Bourke-Dowling (1998: 199) uncovered a picture very far removed from the cynical queue-jumping so frequently alleged; the circumstances of the teenage mothers whom they interviewed were characterised by 'lack of knowledge, long waits on local authority housing lists and an inability to understand the system, let alone manipulate it.'

The terms of the homeless persons legislation are such that if an applicant 'deliberately does or fails to do anything in consequence of which [she] ceases to occupy accommodation' which would otherwise be available to her and reasonable for her to continue to occupy, she is to be treated as becoming homeless 'intentionally'[39] so that she is entitled merely to advice and assistance, and to accommodation for a short period only.[40] This might appear to cover young women who, as a result of purposely getting pregnant, can no longer go on living in their current accommodation, whether it is the parental home or their own shared or independent housing. It is notable, however, that this is not the view of the statute which has been taken in the case law. In *R v Eastleigh Borough Council ex p Beattie (No. 1)* (1983) 10 HLR 134 (at 141) Woolf J ruled out an argument that a couple had rendered themselves intentionally homeless by increasing the size of their family so that their house became unsuitable for their needs, commenting 'it seems to me that such a conclusion would be wholly inconsistent with the whole intent and purpose of this particular section.' The judiciary, at least, seems not to have been seduced into the belief that children are conceived deliberately in order to bring about homelessness and consequent rehousing.

Responses received by the Government to the 1994 Green Paper from organisations working in the housing field, many of which were published by Shelter (1994b) were forthright in pointing out the false premises upon which it was based. The Chartered Institute of Housing regretted the use in the paper of 'language which appears judgmental and moralistic', and refuted the Government's claims of widespread abuse of the legislation, concluding that 'all recent research and relevant statistics . . . comprehensively contradict such assertions.' The submission from the Council of Mortgage Lenders (not a body generally known for its outspoken radicalism) included the following statement: 'Although it is not stated explicitly, the justification for restricting the access of certain priority groups appears to be the belief that the current system is being abused and that it rewards single parents and young women who become pregnant. However, there is no evidence that abuse of the system is a significant problem or that the priority system encourages young women to become pregnant.'

## The consequence of scapegoating: the Housing Act 1996

Despite the lack of substance behind the myth of the queue-jumping teenage mother, this image was nevertheless a powerful force behind the enactment of the Housing Act 1996, the effect of which was a major curtailment of the rights of all homeless people. The pages of *Hansard* show that the debates on the Housing Bill were peppered with references to the prevalent stereotypes of good and bad mothers. Conservative backbencher Dame Elaine Kellett-Bowman, for example, commented on the 'sad . . . cases of young married couples, when one of them is obliged to live with parents and the other with in-laws. They postpone having a family because, being responsible, they do not want to start one before getting their own home – yet see other people, probably in far better circumstances, leaping to the head of the queue.'[41] Mrs Jacqui Lait (another backbench MP) stated: 'I have been struck by the number of honest, decent, respectable people who have . . . endured difficult housing conditions for a long time and then been pipped at the post when it was their turn at the top of the housing list. A recent *Panorama* programme highlighted a 17-year-old girl who was four months pregnant. . . . and who had been given her own flat. This is a result of current policy.'[42] Nor were such stereotypes confined to those on the backbenches. Secretary of State for the Environment John Gummer, who steered the Bill through Parliament, also referred to the need to protect the position of 'married couples who have waited to have children because the conditions in which they lived were unsuitable for having them.'[43]

The debates indicate that the Housing Bill was founded upon a fundamental misconception. As we have seen, it has never been the case that acceptance as homeless and in priority need meant that an applicant received immediate and automatic preference for the offer of council housing. Despite this, members of the Government constantly referred to the existing system as one of 'automaticity', where 'people get to the top of the list by category'.[44] The stated aim of the Bill (and one with which it would be difficult to disagree) was to ensure that council accommodation should be allocated according to individual housing need. However, the language used makes it clear that issues of need were inextricably mixed in the minds of ministers with questions of personal desert, according to received moral values. The Secretary of State wanted to create a system which would work in favour of 'those who most *deserve and need* accommodation'.

In its original form, the Housing (Homeless Persons) Act 1977, subsequently codified as Part III of the Housing Act 1985, placed a duty upon local housing authorities to secure that accommodation became available for the occupation of those persons whom they found to be unintentionally homeless and in priority need.[45]

The proviso that the accommodation arranged should be 'suitable' to the needs of the homeless household was added by the Housing and Planning Act 1986, directly overturning the effect of the House of Lords' decision in the infamous case of *Puhlhofer v Hillingdon London Borough Council* [1986] AC 484. Although this was not explicit in the words of the Act, it was always assumed that discharge of the duty required *permanent* accommodation to be made available to the applicant. It was established that this could be accomplished in two stages, with temporary accommodation being provided in the first instance,[46] but this was only as an interim measure pending the securing of a long-term tenancy. That the accommodation was to be permanent seemed clear from the structure of the legislation itself; the full duty towards the priority homeless contrasted with that owed to those judged to be homeless intentionally, for whom local authorities were merely obliged to secure that accommodation became available 'for such period as they consider will give [them] a reasonable opportunity of securing accommodation' for themselves.[47] Such was certainly the interpretation put upon the duty at the time by government officials. The 1991 edition of the *Code of Guidance* issued under the homelessness legislation regarded it as 'clear that the accommodation secured must be long-term settled accommodation'.[48]

The White Paper (DoE 1995), however, proposed a change to the law, limiting the duty of local authorities to that of securing housing for an initial period of 12 months only, even for those applicants who were unintentionally homeless and in one of the priority need categories. The stated aim was to reduce the role of the homeless persons legislation to that of 'an immediate safety net, . . . separate from a fair system of allocating long term accommodation' (DoE 1995: 36).

The White Paper was issued in June 1995, and within a very few weeks of its publication, on 6 July 1995, the House of Lords handed down a controversial decision which in one respect anticipated the Government's proposals. In the case of *R v Brent London Borough Council ex p Awua* [1996] 1 AC 55 Lord Hoffmann ruled that the local authority duty to secure accommodation to those found to be unintentionally homeless and in priority need did not necessarily mean the supply of a permanent or settled home. By contrast with the lesser duty towards intentionally homeless applicants, the full duty was 'indefinite', but it did not entail 'a duty to provide permanent accommodation' (at 71). What his Lordship seems to have meant by this somewhat arcane distinction was that the local authority could discharge its duty by placing a homeless household in temporary accommodation, which could later be terminated provided that the household would not as a result once again be homeless and in priority need. The example he gave was of an applicant in priority need due to pregnancy; the local authority could meet its obligations to her by placing her in temporary accommodation, and if after giving birth she were to place her child for adoption, that accommodation could then be withdrawn, since the applicant would no longer qualify as being in a priority category. It is interesting that Lord Hoffmann should have chosen as his illustration of the principle he was laying down the case of a pregnant woman, an example which was so central to popular fears about unwarranted priority for housing. At least one commentator has speculated as to whether underlying his Lordship's thinking was the spectre of the queue-jumping teenager, and the suggestion 'that women would become deliberately pregnant just to get a home' (Arden 1995: 23).

In justification of the decision which he reached, Lord Hoffmann cited with approval a *dictum* of Lord Brightman in *Puhlhofer v Hillingdon London Borough Council* [1986] AC 484 (at 517) in which, in a remarkable pre-echo of the 1995 White Paper, he described the homelessness legislation as 'intended to provide for the homeless a lifeline of last resort, not to enable them to make inroads into the local authority's waiting list of applicants for housing'.

The case of *R v Brent London Borough Council ex p Awua* [1996] 1 AC 55 certainly had the effect of blunting opposition to the proposed changes in the legislation. Speaking in Committee during debates on the 1996 Housing Bill, Housing Minister David Curry said that as a result of the Lords' decision 'the legal landscape . . . has . . . changed', and that 'a housing authority's duty could be discharged in as little as 28 days.'[49] Lord Mackay in the House of Lords was even able to argue that the proposed new statutory provisions (which at the time they were drafted were clearly envisaged as cutting back substantially upon the rights of homeless persons) afforded 'a more certain guarantee of assistance than the present legislation provides following the recent *Awua* judgment'.[50]

Nevertheless, Opposition pressure and concerted lobbying led to the securing of an amendment to the original Bill, to extend the minimum period of accommodation to be afforded to priority homeless households from 12 months to two years. Under s 193(2) of the Housing Act 1996, the local authority remains under a duty to 'secure that accommodation is available' for any applicant whom they are satisfied is unintentionally homeless and in priority need. This accommodation, under s 206(1) of the Act is still required to be 'suitable' to the needs of the applicant and, as a consequence of s 176, to any other person who resides or might reasonably be expected to reside with her. However, s 197 of the Housing Act 1996 as originally enacted provided that no such duty arose if the authority were satisfied that other suitable accommodation was available for the applicant in their district. And, most importantly, the duty was limited by s 193(3) to securing housing for a period of two years. Thereafter, under s 194, any continuation of the accommodation was discretionary, was permissible only if the applicant was still in priority need and lacking other suitable accommodation, and had to be for limited periods of up to two years at a time. If the local authority failed to continue the accommodation under these discretionary provisions, the applicant was obliged (if still homeless and in priority need) to make a fresh application under s 193(9).

Section 207 of the 1996 legislation explicitly limited local authorities in the use of their own housing stock in discharging their duties towards the homeless. The accommodation which was made available, if directly supplied by the local authority, could either be hostel accommodation or be leased for the purpose from a private landlord, but could not consist of a secure tenancy of council housing; authorities were not permitted to use their own properties to house the homeless for more than two years (continuously or in aggregate) in any period of three years.[51] The intention of the legislation was that the two years of temporary accommodation afforded to priority homeless households under s 193 should in most cases provide sufficient time for them either to find their own accommodation or to qualify for the offer of a permanent council tenancy under the general allocation scheme in Part VI of the Act.[52]

However, it was clear that not all priority homeless households would qualify for permanent housing allocation before the end of the two-year period of temporary accommodation. The allocations survey by Pawson *et al.* (2001: table 5.3) indeed revealed large numbers of homeless families still in temporary accommodation at the end of two years, especially in London and the south-east of England. In such cases, unless the local authority was prepared to extend their accommodation on a voluntary basis, the applicants had to reapply for further assistance. This may frequently have resulted in their facing the upheaval of being moved to new temporary accommodation, especially in view of the s 207 bar on the use of council stock to house the homeless for periods exceeding two years. Whilst acknowledging that many homeless persons were being allocated long-term accommodation within the statutory two-year period, Secretary of State Stephen Byers, when introducing the Homelessness Bill in 2001, stated that the 1996 framework was nevertheless 'unhelpful and bureaucratic' for local councils, imposing an additional administrative burden and limiting their flexibility in the provision of accommodation, as well as giving homeless households 'cause for great uncertainty about their future and about whether they will continue to have a home.'[53]

Even when homeless persons were allocated long-term accommodation within the two-year period, the 1996 statutory scheme meant that they normally had to move twice, first into temporary accommodation and then again into permanent housing.[54] Ample evidence is available of the highly disruptive effect upon homeless families of having to move through a succession of temporary homes (LRC 1996).[55] Moving house is a stressful event for anyone to cope with, and may be particularly difficult for vulnerable homeless persons, while the delay before a permanent housing solution is reached may prevent applicants from re-establishing themselves in work and their children in schools, and hamper the process of forging vital links with neighbours and the wider community. The rebuilding of lives shattered by the experience of homelessness will be put on hold. Although it is true that two-stage rehousing of homeless households was not uncommon under the pre-1996 law, this was in most cases a result of necessity, and was certainly not a matter of express legislative policy. The periods spent in temporary accommodation under the old statutory regime were in most cases far shorter than two years, and could moreover be endured by the applicant safe in the knowledge (at least until the decision of the House of Lords in *R v Brent London Borough Council ex p Awua* [1996] 1 AC 55) that there was a duty upon the local authority to arrange suitable permanent accommodation as soon as practicable. Under the Housing Act as originally enacted in 1996 there was no such guarantee; homeless persons had to go through the doubly unsettling experience of living in temporary accommodation while facing uncertainty as to the outcome of their application for long-term housing under the council's allocation scheme.

The pregnant teenager whose demonisation was such a strong factor behind the enactment of the 1996 Act now, under that legislation, faced the prospect of losing her priority for permanent housing, not only should she choose to give up the child for adoption (as pointed out by Lord Hoffmann in *R v Brent London Borough Council ex parte Awua*), but also should she miscarry or decide to abort the pregnancy, or should her baby die or be stillborn. It was highly regrettable not only that vulnerable teenage girls should have been placed in such uncertain circumstances at a time when they were most in need of security, but also that their prospects of obtaining settled accommodation should have depended upon the outcome of their pregnancy, particularly so where they may have been considering the complex and difficult question of abortion. It would be appalling if any young woman felt herself under pressure to keep a baby with which she could not cope, out of fear of her accommodation being withdrawn by the local authority. Moreover, commentators have argued that it is unfair to penalise all pregnant homeless women, by forcing them through a period in temporary accommodation, merely because of what might happen in a small minority of cases (Hunter and Miles 1997: 287). One of the motivations behind the passing of the original Housing (Homeless Persons) Act in 1977 was to bring an end to the practice of local authorities placing pregnant women in hostel accommodation until the end result of their pregnancy was known, or refusing to consider them for permanent housing until the baby was born or the pregnancy well advanced.[56] It was to this situation that the 1996 legislative scheme, in its original form, marked a return.

Furthermore, we have seen that young pregnant women form only a very small percentage of all households accepted as homeless and in priority need. The enactment of the Housing Act 1996 may have resulted in a curtailment of the rights of those Bad Mothers who were the popular scapegoats in arguments for the need for changes in the law. It also created serious hardship for the other families and vulnerable single people to whom the local authority owed a duty under s 193 of the Act, who all now had to face a lengthy spell in unsettled accommodation, with uncertainty as to their prospects of being allocated a permanent home.

## The present landscape: the Homelessness Act 2002

When the Labour Government came to power in 1997, a first simple step to reduce the impact of the 1996 legislative changes was taken expeditiously in the November following the General Election. Part VI of the Housing Act 1996 was amended so as to include within the categories of persons to whom local authorities have to give 'reasonable preference' in their allocation schemes (amongst others) 'people who are homeless (within the meaning of Part VII)'[57] and those to whom duties are owed or who are accommodated under the homelessness provisions.[58] It was hoped that this would have the effect of ensuring that most homeless households would qualify for permanent rehousing before the end of the statutory two-year period of temporary accommodation.

It was not until April 2000, however, that Labour's promised major review of housing policy was launched, with the issue of the Housing Green Paper, *Quality and Choice: A Decent Home for All* (DETR 2000). Unlike the discussion documents issued by the Conservatives in 1994 and 1995, Labour's Green Paper was free from any judgmental language about queue-jumping single mothers or the need to reward married couples who wait patiently for a council flat before starting a family. Gone was the moral distinction which was drawn between the Good Mothers on the waiting list and the feckless Bad Mothers presenting themselves for housing via the homeless persons route; indeed, the Green Paper (2000: para 9.46) specifically proposed that people accepted as homeless and placed in temporary accommodation 'should have the same priority for settled social housing as those in urgent . . . need on the housing register'. The Paper's rhetoric was of choice (DETR 2000: paras 9.5–9.7) and the need to give people, including the homeless, so far as practicable,[59] a say in selecting the accommodation which they are to occupy, and it placed emphasis on initiatives aimed at preventing homelessness (DETR 2000: para 9.60–9.65). It proposed removal of the 'two years in three' restriction in s 207 of the 1996 Act upon the use of the local authority's own housing stock to discharge its duty towards the homeless and, most crucially, the abolition of the two-year limit upon the duty to secure accommodation for priority homeless households contained in s 193(3) of the 1996 Act (DETR 2000: para 9.53).

December 2000 saw the publication of a White Paper (ODPM 2000), *The Way Forward for Housing*, together with a parallel draft Bill. The Homes Bill was introduced to the House of Commons on 12 December 2000, but fell due to lack of parliamentary time in the run-up to the 2001 General Election. The planned legislation re-emerged after the Election in the form of the Homelessness Bill and this time, decoupled from controversial proposals respecting vendors' packs for home-owners, the Bill made rapid progress through both Houses, receiving the Royal Assent on 26 February 2002.

The 2001 Homelessness Bill attracted a broad measure of support from both sides of the House, the Conservative front bench having executed a *volte-face* since 1996 and now backing the Government in removing the two-year time limit in s 193(3). Voices of concern were nevertheless raised by some Opposition backbenchers: it is clear that fears about queue-jumping are still far from dead. Julian Brazier MP expressed his support for retention of the two-year rule with the claim that 'had those provisions not been made, almost all the available social housing would have continued to go to those on the homelessness list, while those who had waited years had no chance at all in many boroughs'.[60]

New villains had largely superseded teenage single mothers as the leading stereotypes lending shape to these fears. Several Members professed anxiety that local people were being displaced in the housing queue by those from outside the area, and in particular by immigrants and asylum-seekers,[61] while released prisoners and especially sex offenders were another target of back-bench disapproval.[62] However, the spectre of the feckless young mother was still in evidence and Conservative MP Andrew Turner complained of how 'a young female could well come to the constituency, work as a fruit picker for six months, become pregnant during that time and later present herself as vulnerable because she was pregnant . . . I do not deny the vulnerability, but I deny the responsibility.'[63] This enduring image of the Bad Mother was still being held up in contrast to 'perfectly ordinary decent constituents'[64] waiting their turn on the housing register, typically characterised as a 'young family',[65] implicitly comprising two (married) parents.

Despite such lingering attitudes from a handful of MPs, the Act was passed, and its main provisions regarding homelessness came into force on 31 July 2002. The Homelessness Act 2002 did not create a wholly new statutory regime, but achieved change by amending the terms of the Housing Act 1996. Both s 197 of the 1996 Act[66] and s 207[67] were repealed. A discretionary power to accommodate the non-priority homeless was added to the legislation, in the form of a new s 192(3). And, perhaps most crucially, the central s 193 duty to secure accommodation for those who are homeless and in priority need is no longer time-limited.[68]

However, for all that these changes are very welcome, the Homelessness Act 2002 left unchallenged the central principle of the 1996 Housing Act: namely that homeless households should be entitled to accommodation under Part VII only until they are able to secure access to a long-term council tenancy through the general allocation scheme in Part VI. Hence, although no longer expressly time-limited, Part VII accommodation for the homeless is still constructed as being essentially a temporary staging post on the way to a permanent home, which can only be obtained via the more 'normal' Part VI route. That this remained the intention was evident from statements of Ministers when presenting the legislation to Parliament. Secretary of State Stephen Byers told the Commons that the Bill would ensure 'that local authorities offer everyone in priority need who is unintentionally homeless somewhere suitable to live *until they obtain a settled home*'.[69] The amended law retains the key features of the statutory framework enacted in 1996, with its two-tier access to public housing. Accommodation made available for the homeless is interim only and permanent lettings of council or housing association properties can occur only through the general allocation process.[70] Far from being able to 'jump the queue', homeless households therefore continue to come into public housing via a less privileged and more uncertain route than their non-homeless counterparts.

The Part VII route continues to be characterised by less choice of accommodation, in spite of Government rhetoric.[71] Current government policy aims to ensure that 100 per cent of local authorities operate a choice-based lettings scheme by the end of 2010 (ODPM 2005), but such choice does not apply to the homeless under Part VII. Although it is claimed that 'considerable efforts have been made to guard against disadvantaging homeless households'(ODPM 2005: 7), it is clear that offering choice tends to benefit those whose housing need is less acute, making the exercise of choice a realistic possibility. As Cowan and Marsh (2004: 486) have pointed out, 'the longer households [are] willing to wait, the choosier they could be'.

Retention of the demarcation between Parts VI and VII also means that for the vast majority of homeless people, their route to settled housing will be a two-stage process, involving the upheaval of a move from interim accommodation to a permanent home once they become entitled, with all the attendant disruption to their lives.[72] Their spell in temporary accommodation may no longer be subject to the specific uncertainty to which the two-year time limit gave rise, but they still face the insecurity of knowing that they will have to move again before they have a home they can call their own. Latest statistics still reveal, at the end of 2005, 98,730 homeless households lodged in temporary accommodation and waiting for a long-term home.[73] It is of course possible for a local authority as a matter of practice to offer under Part VI of the Housing Act a secure tenancy of the same house or flat which a homeless person has been occupying pursuant to the s 193 duty, thus eliminating the need for an unsettling move, but as commentators have pointed out, the lack of choice available at the interim stage (with its tendency to mean that homeless applicants under Part VII receive less desirable properties) will then be perpetuated (Luba and Davies 2002: 12).

It is to be noted that the events which will terminate the right to accommodation under s 193 do *not* include the applicant ceasing to be in priority need. This preserves the position reached following the decision of Moses J in *R v Brent London Borough Council ex p Sadiq* (2001) 33 HLR 525, whereby the authority's duty towards a homeless parent accommodated under s 193 does not cease if she[74] loses custody of her child and thus her priority need status; the same would apply to a pregnant applicant who has an abortion or miscarriage or who gives up her child for adoption. Under the 1996 legislation as originally enacted, such a parent would of course face losing her accommodation at the end of the two-year period provided for in s 193(3). Although this specific pitfall has been removed with the abolition of the two-year time limit, it remains the case, as was noted in the previous section, that the loss of her child or children might well reduce the applicant's chances of securing a permanent allocation under Part VI of the Act, leaving her to spend an indefinite period in insecure and frequently poor quality interim accommodation.

Four years on from its coming into effect, it may be argued that the Homelessness Act 2002 has not brought about the 'dramatic improvement'[75] in the rights of homeless people which its proponents claimed for it. Damningly, the Public Services Ombudsman for Wales (2006: 4) reported that a significant number of the 22 Welsh local authorities had made no apparent change in their allocations policy towards the homeless as a result of the 2002 Act. The same report instanced the case of a homeless household provided with temporary accommodation in a motorway service station under Part VII of the Housing Act 1996 and not informed of the right to apply for permanent housing under Part VI, and of a homeless single mother with four children placed in a damp one-roomed caravan for over two years with no offer of permanent accommodation (PSOW 2006: 4 and 7). In the final analysis, the much criticised specific two-year time limit repealed in 2002 may not in fact have been the most damaging of the Conservative reforms. Research by Pawson *et al.* (2001: para 5.21) suggests that the most common outcome for homeless households reaching the end of the two-year period without having received an offer of permanent rehousing, was the offer of a further two years of temporary accommodation under the discretionary provisions of s 194. Perhaps far more pernicious and lasting in its effects was the enshrinement in statutory form of a two-tier system involving vulnerable homeless families in the disruption of two moves, first into the temporary staging post of Part VII accommodation and then on to a permanent allocation under Part VI.

The myth of that popular scapegoat, the teenage mother who leapfrogs the housing queue, which was so all-pervasive during the mid-1990s and which fuelled pressure for the enactment of the Housing Act 1996, has wrought its damage, making fundamental changes in the legal landscape and leaving all priority homeless households in a much more vulnerable and uncertain position than was the case before 1996. And despite some ameliorative changes brought about by the Homelessness Act 2002, the central tenets of the 1996 legislation still stand unaffected, so that the damage seems set to become permanent.

## Notes

1 Extract from a speech by Sir George Young MP, Minister for Housing and Planning, to the Conservative Party Conference, 7 October 1993.

2 Mr W Rees-Davies, MP for Thanet West, *Hansard House of Commons Debates*, 18 February 1977, column 921.
3 Intentional homelessness is now dealt with in ss 190–191 of the Housing Act 1996.
4 See also Mann and Roseneil (1994).
5 Cited in Blackie, A, 'Family Fall-Out', *Times Higher Education Supplement*, 4 March 1994, page 18.
6 Mann and Roseneil (1996) note in particular the views of Melanie Phillips expressed in the *Guardian* (23 and 26 February 1993), and editorials in the *Sunday Times* (28 February 1993) and the *Daily Telegraph* (15 July 1993).
7 *Inside Housing*, 1 October 1993.
8 The male pronoun is used throughout the Act, even when, for example, referring to those experiencing domestic violence. In this chapter I have chosen instead to use the female pronoun to refer to homeless applicants, both for economy of expression and to reflect the focus of my argument.
9 Section 176 of the Housing Act 1996.
10 Section 175(3) of the Housing Act 1996.
11 The Homeless Persons (Priority Need for Accommodation) (England) Order 2002, SI 2051/2002, issued under s 189(2) of the Housing Act 1996, came into force on 31 July 2002. Parallel but slightly different rules applying to Wales are to be found in the Homeless Persons (Priority Need) (Wales) Order 2001, SI 607/2001 (came into force 1 March 2001).
12 Section 189(1)(c) of the Housing Act 1996.
13 Homeless Persons (Priority Need for Accommodation) (England) Order 2002, para 5.
14 Above, para 6.
15 Section 189(1)(d) of the Housing Act 1996.
16 Homeless Persons (Priority Need for Accommodation) (England) Order 2002, para 3.
17 Above, para 4.
18 Section 189(1)(a) of the Housing Act 1996.
19 Section 189(1)(b) of the Housing Act 1996.
20 2005 figures: Live Tables on Homelessness, Department for Communities and Local Government, June 2006 (www.odpm.gov.uk/index.asp?id=1156305), Table 632.
21 The application may be made by the mother or the father. Even in the case of pregnancy, the application may be made by the male partner, who qualifies as in priority need by being someone with whom a pregnant woman 'resides or might reasonably be expected to reside' (s 189(1)(a) of the Housing Act 1996).
22 Unpublished Housing Corporation figures, cited in *Inside Housing*, 15 October 1993.
23 See n 20 above, Table 633.
24 Census 2001, National Report for England and Wales, Part 2, Office for National Statistics, May 2003, Table S007 (www.statistics.gov.uk/StatBase/ssdataset.asp?vlnk=7504&Pos=&ColRank=2&Rank=224).
25 Housing Act 1985, s 65(2).
26 Housing Act 1985, s 69(1)(b).
27 Unpublished figures, cited in *Inside Housing*, 15 October 1993. An even lower proportion of housing association lettings were taken up by statutory homeless persons: 17 per cent in 1992 (*Housing Associations in 1992: Supplementary Tables on Individual Associations*, Housing Corporation, 1993).
28 Over a quarter of authorities reported using a quota system in 1990 (*Housing Allocations: Report of a Survey of Local Authorities in England and Wales*, Institute of Housing, September 1990).

29 It is notable that both percentages are considerably higher than Shelter's 1994 figures, but the homeless are still being treated much less favourably than other applicants.
30 See now s 188 of the Housing Act 1996.
31 See, for example, *Housing the Homeless: the Local Authority Role*, Audit Commission, 1989, at p 33. It should be noted that although the practice of local authorities meeting their obligations to the homeless in two stages was accepted by the courts in circumstances where suitable permanent accommodation was not immediately available (see *R v East Hertfordshire District Council ex p Hunt* (1985) 18 HLR 51), any suggestion of doing so as a matter of general policy was condemned in the *Code of Guidance* on the homelessness legislation, the 1991 edition of which urged that 'temporary accommodation should only be used for the minimum time necessary . . . It should not be used as a deterrent and homeless people should not automatically be placed in temporary accommodation before being found permanent accommodation.' (*Homelessness: Code of Guidance for Local Authorities* 3rd edn, HMSO, 1991, para 13.2). This edition of the Code was current at the time leading up to the introduction of the Housing Act 1996.
32 Hotel accommodation is also very expensive. Keeping homeless families in bed and breakfast accommodation in England cost the public purse a total of over £70.8 million in 1999/2000, for example (*Hansard House of Commons Debates*, Written Answers, 21 March 2002, column 493).
33 *Homelessness Code of Guidance for Local Authorities (England)*, July 2002, para 12.6.
34 Statutory Homelessness: England, Fourth Quarter 2002 (see n 20 above). This number represents a 5 per cent increase upon the previous year, and means that 15 per cent of all homeless households accommodated by local authorities were in bed and breakfast.
35 A consultation paper issued by the Homelessness Directorate in 2003 refers to families in some areas remaining in bed and breakfast accommodation for over a year and, in a few cases, for more than two years (Office of Deputy Prime Minister, *Improving Standards of Accommodation for Homeless Households Placed* in *Temporary Accommodation: A Consultation Paper*, May 2003, p 10).
36 See n 35 above.
37 Speech by Rt Hon Peter Lilley MP to the Conservative Party Conference, 7 October 1992.
38 *Hansard House of Lords Debates*, 8 February 1984, column 1156.
39 Housing Act 1996, s 191(1).
40 Housing Act 1996, s 190(2).
41 *Hansard House of Commons Debates*, 29 January 1996, column 696.
42 Above, column 720.
43 Above, column 651.
44 Mr John Gummer, above n 41, column 661.
45 Housing Act 1985, s 65(2): see n 25 above.
46 *R v East Hertfordshire District Council ex p Hunt* (see n 31 above); *Homelessness: Code of Guidance for Local Authorities*, 3rd edn (see n 31 above) para 13.1(d).
47 Housing Act 1985, s 65(3)(a).
48 *Homelessness: Code of Guidance for Local Authorities*, 3rd edn (see above n 31), para 11.2.
49 *Hansard House of Commons Debates*, Session 1995/96, Standing Committee G, 19 March 1996, column 691.
50 *Hansard House of Lords Debates*, 16 May 1996, column 565.
51 The purpose of this limitation was to ensure that the homelessness provisions of

Part VII of the 1996 Housing Act provided only a temporary safety net, and not an alternative route into the allocation of permanent public sector accommodation. Instead, long-term allocations were dealt with by Part VI of the Act, which required local authorities, under s 162, to establish a unified housing register, and an allocation scheme for determining priority between those registered upon it (s 167(1)), giving reasonable preference to persons in various specified categories of need (s 167(2). The listed categories did not, in the original 1996 Act, specifically include homeless people.

52 The *Code of Guidance* on the Housing Act 1996 Parts VI and VII (Department of Environment/Department of Health, October 1996, revised 20 December 1996 and 7 March 1997), para 20.20 noted that 'in many cases applicants to whom a duty is owed will fall . . . within the reasonable preference categories for housing allocation', adding optimistically in the following paragraph (20.21) that 'the circumstances may be such that the applicant could be allocated long-term accommodation through the local housing authority's allocation scheme within substantially less than two years'.

53 Second Reading of the Homelessness Bill, *Hansard House of Commons Debates*, 2 July 2001, column 37.

54 Where a sufficient supply of council housing permitted, the needs of some homeless households will have given them sufficient priority under Part VI to qualify them for immediate allocation of a permanent home. However, the findings of Pawson *et al.* (2001: Table 5.2) suggest that this happened only in a minority of cases.

55 See, for example, London Research Centre (1996)

56 The 1991 edition of the Code of Guidance (see above, n 31) stated that all pregnant women should be treated as in priority need 'regardless of the length of time they have been pregnant' (para 6.2). The same words were repeated in the 1996 edition of the Code of Guidance (see above, n 52) following enactment of the 1996 Housing Act (para 14.4). However, they now offered little realistic protection: the two-year period of temporary accommodation enabled the local authority to await the outcome of the pregnancy before offering a permanent tenancy, and thus removed the previous incentive to defer acceptance until it appeared that the pregnancy would come to term.

57 Housing Act 1996, s 167(2)(a).

58 Section 167(2)(b). Both paragraphs were added to the section by the Allocation of Housing (Reasonable and Additional Preference) Regulations 1997, SI 1902/1997.

59 However, the Green Paper explicitly recognised that pressures upon the supply of emergency housing would 'impose constraints on the extent to which homeless people can be allowed free choice' (DETR 2000: para 9.43).

60 *Hansard House of Commons Debates*, 2 July 2001, column 100. That this claim is unsupported by the evidence is demonstrated above, see in particular n 27.

61 See, for example, Jonathan Djanogly MP, *Hansard House of Commons Debates*, 2 July 2001, column 78; Geoffrey Clifton-Brown MP, *Hansard House of Commons Debates*, 25 February 2002, column 458.

62 See, for example, Geoffrey Clifton-Brown MP, *Hansard House of Commons Debates*, 22 October 2001, column 42; Andrew Turner MP, *Hansard House of Commons Debates*, 22 October 2001, column 51.

63 *Hansard House of Commons Debates*, 22 October 2001, column 58.

64 Geoffrey Clifton Brown MP, *Hansard House of Commons Debates*, 22 October 2001, column 42

65 Mark Simmonds MP, *Hansard House of Commons Debates*, 22 October 2001, column 61.

66 Section 197 of the Housing Act 1996 imposed no duty upon the local authority for the homeless if satisfied of the availability locally of other suitable accommodation.
67 Under s 207 of the Housing Act 1996 there was a limit upon the use of council stock to accommodate the homeless for more than two years out of three.
68 The specific two-year rule in s 193(3) of the Housing Act 1996 was deleted from the statute; instead, the duty to secure that accommodation is available for the applicant's occupation will come to an end only upon the occurrence of certain specified events, including in particular the applicant receiving an offer of permanent accommodation under Part VI of the Act (s 193(6)(c)).
69 *Hansard House of Commons Debates*, 2 July 2001, column 39 (emphasis added). In the upper House Lord Falconer made it clear that accommodation under Part VII of the Housing Act 1996 was intended to remain as a temporary safety-net, the Homelessness Bill simply aiming to achieve 'a sensible arrangement of what the safety-net consists of' *Hansard House of Lords Debates*, 10 December 2001, column 25.
70 Housing Act 1985, Sched 1, para 4 states that a tenancy granted in pursuance of any duty to accommodate the homeless will not be secure; the local authority can only give notice that it is to become a secure tenancy once the homeless person becomes entitled to an allocation under Part VI of the Housing Act 1996. Note that under the Law Commission's draft Rented Homes Bill, homeless households accommodated under Part VII of the Act will similarly be entitled only to a 'standard contract' and not a 'secure contract' ('Renting Homes: The Final Report', Volume 2: Draft Bill, Sched 2, para 6 (Law Com No. 297, Cm 6781, May 2006).
71 A new s 167(1A), requiring local authorities to issue a policy statement about applicants' chance to choose or express preferences about the housing which they are to be offered, applies only to allocations under Part VI, and not to the provision of front line accommodation for the homeless under Part VII. There are improved safeguards about rights of review and the local authority must now inform the applicant of the right to a review of suitability when making an offer of accommodation under s 193, and a new s 202(1A) makes it clear that a review is possible even when an offer of accommodation has been accepted, reversing the effect of the Court of Appeal's decision in *Alghile v Westminster County Council* [2001] EWCA Civ 363. However, it remains the case that the refusal of even one offer of suitable accommodation will terminate the authority's duty – see s 193(5).
72 See London Research Centre (1996).
73 See n 20 above, table 623.
74 In fact, unusually the homeless single parent in *R v Brent London Borough Council ex p Sadiq* (2001) 33 HLR 525 was male.
75 Under-Secretary of State Sally Keeble, *Hansard House of Commons Debates*, 25 February 2002, column 499.

Chapter 6

# Women's work

## Locating gender in the discourse of anti-social behaviour

*Helen Carr*

### Introduction

Anti-social behaviour, particularly on housing estates, has been a persistent target of government activity in the UK for the past ten years. The penalties devised by the Crime and Disorder Act 1998, in particular the anti-social behaviour order (ASBO), have attracted extensive critical comment particularly from criminal lawyers (see most recently MacDonald 2006). Housing lawyers have been equally concerned with the transformations to security of tenure provoked by anti-social behaviour initiatives implemented within the Housing Act 1996. Security of tenure, which can be summarised as the right to remain in your home unless you receive adequate notice of eviction proceedings, which can only be based upon limited and specified grounds and requires a court to decide that it is reasonable to evict you, has been the hallmark of social housing since the Housing Act 1980. However the Housing Act 1996 began an erosion of this right. Now there is no requirement for notice if the landlord is making allegations of anti-social behaviour and the original formulation of the ground, which was limited to nuisance or annoyance to neighbours, has been extended. The current version includes the conduct of visitors and the impact of the conduct upon residents, visitors and those engaged in lawful activities in the locality, and the meaning of neighbour embraces everyone who lives in the locality. Moreover, the court's discretion in anti-social behaviour cases has been legislatively redirected. Instead of focusing on the individual circumstances of a case, the court is required to consider the past impact of the anti-social conduct on other people, the likely continuing effect of the nuisance and the likely future effect of any repetition of the conduct when considering whether it is reasonable to make an order for possession. The objects of law reform have been two-fold. First, dismantling the barriers to possession proceedings where a tenant is alleged to be responsible for anti-social behaviour means that landlords can no longer justify inaction, and second, remedies have been made available which not only punish past behaviour but are designed to prevent future problematic behaviour.

Eviction is not only more readily available as a tool to prevent anti-social behaviour, but also it frequently is a much more draconian punishment than a criminal conviction. It is particularly severe if the tenant's responsibility is limited to a failure to prevent anti-social behaviour by others. Single mothers seem to be especially vulnerable to eviction in these circumstances (Hunter and Nixon 2001). Young has observed that, 'Governmental and criminological discourses pick out the figure of the single mother as the contemporary embodiment of responsibility for the criminal child' (Young 1996: 147). This chapter points out that this also applies to the single mother of the anti-social child. Moreover, her reliance on the social provision of housing enables her to be disciplined through the loss of her home. The focus on the responsibility of the single mother dependent upon welfare resources seems more than coincidental. The purpose of this chapter is to highlight the disciplinary manifestations of social interventions in housing and draw attention to the contemporary role of the social construction of gender as a disciplinary mechanism. The chapter begins by considering the Victorian origins of housing policy and demonstrates that the discursive themes, including the critical disciplinary role of gender, which inform contemporary approaches to anti-social behaviour, were evident in the early stages of government interventions. The discussion then turns to an analysis of two examples of contemporary discourse on anti-social behaviour. The first example is judicial discourse, which is powerful because it is authoritative. After a general consideration of the role of judicial narrative in constructing gender I provide a close analysis of two recent housing cases where the anti-social behaviour of the children prompted the landlords to initiate possession proceedings. I then turn to the complementary public discourse of the media as I consider *Take a Break's* 'Mum's Army', a discursive construct which draws it power from its authenticity. It links motherhood and the survival of civil society in a particularly potent way that resonates with Victorian fears of the irresponsibility and contagiousness of the 'residuum'.

## Discursive origins

It is well established that the origins of housing policy can be found within the massive industrialisation and urbanisation of the Victorian era – see for instance Burnett (1980). However, the form of government intervention into housing in the nineteenth century was neither stable nor consensual. The plurality of the discursive strands which made up the housing problem, each claiming a distinct authority – perhaps from religion, science or economics – was reflected in slow and uncertain evolution of housing policy, whilst the competing and contradictory forces of *laissez faire* individualism, charitable enterprise and national and local state endeavour produced at most a fragile compromise at its core. Not only were the debates intensive; they were extensive, covering for instance novels, social surveys, journalism, government reports and professional advice. The complexity, the variety and the sheer volume of the discursive outputs make an analysis difficult to manage. Nonetheless it is important to understand the contradictory forces of the past in order to make sense of the present. As Bakhtin explains in his notion of dialogism inherent historical tensions are revealed in our language even at the level of individual utterances (Bakhtin 1981). Holquist points out, for Bakhtin, language reflects, 'a ceaseless battle between centrifugal forces that seek to keep things apart, and centripetal forces that strive to make things cohere' (Holquist 1981: xviii). What this means is that the conflicts within the history of housing policy are always present and inform the language, perhaps more accurately the languages, of contemporary debate.

I have observed elsewhere (Carr and Cowan 2006) that it is noticeable that housing policy discourse, from its origins, appears to have adhered to particular dialectic themes of 'property and people' and 'quality and quantity'. The resulting matrix produces relatively limited possibilities for discursive couplings which explain why each turn of housing discourse apparently exploring a new theme seems nonetheless to be remarkably familiar. So the quantity of people requiring to be housed for instance forces attention on mass housing solutions whilst the quality of property stimulates debates about the inadequacies of speculative building and the need for new designs for workers homes. From the perspective of anti-social behaviour the discursive theme of the problematic quality of the people who made up the housing problem was fully explored in Victorian times, particularly by the evangelically inspired social reformers, and has remained a strong discursive force, despite at various times being apparently overshadowed by demands for quantitative and property based solutions to the housing problem (see Carr and Cowan 2006). As Davidoff observes, 'Victorians visualised the "Nether Regions" of society which, by their definition, were inhabited by the criminal classes, paupers, beggars and the work-shy as "stagnant pools of moral filth" comprising the "effluvia of our wretched cities" ' (Davidoff 1995: 105). Such images emphasised the powerlessness and the degradation of the slum dwellers as well as their 'potentially threatening and polluting effects' (Davidoff 1995: 104).

Of course demands for discipline were inherent in all discursive constructions of the housing problem. However, 'property' and 'quantity' were susceptible to the traditional economic disciplines of the market – so the model dwelling movement was constrained by the requirement for some modest return on investment for instance, and improvements to the standards of property were limited by the affordability of the rent. What was new in the Victorian origins of housing policy was social discipline and surveillance imposed upon tenants. Behaviour could be improved for instance through the rules imposed on the tenants of the model dwellings. Crucially for this chapter, gender and the Victorian creation of the marital ideal of disciplinary father and loving mother provided a potent social disciplinary mechanism for the poor. These ideas emerged largely from evangelicalism which considered that a critical role of the family was the moral education and discipline of children tainted by original sin (Hendrick 2002). Moreover, Victorian constructions of gender meant that the father functioned in the public sphere and was a conduit between the public realm and the private life of the family, whilst the mother took prime responsibility for the home. Failure to appropriately socialise children and run a good home made her a 'bad mother' (Lewis 1986, Davidoff 1995). This was essential not just for the well-being of individual families but for society as a whole As Rose puts it, the new mode of social government relied upon:

> A revised ethic of womanhood, of the respectable and educated woman who was best suited to staff the devices that would relay government into the household, of the decent and educable woman who was to enact government with the domestic space, of the feckless and irresponsible woman whose character was impermeable to education.
>
> (Rose 1999: 129)

Rose here also alerts us to a particular twist of gender. A new role for middle-class women as inspectors of domesticity emerged. Davidoff explains this as, 'a result of negotiation and protest from politically active women seeking to gain entry into the public arena through engagement with local issues and philanthropy, seen as extension of familial concerns' (Davidoff 1995: 257). This led from the 1870s onwards to what Lewis describes as 'the invasions of the working class family . . . chiefly through the agency of voluntary visitors' (Lewis 1986: 101).

Considerable discursive effort has had to be expended in order to maintain this ethic of womanhood. As Butler reminds us, gender is socially created through repeated ritualised and mundane acts, 'the body becomes its gender through a series of acts which are renewed, revised and consolidated through time' (Butler 1990: 274). Moreover, it is disciplinary because, 'the ascription of interiority is itself a publicly regulated and sanctioned form of essence fabrication' (Butler 1990: 29). The result is that 'those who fail to do their gender right are regularly punished' (Butler 1990: 273). My point here, drawing on Bakhtin, is that whenever there is a discursive turn to the anti-social quality of the people who constitute the housing problem and a call for disciplinary interventions, then gender, a critical element within the emergence of housing policy, is revitalised. So just as the evangelicals blamed mothers for juvenile delinquency and Octavia Hill used the housekeeping standards of women as selection criteria for her properties, responsible motherhood plays a crucial role in the contemporary problematisation of anti-social behaviour. This is exemplified by judicial discourse.

## Compelling motherhood

The empirical work of Hunter and Nixon provides a valuable exception to the almost complete silence of housing theorists on the role of gender within anti-social behaviour. In an analysis of landlords' files and Court of Appeal cases relating to possession proceedings for anti-social behaviour they observe, 'Notwithstanding the fact that in the majority of cases involving women-headed households, the main perpetrator of the behaviour complained about was not the woman, women were still held to be responsible for the anti-social behaviour' (Hunter and Nixon 2001: 401). They illustrate their point with a particularly telling quotation from a judge who is responding to a single mother's claim that she had tried to control her adolescent son's behaviour and therefore should not be evicted:

> I have to say that I find her protests are not persuasive. At a time when her son was getting into deeper trouble at the school, and his offending was deteriorating, and he was video'd . . . scrawling graffiti on the wall, her attention was elsewhere . . . [S]he conceived a child in the summer of 1999 (that baby is now five months old) and will have been at the very least, visibly pregnant to her son, who might be forgiven for thinking that her attention, if not her affection, was elsewhere.
>
> (Hunter and Nixon 2001: 404)

Drawing on the observations of feminist geographers, they point out that in the ideal family of a married couple with children of government's imagination, 'the man will be able to control behaviour, but where it does not exist and there is a failure of control, a woman will be doubly at fault for the failure to provide the ideal state and the failure to exercise authority in the absence of a man to do so' (Hunter and Nixon 2001: 407). However, the point can be developed. The judge's comment can be read as a condemnation of the inappropriate fecundity of the single mother, resonating with the sexualised fear of the other. It fits in with traditional criminological theories concerning the narcissistic woman offender, who, ceasing 'to be the self-sacrificing altruist is renamed as destructive of the masculine ego' (Young 1996: 31). Moreover, the comment illustrates that judicial pronouncements are a rich resource for feminist analysis. Diamond points out the significance of narrative for feminist analysis, 'With its relentless teleology, its ordering of meaning, narrative accrues to itself the power to define and legislate' (Diamond 1990: 95). Judicial narratives are particularly powerful and their power is employed, in Butler's terms, to perform gender. Significantly, as I have already noted, performance has consequences, an observation exemplified by successful possession proceedings taken against Mrs Higgins by her landlord, Manchester City Council.

## The indifferent mother

*Manchester City Council v Higgins* [2005] EWCA Civ 1423; [2006] 1 All ER 841 was a possession case based upon Mrs Higgins's breach of the anti-social behaviour term of her tenancy with Manchester City Council. Mrs Higgins was a single mother of three children including a two-year-old suffering from a heart condition, and a 12-year-old son James who had victimised a neighbouring family, damaging their property, bullying the sons and generally abusing the family. James became the subject of an anti-social behaviour order, the council got an anti-social behaviour injunction against Mrs Higgins and eventually issued possession proceedings.

The judgment is particularly fruitful discursively because the Court of Appeal paid close attention to the initial judicial evaluation of Mrs Higgins's evidence – something which is often hidden in reported cases. The paragraph numbers are taken from the Court of Appeal decision. We learn that the judge:

> . . . found the evidence of the defendant to be quite inadequate. Not only was she not able to bring to mind any of the complaints relied upon, but she seemingly took the view, regardless of the nature of the complaints that had been made, that if James said he did not do it, then he did not do it. From a son who she knew had been truanting from school, had been engaging in damaging and destructive behaviour behind her back (conduct which she initially denied he had been involved in) in the early hours of the morning, any reliance on his account in such a way would be self-evidently preposterous (para 15).

Mrs Higgins inappropriately, indeed preposterously, supported her son. This resonates with Young's observation of the deviance typically ascribed to the single mother: 'The mother–child relation is no longer secondary to the marital relation, because she responds to the child as child, rather than as surrogate for the husband, or the law, or the community. This is the key to the single mother's assertion of difference and also to the way in which she has been condemned' (Young 1996: 172). The judge's comments upon Mrs Higgins' parenting skills continue the notion of her inappropriate prioritising of her son, in particular above the needs of the community:

> The issue of parental supervision, restricting his activities seems not even to have crossed her mind. James self-evidently, and I find, was allowed to go out and play out whenever he liked and mix with whomsoever happened to be on the street corner and engage in any activity of his choosing, good or ill, without any apparent supervision (para 17).

This inappropriate support for her son is fused with a notion of abandonment of her responsibilities as a mother which is reflected in the emphasis upon her indifference to his behaviour. Fascinatingly, the judge 'ventriloquises' her carelessness on her behalf:

> Regrettably I am driven to the conclusion that the defendant has exhibited what I will describe as a '*belle indifference*' to the supervision of her son and in the controlling of his activities. I also find, having heard the evidence and accepted the evidence of Mrs Copeland that when on one occasion she was confronted with James's behaviour in May 2004, her attitude was just to laugh it off, with a care-less or care-free attitude, more or less saying: 'I am going out. If the police arrive, no doubt they will be confronting an empty door' (para 17).

Abandonment and evasion of appropriate suffering are themes within representations of aberrant motherhood. As Young puts it, the mother 'is a non-mother, absent, ineffective, destructive . . . [Her] image operates as an allegory of absence and indifference' (Young 1996: 124). The use of the French phrase works to extend the distance between her and us. Her failure to apologise is particularly symbolic of her indifference: 'What I also find extraordinary and as an indication of her complete incompetence to address these issues, she never once spoke any remorse or apology to Mrs Copeland about it and her excuse when she was asked about it specifically was that she did not have the time. I regard that statement as lame in the extreme' (para 17). Mrs Higgins' failure to apologise for the behaviour of her son exacerbates her failure to perform her conventional duty, and enhances her responsibility for the gap between the requisite image of motherhood and its inadequate realisation. Her failure means that she has failed to embrace the essential sacrifice of motherhood and justifies the judicial imposition of a material sacrifice upon her, the sacrifice of her home. As the judge put it, Mrs Higgins had, 'significant personal responsibility for what unfolded' (para 17).

Nonetheless the judge was uneasy granting immediate possession, particularly because James was at that time in custody. He suspended the order but at the same time gave permission to the council to appeal to the Court of Appeal. The Court focused on the judicial exercise of the discretion to suspend and the necessity to consider the future impact upon the community: 'When deciding whether or not to suspend the order the court will amongst other things be concerned to devise the best method of protecting the needs of neighbours against the re-occurrence of the anti-social behaviour which gave rise to the order for possession being made' (para 55). As Carr and Cowan argue:

> As a consequence the concept of rights is refocused. It no longer guarantees security for the tenant challenged by her landlord. Instead it is used to work for the security of others. At paragraph 38 of the judgment the Court explains, 'Ultimately, given the art 8 ECHR respect for the

> tenant's home, the question is whether an immediate possession order is necessary in order to meet the need to protect the rights and freedoms of others – the neighbours – and is proportionate to it.
>
> (Carr and Cowan 2006)

A further observation is appropriate. The protection of the community is prompted in part by left realist criminology's preoccupation with crime in the public arena. As Naffine points out, 'It suggests that the proper object of concern is crime whose public nature offends and threatens local residents or passers-by. Authentic (usually working class) victims are those decent citizens who do not give their consent to crimes occurring on their streets, such as drug-dealing or assault' (Naffine 1997: 65). Resistance to gender through indifference, just like resistance through fecundity, is meaningless. Not only is Mrs Higgins not an authentic victim, it is her perceived inadequacy as a mother which threatens the rights of the community and must be punished. For Young she becomes the 'symbolically sacrificed outlaw [and] is thus the victim of our desire for community (through shared victimization)' (Young 1996: 9).

## The loving mother

Consideration of another anti-social behaviour case provides a useful contrast. In *Moat Housing Group South Ltd v Harris* [2005] EWCA Civ 287; [2005] 3 WLR 691 we are reassured that judicial protection is available to those who do gender right when the Court of Appeal intervened to overturn an ASBO and suspend a possession order made against the mother of four young children. The first two paragraphs of the Court of Appeal judgment explain the events of the night of 29 October 2004 when an anti-social behaviour injunction with ouster and exclusion provisions was served on the family:

> The second defendant, Susan Hartless, lives at 49 Midhurst Road, Liphook with her four children, whose ages ranged between six and 14 years. The first defendant, Carl Harris, is the children's father. He lived with his parents in Hindhead and was estranged from Ms Hartless during the period to which these proceedings relate, but he often visited the family in Liphook. Ms Hartless has occupied her home since May 2001 on an assured tenancy from the claimants, Moat Housing Group-South Ltd, who are registered social landlords. She and her growing family had lived in Liphook since 1992. . . . On the evening of Friday, 29 October 2004 her eight-year-old daughter was looking forward to joining the other Brownies who had been chosen to represent their pack on a float at the village carnival the following day. Her son CH was looking forward to his seventh birthday party the following Monday. She

> had never received any notice or other warning from her landlords that her behaviour, or the behaviour of Mr Harris or her children, was such that the family might be at risk of being evicted from their home. It was therefore an enormous surprise to her when representatives of her landlords called at her house without prior notice at about 9 pm that evening, accompanied by the police and a television cameraman (para 1–2).

The privacy of a loving domestic scene is sundered. The intrusion is increased by the presence of the cameraman which, we learn, cannot be explained by the anti-social behaviour adviser employed by the social landlord. Ms Hartless's solicitor obtained an order staying the effects of the original order over the telephone from a High Court Judge at 1.30 am the following morning. However, on 3 November 2004 the claimants served a notice of possession proceedings on Ms Hartless, alleging 19 different examples of nuisance and a possession order and an anti-social behaviour order was obtained against Ms Hartless at the end of November. The court remarks upon the spelling mistakes in the court papers: 'Apart from the misspelling of the words "part" [aprt], "area" [aream], "assaulting" [assulting] and "occupying" [occuping], it contained no particularly noteworthy features' (para 5). This operates to subtly subvert the landlord as an agent of justice 'imbued with knowledge, determination, rationality and objectivity' (Young 1996: 8). This continues throughout the case when the Court belittles the evidence of the claimant's expert, 'who likes to describe himself as an anti-social behaviour adviser', because of its generality. It remarks upon the failure to provide the family with notice of its actions and the landlord's poor record-keeping.

More significantly, however, the Court of Appeal's narrative of normal mothering is substituted for the social landlord's story of deviance. Instead of an indifferent mother we learn that an alternative formulation of the state has vindicated her achievements in relation to two of her children:

> DH, Ms Hartless's daughter, attracted virtually no attention at all from any complainant. Her excellent school report, which was with the court's papers, described her as co-operative and friendly, and someone who followed school rules and social codes. Although there was an occasional mention of her second brother BH in some of the hearsay evidence, it certainly could not have justified a finding that he was out of control. He, too, had a good school report: 'a very pleasant and co-operative pupil who has made satisfactory progress this year' (para 154).

Whilst this could be understood as the court resisting the dominant narrative of populist authoritarianism, my argument is that it is only able to do so by performing gender which appeals to a particular conservative and moral authority. Significantly, and in contrast with *Manchester City Council v Higgins*, the order can be suspended because the Court sees a particular hope for the future: 'Perhaps quite importantly, we were told that Mr Harris is now living with Ms Hartless where he ought to be able, if he is so inclined, to instil in his oldest and youngest sons a degree of discipline which seems to have been sadly lacking when they did not have a father living permanently in their home' (para 160).

A woman alone with children is not sufficient for the court. Her resistance to conventional family structures cannot be tolerated. So as Young puts it, the absent father is 'made present; his presence as a stern lawgiver would be coupled with his opposite terms: the loving mother' (Young 1996: 127). There is now the possibility that order will be restored within the family and therefore to the community. The linkage of family and community reminds us that judicial discourse is not simply concerned with the individual family that is the subject of litigation. It is importantly a public discourse so its achievements work to buttress the symbolic role of motherhood. Yet its dissemination is limited, a point which is particularly pertinent in the context of the extreme anxiety provoked by anti-social behaviour and highlighted by the presence of the television crew in Mrs Hartless's home at the time of the failed eviction. The media, and in particular women's magazines, have always had a crucial role in gender performativity, and it is to this that the chapter now turns.

## Of motherhood and death

Young provides one way to understand the role of the media in the sphere of gender. Writing in the context of mothers of criminal children, she explains stories of motherhood as responses to the 'crisis in the cultural representation of the maternal relationship. This crisis takes the form of a rupture or breach in the permitted representations of this relationship. Such a rupture causes extreme anxiety, resulting in frantic attempts, within the public discourse of the media, to efface the rupture and restore a sense of order to the maternal and the familial relation' (Young 1996: 117). Of course the role of women's magazines is inevitably complex. They must entertain their readers with incidents of transgression at the same time as provide the constituent work of gender. Presdee's take on the function of carnival derived from Bakhtin provides valuable theoretical insights here (see Presdee 2000) and *Take a Break* – the UK's best selling women's weekly – embraces both of these roles. In a feature in its media pages, *The Independent* explains:

> *Take a Break* has eschewed celebrity tittle-tattle in favour of political campaigning. With sales of 1.2 million almost double those of its closest rival, IC's *Chat*, [the editor has] shown that it takes more than the insights of a C list celeb to claim the top weekly slot. Leaving others to fight over Big Brother exclusives, *Take a Break* has recently been busy

> recruiting readers to Mum's Army, the UK's newest and fastest-growing political party.
>
> (*The Independent*, 7 March 2006)

In a discursive move echoing judicial concerns, the editor claims also a particular community: 'Something's gone wrong he says. Mum's Army is a response. The decent majority – I choose my words deliberately – want to restore values. It's about community and self-help and mutual respect. The best role model is the woman down the street, not Jordan' (*The Independent* 7 March 2006).

The magazine's prescription of gender is rich and does not forget its role in carnivalising transgression to be consumed during breaks in the domestic routine as well as its disciplinary role:

> Alongside Mum's Army, *Take a Break* is in the second year of its Kitchen Table Tycoon competition, which helps women set up their own businesses, and its Women's Orgasm Liberation campaign, to help the 25% of the female population who don't have them. Previous campaigns include Mums on Drugs which encouraged kids to take pictures of their mothers doing crack. 'Imagine if Oliver Twist had been given a Nikon', Dale says. – Did we use those pictures big – You bet!
>
> (*The Independent*, 7 March 2006)

The cover of the 16 March 2006 issue illustrates its particular discursive approach to motherhood emphasising its quintessential sacrificial quality: 'Mum's dying words to love rival – I forgive you, Linda' (*Take a Break*, 16 March 2006) and reminding us of Butler's observation, 'that [gender] operates as an interior essence that might be disclosed, an expectation that ends up producing the very phenomenon that it anticipates' (Butler 1999: xiv). It also introduces the focus of my interest with the words, 'Mum's Army Down's Bride latest victim of yobs' (*Take a Break*, 16 March 2006).

Inside the magazine the story is headlined, 'Down's Bride's Mother Says: Why we Back Mum's Army'. The story is told in the words of the mother, stressing the authenticity of her experience. The story opens by stressing the dangers inherent in the familial: 'My daughter Maryanne was 12 years old when she saw her younger brother Philip being pushed into a swimming pool by a group of kids. He banged his head and died. We were devastated. It was a terrible lesson in the effects of bullying, one that was even more pertinent to her because of her nature. Maryanne had Down's syndrome' (*Take a Break*, 16 March 2006). This mother is both ordinary in her domesticity and care and special, because one child has died and another is disabled. However, this makes her a particularly potent symbol of sacrificial motherhood. Moreover, she achieves for her daughter the marital ideal:

> One day she returned home with a big smile and said, Mum, I've met someone very special today . . . he also had Downs. It was love at first sight and it wasn't long before Tommy came to see me and said: I want to marry Maryanne. He was clutching the ring he'd bought her as a surprise. They were perfect for each other. Tommy offered the constant love, security and support that Maryanne needed.
>
> (*Take a Break*, 16 March 2006)

However, that cannot eradicate the fear and insecurity:

> But the bullies persist. They seem determined to take away the little independence Maryanne and Tommy have, making them prisoners in their own home. Their foul behaviour shames our society. Maryanne and Tommy are two of the gentlest people you could ever meet and yet they live in fear. . . . Something has to be done to stop these yobs. We're always looking over our shoulder. Why should we have to live like this? That's why I am supporting Mum's Army in *Take a Break*. I want to get involved. We as parents cannot sit back and let these yobs destroy our family life. I am going to do all I can to get justice for my children and make my neighbourhood a safer place to live.
>
> (*Take a Break*, 16 March 2006).

The magazine has a strategy to enlist the fear and frustration. It is organising a Mum's Army: 'We give Mother's Day a new name – Mum's Army Day. They with our 10,000 supporters are determined to vent their frustration at the continuing growth of yob culture and demand that every effort is made to restore decent community values' (*Take a Break*, 16 March 2006). As Young points out however: 'The community that results is, of course, a simulacrum of a community; a phantasm that speaks of a nostalgic desire for oneness and unity, while at the same time structuring itself around its dependence upon fear, alienation and separateness for its elements to make sense' (Young 1996: 10). One essential building block for the construction of such a community is the magazine's performance of gender. It demands activity of the reader. (There is a cut-out coupon to be completed and sent to the editor. Readers' names are to be added to the *Women Stand Up* petition which is to be forwarded to the Prime Minister on Mother's day. The most motivated are encouraged to stand as candidates for Mum's Army in the forthcoming local elections.) This simultaneously constructs the social, the engaged mother and the anti-social, indifferent mother. Women are thus implicated in the marking of the boundaries of the respectable and the other. Davidoff makes a similar point about Victorian philanthropy. She observes that middle-class women's activities, 'were intimately bound up with the relational aspects of class. In their social rounds, in philanthropic activities and dispensing charity, they were cultivating, smoothing and negotiating the relationships created and sustained by the productive sphere' (Davidoff 1995: 252). So there are crucial continuities of gender in the government of the poor.

Yet another story is presented in the context of the petition, 'The handover will be made by 12 year old Donna Stocker, who witnessed the bullying of her mother Debra even as she was dying of breast cancer' (*Take a Break*, 16 March 2006). The constant intertwining of death with stories of the anti-social emphasises both moral repugnance for the behaviour and the essential insecurity of social life. The fear is utilised by the magazine, which seeks security in recreating gender in its traditional and reassuring role whilst simultaneously provoking the state to further authoritarian postures. The metaphor of an army is significant; and this is a Mum's army, an army on behalf of mothers which pursues the impossible goal of mothers being protected from their unspoken fears through the annihilation of yob culture. The words employed reflect a Bakhtinian hidden dialogicality. When we hear a woman's response to the Prime Minister's launch of the Respect agenda in January 2006, we note the similarities:

> People have got away with murder for too long and we've been powerless to stop it. Young people have a protection ring around them and you become frightened to report them – it's your word against theirs. It starts with things like graffiti and spitting and before too long they're fighting in gangs, intimidating and mugging old people and even worse. The government should have done something a long time ago.
>
> (Swindon Web 2006)

Then, as Wertsch puts it:

> We sense that this is a conversation, although one person is speaking, and it is a conversation of the most intense kind, for each present, uttered word respond and reacts with its every fibre to the invisible speaker, points to something outside itself, beyond its own limits, to the unspoken words of another person.
>
> (Wertsch 2001: 230)

The unspoken words are of death. As Neocleous says, '[the] terror of death can be thought of as a terror of social death – the death of civil society itself. The history of security is a history of the state seeking an impossible security from the terror of the death of civil society' (Neocleous 2000: 61). If death of civil society is the risk then a response which provokes the elimination of the risk is proportionate. As Carr and Cowan put it, 'Common sense therefore justifies the death of the social existence of the "other" because of the need to enhance the protections of the "innocent" and "the law abiding" (Carr and Cowan 2006). The consequences of such a discourse seem irreversible. The only progress will be the amplification of both the fear and the response to it.

## Conclusion

Close examination of two powerful and complementary examples of discourse, one speaking with an authoritative voice, the other with an authentic voice demonstrates that gender permeates government's problematisation of and response to anti-social behaviour. There are strong continuities with Victorian concerns, as Davidoff puts it, the 'residuum was at least partially defined by deviance from expected gender behaviour' (Davidoff 1995: 256). The observation of Anna Martin, an active suffragist at the end of the nineteenth century who described early state interventions into mothering as 'mothers being ordered by law to perform the impossible and punished if they fail' (quoted in Lewis 1986: 109) is particularly compelling in the context of mothers restraining the behaviour of their adolescent sons. The anti-social behaviour agenda marks a revitalisation of a moralising and punitive discourse of welfare which relies in part upon the constituent work of gender. This sits uneasily with the apparent liberalisation of family structures that the Civil Partnership Act 2004 and other recent government initiatives represent, perhaps indicating that such freedoms are not available to the welfare recipient. More significantly the discursive linkage of anti-social behaviour with death actively animates the community in whose name government seeks to act. It speaks of Foucault's 'new technology of power, this biopolitics, this biopower' (Foucault 2004: 243) which permits in the cause of survival the extermination of the anti-social 'other', suggesting perhaps that rights to live lives which fall outside of the constraints of the norm may be short-lived.

Chapter 7

# Women Travellers and the paradox of the settled nomad

*Margaret Greenfields and Robert Home*

## Introduction

A Gypsy family had planning permission (won on appeal) for placing two caravans on land they owned. Wanting to look after the husband's widowed mother, who was 86 years old, blind and barely able to walk, they applied for permission to add a third caravan for her to live in. The council refused the application: although the site complied with its criterion-based policy on Gypsy sites, 'countryside policy' (preserving the amenities of the rural environment) prevailed. The family appealed. When the appeal hearing opened at the council offices in 2003, the chairperson of the planning committee obtained an adjournment by introducing the case of *Wrexham County Borough v National Assembly of Wales, Michael Berry and Florence Berry* [2003] UKHL 26, and arguing that the elderly woman could not now claim 'gypsy' status as she had surrendered her nomadic way of life and had no intention of resuming it. She attended the hearing, using the council's stair lift to reach the room where the hearing was being held, and sat largely unaware of the proceedings. This elderly woman, had she been more able to understand the proceedings taking place, was being told that, irrespective of her state of health, to be able to be defined as a 'gypsy' in law, she would have to be able to continue to travel. Such is the world of planning law and policy that Gypsies inhabit, a world worthy of Kafka.

This chapter will explore the paradox of the 'settled nomad', the particular implications it has for Gypsy and Traveller women and the broader issues arising for a feminist analysis of gender and land use. The legal definition of 'gypsy' is a crucial factor in gaining access to land when Travellers seek permission to 'develop' land they own by placing caravans on the land in which to live. We will explore the reasons why it has become increasingly important for Travellers to be able to obtain such planning permission, and increasingly difficult for them to do so.

## A history of the 'outside'

The relationship between Gypsies, Travellers and the state in the United Kingdom has for many centuries been 'marked by confusion, ambiguity, harsh persecution and qualified tolerance' (Mayall 1995: 7). Identities which touch on issues as diverse as occultism, dirt, criminal activity and promiscuous behaviour have consistently been imposed on Gypsies and Travellers by non-Gypsies (the settled 'other' known to Romanies as 'gadje' – those who are not of 'The People') (Clark 2005). These identities have been constituted by, and reflected in, legislation targeted at Gypsies for some five centuries. In law, the romantic idea of the Gypsy derived from such writers as Borrow (1851 and 1857) is less evident than a perception of them as an anti-social nuisance to settled society, which must be subjected to state control. Mayall (1995) lists 29 laws concerning Gypsies passed in England and Wales between 1530 and 1908. Early legislation sought to expel or even execute 'outlandish people callynge themselves Egyptians' and severe criminal penalties stayed on the statute books until repealed in 1783, returning with the Vagrancy Acts of 1822–4 (Mayall 1995, Rickard 1995). This 'most pernicious piece of legislation' (Mayall 1995: 29) imposed a three-fold classification of vagrants: 'idle and disorderly persons', 'rogues and vagabonds' and 'incorrigible rogues'. Gypsies were explicitly grouped with rogues and vagabonds and, if 'not having any visible means of subsistence and not giving a good account of himself', subject to imprisonment (Beier 1974, 1985).

Quite apart from the suspicion and fear engendered by these folkloric identities, there is always the vexed question of where Gypsies and Travellers can stop, what material space they can occupy and what place they can have in the world, when not required for farm labour, scrap work or the 'traditional' activities followed by such nomadic people. Confronting this question has led to conflicts over land-use and acceptable halting places and has engendered complex state processes of confinement and exclusion, in which legal definitions of spatiality (although often met with various forms of resistance) have important effects upon the social reality and practices of Gypsies and Travellers. Modern legislative activity exemplifies this constitutive effect of law and the intricate relationships between law, power and space (Delaney *et al.* 2001).

The Highways Act 1835 introduced fines for a Gypsy 'or any other person travelling' who 'pitches a booth, stall or stand, or encamps on a highway', and the consolidating Highways Act 1959 retained the offence, omitting however the phrase 'or other person travelling'. In *Mills v Cooper* [1967] 2 All ER 100, Mr Cooper pleaded not guilty, claiming that he was not an ethnic Gypsy and therefore not covered by the legislation. The court found against him, on the argument that to be a Gypsy was a way of life rather than a racial category: 'gypsy means no more than a person leading a nomadic way of life with no, or no fixed, employment and with no fixed abode'. The following year this judicial interpretation formed the basis of the statutory definition given in the Caravan Sites Act 1968.

Caravan sites have become an integral part of the state's regulatory power over Gypsies. In the nineteenth century, legislation intended to encourage Gypsies to settle was proposed, but not enacted (Mayall 1995). In 1960, the Caravan Sites Act brought caravans under closer control and, to compensate for the reduction in legal stopping places for Gypsies, gave local authorities a discretionary power to establish sites for them. During the early 1960s, a number of heated Parliamentary debates followed high-profile evictions from large sites established on traditional stopping places (some used for hundreds of years), the prosecution of landowners willing to allow Gypsies to stop on their land and the compulsory purchase of Gypsies' land. Gypsies were increasingly unable to find places to lawfully stop. A public outcry about the 'inhuman' treatment of Britain's 'oldest ethnic minority' (Acton 1974) led to the enactment of the Caravan Sites Act 1968, a significant intervention aimed at ensuring local authorities provided sites for Gypsies to legally stop. However, the Act also empowered the Secretary of State to make designation orders for areas where s/he was satisfied that there was adequate accommodation or on grounds of 'expediency', thus extending control over informal sites or applications for sites not controlled by the local authority. Local authorities were given additional powers to remove unlawful encampments and, although the 1968 Act had been intended to encourage a more positive approach, it was widely regarded by Gypsies as implementing a form of apartheid or separate treatment. By 2000 nearly half of all Gypsy caravans were accommodated on council sites, mostly developed with central government capital grant support.

However, it is the statutory definition of 'Gypsy', around which the 1968 Act was organised, that is of particular interest here. The dictionary definition of 'a member of the Romany ethnic group', was substituted by a definition of Gypsies as 'persons of nomadic habit of life, whatever their race or origin' (Fraser 1992: 3). By this means ethnic Gypsies could lose their legal status if they ceased to travel and any individual who adopted a nomadic way of life might be classed as 'gipsies'. The rewriting of a cultural history with all of its multiple layers of meaning has exercised Traveller activists and planning inspectors, local authorities and the judiciary ever since.

The Criminal Justice and Public Order Act 1994 (trailed in the Conservative Party manifesto for the 1992 General Election) abolished any statutory obligation to provide accommodation for Gypsies, discontinued government grants for caravan sites, and made it a criminal offence, with heavy sanctions, to camp on land without the owner's consent. As the consultation paper said: 'The problem has grown faster than its remedy' (DETR 1998). With unauthorised encampment now criminalised, large sums of public money were spent evicting Gypsies and Travellers (Morris and Clements 2002). Further, the criminalisation of certain activities associated with the Gypsy way of life (usually under the argument of the need to protect private property) also threatened the culture of travelling. Yet, the contentious relabelling of Gypsy remains, as alluded to by Tony Baldry (then Minister of the Environment) when introducing the Parliamentary debate on the Criminal Justice and Public Order Bill in 1994: 'not all gypsies are Travellers, and not all Travellers are gypsies'. Official insistence on 'nomadism' as a prerequisite for 'gypsy' status blurred the understanding of 'Gypsies' as an ethnic group (Greenfields 2002, Clark and Dearling 2000), creating a hierarchy of 'deserving' and 'undeserving nomads', with Romany Gypsies being perceived as a 'respectable' minority (Morris 2000). Thus the word 'gypsy' has become a convenient policy categorisation for a wide variety of people who have never constituted a homogenous group, and who themselves often prefer to be called Travellers.

Other legal codes of spatiality have served to control and shape the lives of Gypsies and Travellers. The Planning Acts, controlling land use and enforcing against breaches of planning control, represent in themselves 'a crucial blow to the traditional, if hazardous, life which modern Gypsies had carved out for themselves' (Hawes and Perez 1996: 18). Planning policies in development plans designed to protect the countryside, and even mild encouragement to gypsies to set up self-help sites (Circular 28/77), met resistance from local authorities and residents eager to object under the public consultation provisions. A growing public intolerance of gypsies was reflected in new legislation: the Planning and Compensation Act 1991 strengthens local government enforcement powers against breaches of planning control and some of its provisions are targeted specifically at gypsies, even when occupying land they own. Further, another legal definition, that of 'homelessness', also constitutes and affects the Gypsy way of life: s 172(2(b) of the Housing Act 1996 includes as homeless someone whose accommodation is a 'moveable structure, vehicle or vessel, designed or adapted for living in, caravan, houseboat or other mobile structure and she has no place where she is entitled or permitted to put it and live on it'. However, as the Homelessness Code of Practice indicates, a local authority is not required to make equivalent accommodation available to a 'homeless' Gypsy and, if no pitch on a legitimate site is available, can arrange for some other 'suitable' form of housing (Arden and Hunter 2002).

In sharp contrast to legal definitions, Hawes and Perez (1996: 7) define Gypsies or Travellers as a loose affiliation of individuals, families and social groups (some of whom may not even want to be classified as 'gipsies'), who 'possess a continuity, rather than a community, of culture' and whose rights to secure accommodation are often denied or contested by the state and society. For much of sedentary society, the media and the state, 'gipsies' of all ethnicities are perceived as sharing (to a greater or lesser extent) five overlapping characteristics:

i) nomadism, vagrancy or itinerancy (Mayall 1995, Acton 1974, Beier 1985);
ii) race or ethnicity – English Romanies have been recognised as an ethnic minority since the case of *CRE v Dutton* [1989] 1 QB 783 and Irish Travellers have followed (but not Welsh, Scottish, or 'New' Travellers);
iii) deviancy or some forms of anti-social behaviour (Clark 2004);
iv) social and physical marginalization (Kendall 1997, Halfacree 1996); and
v) homelessness (when travelling or not having a settled home-base) (Arden and Hunter 2002).

It is the intersection between these paradigms and definitions, including the use of the term 'Gypsy' as a metonym for the entire complex cultural existence of Travellers, which the state seeks to control by the synecdochic use of 'nomadism' as a prerequisite of 'gypsy status', with which this chapter is concerned. By redefining *all* Travellers (ethnic Romany Gypsies as well as 'legislative' gipsies) purely on the basis of what they do (or folkloric expectations of their behaviour) it is possible to control access to land-use. A hierarchy of authenticity, and the pre-conceptions which sedentary populations bring to their engagements with members of these communities, are legitimated. Therefore, within this chapter we explore the interactions between law, power and space around the legal definition of 'gypsy' as (only) a nomadic person. At a more general level these interactions have concerned critical legal thinking, legal geography and feminisms, the latter most obviously with respect to the spatial and ideological division between the public and the private. The discussion presented here takes as a specific focus the position of women whose lives are shaped at the intersections of legal, political and cultural paradigms.

Women are caught up within the paradox of legal Gypsy status, but have found ways of resisting state power and developing complex spatial negotiations. Traveller women, who historically and culturally tend to occupy the role of transmitters of culture (Oprea 2003, Lackova 1999), are becoming increasingly politically radicalised within the forum of 'Traveller politics' (Bancroft 1999). The policy and legislative fixation on nomadism is particularly problematic for them, as a desire to stop travelling (perhaps for children's educational opportunities, or to ensure care for the elderly) is interpreted by the law as ceasing to be a 'gypsy', regardless of whether the woman in question has no intention of giving up her traditional cultural practices, or if she ever resided in a house. For all Travellers, let alone those women who are ethnically Romany Gypsies and are now told they have lost their 'gypsy status', by defining them by what they do (or by stereotypical expectations of behaviour), the state imposes a dichotomy, between stability, security on the one hand and cultural identity on the other, which ensures that access to land is inevitably and overtly politicised.

## Traveller cultures and gender roles

Research on Gypsies and Travellers (Okely 1983, Fraser 1992, Weyrauch 2001 and Williams 1999) makes it clear that although they lack a 'homeland' (unlike, for instance, racial groups who may be 'exiled' from a grounded, original location), they have 'created their own semi-autonomous cultural space rather than a legally politically defined territory' (Okely 1997: 189). They may be regarded as the archetypical *bricoleurs* (Levi-Strauss 1966: 17–21), who sort, discard and integrate elements from the surrounding systems within which they live, but adapt and synthesise these elements to create a world in which they can exist, whilst retaining their own cultural integrity. Research to date has tended to focus upon questions of ethnicity rather than gender, although there has been some interest in Gypsy women's responses and adaptations to their increasingly sedentary lives (Willoughby 1996).

Within the 'traditional' Traveller cultures, gender roles are strongly differentiated, and both men and women adhere to a set of core behaviours which place the 'family' and 'home' at the centre of their value system. A couple do not regard themselves as being in competition, but part of a mutually complementary relationship, with men being primarily responsible for supporting their family financially and practically (for example, through making connections with other relatives so that employment opportunities exist) and women taking overall responsibility for the home and children. Certain aspects of life (for example, matters relating to pregnancy, personal care for elders, and teaching appropriate household and hygiene skills to daughters) are very much the role of women, and it would be inappropriate and cause offence to both men and women if a man were to intervene in these matters. Similarly, a man will take care of his sons' training in employment skills, negotiate over finances, deal with land purchases (although the land will, as discussed in the later, usually be formally registered in the name of his wife) and other practical issues such as vehicle repairs and employment opportunities, as well as matters involving family reputation (Clark and Greenfields 2006, Levinson and Sparkes 2003). While a woman will generally take a lesser part in public discussions about these matters, in private the couple will be equally involved in decision making and debate as the women are as strong and confident in their roles as their men. In public, however, women are expected, and are willing, to appear to be subservient to men, although much joking to the opposite sometimes occurs. At social gatherings, weddings, funerals etc, men and women will always split into separate gender groups.

Among traditional Travellers there is a strong adherence to strict moral codes governing the relationships between men and women. Young women are expected to be chaste before marriage and families will 'watch out' for their relatives to ensure that gossip will not adhere to the young person about their behaviour. With the close-knit family structure, presence of relatives during social interactions, and knowledge that community is central to their way of life, traditional values remain central to the upbringing and behaviour of both men and women (Clark and Greenfields 2006). Generally persons of the opposite gender (unless they are very closely related) must not be alone together, and discussions on matters pertaining to sexuality and reproduction are highly inappropriate between men and women, particularly those of different generations. Concerns about sex education at school, and about youngsters mixing with teenagers with different cultural beliefs (pertaining to sexuality, gender roles and drug use) are often cited as a reason for disliking sending children to secondary school, as exposure to such issues is contrary to the values and cultures of traditional travelling communities (Levinson and Sparkes 2003). Lone parenthood is very rarely found among Gypsies and traditional Travellers, and where this does occur, is almost always as a result of the (unusual, but very slowly increasing) separation of a married couple. Within traditional communities an unmarried woman with a child would always require the presence of family members (and particularly a close male relative) to ensure social integration and the protection of her reputation.

Crucially, women are seen (and are proud to regard themselves) as the upholders of cultural and ethical traditions (Weyrauch and Bell 2001, Fraser 1992: 238–47, Acton, Caffrey, Dunn and Vinson 1997), and hold responsibility for ensuring the physical and moral hygiene of what Kendall (1997) calls the 'homespace' (whether trailer, caravan or house). Much has been written about the concepts of cleanliness and pollution (in both the moral and physical sense) among Romany Travellers, although over time, and within individual families, some practices have altered or fallen into disuse. There are variations in how strictly these rules of '*mochadi*' are interpreted and, for example, Travellers in houses and static mobile homes will not generally be able (or may not wish) to have the structures adapted to follow traditional notions of where hygiene facilities are placed. Nevertheless, even among families who do not outwardly appear particularly traditional, rules about behaviour between generations, how and when hands should be washed, the handling of food, cleaning implements and items pertaining to the family animals, etc will generally be firmly adhered to.

It can be argued that knowledge of '*mochadi*' (that which is polluting) is a form of cultural boundary, providing a guide to who and what are included into, or rejected from, the society. By extension the 'homespace' must at all times be '*wuzho*' (clean). Homespace cannot, however, be viewed in any simplistic way as the site of oppression: constructing a homespace within the cultural and moral norms of Romany society represents 'a method of cultural survival and resistance for the marginal group . . . somewhere that Traveller women can restore their dignity, providing a "safe" spatial area in which to learn to love and respect their culture outside the hostility of the sedentary culture' (Kendall 1997: 83). Thus, traditional Travellers, regardless of their physical surroundings (many 'authorised' sites are placed at the margins of society, in close proximity to motorways, sewage recycling plants and rubbish tips where settled populations would not be permitted to build) are very far from the imposed identities of 'homeless' or 'dirty'.

Not only do the cultural landscapes which Gypsies and traditional Travellers inhabit require adherence to rules of morality and hygiene, but traditional gender expectations exist in terms of income generation. Whilst in some Travelling cultures women and men are both expected to contribute to the family income through undertaking different (gender appropriate) work, in Britain Romany women are (at least currently) more likely to remain home-based, caring for children and the elderly, while men occupy a more visible role, moving between the homespace and the outside world while engaged in physical work such as trading their skills or selling their labour. However, for those families who are able to access stability of site, women are proving more adaptable to changing economic circumstances than are most Traveller men, and in some cases are returning to education, skills training or (unusually for Travellers) entering the formal labour market (Clark and Greenfields 2006).

Conversely, 'New Travellers', who whilst not ethnically Gypsies may be 'gipsies' in law, have a distinct cultural pattern which is unique among nomadic groups and would appear to owe much to the recent nature of this group's travelling history, as well as their tendency to aspire to a non-hierarchical, 'green' and often feminist political belief system (Greenfields 2002). 'Gender appropriate' roles are rare and it is not uncommon to see women mechanics and men involved in childcare work. Men and women engage equally in a variety of work, often similar in nature to that practised by 'traditional' Traveller men. In sharp contrast to 'traditional' Travellers, marriage is not the norm and patterns of serial monogamy (perhaps interspersed with lone parenthood) are fairly common amongst this community. Where partnerships do break down, a strong ethic exists that fathers will be involved in childcare, often having children to live with them for blocks of several months at a time. Lone parenthood, among both men and women, is not uncommon and appears to be no barrier to repartnering (Greenfields 2002). Support with childcare is usually available (and expected) from other Travellers.

Perhaps as a result of the feminist ethic of many women New Travellers, as well as a realistic awareness of the potential for relationship breakdown within their community, many women own and maintain their living vehicles or trailers, and retain separate 'spaces' even within a stable relationship. New Traveller behaviour is very different from the highly structured and gender differentiated cultures of traditional Travellers. This has sometimes led to a reluctance by Gypsies and other nomadic people to share sites with New Travellers, who are sometimes perceived, in a hostile manner, as being both *mochadi* and responsible for the bad reputation which media, politicians and members of the sedentary community impose on all groups of Travellers. However, with the recent upsurge in Traveller political engagement focusing on equality of access to site provision, groups of traditional and New Travellers have begun to work more closely together with a view to ensuring that Traveller issues remain on the political agenda.

## Land holding and access to sites

Access to land is a vital issue for all Travellers. Authorised accommodation comes from a range of sources, including council sites, private sites (with planning permission granted by councils or on appeal), and movement onto non-gypsy caravan sites and mobile home parks. In addition, as will be explored in more detail below, there is some movement into conventional housing. The number of Gypsies in the UK is small, arguably quite disproportionate to the public resources expended in controlling and regulating them (Morris and Clements 2002, Crawley 2004). Since the most 'visible' Gypsy and Traveller populations typically live in caravans, central government has, since 1979, required 'gypsy caravans' (distinguished from other types of caravan or mobile homes) to be counted six-monthly by local authorities under three categories (council authorised, private authorised and unauthorised) according to the land on which they are placed. The first official count in 1979 recorded about 8,000 caravans in England, but this rose to over 15,000 in 2005, of which approximately 26 per cent were on unauthorised sites (Greenfields and Home 2006). The figure of 13,000 caravans recorded in the 1990s was considered to represent about 10,000 families (Green 1991, Halfacree 1996) and emerging evidence from on-going Gypsy Traveller Accommodation Assessments indicates that the calculation of 1.3–1.5 caravans per family is still accurate, although with many households consisting of four or five persons it may be more reflective of family size to refer to the fact that perhaps 40–50,000 Gypsies and Travellers are currently residing in caravans (Greenfields and Home 2006).

England currently has about 300 council sites, providing in the region of 5,000 pitches. Ninety-five per cent of these pitches are classed as residential (that is for 'long-term' use) and there is a generally recognised trend towards long stay and more settled habits (a number of respondents interviewed for needs assessments and planning appeals assert that 'the Traveller way of life is dying'), rather than the provision of transit sites. However, the distinction that is sometimes made, between 'settled' Gypsies needing residential pitches, and those resorting to an area for a short period and so apparently needing only transit accommodation, is hard to maintain in practice as many families travel around a cluster of counties or districts, and may be classified everywhere as 'passing through' (Gypsies and Travellers were recorded as passing through 91 per cent of local authorities in the 2006 Commission for Racial Equality research), but want and need a settled base, which could be in any of the areas where they travel. Although, legal definitions mean that a decision to settle and cease the nomadic habit of life may lead to individuals forfeiting

Gypsy status and that central government policy guidance acknowledges that sites might be for 'long-stay use' (Circular 1/94), nowhere in the law or central government guidance is it stated that there is a policy of encouraging gypsies to settle down.

There is abundant evidence that there is a shortage of sites for Gypsy families (Niner 2004, Drakakis-Smith and Mason 2001) and ironically, given the popular conception of 'Gypsies' as landless wanderers, they have increasingly turned to 'private' land ownership in order to provide themselves with sites. Private sites, owned and maintained by traditional Travellers, now accommodate about a third of all caravans, but the decrease in local authority provision (since the statutory duty on local authorities to provide sites for 'Gypsies' was repealed by the Criminal Justice and Public Order Act 1994) has not been compensated for by this slight increase in private provision. New private sites can only be achieved through having the cash to purchase land (and an owner willing to sell), as well as the grant of planning permission, with a wide degree of discretion afforded to the local authority within a framework of central government policy. Gypsies have gradually, and only reluctantly, been accorded special policy consideration in the 'plan-led' planning system and most local authorities now have specific criterion-based planning policies for them, although the system allows for wide variations and inconsistencies of approach. The planning system has to balance a concern with protecting the rural character of the countryside against the accommodation needs of a small minority group, and operates on a case-by-case basis. Research indicates that councils approve as few as 5 per cent of planning applications for private Gypsy sites, with about 30–35 per cent subsequently succeeding on appeal (FFT 1996, Williams 1999). University of Birmingham research recently estimated that the overall need for caravan pitches in England is for 1,000–2,000 more residential, and 2,000–2,500 more transit or stopping places (Niner 2003).

Access to land (obtaining planning permission for a 'Gypsy Site' or obtaining a pitch on a local authority or private licensed site) is of paramount importance for Travellers of *all* ethnicities and cultures, but in practical terms the situation for New Travellers is even harder than for other groups. Although, technically, under the 'nomadism' clause (inserted into the Caravan Sites Act 1968 and subsequently imported into planning law and the Criminal Justice and Public Order Act 1994) New Travellers can be 'legal gipsies', the likelihood of a planning inspector or owner of a private site allowing 'non-ethnic' Travellers the opportunity to obtain a pitch or a site licence remains extremely slim. When pitches become available on private sites, our experience is that, given the pressure on accommodation and the demographics of the traditional Traveller populations (early marriage leading to the formation of new family units), any available pitch tends to be offered to immediate relatives of the site owners. (Indeed site owners may ask a more distant relative, or unrelated Traveller, to vacate a site when a son or daughter marries and requires a pitch, an understandable, socially acceptable behaviour among traditional Travellers, given the importance of kin-groups.)

## A gendered perspective

Among the Romany population in particular, when land has been bought to provide a family base, it is generally registered in the woman's name regardless of which partner to a marriage (or their extended family members) have paid the purchase price. Although women may not be engaged in waged employment and therefore able to acquire wealth through those means, inheritance from parents is equal for both genders, ensuring that women may retain financial independence from their spouse. Accordingly, if property is bought to provide a base for ageing parents, who with increasing infirmity are unable to withstand the rigours of roadside life on a year-round basis, daughters as well as sons will usually contribute equally to the cost of buying land and applying for planning permission.

It may seem surprising that women will generally own the family land, given that it is men who will usually undertake negotiations in the public arena in their role as 'head' of the household. Land ownership has developed among Traveller communities largely over the past 30–50 years and has been accelerated with the turn towards private land use driven by recent legislation. One explanation for an emerging pattern of women as landowners is that women's status and authority in the arena of the 'homespace', entitles them to be recognised in the *gorje* legal context as responsible for owning the family land. Further, 'dealing with paperwork' is often a female responsibility (Okely 1983). More prosaically, it has also been suggested to us by a leading member of a Romany community that women's landholding can represent either a cautious approach to ensuring that essential assets such as tools, vehicles and land are owned by separate individuals (in case of such issues as debt) or a practical response to the problems posed by limited literacy (Levinson and Sparkes 2003). One outcome is that while formerly having only a minor role in case law on Gypsies, as will be discussed later in this chapter, women have been the named protagonists in recent high-profile court cases.

## 'Bricks and mortar'

Overwhelmingly, Traveller cultures, their home and family life are now shaped less by the communities' own preferences, and more by their responses to the legal constraints imposed by law and state (despite the strength of cultural tradition, home and family life). The shortage of legal sites and the criminalisation of 'unauthorised encampment' since the 1994 Act, has forced many Gypsies to overcome their aversion to 'bricks and mortar accommodation', thereby striking at the heart of traditional Traveller culture. While some traditional Travellers have willingly exchanged the hardship and inconvenience of roadside life for running water and plentiful heating, many living in houses are distressed at the constraints imposed by such an alien way of living, with the loss of community ties, shared values, physical isolation and loneliness (Thomas and Campbell 1992, Davis and Hoult 2000, Kenrick and Clark 1999).

Travellers often associate bricks and mortar with negative experiences: going into hospital (a place to be avoided, where people go to die and 'mochadi' things occur) (DGLG 2003), or attending at council offices, police stations, or other hostile places of encounters with officialdom. Gypsies and Travellers say that houses 'sound' unnervingly different from trailers, with heating pipes banging, or creaking doors and floorboards. Even becoming used to negotiating stairs, or living on an upper floor after a lifetime spent near to the ground and hearing trees move or people passing within a few feet of sleeping quarters can prove traumatic. Further, the lay-out of the built home may make it difficult to maintain the traditions and practices of cleanliness. For women the pressures in such an environment can be particularly traumatic. Financial issues too, are a frequent source of distress, as credit needs to be negotiated for bills which need to be met on a regular quarterly or monthly basis, instead of paying for a gas bottle and filling up with fuel when needed. Indeed for families with limited literacy the extent of the bureaucracy involved in obtaining, moving into and retaining a property, can prove astonishing and alarming. Not only are these experiences strange, but the sense of cultural isolation and 'differentness' from neighbours can be frightening (O'Dwyer 1997). Contacts with neighbours may often be fraught with difficulties, whether because of simple culture clashes (for example, over ownership of dogs or trailers parked by a house), or young Travellers encountering drugs or racism. Inevitably the burden of supporting the family through potentially traumatic moves into housing falls primarily on the woman of the household, who in herself may be experiencing depression as a result of the unwanted 'settlement'. While Travellers and Gypsies tend to marry for life, separation occurring only rarely, we are aware anecdotally that the pressure of moving into accommodation has in some cases led to family breakdown.

Unsurprisingly many Travellers fail to remain in 'bricks and mortar' accommodation. Davies (1987) found, in the period 1981–5, that around 20 per cent of Traveller families in housed accommodation were unable to settle and soon returned to their traditional way of life. Men frequently say that 'it is the women who insist we go back on the road', while women refer in strong terms to a determination not to lose their culture, community or freedom to live a traditional lifestyle, despite the fact that they experience deeply felt anxiety at the prospect of the family attempting to access educational and medical facilities while living on the roadside. The courts have also, belatedly, recognised the risk of psychological damage caused by forced settlement. In *Clarke v Secretary of State for the Environment, Transport and the Regions and Tunbridge Wells Borough Council* [2001] EWHC 800 Admin a Traveller who had been refused planning permission for a Gypsy site on the grounds that he had been offered conventional housing as statutorily homeless, had his 'deep cultural aversion to bricks and mortar accommodation' upheld as a valid cultural reason to refuse the local authority's offer of housing.

## A settled nomad?

Conventional accommodation is usually a 'last resort' for nomadic people, so why do families decide to 'settle' – either into housing or (by preference) onto a pitch at an authorised site? Indeed the very notion of settlement and pressure to settle is a vexed trope in Gypsy discourse, for how can a nomadic person 'settle'? Some families have been forced to leave a licensed site on marriage, because planning restrictions or lack of available plots on local authority facilities, means that they cannot live among their kin-group. Other families have remained nomadic, perhaps through choice, or simply because (perhaps due to lack of money, family contacts, or being evicted too rapidly to ever reach the top of a lengthy waiting list) they have never been able to access a licensed pitch. The Criminal Justice and Public Order Act 1994 has led to a situation where Travellers can be criminalised for stopping at unauthorised locations, and families often have to engage in a game of 'cat and mouse' with local authorities who force them to move on repeatedly, until at last they leave the area or cross the local authority border. However, it is not merely the constant stress of eviction, and being unable to plan for the future as a result of not knowing how long they can stop prior to being moved on, which leads Travellers to seek to obtain a licensed pitch. Despite the best efforts of Travellers themselves, the travelling way of life is not sympathetic to disability, or vulnerability from old age or other cause.

In modern society a settled address is increasingly important for receiving post and obtaining access to medical, educational and welfare services; researchers (Cornwell 1984, Feder 1989, Hawes 1997, Van Cleemput 2000) have found that unsited Travellers experience inequality in matters such as registering with a GP, obtaining hospital appointments and contact with health services, with obvious health implications. For Travellers without a stable site, the risk of ill health exists from cradle to grave. Miscarriage, infant and perinatal death rates are inflated among Traveller communities (Parry *et al.* 2004), and Beach (1999) recorded greater numbers of child accident and injury rates associated with instability of site and lack of access to appropriate health care.

It was concerns with health issues and access to medical treatment which contributed to the growth of a Women's Movement among Gypsies in the late 1970s (Acton *et al.* 1997) and in terms of Gypsy and Traveller women's engagement with mainstream agencies (including the legal system), as a direct result of the inequalities experienced by their communities, there is now something of an upsurge in female militancy and an increased awareness of their power as protagonists in emerging social change.

Access to education is also problematic for many un- (or insecurely) sited families, and many Travellers, especially women, are concerned about how best to equip their children for dealing with an increasingly bureaucratised and literate society. Traveller children are seriously disadvantaged in the education system (Save the Children Fund 2001, OFSTED 1996, Dept of Education and Science 1985) and national figures from the Department for Education indicate only 60 per cent attendance rate in schools for Traveller children, although for secondary age children this is thought to be nearer 20 per cent or less (OFSTED 1996, 1999, Waterson 1997). The Parekh Report (2000) noted the 'generally low educational attainment' of Gypsy/Traveller children who move from school to school according to patterns of seasonal mobility and eviction patterns and Webster (1995) found a strong correlation between access to education facilities and the eviction policies of local authorities: 77 per cent of children of Traveller families on relatively stable sites attended school regularly, but for families subject to evictions, only 15 per cent had school places.

Research evidence suggests that Traveller mothers on long-term sites are likely to undertake adult education classes if they are in a supportive environment (for example, living among other Travellers who value education) and their children are retaining continuity of education. Kendall (1997: 86) notes that '[children's] attendance at school may prompt non-literate parents, particularly women, to learn to read in order to help their children's learning and because they feel embarrassed that they have to rely on their children to read e.g. food labels in shops'.

All these factors make it is unsurprising that women Travellers are increasingly acknowledging the necessity of obtaining a 'settled' site despite (or perhaps because of) Travellers' extended family patterns, responsibility for obtaining schooling for children and ensuring care for the sick and elderly. This places women under particular pressure to become settled, and both engage with (and at times resist) assimilation into the dominant society. The somewhat ambivalent feelings that women may have about settling, particularly in conventional housing, as well as the pressures felt by them to settle, have been frequently expressed to the authors of this chapter.

## Changing gender roles?

Levinson and Sparkes (2003: 597–9) have ambivalent views as to the extent to which gender relations amongst Gypsies have changed in the context of an increasingly sedentary lifestyle and to the meaning which can be ascribed to women's apparent adoption of hitherto male public roles. Their research upon Gypsy masculinities amongst male children shuttling between the contrasting value systems of home and school, focused on the male perspective and they suggest that 'changing economic circumstances in the past 50 years have augmented the male power base within the family' (Levinson and Sparkes 2003: 597). Despite noting a defensiveness of their traditional masculinities by Gypsy men in the face of outside pressures, Levinson and Sparkes (2003: 598) also acknowledge that 'forces, both internal and external, are leading to gradual compromises and the growth of more radical ideas'. They suggest that too much emphasis should not be put upon apparent shifts in how 'gender is done' in Gypsy communities, but at the same time changes in women's responsibilities should not be underestimated. This includes women's increasing participation as land owners and legal protagonists, although again the social meaning that can be ascribed to this seemingly greater intervention into the public, as suggested earlier, is fraught with ambiguity and may be little more than a convenient and practical response by Gypsy communities to external forces.

## Exclusion through judge-made law

Since 1984 judicial attention has repeatedly turned to the statutory definition of 'persons of nomadic habit of life, whatever their race of origin' in relation to planning applications and judicial interpretation has imposed an increasingly restrictive reading of the definition making it harder for Traveller families to set up legal sites. Challenges to decisions have utilised human rights law (Art 8 of the European Convention on Human Rights and Fundamental Freedoms: the 'right to family life'), but have enjoyed little success.

The exclusion of an ethnic component from the statutory definition has not prevented the occasional intrusion of ethnic or racial arguments in case law, and the continuing demand from the Romany community for recognition of their ethnic status. Various resolutions of European government bodies have indicated support for the Gypsy way of life, including the 'special responsibility' of local and regional authorities towards Rom/Gypsies for accommodation and the promotion of their culture (Danbakli 1994). The European Court of Human Rights, while determining that the case of *Linda Porter v United Kingdom* (2001) 10 BHRC 48 was inadmissible, did concede that 'the vulnerable position of Gypsies as a minority means that some special consideration should be given to their needs and their different lifestyle both in the relevant regulatory planning framework and in arriving at the decisions in particular cases'. New Travellers have effectively been excluded from the definition in *R v South Hams District Council ex p Gibb* [1993] 3 WLR 115, which added a further employment test, by redefining Gypsies as: 'persons who wandered or travelled for the purpose of making or seeking their livelihood, and did not include persons who moved from place to place without any connection between their movement and their means of livelihood'. However, the court also took the view that whether a person was nomadic or not was a matter of fact and degree, depending upon the circumstances of the case, and that a factor to be taken into account was the level of connection or links between the group of Travellers and other nomadic groups.

The growing number of applications for private sites raised the possibility that a Gypsy could gain a valuable benefit from a public authority in the form of planning permission to live in the countryside, even in the Green Belt. The perception within the settled community that, in this regard, Gypsies have a 'privileged' position coupled with the accelerating price of land for housing, has meant that this benefit is deemed significant enough for local authorities to regularly challenge awards of planning permission. Eligibility has continued to be contested in the courts, whether by questioning whether the individual or individuals (often women) concerned qualify as nomadic people or questioning whether their nomadic lifestyle has been lost through settlement (as a consequence, for instance, of age, vulnerability or to permit children's attendance at school). Early, if not widely reported, examples include *R v Shropshire County Council ex p Bungay* [1990] 23 HLR 195 and *Horsham District Council v Secretary of State for the Environment ex p Giles* (1989) (unreported). In the latter case McCullough LJ set the tone: 'Clearly there can, and indeed must, come a time when as a matter of fact the nomadic habit of life has been lost. When it is lost the Gypsy is no longer a Gypsy for the purposes of [legislation]. He remains of course a Gypsy by descent, by culture and by tradition, but that is not the issue' (quoted in Goodman 2005).

Whether the nomadic way of life was merely in abeyance, and whether there was intent to resume it, was raised in *R v Shropshire CC ex p Bungay*, which found that a Gypsy family who had ceased travelling on grounds of age and ill health, could settle for long periods and yet still be held to retain their nomadic way of life. Nevertheless, in *Hearne v National Assembly of Wales, The Times*, November, 1999, the date when the decision was made on the relevant planning application or appeal became crucial, on the basis that the applicant could not rely on his former nomadic habit of life if he now intended to settle permanently on the land in question. In other words, his future intentions were a factor in establishing whether or not he was a nomad. Two years later, in *Chapman v United Kingdom* [2001] ECHR 43, Mrs Chapman having been refused planning permission to remain on Green Belt land, was held to retain her legal Gypsy status despite spending settled periods to permit her children to attend school regularly. However, the argument was developed, to the disadvantage of Gypsies, in *Wrexham County Borough Council v National Assembly of Wales, Michael Berry and Florence Berry*. Mr and Mrs Berry sought permission for a site for a caravan since they wanted to give up travelling in consequence of Mr Berry's poor health. The court acknowledged that a Gypsy may become too old or infirm to travel for work and that it would be 'inhuman pedantry' to regard him as no longer a Gypsy, but if they 'have retired from travelling for whatever reason, ill health, age or simply because they no longer wish to follow that way of life, they no longer have a nomadic habit of life'. They may recover such a way of life later, the test being whether they have 'an honest and realistically realizable intention of resuming traveling and, if they do, how soon and in what circumstances'.

In *O'Connor v Secretary of State for Transport, Local Government and The Regions and Bath and North East Somerset Council* [2002] EWHC 2649 Admin, Mrs O'Connor appealed the decision of a planning inspector to refuse planning permission and again her case hinged upon her Gypsy status in law. She had a long history of travelling, but sought to settle, at least in the medium term, because of her diabetes and other health problems, the special health needs of one of her children (who was deaf) and the educational needs of her other children. Four factors were identified in deciding whether the nomadic way of life had been surrendered: history, reasons for ceasing to travel, future intentions and attitude to living in a caravan rather than a house. Mrs O'Connor was deemed to still have a nomadic lifestyle: some recognition, perhaps, that a 'gypsy retired by age or ill health may still rove the countryside in his or her imagination, if no longer able to do so in practice' and 'a parent who has settled down for the sake of the children's education may also still rove, or intend to do so in the future at some indeterminate date' (Goodman 2005). However, Circular 1/94 requires 'very special circumstances' to justify overriding restrictive planning policies such as Green Belt and cases have turned on what would be sufficiently overriding, again to Gypsies' disadvantage. Two decisions by Sullivan J as to whether the educational needs of Gypsy children amount to 'very special circumstances' are revealing: *Doncaster Metropolitan Borough Council v Secretary of State for the Environment, Transport and the Regions* [2002] EWHC 808 (Admin) and *R (On the Application of Chelmsford Borough Council) v First Secretary of State* [2004] 2 P & CR 34. In the latter case where Mrs Draper sought planning permission for caravans for the benefit of her family including her husband, the judge confirmed that the mere fact that the children were settled into schools close to the relevant site did not amount to very special or exceptional circumstances to overcome Green Belt objections.

Human rights arguments on behalf of Gypsies, claiming possible violation of Art 8 of the European Convention on Human Rights have enjoyed only limited success. In the high-profile case of *Buckley v United Kingdom* [1996] 23 EHRR 101, the planning system was found to override Art 8 rights and that there was no breach of those rights for Mrs Buckley who had been refused planning permission for three caravans for herself and her family on land which she had purchased. *Chapman v United Kingdom* offered some assistance to Gypsies, finding that measures affecting the stationing of the caravan had an impact upon Mrs Chapman's 'ability to maintain her identity as a Gypsy and to lead her private and family life in accordance with that tradition'. Finally, in *Connors v United Kingdom* [2004] ECHR 223 the eviction of a family from a council site, contributing to the break up of the marriage, interruptions to the children's education and other hardships, including the exacerbation of ill health, was held to be a breach of Art 8 rights, with insufficient procedural protection existing for a category of people, especially having regard to the positive obligation placed on states to facilitate the Gypsy way of life. The local authority in that case was found to have failed to establish a proper justification for a serious interference with Article 8 rights, when these were not justified by any pressing social need.

## Conclusion

Gypsies and Travellers find their way of life caught within a bureaucratic and legal net, in which their cultures are fashioned not by individual or community choices but by legislative constraints and an accumulation of case law which is generally hostile towards them. The case law has involved a forensic deconstruction of the statutory definition, each time seeming to add a new hurdle to be overcome for anyone wishing to be recognised as a Gypsy and receive the few benefits this status gives them in relation to planning law. The frustration felt by 'pro-gypsy' elements at this negative development has been described as: 'tortuous intellectual wrangling to which the state and the courts have had to resort in their pursuit of pointless categorising' (Morris and Clements 1999: 11). The overall effect is that it is increasingly difficult for Gypsies to find land on which they can legally encamp. A Gypsy who settles ceases to be a 'Gypsy', unless she can show that her 'nomadic habit of life' is only temporarily in abeyance and thus factors such as old age, illness, education of her children and other family responsibilities, do not receive significant consideration in allowing for the legally permitted change from 'roving' to 'roving in the mind'.

Pitches on council sites are reducing in number, yet it is very difficult to get permission for private sites because of opposition from local planning authorities (often supported by local people who do not wish to encourage a 'Gypsy' presence, FFT 1996). Government policy recognises that Gypsies and Travellers need somewhere to live, but in practice, if they intend long-stay 'settled' accommodation on land which they own, they risk forfeiting their 'Gypsy' status and (presumably) being forced back on the road, to a way of life which is increasingly difficult to lead and now criminalised (Clark and Greenfields 2006). Local authorities are increasingly willing to contest Gypsy status at planning appeals and subsequently by legal challenge, and judges have imposed further tests upon the statutory definition.

For Gypsy and traditional Traveller women caught up in the paradox of the settled nomad, it is increasingly them, both as landowners and defenders of the home space, who are representing their families in attempts to cut a way through the tortuous legalistic net. In this, they act not only as the landowners, and therefore as the protagonists in legal proceedings, but as the bearers and protectors of cultural traditions: It is they who have been at the forefront of negotiating a new *modus vivendi* with the settled world and finding patterns of resistance. However, from the cases, it is clear that the settled world, a world still dominated by masculinist values, makes it all too difficult for those factors which are important to them to be fully recognised in case law.

From a feminist perspective it is not easy to assess this enhanced role for women coming from traditional Traveller families in negotiating legal definitions and spatialities: On the one hand, for some women, the move into a more overtly public space may be evidence of a shift in power relations and subtle changes in value systems concerning gender. On the other hand, for other women, their changed roles may be simply a response to the settled communities marked hostility to Gypsies and particularly Gypsy masculinities, adopting a public façade behind which traditional values, including the orthodox gender divide and relations remain firmly intact and protected. Either way, women are increasingly bearing new responsibilities and the extent to which this will change gender roles within their community is moot. What might be more important for feminists to consider is not so much the impact on gender within these communities, but rather the impossibility the socio-legal order displays in understanding and accepting forms of living which do not conform to a settled existence: and this may be particularly threatening when it brings together the tropes of nomadic life with a wish to purse the vestiges of this lifestyle on private property, even when that property is owned by those who wish to pursue their own lifestyle. Being 'encouraged' to settle means, in practice, accepting the unpalatable choice of 'bricks and mortar' or accepting marginalisation back on the road and the constant fear of being evicted from unauthorised sites. A 'liminal' existence on the borders of society seems to be threatening to the social ordering required by modern state practices as well as the mores of the settled 'insiders'. To insist upon conformity not only threatens the culture of Travellers and places a particular burden upon their women, it also speaks of a socio-legal ideology which is sustained by, and sustains, rigid boundaries between 'inside' and 'outside': An ideology which has long been the object of feminist critique and to which, it is hoped, the plight of Travellers can now be added as both further data and, conversely, to bring to bear a critique to further expose the paradox of the settled nomad.

**Note**: Since the above was written, central government policy has been changed with new policy guidance issued in February 2006 (Circular 1/2006 *Planning for Gypsy and Traveller Sites*, ODPM). Local authorities now have to undertake statutory local assessments of the accommodation needs of Gypsies and Travellers. At the time of writing an additional consultation is under way to consider whether ethnic Gypsies and Travellers should continue to retain their 'gypsy status' if they have ceased travelling 'on grounds only of their own or their family's or dependants' educational or health needs or old age have ceased to travel temporarily or permanently' (*Definition of the term 'gypsies and Travellers' for the purposes of the Housing Act 2004*; ODPM: http: //www.communities.gov.uk/pub/401/Definitionofthetermgypsiesand travellersforthepurposesoftheHousingAct2004PDF294Kb_id1163401.pdf). It remains to be seen whether the new measures will improve the situation.

Chapter 8

# 'Land doesn't come from your mother, she didn't make it with her hands'

## Challenging matriliny in Papua New Guinea

*Melissa Demian*

### Introduction

In November of 1969, A$50,000 was paid by the Australian colonial administration to a number of 'landowners' in the Suau census division of Milne Bay District (now Province), Papua New Guinea, in exchange for timber extraction rights. The government patrol officer at the time, one John Balderson, noted in his annual report that there was some dissatisfaction amongst 'people belonging to one of the Clans holding full rights over the timber in question, but residing in another village at the time of purchase, thereby receiving no monetary compensation' (Balderson 1970: 9). He also remarked that one plantation owner[1] at the village of Maliawate expressed concern that he wouldn't be able to log because the 'real' owners of the land in question hadn't been paid (1970: 10). However, Balderson wrote that 'Overall satisfaction with the sale was expressed nonetheless, and the impression gained was that the payees are now waiting patiently for the Government's second move to see if it is as silly as its first' (1970: 10).

Twelve years later, in a report written as a result of a social feasibility study for the introduction of oil palm to the province, the anthropologist Michael Young noted that land tenure among the peoples of the southern mainland was remarkably 'insecure' in comparison with the island peoples with whom he had the most experience (Young 1981: 15). By 'insecurity' he meant the flexibility with which land could be transmitted. Although the default is inheritance through the matriline, several mechanisms exist for obtaining use-rights and even 'permanent' transferral of land ownership through the father, or more precisely, from the mother's matrilineage to the father's. As one of his informants told him, 'We have *too many* ways of getting land' (1981: 15, emphasis in original). Young noted that the issue was not simply one of matrilineal versus patrilineal inheritance, but also one of mytho-historical relationships to the land. The Goodenough Islanders with whom he had worked before could be claimed to have a more 'secure' or 'stable' system of land tenure not only because patriliny and virilocality meant that the same lineage remained on the same land for generation after generation, but because each patrilineage could claim its origin in a cave opening on that land. Origin accounts among mainland peoples such as Suau can be far more ambiguous, as I will illustrate.

When I first went to work in the area in 1996, I had been invited by a local activist and sometime politician named Matilda Pilacapio, who told me on several occasions that my job would be to record 'the matrilineal kinship'.[2] Her use of this phrase was clearly a shorthand reference to something more complex, and in true Papua New Guinean fashion she left it to me to work out what it was. My eventual conclusion was that she perceived Suau matriliny to be under threat, particularly as it pertained to the transmission of land rights. The threat in this case was the possibility of land being claimed through patrilateral ties, and perhaps even legally registered as such, although the cost of hiring a surveyor and filing a legal claim would have been prohibitive to most people on the Suau Coast. Her concerns, as I ultimately learned, were inflated but not baseless. The Suau Coast had been heavily missionised in the late nineteenth and early twentieth centuries, and was the site of numerous Australian-owned rubber and copra plantations to which people came from all over the region to work. Suau-speakers and their hinterland neighbours[3] were thus exposed early and intensively not only to the property regimes of Europeans, but to those of people from non-matrilineal societies. While it could be argued that the former was more vigorously 'imposed' on Suau, the impact of the latter could not be discounted, if only for the way in which it enabled them to imagine how outsiders might perceive them, and in what terms they might or might not continue to differentiate themselves from those outsiders.

Suau belong to a matrilineal minority within the panoply of systems by which Papua New Guinean societies reckon descent and inheritance.[4] Matriliny tends to be found among coastal and island peoples speaking Austronesian languages, while the majority of non-Austronesian language speakers on the mainland (and on some islands) reckon inheritance along patrilineal or cognatic lines.[5] The culture area to which Suau belongs, the Massim, is, with two known exceptions, entirely matrilineal. Along with matriliny, Massim societies are anthropologically renowned for their elaborate mortuary sequences and their extensive networks for the exchange of prestigious wealth items as well as trade in everyday goods and consumables. But underscoring discussions of these and other phenomena is the notion that matriliny provides the 'blueprint' for a particular configuration of relations between men and women in the Massim, and the forms those relations are likely to take. In the latter half of the twentieth century, anthropologists were concerned to elaborate the ways in which matriliny contributed to the political and economic influence of women in Massim societies (Weiner 1976, Kahn 1986, Lepowsky 1993). Not unreasonably, all of these studies took as their object of analysis women's control over particular material forms, from food to valuables to land. For while it had to a certain extent been recognised all along that Massim women enjoyed a more active role in the 'public sphere' than did women in most other Papua New Guinean societies, it was not until the dual emergence of feminist and Marxist thought in anthropology that matriliny was construed as playing a significant role in women's lives outside of their obligation to reproduce the lineage and their status as future ancestresses through whom property and identity would flow.

In fact, until the 1970s, the focus had for the most part been on the implications of matriliny for men. Matriliny appeared to present a peculiarly difficult situation for fathers, who were assumed to be torn between the interests of their children and those of their sisters' children, that is, their heirs (Richards 1950: 246). Later studies, notably those from Melanesia, suggested that fathers in matrilineal societies are not as conflicted about their obligations as previously accepted (Clay 1977, Battaglia 1985, Bolyanatz 1996, Sykes 2001). The imperatives of reciprocity through which fathers are compensated for their fathering work, provisions for particular property forms that fathers can transmit to their own children, and new obligations to the nation-state, all contribute to a picture of relationships in which fathers can quite comfortably distribute resources of various kinds among their children and their sisters' children. Too, the assumption that fathers invariably prefer to devolve property to their own children, and are only prevented from doing so by the demands of matriliny, has been called into question (Levine 1987), and the idea has even come full circle to meet its mirror image. Matriliny has now been conceived as promoting solidarity between lineages, rather than fission within them, by means of the 'dual role played by men: on the one hand, father and husband, on the other hand, mother's brother and brother' (Petersen 1982: 138). Far from the splitting or diluting of men's kin identity imagined in the 1950s, their identity is now thought to be doubled by the provisions of matriliny. Key to both images, of course, is the notion that kinship can be added or subtracted by the 'rules' of unilineal descent. With the addition or subtraction of kin relations is implied the addition or subtraction of property relations.

In the 1960s, an apparently new problem emerged: matriliny appeared to be on the verge of dissolution in the face of capitalism's inexorable advent (Gough 1961). If, as the theory went, matriliny was associated with 'abundance and unrestricted access to resources' while capitalism was associated with 'scarcity and restricted access to resources' (Poewe 1980: 342), then matriliny stood no chance of survival. Later assessments of the death-of-matriliny announcements noted that they were based on the modernisation theory prevalent at the time (Colson 1980: 359) which proceeded from the assumption, on the one hand, that capitalism would sweep all before it and, on the other hand, that it would reproduce the social forms which had produced it, namely, private property and patrilineal inheritance. Underpinning the second assumption was in turn the evolutionist sensibilities of Victorian anthropology, to which the association between matriliny and the absence of private property can be traced. For Lewis Henry Morgan (and those influenced by him, most notably Engels), both kinship and resources were imagined to undergo incremental 'enclosures' progressing from a state of 'primitive promiscuity' to polygamous matriliny and finally to monogamous patriliny, with the final stage accompanied by full-blown private property regimes (McKinnon 2001). The final two social and economic forms brought each other about because: 'In contrast to the maternal relation, which was thought to generate a natural form of social relation in the matrilineal gens (but one whose maternal communalism was inherently antithetical to ideas of individual property), the paternal relation was seen as incapable of generating any social form *until property was added to it*' (2001: 284, emphasis in original). A century after Morgan, social theorists still assumed that private property and matriliny were fundamentally incompatible; although that belief has been tempered by abundant evidence to the contrary, it still lurks behind the concerns of those who would 'preserve' matriliny from the depredations of capitalism.

So while reports of matriliny's demise have been greatly exaggerated, I was initially obliged, out of the absence of any ethnographic knowledge about the people with whom I would be working, to confront the problem as Matilda Pilacapio presented it to me in her coded manner. If people could now claim land through their fathers, what future was there for matrilineal kinship reckoning, and by implication, for the political and economic influence historically wielded by women in this quintessentially matrilineal corner of Papua New Guinea? My concern in this chapter is therefore twofold. The first is to question whether matriliny is most accurately defined as a rule of inheritance in Suau conceptualisations of it. The second is to ask whether, in the event that Suau land claims become as 'chaotic' as some predict they will, matriliny is itself actually under threat. The first concern obviously delineates the second.

## Land, movement and precedence

> Our *ulutubu* (matrilineage) came from Ware Island. We came from Ware and later went to Suau. At Suau there is a little village called Gadawiwi. There at Gadawiwi we lived. That was our grandparents, our *ulutubu*. At Gadawiwi they lived until . . . they went to Pwa'iu. They went to Pwa'iu and then they went to Saga'afo and lived there. At Saga'afo they lived until they had children. There was a big death [epidemic?] there. Finally all the people at Saga'afo died, with one left who came up to Buhutu. At Buhutu that person lived, got married, and had one girl child. There was one girl child, and it went until that woman herself had a child. She also had one girl child. After that one girl child she gave birth again: a boy . . . They lived until they had another boy. They had another child. Giuwede. They had Giuwede. Then they had another, Waileya. Then they wanted to stay together, and they came down to the foot of Monailo River . . . They built

> a house and time passed while they lived there. Then they gave birth to Laukapore. After that they also gave birth to me. They bore Tauyabuna. There we lived and then later we lived at what's-it-called. At Puyuwa. Another hamlet called Puyuwa. There we lived until we lived at Daiyela. Later we lived at what's-it-called. Boboulo, a place called Boboulo. We lived at Boboulo until Misibibi came and gathered us together. The government. Misibibi came and gathered us together, in the mountains where we were all living at the time. We came here to Bwabwatiti. At Bwabwatiti we stayed together.
>
> (Tauyabuna, ~70, recounting the history of his *ulutubu*)

If you ask a person on the Suau Coast to tell you about his or her lineage, you will be regaled with a catalogue of places and people in the order that they were born. Tauyabuna's narrative shifts seamlessly between a progression from place to place and from sibling to sibling, each 'movement' between locations and persons denoting the passage of time. His own birth is embedded in a sequence of births and deaths of which the flow of time from past to present is constituted. As the oldest living member of his lineage, to whom younger members could come for accounts like the one I have excerpted, he was more than entitled to locate himself as an ancestor-to-be in his telling. The other siblings named in the history were all dead.[6] The names of ancestors and the names of abandoned hamlets form a constellation of reference-points from which people can take their spatiotemporal bearings. As Küchler writes of New Ireland: 'In the absence of any emphasis on genealogy, the history of social relations is embedded in the process of mapping. Mapping is the product of place transmission which, together with the transmission of personal names and skills, effects the virtual reconstitution of social relations over time' (Küchler 1993: 96). Places and deceased people become nearly interchangeable in this conceptualisation, as they serve the same purpose of orienting the present generation in the history of its lineages.

What characterises all Suau lineage histories is that they are narratives of movement across the land (and sometimes the sea, as in Tauyabuna's history); the names of lineages are themselves place names, typically an 'earliest known address' for an apical ancestress. Lineages moved as a consequence of marriage, adoption, exile, kidnapping, warfare, and in the twentieth century, government intervention. The person identified as 'Misibibi' in Tauyabuna's narrative was Mr Vivian, a Resident Magistrate of the Australian administration in the 1920s, who is credited with having relocated entire lineages from the hinterland to the coast in order to render them more accessible to government patrols. This policy probably saw the relocation of the most people at any one time in Suau history, and gave rise to the emergence of villages which had not previously existed or had only existed as hamlets occupied by members of a single lineage. Land disputes in such villages are, needless to say, endemic. But the government relocations of the early twentieth century were duly incorporated into the histories of the relocated lineages, a new kind of 'road' along which lineages might travel.[7] There can be no doubt that the relocations exacerbated the already transient nature of Suau land claims, but they did not generate it. Mobility as a component of lineage identity is a product of the combination of matriliny and virilocality. It is granted, unsurprisingly, a distinctive moral value.

Stationary and mobile states mark particular phases in the lives of Suau people, and the movement of lineages may ultimately be affected by one of these phases. The elaboration of 'mobility ideology' on an individual level may be seen as reflective of movement through and claiming of land by lineages. Three elements of varying strictness: matriliny (non-negotiable), exogamy (often violated at clan level but never at that of lineage), and virilocality (normative but flexible), combine to produce highly mobile lineage populations which nonetheless place a heavy emphasis on identification with specific places. This is not as paradoxical as it might seem, although it does necessitate an ideological acknowledgement of principles of both rootedness and travel. These typically Austronesian concerns with origins and precedence (Fox and Sather 1996) are elaborated further at the level of birth order. Firstborn children (*taubaguna*, 'leader'), whether male or female, are understood to be the 'bosses' or stewards of their junior siblings (*taumulita*, 'follower'), requiring particular respect from the junior siblings and their spouses. Married couples address each other by the names of their respective hamlets or lineages until the birth of their first child, after which they practise teknonymy using the name of this child. Firstborn children are often also the holders of lineage origin stories. In the event of the death of a firstborn sibling, authority transfers to the second-eldest, and so on down the 'line' of birth order. Sibling groups are thus metaphorically conceived as travelling single-file, which is the preferred spatial arrangement for people journeying from one place to another. Generations are also conceived in this way, as a woman might speak of her ancestors as 'the women behind me' and her descendents as 'the women in front of me'.

The special status of firstborn children is also condensed in the unique relationship they have with their fathers, to whom they are said to 'belong'.[8] This relationship contains as much potential for the mobility of a lineage as does virilocality, for in both cases the land available for inheritance or usufruct is shifted from one location to another. A firstborn's 'belongingness' can, in certain cases, be expressed as an option to inherit land from the father's matrilineage rather than the mother's. The option is not always invoked, but remains as a latent relationship between a father and his firstborn child. It may be invoked if a firstborn son has no sisters, if a firstborn daughter prefers to stay on land belonging to her father's lineage rather than her mother's, or for other circumstantial and political reasons. The definition of this type of inheritance is not universally agreed upon, and a firstborn-rule land claim may be overridden by someone claiming the same land through a female ancestor. But in this respect, a firstborn child can truly be said to 'lead' his or her siblings to a new home, should the option of inheritance from the father's matrilineage be exercised. It also creates additional tensions in a system of land tenure which is already laden with contingencies. The burden of firstborn children is to embody both principles of rootedness, in that they are usually the holders of lineage origin knowledge and authority over the disposal of their land; and mobility, in that they may or may not ultimately occupy and work this land. In the case of a firstborn woman, the issue is compounded by the fact that she may potentially claim identification with land belonging to her own lineage, her father's lineage, her husband's lineage, or any or all of these at different stages in her life! Firstborns are *par excellence* the creators of new 'roads' for their lineage to traverse, but each time a lineage moves, a renegotiation of old and new relationships must take place in order for the land on which the lineage resides to belong to that lineage.

## What kind of landowner?

I refer to 'belonging' rather than 'ownership' throughout this chapter for a reason. I wish to maintain a distinction between the kind of relationship Suau people have historically had with land, and that implied by ownership, that is, the fee simple estate. Eighty-five per cent of land in Papua New Guinea is still held under customary tenure, which includes all but very small portions of the Suau Coast. As the Australian administration learned, and as oil palm and timber companies may yet learn, Suau land tenure is remarkably hard to pin down in such a way that 'landowning' individuals, or corporate groups acting as if they were individuals, may be negotiated with. Or rather, individuals claiming to be 'landowners' may readily be found, but it is guaranteed that at some point in the future their claim will be contested, either by lineages claiming to be the true owners of the land or by a member of that person's own lineage claiming to be the true 'boss' of the land.

'Boss' is in fact the preferred gloss offered by English-speaking Suau for their word *tanuwaga*. A *tanuwaga* is an elder member of a lineage who is resident on that lineage's land and, crucially, knows the lineage history including the means by which they came into stewardship of the land.[9] A *tanuwaga* cannot order the members of his or her lineage to dispose of resources in a particular way, but can only cajole and persuade, either by means of meetings with individual lineage members or by mustering the entire lineage to confer together. The status of a *tanuwaga* is not even entirely secure if there are several senior members of the lineage who know the relevant history; sometimes the title is shared peaceably between them, and sometimes it is acrimoniously contested, particularly if there arises dissent in the lineage over how land is to be used. But whatever a *tanuwaga* is, he or she is not a landowner in the sense of a person with absolute and exclusive authority to dispose of a piece of land or its resources and reap their benefits. This ethnographic fact, along with the combination of matriliny and virilocality described above, makes for difficult negotiations with companies desirous of making a one-time deal with 'owners' of land who are acting in a corporate capacity. However many 'owners' may appear on the day of the contract signing, several dozen more are bound to appear in the following months and years, indignant that they have not been consulted or compensated.

Suau are themselves trying to come up with a solution to this problem. That they, or at least those who have had some education or other exposure to Euro-American property regimes, regard it as a problem was evident at a meeting I attended in December of 1999, in the village of Saga'aho. Several men in their thirties or forties, all educated to some degree, were convening a series of meetings to discuss the possibility of forming a company called 'Saeleu', a contraction of the names Duiduisae and Duiduileu, which Suau use to designate the eastern and western halves of the coast, respectively. Saeleu would be a logging company, they said. However, they did not want to repeat the experiences of nearby villages which had had unfortunate dealings with Malaysian timber companies who paid below the market value for logs, built shoddy roads that washed away with the next rainy season, and left behind scorched grassland.[10] So the meeting organisers were travelling up and down the coast to try to get 'landowners' interested. 'Landowner' was an English word used liberally throughout the meeting; another was 'clan'. When I pressed one of the organisers to define what he meant by these terms, he said a 'landowner' was the oldest member of a 'clan', which is in turn, he said, 'one family, one *ulutubu*'.[11]

There seemed to be, in his account, some slippage between the notions of landowner and *tanuwaga. Tanuwaga* can just as easily be women or men, but there were three women present at the meeting, and roughly forty men. And the convenors sometimes appeared to use the terms 'landowner' and *tanuwaga* as if they meant different things. Clearly they do. *Tanuwaga* is a profoundly contingent office; one is only *tanuwaga* if one is appropriately placed at or near the top of the birth order, has been taught where the land boundaries are and the history of one's lineage, and is demonstrably committed to living on the land. Finally, it cannot be emphasised enough that *tanuwaga* do not own the land so much as they orchestrate its use. But 'landowner' carries the notion of fixity, of something that a person is, rather than something he or she superintends for the time being. Landownership is a crystallisation, a freeze-frame, of the ephemeral nature of *tanuwaga*-ship.

The convenors were also conversant in the language of 'the individual' versus 'the community', again employing the English words. Continuing with their negative examples of logging villages where all the money went into beer and other consumables, they stressed that they wanted a percentage of Saeleu's proceeds to go toward schools, churches and aid posts, with the remainder going to the 'landowner'. One of the convenors suggested, improbably, that those who withheld their 'community' percentage or wouldn't participate in the logging at all, couldn't send their children to the resulting schools. It was classic Suau coercive consensus-building: either we all do it, or nobody does it. Finally, they stressed their desire to pre-empt the land disputes that would invariably arise as a consequence of land bringing in money. They exhorted their audience to go home, hold meetings with their 'clans', and try to come to an agreement (*nua esega*, 'one mind') about the logging project so that discord wouldn't arise later. That they anticipated discord seemed both a reverberation of Balderson's wry remark in his 1970 report, and an acknowledgment that decisions to dispose of land in particular ways would without fail lead to contestations of who could rightfully claim to be the 'boss' of the land and its resources.

## Matriliny tested: a land dispute

Rural land disputes in Papua New Guinea are not handled by the legal system, not even the village courts whose mandate is the maintenance of 'law and order' using a combination of statutory and 'customary' law (Demian 2003). They are instead overseen by land mediators, knowledgeable and often elderly local persons who are conversant with the history of the families resident on the land within their jurisdiction and, perhaps more importantly, with the way that devolution of rights to land is handled by their own society. They do not adjudicate, but can only mediate between disputing parties. If a dispute brought to them proves itself to be intractable, they can recommend that it be taken to a district court. Such a solution is, however, beyond the means of most rural people, and it has been my experience that Suau people at least are keen to settle in the course of a land mediation hearing. Suau land mediations are almost festive occasions, months in the planning, accompanied by feasting and prayers, and hosted at no small expense. A single land mediation hearing may cover several disputes and continue for over twenty-four hours without interruption (alas for the exhausted anthropologist).

The quotation in the title of this chapter came from a man present at a land mediation hearing at Duhumodawa hamlet in November of 1999. This man, a political activist,[12] divided his time between the village and the provincial capital, Alotau. My first encounter with him in 1997 involved a meeting not unlike the one just described, in which he proposed a downstream processing operation through which people would be able to sell their timber, already sawn, to contractors in Papua New Guinea. I was struck by the fact that at his meeting, he insisted on the presence of women and their consent to the proposed plans (which never came to fruition), although he explained to me afterwards that this was to ensure no witches would sabotage the business out of jealousy. The remark he made two years later at the land mediation was, however, somewhat surprising to me, as he had previously taken an idealistic 'conducting business in accordance with traditional values' line. 'Tradition' apparently had its limits for him, however, and during the conclusion of the 1999 mediation hearing he exclaimed, 'Land doesn't come from your mother, she didn't make it with her hands. God made it in six days.' The land mediator presiding, a canny and eloquent old gentleman, appeared to agree with him by responding that indeed, God had made the world and distributed its lands amongst different people. But he then proceeded to spend the next dispute much as he had the previous one: in lecturing the youthful disputants about the ins and outs of matrilineal inheritance.

The mediator had opened the proceedings with a speech emphasising 'development' and the future; land belongs, he said, 'to our children, it's not ours'. He gave a condensed history lesson, from 'the time before' to the colonial era when missionaries and government 'gathered us together' from every corner of the province. He took pains to acknowledge that the mobility, voluntary and otherwise, ushered in by the colonial encounter made the land situation more complicated than it might otherwise have been. He listed the ways people might have come by their land, through bridewealth, other marriage-related payments, or in exchange for pigs and shell wealth. Finally, he urged people not to be petty, but to make their decisions in a way which would 'lift' the name of Buhutu, the hinterland people who speak a dialect mutually intelligible with coastal Suau and for whom he acted as mediator.

In the first dispute heard, Bina,[13] a man acting as *tanuwaga* for his lineage, supplied a bit of history in which his grandmother from Mahimahina got married to a man from Magaya and went to live with him there. At Magaya there was a *mata'asi*, a large-scale feast for the exchange of wealth items through which lineages and their influential members would build on their fame and demonstrate their economic efficacy.[14] So the grandmother went to her relations at Mahimahina, who supplied a number of pigs for the *mata'asi*. But the people of Magaya were not able to repay the pigs, so instead they gave the Mahimahina people a piece of land, Bunalele Panepane, and a stand of sago palms. Bina himself grew up at Bunalele Panepane. His family cleared bush there in order to plant gardens and coconuts; when Bina was grown and the coconuts mature he began to plant oil palm. When Galuboi, a Magaya man, returned from work at a commercial oil palm plantation, he too began to plant oil palm at Bunalele Panepane.[15] Bina complained about this, whereupon Galuboi's nephew chopped down some of Bina's oil palm and damaged his house. The actions of the nephew were dealt with in a separate village court case, and Bina emphasised that he was not trying to re-prosecute that case[16] but trying to resolve the dispute between himself and Galuboi.

Once Bina had finished speaking his sister spoke up to clarify that because their grandmother had had no children of her own,[17] Bina was entitled to act as *tanuwaga*. After some discussion with the land mediator over the precise relationship between the grandmother and the people at Magaya, which accounted for her obligation to supply pigs for the *mata'asi*, Bina suggested that the unreciprocated pigs were ultimately the source of the present dispute, because of the substitution of land as payment for the pigs.[18] He described the boundaries of the land his lineage claimed at Bunalele Panepane, and asserted that two of his Magaya uncles, that is to say his father's brothers, had walked the boundaries with him.

The land mediator reminded Bina that he could not claim all of Magaya, only the 'block' (an English term probably introduced by early twentieth-century copra and rubber planters) at Bunalele Panepane. He then mentioned that one of Galuboi's objections to Bina having planted oil palm there was that there were graves in the 'block' belonging to the Magaya lineage. Graves, like fruiting trees, are pre-eminent indicia of a long-standing land claim, as it is preferable to be buried on land belonging to one's own lineage. The land mediator chastised Bina for his thoughtlessness in planting oil palm over the graves, but said again that he had no power to grant land either to him or to Galuboi, and that they had to agree on a settlement between them. A second land mediator, who had been silent up to this point, encouraged the disputing parties to decide that the dispute had gone on long enough, to pray together, 'shake hands' and thereby arrive at 'one mind' together. Both mediators, in other words, didn't seem to think there was an especially complex problem before them, only a case of the non-recognition of a land claim which should in the course of the mediation become recognised. At that point Galuboi admitted that because his sister's son (his heir according to matrilineal reckoning) did not have any land on which to plant oil palm, he had cajoled Galuboi into giving him some – but the land given him was part of Bina's 'block' at Bunalele Panepane. Galuboi said that he was finished arguing, and implicitly blamed his nephew for talking him into a course of action that he now regretted.

The first land mediator then lectured both disputing parties, something he did frequently while presiding. He noted that Bina's paternal uncles should have shown both Bina and Galuboi the boundaries of the land given to Bina's grandmother, because, he said:

> The people who came before us didn't know if the people to come after them would be few or many. These days education has made us all very clever. If a mother gives birth to a baby boy we know he'll marry a woman who is different from the family. But if she gives birth to a girl, then we know that she will be the 'boss' of the land. We should recognise that the children of our sisters will 'boss' the land. Our own children will not 'boss' because they are of a different kind.

The second mediator also ended with a lecture, saying that 'a woman's payment is land'. He did not mean that land is given as bridewealth, which it is not, but rather that marriage entails consideration of how future generations will divide up land between them. He exhorted the young men present to think carefully about how they would marry:

> At Gelemalaiya [the village he was from] I have a lot of sons-in-law, but we cannot work their land. Their children will look for land one day. If you get married in your own village you must be of one mind and work together properly. You should marry a woman from your own place so that you'll hold onto the land. But if you marry someone from far away, there won't be any land for her. So remember that a woman's payment is land. Because business requires land and education requires foresight.

## Conclusions

The harangues by the two mediators suggest why they thought this dispute, which should not have arisen, did arise. First, both referred obliquely to a problem felt by many contemporary Suau, namely, that the Suau Coast has experienced a 'population explosion' (the English phrase is regularly used) in the past thirty years or so. The rise in population and the artificial concentration of villages near the coast stemming from Australian government policies have combined to generate something previously unknown in the Suau material repertoire: scarcity. This has not yet spelled the end of matriliny; as has been demonstrated in other contexts, matriliny can respond to pressure on resources through the idea of ancestral interests in land which their descendants construe as a form of 'profit' (Pavanello 1995). Some Suau lineages have started to address the problem by reappropriating their historical territories in the hinterland, but these are frequently only accessible by foot, and so less desirable to younger people who value road and water connections to oil palm plantations, towns, and other villages. More often, what happens is that lineages arrive at *ad hoc* land-sharing agreements with each other, or attempt to make land claims on increasingly 'creative' grounds. The land mediators' reproof to Bina for trying to claim all of Magaya on the basis of the payment to his grandmother is an example of the latter strategy, although Bina did not pursue it very aggressively.

I attended a land dispute three years earlier in which a patrilateral connection was offered to account for a land claim, but this connection was rejected outright by the land mediators. One of the victorious disputants told me afterwards with evident amazement at his opponents' audacity: 'Those people tried to claim the land through their father. But the father is a completely different person.' Like the exhortations of the mediator in the case of Bina and Galuboi, who insisted that 'Our own children will not "boss" because they are of a different kind,' this man was asserting that patrilateral claims were illegitimate on nothing less than taxonomic grounds. But the taxonomy, the 'kindedness' of persons, was primarily, and perhaps exclusively, relevant in the context of land claims. I should clarify that I say this only because I have never heard a Suau person make taxonomic distinctions between people based on anything other than the inheritance of land; it is of course possible that they do so on other occasions. But their unerring attention to this point when discussing or conducting land disputes is noteworthy. The effect conveyed is not so much one of matriliny separating people into heirs and non-heirs, as one of *land* separating people into belonging and non-belonging. I am not the first to offer such a formulation; some time ago de Coppet (1985) proposed that for 'Are'Are in the Solomon Islands, people mediate relations between lands as much as, if not more so than, land mediates relations between people. 'Are'Are do not posit the relationship in the crude one-way fashion that I have just done, but note that the trajectory of 'ownership' between land and people is never reducible to 'people own land' or 'land owns people'. Both forms are available at all times; which one is active and which one is suppressed at any given moment is a matter of expediency. And it is not only in Melanesia that the contingent nature of differentiation comes into play; Şaul (1992: 359) has documented in a West African society the fact that debates over the matrilineal inheritance default arise only upon the deaths of wealthy and influential personages.

Suau people can and do attempt to claim land through their fathers. There are as I mentioned a handful of permissible ways to do so, although all presume a matrilineal default to which claims revert if none of the following conditions obtain. If a couple has only sons and no daughters, the children of the eldest son (*taubaguna*) can claim their father's mother's land – but the son cannot claim it himself. Alternatively, a person assiduously making contributions to events in the father's lineage, such as bridewealth and mortuary payments, would in so doing add (weight) *polohe* to the land, and might proceed from there to a land claim. Finally, one can adopt a child from one's father's sister. The lineage status of adopted children is elastic, but so is the status of the adopter in a few cases. Suau draw many metaphoric connections between children and land, and claiming a parental interest in a child may be read as claiming an interest in the land of that child's lineage. All of these strategies can, however, be overturned by a convincingly argued matrilineal claim, and some of them only 'stick' for a generation or two before control over the land is wrested back by members of the matrilineage to which it originally belonged. Matriliny is therefore not so much a 'rule of inheritance' as it is a constitutive configuration of persons, land, and identity which allows any one element to generate distinctions between any of the other two elements.

There is another factor to take into consideration, however. Land now has the capacity to generate money. Land planted in oil palm, cocoa or coconuts is taken more or less permanently out of horticultural circulation.[19] And oil palm, currently the most lucrative but also the most ecologically disruptive cash crop, renders soil useless for any other purpose long after the palms have stopped producing commercially viable fruit. But oil palm is popular in the Buhutu region, and the small-scale plantations established by Buhutu appear to have generated a deluge of land disputes. Most people predict that with the dual pressure of population and cash cropping, the number of disputes is bound to escalate. This concern forms half of the cautions voiced by the land mediators in the case described above. The other half stems from the increasing tendency of people to try to claim land by means other than the matrilineal default. Bina did not explicitly do this, although he claimed, somewhat disingenuously, that since his paternal uncles gave him control over Bunalele Panepane he thought they were his maternal uncles, that is, that he would inherit from them all the land at Magaya. The lectures from the land mediators indirectly reminded him that he could not make such a claim, that his paternal uncles had parceled out Bunalele Panepane to Bina's lineage strictly on account of the pig debt incurred at the *mata'asi*. He capitulated to this argument, but it was clear to everyone present that his half-hearted bid to claim all of Magaya was motivated by the fact that it was heavily planted in oil palm. Strathern (1999: 57) has noted that: 'Money has become visible [in the Papua New Guinea Highlands] all the time, a medium whose enabling capacities cannot be hidden.' Its mediations appear to be, I would add, one-way: money is a latent capacity of oil palms, but oil palms are not a latent capacity of money. One form cannot be subsumed, even temporarily, by the other.

If capitalism and colonialism have had an effect on 'the matrilineal kinship', it is to be found both in the increasingly far-fetched nature of some land claims, and in the countervailing desire of people to be reminded of how things 'ought' to be, when they are exhausted from dealing with far-fetched land claims. While there have been signs of some accommodation on the part of Suau to make (exclusive, male) 'landowners' appear in order to conduct relationships with non-Suau commercial interests, we should not assume that these performances are anything more than that: performances. The performances have a value which is limited to particular contemporary contexts of life in a Papua New Guinea where resources in the form of money must be extracted from those who would extract resources in the form of timber, minerals, or whatever (Toft 1997). But for Suau, governance of land by matrilineages under the stewardship of their *tanuwaga* is still the default when no one else is looking, so to speak. Their compliance with the assumptions of exogenous agents is invariably followed by feuding over who can legitimately lay claim to the land; it is in these disputes that people have the opportunity to sort out the proper set of relations between land and people. Was the challenge of the theologically minded man at the land dispute a declaration that since divine authorship confers ownership (Delaney 1986), all land devolves through God rather than women? Is 'God made it in six days' an assertion that land should be held in common or that land should be devolved through men? He did not appear to assert either of these positions. Instead, I had the impression that he was asking the land mediators to be more forthcoming about the basis for any sort of land claim, full stop. In the time-honoured manner of senior Papua New Guineans being interrogated by their callow juniors, they declined.

## Acknowledgements

This chapter is based primarily on fieldwork conducted in Papua New Guinea in 1999–2000, whilst I was a member of the research project 'Property, Transactions and Creations: New Economic Relations in the Pacific', ESRC grant no. R000 23 7838. I would like to acknowledge gratefully the work of Kiukiuna Yokotali in assisting with translation of the land dispute transcripts. Thanks are due also to Michael Young for being so generous with his unpublished research materials and a previously 'classified' report. Finally, Sandra Bamford supplied insight at a critical juncture in the writing of the chapter, without which the discussion might not have taken the form that it did.

## Notes

1 While Balderson does not specify whether this plantation owner was Suau or expatriate, the historical context would suggest the latter. Balderson himself is recalled with affection by Suau old enough to have known him; he was the last patrol officer posted to the Suau Coast prior to Papua New Guinea's independence in 1975.

2 She also apparently told my PhD supervisor that she 'didn't want a feminist, but someone who would get the job done'. Although the precise meaning of her expressed preference is still unclear to me, I can only hope that she was not disappointed with the efforts of the person she got.

3 I use 'Suau' to denote all members of the Suau language cluster on the southeastern mainland of Milne Bay Province, both coastal and inland. While this designation probably would not be acceptable to local sensibilities, which tend to emphasise the differences between speakers of the six (mutually intelligible) Suau dialects rather than emphasising their similarities, there is no readily available term to use in its place.

4 As the most internally diverse country in the Pacific, with over 750 vernacular languages spoken, Papua New Guinea represents a challenge to any attempt to generalise about its social organisation or cultural perspective. Consequently, it is in almost all cases more accurate to refer to Papua New Guinea 'societies' in the plural.

5 That is to say, in cases where 'lines' of any kind can be perceived in the first place. The 1960s saw a heated debate question the existence of unilineal descent groups in parts of New Guinea, which until then were assumed by anthropologists to be a nearly universal characteristic of 'tribal' social organisation. See Lawrence 1984, Wagner 1974, and Barnes 1962 for key instances of this debate.

6 Tauyabuna himself died in 1998. My field assistant, a member of the same lineage, asked for a copy of the cassette tape on which that particular interview was recorded, in case her family needed it in the event of a land dispute, as she was uncertain whether he had taught the entire history to anyone else.

7 The use of 'roads' as an idiom for relationships of various kinds is extremely common in Papua New Guinea. For Suau, roads (*'eda* or *dobila*) are most often invoked to speak of marriage, although I have also heard people use them to describe social and cultural changes on the Suau Coast in general.

8 It is not uncommon in matrilineal societies for a father to be compensated for his work and nurturance on behalf of children belonging to his wife's lineage. Among Suau, a father is usually given a live pig at his child's bridewealth feast, and the

firstborn child is understood to enjoy a special relationship with him, and should be given a name from his lineage.

9 The term *tanuwaga* is used by a neighbouring language group to denote the 'manager' (note the gloss) of a clan's sea-going canoes (Macintyre 1989: 160) in particular, but also all the clan's valuable resources in general. Another cognate term from Vanatinai Island, *tanuwagai*, is glossed by Lepowsky (1993: 129) simply as 'owner'.

10 It should be noted that the Suau Coast is heavily forested. Grassland, apart from being alien to the Suau conception of what 'land' should look like, does not yield anything in the way of subsistence resources that the forest does: material for houses, medicines, animals and birds for hunting, wild fruits, nuts and greens, shade for cocoa cultivation, swamps for sago cultivation. Grassland harbours only one type of edible animal (bandicoots), is difficult to clear for gardens, and attracts snakes.

11 I have chosen to gloss *ulutubu* as 'lineage' rather than 'clan' because it better matches the distinction anthropologists traditionally draw between these two terms. Both connote a common identity and a certain degree of shared substance, but are reckoned differently. A lineage is a group of people which can trace its descent more or less 'genealogically' to a known ancestor, while a clan is a group of people who claim a common ancestry or substance, but cannot necessarily demonstrate their precise relationships to one another or identify the ancestors through whom they are related. It is possible for a group to have both clans and lineages, as Suau do. 'Clan' has, however, become the popular term in Papua New Guinea for referring to all forms of common 'family' identity regardless of its origins.

12 He called himself a 'nationalist' when I first met him in 1997. It is a term infrequently invoked in Papua New Guinea, and perhaps because of this, does not carry the negative connotations attached to it in many other parts of the world.

13 I have substituted the names of the disputants' clan totems for their actual names.

14 The last reported *mata'asi* happened over 20 years ago. It is not clear now whether the practice is moribund, or whether this length of time normally lapses between *mata'asi* which, by all accounts, require an extraordinary level of commitment and effort from lineages participating in them.

15 There is a horticultural hierarchy in Suau, in which fruit-bearing trees (and, these days, 'money-bearing' trees such as cocoa and oil palm) are weighted more heavily than gardens in terms of significance to a lineage's land claims.

16 See Demian (2004) for a consideration of the assiduous distinctions Suau maintain between litigating damage to property as opposed to disputing claims to property.

17 This is not a paradox; the ancestress in question will have been a classificatory rather than a lineal grandmother. All members of the third ascending and descending generations from Ego are called *tubu-*. All members of the fourth ascending and descending generations are called *waha-*. Both terms always take an 'inalienable' possessive suffix, for example, 'my great-grandparent' would be *wahagu*. Bina used this term in reference to his ancestress, implying that she was at least four generations removed from him.

18 Older Suau occasionally express dismay at the way the younger generations 'mix' forms of wealth, in contrast with the strict exchange regimes of the past in which a pig had to be repaid with a pig, a shell valuable with a shell valuable, and so on.

19 I use 'circulation' advisedly, since the practice is to cultivate a swidden garden for about two years, and then abandon it for two to five years while cultivating other gardens. This practice of rotating garden sites also explains why people need more land for gardening than they would if they cultivated the same site year after year. (To do so would be a recipe for famine without the use of fertilisers, as soil on the Suau Coast is fairly poor.)

Chapter 9

# Unfair shares for women

## The rhetoric of equality and the reality of inequality

*Rosemary Auchmuty*

### Introduction

In the Law Commission's Consultation Paper on *Cohabitation: the Financial Consequences of Relationship Breakdown*, extensive consideration was given to the inadequacies of English land law's methods of dealing with informal shares in the family home (Law Commission 2006).[1] This Consultation Paper was, of course, concerned only with unmarried cohabitants. Divorcing married couples were taken out of the land law regime following the Matrimonial Proceedings and Property Act 1970,[2] which also recognised spouses who paid for improvements to the home;[3] these provisions were extended to same-sex civil partners in December 2005.[4] Prior to 1970, however, the courts had no clear power to adjust shares in the family home between married litigants.[5] Where the home was legally owned by one party and the other claimed a share, all the courts could do was to identify *existing* interests under an implied trust. Married couples and civil partners in dispute with third parties, however, continue to fall under the land law jurisdiction. The Law Commission's proposals, which would impose a family law-style regime on separating unmarried couples, had nothing to offer these people.

This was by no means the first time the Law Commission had noted the shortcomings of land law in dealing with family home disputes. Throughout the 1970s the Commission was a strong advocate of statutory joint ownership of the matrimonial home[6] and a Bill based on their draft legislation twice received a second reading in Parliament but failed to pass into law.[7] It is often claimed that the failure of the movement for joint ownership, which would have brought England and Wales more closely into line with continental and American jurisdictions on this issue, was due to the fact that, after *Williams & Glyn's Bank v Boland* [1981] AC 487, where a mortgagee's possession of the family home was thwarted by the court's recognition of the wife's overriding interest, most matrimonial homes were put into joint names as a matter of course (Cretney 2003: 141). This is undoubtedly part of the explanation, but an even more important reason was the strength of male resistance, especially in Parliament and the courts, to the idea of giving wives *as of right* a half-share in the value of the home. As well as being the couple's greatest (or only) asset of worth, the home was the primary site of men's exercise of power. Symbolically as well as practically, it represented the last bastion of an outmoded patriarchal rule that lasted well beyond the implementation of sex equality legislation.[8]

The aim of this chapter is to examine the ways in which the courts, while responding to an increasing rhetoric of equality in English society throughout the twentieth century, still managed to continue to restrict women's access to a fair share in the matrimonial home. Property disputes between couples and against mortgagees certainly provided judges with splendid opportunities for creative law-making. And creative they were, evolving mechanisms rooted in existing trust law by which informal co-owners could claim a share in the family home, and rules by which they could defend their property from repossession by the bank where a mortgage had been obtained by undue influence. This chapter argues, however, that judges have been even more creative in the way they have managed to limit women's rights to a successful claim or defence, to limit women's claims even when they appear to 'win' their case, and to ensure that men generally do better out of these disputes than women – all in the context of a rhetoric of equality and justice it is impossible to sustain on the facts.

The focus of this chapter is the idea of 'equal treatment' for the sexes in property disputes. I take as my starting-point the idea that English women have not been treated equally in relation to property; that they have consistently been denied their fair shares in property ownership. Explanations for this have been well-explored in feminist literature: the sexual division of labour, the lack of financial value accorded to housework and childcare, women's unequal access to capital, inequalities of pay, marriage laws and customs, ideas of romance and trust (Auchmuty 2002, Belcher 2000, Bottomley 1993, 1998, Diduck and Kaganas 2006, Fehlberg 1997, Fineman 1998, Kaye 1997, Lawson 1996 and Probert 2005). My interest, however, is in the *legal rhetoric* and *legal reasoning* which have justified unfair apportioning of shares in court resolutions of informal co-ownership disputes and unfair outcomes in undue influence cases involving mortgagees. When the legal/equitable rules are expressed as gender-neutral, judges can and do argue that they are being fair to women, when really they are being unfair.

To illustrate my argument, I have chosen two areas of English land law from the many that could bear out my points. The chapter is therefore divided into two parts. The first, focusing on undue influence, analyses the common view that married women's present legal equality with men obviates any need for special equitable protection. In a discussion of *Barclay's Bank plc v O'Brien* [1993] 4 All ER 417, for example, Graham Battersby wrote: '[T]he conferment of special protection on married women, differentiating them from other sureties, is unacceptably patronising and wholly inconsistent with modern notions of the status of women' (Battersby 1995: 36). The effect of this kind of statement is to close off discussion of the reasons why, in fact, married women could and possibly *should* benefit from special protection in property law: that is, because married women suffer special disadvantage on account of their structural position, as women and in marriage, in relation to property.

The second part of the chapter is devoted to an examination of a small group of family home disputes between 1958 and 1970 in which men were the claimants. This is an interesting group, partly because one generally expects to see *women* claiming shares from *male* co-owners, but chiefly, from the point of view of this chapter, because these husband-plaintiffs faced a gender-specific obstacle to a successful claim: the presumption of advancement. This is the equitable principle which presumed, in the absence of evidence to the contrary, that a voluntary conveyance of property by a husband to a wife is a gift. Though rebuttable, it meant that husband-plaintiffs who had made financial contributions to the home started at a disadvantage by comparison to wives, whose contributions raised a presumption of a resulting trust. The presumption of advancement was regarded as more or less binding until about 1960. But then it came to be seen as standing in the way of equal justice for *men*. As a result, rather than painstakingly attempt to rebut the presumption on a case by case basis, the courts in the 1960s chose to reduce its significance to the point that, by the end of the decade, it had in Lord Denning's words 'no place, or, at any rate, very little place, in our law today' (*Falconer v Falconer* [1970] 1 WLR 1333, at 1335). The reason given for its virtual abolition in husband-to-wife transactions was that 'marriage is really a partnership of equals'[9] – thus, wives no longer needed the special protection afforded by the presumption of advancement. In fact, marriage was far from being a partnership of *economic* equals in 1970.[10] Once again, the effect of giving legal substance to what was largely a rhetorical gesture was to *increase*, not diminish, women's actual *in*equality in marriage.

The husband-plaintiff cases also illustrate the problem of the status of indirect contributions to the matrimonial home in co-ownership claims. The chapter considers the fate of the 'D-I-Y' cases of the 1960s and the relationship between do-it-yourself home improvements (men's work) and housework (women's work). These cases reveal how choices of legal rule and evidence are not accidental and not neutral. Too much success by women at law leads very often to a curtailment of their rights as the courts revert to a more restrictive interpretation of the rules, or change the rules altogether. As Robin MacKenzie puts it: 'advances towards independence, as in the Married Women's Property Acts, provoke an institutional repression of earlier protective measures as an unconscious backlash' (MacKenzie 1996: 168). The focus of this chapter is on the way that this backlash is invariably represented (and generally accepted) as *progressive*, and justified in the interests of gender *equality*.

## Undue influence

In *Howes v Bishop and Wife* [1909] 2 KB 390, Farwell LJ observed (at 394) that, since the passing of the Married Women's Property Act of 1882, he could see no way that the relationship of husband and wife could give rise to a presumption of undue influence. Though wives might have been considered as having a prima facie entitlement to the protection of equity before 1882, his view was that now they had legal rights over their own property, any automatic entitlement had gone.

Farwell LJ's comment is typical of the debate, long-standing even then, and still around today, over whether women need the 'protection' of equity in property disputes, or whether such interventions are undesirable and unnecessary, since women were then/are now 'equal' to men. When the laws were substantively loaded against wives, as in the days before the Married Women's Property Acts 1870–93, equity's interventions were regarded as natural, if not inevitable. Prior to the Acts, married women were very clearly a protected class in law – or, more correctly, a class whose disadvantage was seen as needing the attention of equity, whose role was, not exactly to protect the woman against her husband, but to mitigate her disadvantage. Equity intervened, for example, to allow women to hold property of their own under trusts, and then, when it emerged that many wives simply handed over their 'separate' estate to their husbands, to impose a restraint upon anticipation on the settlement.[11] In those days, then, married women were self-evidently not equal to men, as far as property was concerned.

But once the law recognised married women's right to hold and dispose of their separate property as they wished, there was no room for its paternalistic intervention, and no more special treatment for wives. So Farwell LJ argued. But other judges disagreed. In *Bischoff's Trustee v Frank* [1903] 39 *Law Times* 188. Wright J found it 'very singular' that neither case reports nor textbooks regarded the relationship of husband and wife as meriting an automatic presumption of undue influence (at 190). This led him to conclude that the Married Women's Property Acts had plunged the law into 'a somewhat unsatisfactory condition', and he preferred to hold that the husband–wife relationship *was* 'one where in the case of a large voluntary benefit influence was presumed to exist' (at 188).

I have often wondered about the true significance of the Married Women's Property Acts. Certainly the symbolic value of these Acts was enormous, because they broke the back of coverture, the concept that in marriage a woman's legal personality was subsumed in her husband's. For employed and propertied women, the ability to retain legal control of their property and earnings could mean the difference between independence and subservience, comfort and penury, even life and death. Lee Holcombe, the historian of the Acts, claims that they represented the largest ever transfer of property in English history (Holcombe 1980: 27). It is unclear, however, precisely how much property was transferred. How much property did Victorian wives actually possess? The ability to hold your own property is of little use to the woman who has none. Without financial resources, one cannot purchase property; and married women have tended to lack financial resources in a society which discourages, and sometimes forbids, the employment of wives, while consistently paying women less than their labour is worth – in the case of wives' domestic labour, nothing at all. And legal control of one's property, as a century of undue influence cases has demonstrated, offers insufficient protection to women whose social and emotional dependency leads them to do whatever their husbands want them to do with it.

In 1909, the rejection of a special equity for married women was in many ways progressive. (Remember that this was before women had the vote.) Certainly the feminists who had campaigned for the Married Women's Property Acts wanted wives to be treated just like everyone else in the management of their financial affairs (Holcombe 1983). If a married woman wished to give her property to her husband (or anyone else), or to mortgage it to support her husband's business (or set up her own), she should, they argued, be allowed to do so: only then, they believed, would married women be taken seriously as independent financial agents, and enjoy real equality with men. Feminists were anxious to rid married women of their reputation for being gullible, vulnerable and weak. As Robin MacKenzie explains:

> The rhetoric in the earlier [undue influence] cases had as its focus the image of woman as victim, completely dependent on her husband and without a will of her own, having to be saved from her soft-hearted and soft-headed misguided loyalties by equitable intervention, the very icon of the Victorian bourgeois woman.
>
> (MacKenzie 1996: 166)

But this, I would argue, was the rhetoric of the textbooks, not of the case reports themselves. What the latter described was not so much feeble women as brutal husbands who took advantage of them. For the fact remained that the great majority of married women were not in a position of equal bargaining power with their husbands or with commercial third parties. Less educated, less experienced, and with the 'wrong' priorities, they were easy prey for pressure and bullying. The result was that married women continued to feature as victims of undue influence and misrepresentation as the case law of the twentieth century unfolded.

As MacKenzie observes, the problem was one of transition. 'While the Married Women's Property Acts afforded women significant rights, they did not of themselves reform the institution of marriage in such a way that the perils against which equity sought to defend wives vanished' (MacKenzie

1996: 167). The question was, for how long could the previously disadvantaged group expect to continue to receive the protection and assistance of equity to tide them over until the attainment of full equality?

I have lost count of the number of times the moment of equality has been announced. With each legal advance – the vote,[12] entry to the professions,[13] the abolition of the restraint upon anticipation[14] – commentators proclaimed the end of the need for any special legal treatment for married women. 'Equality has been largely achieved', declared Erna Reiss (1936: 137) in her 1936 survey of women and law. And in 1980, after the passing of the Equal Pay Act 1970 and the Sex Discrimination Act 1975, Lord Denning (1980: 200) reiterated: 'By a series of Acts of Parliament . . . starting in 1870, all the disabilities of wives in regard to property have been swept away. . . . No longer is she dependent on her husband. . . . Her equality is complete.'

Hand in hand with these assertions of women's legal equality come other, more ominous allegations. Reforms that have benefited women are accused of leaving men worse off. Of married women's property rights, Pollock and Maitland (1898: 433) wrote: 'A law which was preeminently favourable to the husband has become a law which is preeminently favourable to the wife.' 'She certainly is to-day entitled to be called "the favourite of the law" ', concurred Montague Lush (1901: 344), in a not-unconscious echo of Blackstone's famous dictum. Fifty years and several pertinent reforms later, Sir Alfred Denning (as he then was) was still complaining about the wife's unfair advantage over the husband: 'If she is the "spoilt darling" of the law, he is the patient pack-horse' (Denning 1953: 98). Pollock, Maitland and Lush may have been concerned about the husband's continuing liability for his wife's debts and torts which, in spite of the Married Women's Property Acts, was not abolished until 1935.[15] Denning's remark presumably referred to men's largely social responsibility as family breadwinners.

Yet the criticisms were not really rational: what was left unsaid was that men enjoyed substantial benefits as a result of this social arrangement, which they showed little eagerness to forgo. Indeed, one begins to note an underlying masculine irritation at the pace of social and legal change, which in relieving women of some of their disabilities threatened also to remove some of the associated privileges for men. As long as husbands had access to their wives' property, the expectation that they would maintain those wives and settle their debts and torts seemed reasonable and fair. The fact that there was no legal enforcement of this expectation, however, left many women in a parlous situation (Cobbe 1868: 117). It was quite a different thing when wives could control their own property, but *still* men were bound to look after them financially. Even in cases where the wife actually owned very little, the Married Women's Property Acts removed a significant privilege from husbands: the privilege of unassailable financial dictatorship. To many men it must have seemed as if wives could have their cake and eat it too. Such men should, in principle, have supported the idea of genuine financial independence for married women, since this would free husbands from responsibility to support them. In practice, however, they were apprehensive. If women had equal access to employments hitherto reserved for men, and if wives had equal economic power within marriage, then men would lose a large part of their power over women *and* might have to share the responsibilities currently allocated to women.

On balance, this threat has proved the more potent. Thus, when Farwell LJ argued in *Howes v Bishop and Wife* [1909] 2 KB 390 against an automatic presumption of undue influence between wives and husbands, his expressed reason (that the Married Women's Property Acts had removed the need for any special equitable treatment for wives) masked a scarcely concealed concern, offered *obiter*, that equitable enquiry into women's motives for transferring property to their husbands might reveal a set of gendered power dynamics best left unexamined. '[I]t is clear that business could not go on if in every transaction by way of gift by a wife to her husband the onus were on the husband to shew that the wife had had independent advice,' he remarked; 'such a position *would render married life intolerable*' (at 402, emphasis added). The same sort of reasoning justified the law's refusal, much later in the century, to distinguish women's property rights from their husband's as overriding interests[16] and, again until recently, to take domestic violence seriously.[17]

This suggests to me that the argument that women no longer need the special protection of equity has been deployed more often and more successfully by those who feel that reform has gone far enough, than by those who would welcome it. Withholding 'special' treatment from women in property disputes, in consequence of their new 'equality' – that is, removing gender and marriage from the equation – has always been more likely to result in a disadvantageous outcome for women simply because, whatever their *formal* equality, women were and, in general, remain *not* equal in fact. More than half a century after the Married Women's Property Act 1882, Dixon J in the influential Australian case *Yerkey v Jones* [1940] 63 CLR 647 demonstrated how the modern law of undue influence lay in a direct line of succession from the married woman's settlement and the restraint upon anticipation, all three devices designed to protect the married woman from husbands intent upon getting their hands on her property. He quoted Story's *Equity Jurisprudence* of 1835, which explained that courts of equity examined all property transactions between wives and husbands 'with an anxious watchfulness and caution, and dread of undue influence', and added: 'In substance this position has been maintained until the present day [i.e. 1939]' (at 674).

Later still, in *Heseltine v Heseltine* [1971] 1 WLR 342, the court was obliged to have recourse to a resulting trust remedy precisely because the law refused to recognise a presumption of undue influence between husband and wife. In this case the wife was much wealthier than her husband. She paid four-fifths of the purchase price and guaranteed her husband's mortgage for the final one-fifth on the Hampstead property which was their family home. Four other properties were bought outright with her money, but conveyed into his name. Trusting her husband 'implicitly' in all financial matters, and not bothering to get independent legal advice, Mrs Heseltine also transferred a total of £60,000 in cash to her husband. After 21 years of marriage and four children, he went off with another woman. Mrs Heseltine sought to recover her property. Mr Heseltine denied that she had any beneficial interest whatsoever: it was all his.

It was a shame for Mr Heseltine that he did not live in the nineteenth century before the passing of the Married Women's Property Acts; he would so clearly have appreciated the automatic entitlement of Victorian husbands to their wife's property in law. On the other hand, had they lived in the nineteenth century, Mrs Heseltine's father would almost certainly have placed her fortune in a prudent settlement, with a restraint upon anticipation attached, precisely to prevent the transactions that occurred, unfettered, in the twentieth century. As it was, the courts rallied to Mrs Heseltine's defence, and she got most of her property back. The significance of this case lies not in any unfair outcome but in showing that, at the very moment when the need for special protection for married women was being denied because of their assumed equal status in marriage, this married woman did *exactly* what all those special equitable protections were designed to avoid. What price, then, equality in modern marriage? If wealthy women like Mrs Heseltine could voluntarily choose to order their finances in such self-evidently unprotective ways, what hope could there be for ordinary housewives?

Twenty years on, and Scott LJ in *Barclay's Bank v O'Brien* [1992] 4 All ER 983, at 1009 sees little advance:

> The likelihood of influence by a husband over his wife and of reliance by a wife on her husband to make business decisions for the family was the justification in the first place for the tenderness of equity toward married women who gave their property as security for their husband's debts. In my opinion, that justification is still present.

Belinda Fehlberg's interviews with 'surety wives' bore out the truth of his remarks. 'When you love someone, you just do as they ask you to do,' one confessed. 'The issue of choice never crossed my mind . . . It was just assumed I'd sign,' said another; and 'It was sort of . . . emotional commitment,' a third attempted to explain (Fehlberg 1997: 148, 181 and 187). Yet Bill Swadling professed to find Lord Justice Scott's concern for wives outdated and unreasonable. 'It may well have been the case that the paternalistic attitude of equity towards wives who guaranteed their husband's debts was an appropriate one to take at the turn of the [twentieth] century,' he declared; 'it is more questionable whether equity need still adopt this attitude as we approach the beginning of the next' (Swadling, 1992: 269). We need to be suspicious of statements like this.

For here we are in the twenty-first century faced with the recognition that, despite the widening out of the undue influence rules in *Royal Bank of Scotland v Etridge (No 2) and other appeals* [2001] 4 All ER 449 to encompass all non-commercial relationships, undue influence in mortgage situations remains a jurisdiction bounded by marriage. All eight appeals in *Etridge* concerned wives who had alleged undue influence by their husbands, and the judicial narrative focused entirely on husbands and wives except when laying down the broader principle. I am not arguing that the House of Lords was wrong to extend the equitable protection beyond wives: remedies should of course be available to husbands, to heterosexual and gay and lesbian partners, to employees, parents and all other groups who can be and have been victims of undue influence. What I am saying is that the egalitarian principle, and the existence of these other cases, should not blind us to the fact that the problem is largely one of a specific gender, a specific sexuality, and a specific relationship. It is still a problem of married women.

The reason is simple. The conditions of marriage that conduce to the exercise of undue influence by husbands on wives, while not exclusive to this relationship, nor inevitably present within it, are such an integral and assumed part of the institution as it is generally perceived that undue influence becomes almost a *normal* feature of it. This is, of course, why it is so difficult to prove. Consider Dixon J's statement in *Yerkey v Jones* [1940] 63 CLR 647, at 675:

> the reason for excluding the relation of husband and wife from the category to which the presumption applies is to be found in the consideration that there is nothing unusual or strange in a wife from motives of affection or even of prudence conferring a large proprietary or pecuniary benefit upon her husband.

Indeed, there is nothing unusual in this. It is normal for wives to want to please their husbands, to do what he wants. This is partly because of the love and trust assumed to exist between the partners. But where property and money are concerned, it is also because of the relative *power* of the parties. A woman is more likely to go along with her husband's designs if he runs the business that brings in the greater part of the family income, for this, together with the mere fact of his being male, allows him to claim the greater financial knowledge and expertise (Arber 1999: 177). And if (as much case law shows) she disagrees, it is always open to him to beat her up or make her life hell (Auchmuty 2005).

All this is not to deny that there are good arguments against special treatment for women, arguments I generally accept and espouse. My point here is that we have to note and analyse the use of a particular rhetorical device so that we are alert to what it really means and can guard against being taken in by it. The rhetoric of equality is laudable in its way, for it can encourage society to live up to its promise. It is certainly to be preferred to legal discrimination. But it can work to our disadvantage when the reality fails to match the rhetoric. *Simply declaring our equality does not make us equal.* In fact, it can remove all justification for protection in situations where protection is, in fact, still needed. If women continue to suffer structural social and economic disadvantage at the hands of men, then the removal of a gendered basis for intervention can place them at a *legal* disadvantage too.

## Informal co-ownership claims by men

Marriages breaking up after the Second World War precipitated the first co-ownership claims by wives who had contributed to the purchase of the matrimonial home held in their husband's name. At first the courts were not sure how to deal with the problem. In *Re Rogers' Question* [1948] 1 All ER 328 they took a cautious resulting trust approach. In *Rimmer v Rimmer* [1953] 1 QB 63 – where Denning LJ was among the judges – they went for equal division, the maxim 'equity is equality' providing a principled foundation for the development of Denning's 'family assets' solution, which was later to be decisively struck down in *Gissing v Gissing* [1971] AC 886.

As long as the plaintiffs were 'deserving' wives, few difficulties were encountered in the application of either rule. The only uncertainty in outcome derived from the constitution of the court that was to hear it, many Chancery judges being resistant to Lord Denning's family law-style importations into property law. In 1958, however, a Mr Silver applied for a share in his *wife's* home on the basis of his contributions to the mortgage repayments. He was the first husband-plaintiff to present himself. His case came on appeal to a court presided over by the then Master of the Rolls, Lord Evershed, who had sat in both *Rogers* and *Rimmer* with their disparate approaches to co-ownership disputes.

In *Silver v Silver* [1958] 1 All ER 523, the couple's original house had been bought with a deposit provided by Mrs Silver's parents and as a result was conveyed into her name. The mortgage was also in her name as legal owner though, as was usually required in those days, her husband acted as guarantor. The property in dispute was the fourth residence the couple had owned, each one bought with the proceeds of sale of its predecessor and each in turn conveyed to the wife. It was the husband, however, who actually *paid* the mortgage instalments, either directly or indirectly through his wife's housekeeping allowance. She had never been in paid employment and, being by the time of the hearing 'crippled by arthritis', was, in the view of the court, unlikely ever to be so.

After the couple separated, Mr Silver claimed beneficial entitlement to the current home. His case was dismissed in the county court. On appeal he contended that his wife held the property on trust for the two of them jointly. Once again he lost: the Court of Appeal found no evidence that ownership was ever intended to be shared, and no legal basis on which he might acquire a share. Had the house been purchased in *his* name, then 'common sense' might have dictated that the asset 'should be treated as the joint property of both, in the absence of evidence to the contrary,' Parker LJ observed, citing *Rimmer*. 'When, however, the house is bought in the wife's name as here, there is no doubt that the presumption of advancement applies; it is presumed to be a gift, in the absence of a contrary intention' (at 527).

Thus, although he had paid all the mortgage instalments on all the houses, Mr Silver emerged with no proprietary interest. This self-evidently 'unfair' outcome clearly worried all three judges. Lord Evershed gave the case 'anxious consideration' (at 525); Parker LJ reached with decision 'with considerable reluctance' (at 527) and Sellers LJ 'with no feeling of satisfaction' (at 528). Lord Evershed declared himself tempted to go along the 'equality is equity' route. (Good Chancery lawyer that he was, he could not bring himself to speak of 'family assets'.) But to embrace the equitable maxim would be to pre-determine the outcome of all future matrimonial property disputes, an innovation that went beyond his view of the limits of legitimate judicial law-making. If society wished to introduce this form of community of property in relation to the family home, he felt, the legislature must take the lead (at 525).

So the presumption of advancement won the day, but all indications were that the application of the presumption was beginning to be seen as an impediment to equal rights for *men*. It could not survive the advent of a significant number of husband-claimants in the 1960s, and by 1970 it was gone. In *Pettitt v Pettitt* [1970] AC 777 at 793, Lord Reid observed:

> It was said that if a husband spends money on improving his wife's property, then, in the absence of evidence to the contrary, this must be regarded as a gift to the wife. I do not know how this presumption first arose, but it would seem that the judges who first gave effect to it must have thought either that husbands so commonly intended to make gifts in the circumstances in which the presumption arises that it was proper to assume this where there was no evidence, or that wives' economic dependence on their husbands made it necessary as a matter of public policy to give them this advantage.

The second of these explanations raises the old spectre of *special rules for married women*, so we will not be surprised to find that Lord Reid promptly rejects the idea. 'These considerations have largely lost their force under present conditions . . .' (at 793) – that is, *women are equal now* and no longer need special protection. Lord Hodson in the same case voiced a similar sentiment. 'In old days when a wife's right to property was limited, the presumption, no doubt, had great importance' (at 811). But not any more. Lord Diplock added his own, rather muddled, contribution to the anti-advancement campaign:

> It would in my view be an abuse of the legal technique for ascertaining or imputing intention to apply to transactions between the post-war generation of married couples 'presumptions' which are based upon inferences of fact which an earlier generation of judges drew as the most likely intentions of earlier generations of spouses belonging to the propertied classes of a different social era.
>
> (At 824)

In the face of this determined opposition, the presumption's largely unmourned exit is not difficult to understand. The very fact that it was raised in cases involving female property-owners gave an impression that women were already equal to men. Despite the numbers of husband-plaintiff cases, however, wealthy wives were very much in the minority. In statistical terms the percentage of male claimants was negligible, but these cases received disproportionate attention because of their novelty value, because they presented a challenge to an established equitable principle, and probably also because the things men do are generally accorded more attention than the things women do. Thus there probably seemed to be many more of these cases – and many more women home-owners – than there actually were. Then, it is likely that most women supported the removal of the presumption. With the advent of the women's liberation movement in the late 1960s there was a clear sense that women did not want to be patronised and did not want special treatment; they knew that special treatment generally meant *inferior* treatment, condescension and exclusion from areas of male privilege.

The consequence was that, where in *Silver* the Court of Appeal had felt unable to depart from the unswervable principle that voluntary transfers from husbands to wives were gifts, and Lord Evershed had expressed the view that only Parliament could change the law in this area, in *Falconer v Falconer* [1970] 1 WLR 1333 at 1335 only 12 years later his successor as Master of the Rolls, Lord Denning, could confidently observe:

> If this case had come up for decision twenty years ago, there would undoubtedly have been a presumption of advancement. . . . That presumption found its place in the law in Victorian days when a woman was utterly subordinate to her husband. It has no place, or, at any rate, very little place, in our law today . . .

But was he right? Was the presumption of advancement *really* outmoded and redundant? Hardly. Women like Mrs Silver and Mrs Pettitt may have owned the family home but in other respects they were not well-off. Mrs Silver was an invalid. Mrs Pettitt, like Mrs Silver, was dependent on her husband for an income. It is true that the 1960s were in many respects a progressive era for women, with greater sexual freedom and increasing numbers of married women entering the paid workforce. But this was still before the coming into force of the Equal Pay and Sex Discrimination Acts. The women who came before the courts in these co-ownership disputes, notwithstanding Lord Diplock's remarks, had mostly been born before the war and had grown up in the expectation of becoming full-time housewives after marriage or, if they had a job, working part-time for low wages (Klein 1965, Hunt 1968). The Pettitts, for example, had married in 1952. What could be the rationale, then, for removing the special protection afforded by the presumption of advancement *before* the problem of women's economic dependence on their husbands had been solved?

One is forced to conclude that the demise of the presumption was due less to improved conditions of marriage that rendered special protection for married women unnecessary than to the general perception that its continued use was *unfair to men*. As became clear following the enactment of non-discrimination legislation in the 1970s, whenever there are sex equality measures, *men* will avail themselves of them in disproportionate numbers and with disproportionate success. And if the rules appear to discriminate against them, they will change them.

This is in effect what happened to the presumption of advancement. It stood in the way of equality for men, so it had to go. In an article in the *Cambridge Law Journal* John Tiley (1969: 263) described how this happened. The first stage was to emphasise the rebuttable nature of the presumption, as Lord Evershed did in *Silver*. Next came a denial of the presumption's importance. Tiley quoted Harman LJ in *Loades-Carter v Loades-Carter* [1965] 1 WLR 25:

> The presumptions of resulting trust and of advancement are useful crutches to help the court over the stile in the many cases which there are where it has to make bricks without straw. . . . When all the parties are alive and can give evidence as to what they intended and what did happen then these artificial aids are of little use and can be discarded.

Fine; but the whole point of the presumptions is to give guidance where the parties never established their intentions! The final step was when the presumption was replaced by a new one. Here Tiley instanced Lord Denning's family assets rule that any contribution by either husband or wife to the purchase of the matrimonial home should give rise to a presumption that the property would belong to them beneficially in equal shares. As we now know, Lord Denning's formulation was resisted and eventually rejected by the House of Lords in *Gissing*. But the presumption of advancement never recovered.

Notwithstanding the rejection of the presumption of advancement in his case, however, Mr Pettitt did not win his claim to a share in his wife's home. This was because his contributions took the form of home improvements rather than payments towards the purchase price, and the House of Lords (reversing the lower courts) felt that such 'ephemeral' offerings should not guarantee him a *permanent* interest in the property.

This brings us to the little sub-group of 'D-I-Y' cases, of which *Pettitt* was the culmination. They were much discussed in the critical literature at the time, but their gender implications remained almost entirely unexplored. The vogue for do-it-yourself home improvements in the 1960s (MacDonald and Porter 1990) unwittingly provided the means by which a small number of men could assert their right to a share in their wife's property. In *Appleton v Appleton* [1965] 1 WLR 25 the original family home had been purchased by the wife out of money left to her by her mother. The whole family undertook substantial renovations on it before it was sold and another property purchased which, once again, they all worked on. Then one day Mrs Appleton left, leaving a note on the table for her husband and son: 'Dog at kennels, Chelmsford' (at 27). No doubt this little detail helped to prejudice Lord Denning MR against the woman. In a judgment with which his fellow judges agreed, he reversed the county court's finding that the husband's work on the houses was a gift to his wife (the old presumption of advancement) and decided that Mr Appleton should get an interest in the proceeds of sale of the current home in proportion to his contribution to its value. Not an unreasonable conclusion, perhaps, but Lord Denning raised eyebrows when he denied that the court should necessarily look for any evidence of an express or implied bargain between the parties as to ownership of the property. 'A judge can only do what is fair and reasonable in the circumstances', he declared with characteristic rashness (at 28).

In *Jansen v Jansen* [1965] P 478, Lord Denning built on the insecure foundation of *Appleton*. The facts of this case were unusual: the couple had met when the woman responded to the man's advertisement for a wife who would keep him for four years as a student. She was a 38-year-old divorcee with two children, her own home, and a burgeoning career as a psychiatric social worker. He was 31 and had been a planter in Malaysia. Soon after the marriage he abandoned his studies and devoted himself to the conversion of a freehold property purchased by his wife into flats for sale. When they divorced, each alleging cruelty on the part of the other, he claimed a half-share in the property he had renovated. The Registrar denied him a proprietary interest but awarded him £1,000 in compensation. Lord Denning, with whom Davies LJ concurred, agreed that a half-share was too much, but that the man deserved some recompense for his labour. The £1,000 was confirmed, with not a word about the presumption of advancement.

Russell LJ, in the longest judgment of the three, sounded a sharp note of opposition to the idea of rewarding D-I-Y improvements:

> Admittedly [Mr Jansen] has done a great deal of work on his wife's property, work which would otherwise have had to be paid for to a builder [*sic*]. On the other hand, he would otherwise have been expected – having abandoned his studies – to have worked to earn an income with which to support his wife and family.
>
> (At 487)

Russell LJ gave as his opinion that Appleton had been wrongly decided, a view with which the judges in all subsequent cases agreed. Nevertheless, in *Pettitt v Pettitt* [1968] 1 WLR 443 the Court of Appeal felt constrained to follow *Appleton*, thereby granting Mr Pettitt a beneficial interest in the house. It was left to the House of Lords in *Pettitt v Pettitt* [1970] AC 777 to deliver the death-blow to the notion that D-I-Y renovations by hopeful husbands might enable them to acquire a share in their wife's property, by overturning the Court of Appeal's judgment in February 1969.

More than a year before this, however – indeed, the very day after the Court of Appeal delivered its judgment in *Pettitt* – a differently constituted Court of Appeal decided a case in which a *wife* claimed an interest in her *husband's* property on the basis of her contribution to home improvements. Coming in the wake of three successful claims by husbands on similar facts, *Button v Button* [1968] 1 WLR 457 might have been assumed to produce an easy victory for Mrs Button, since the presumption of advancement did not apply to gifts by wives to husbands and the implied trust rules were otherwise gender-neutral. Not so, however: she lost.

There were two reasons why Mrs Button failed to establish a proprietary interest. The first was undoubtedly the turning tide of opinion against D-I-Y as an eligible contribution to the home. Lord Denning's two fellow-judges, Danckwerts and Widgery LJJ, quite plainly put him under pressure to distinguish *Appleton* and *Jansen* and (by implication) to abandon the line of reasoning that had justified them. The second explanation was the novel construction now placed upon the activity of D-I-Y itself:

> I was inclined during the argument to accept that [Mrs Button's] work was so great as to entitle her at least to a share in the house . . . But after discussion with my brethren, I have come to the conclusion that the proper inference from the evidence is that it was *the ordinary kind of work which a husband or wife may do on the matrimonial home without giving the other* [he meant *himself or herself*] *a share or interest in it*.
>
> (At 462) (emphasis added)

There are a number of interesting features in this new definition of D-I-Y. First, Lord Denning was at pains to distinguish the renovations done by Mrs Button from the more heavy-duty work of Mr Appleton and Mr Jansen, which was similar to that which a contractor might do. The *Law Quarterly Review* case-note writer at the time found this 'a novel distinction, and a gloss on the simple test propounded in *Appleton v Appleton*' (Baker 1968: 308). The commentator did not link this observation to the gender of the persons performing the labour, but we all know that women's work is very often belittled and undervalued while men's is inflated to professional status. Second, D-I-Y was now seen as an activity that husbands or wives might equally or interchangeably perform. Yet when D-I-Y was first advanced as a means of obtaining an interest in property, it was clearly perceived as *men's* work, which may help to explain why, in *Appleton* and *Jansen*, it was accepted as conferring value on (and hence an interest in) the home. In *Pettitt v Pettitt* [1968] 1 WLR 443 at 448, however, the Court of Appeal drew a parallel between men's unpaid home improvements and women's unpaid domestic labour, which resulted in a loss of status for the former. As Willmer LJ phrased it:

> I would not regard the work which the husband did as having gone beyond what any reasonable husband would be expected to do, either with his own hands or by paying a contractor to do it, if he had the benefit of living rent-free in a house provided by his wife. In the same way, a wife who has the benefit of living in a house provided by her husband must be expected to do her part in preserving the property, keeping it clean, and so forth.
>
> (At 453)

Yet Lord Denning in the same case allowed the plaintiff a share precisely *because*, like Mr Appleton, he had done work that a contractor might have done!

The actual tasks undertaken by Mr Pettitt are detailed in the Court of Appeal report, and fascinating reading it makes. In the bedroom, we are told, he built a double wardrobe; in the kitchen, replaced the cupboard doors and fitted Venetian blinds; in the garden, laid a patio and planted bulbs. He also installed a cupboard under the bathroom washbasin. The cost of labour and materials for all this, including redecorating throughout 'in Regency style', came to about £725. He based his claim for a share in the house on the enhanced value that his work conferred, which he estimated at £1,000. (The house had originally cost £3,800.) John Tiley (1969: 99) remarked that 'one of the curiosities of *Pettit* [*sic*] is to wonder how the works carried out by the husband could have increased the value of the house by £1,000'. All this helps to explain how the status of D-I-Y contributions to the home became ambiguous in subsequent co-ownership disputes.

What happened next was that, in *Pettitt v Pettitt* [1970] AC 777 in the House of Lords, D-I-Y was reduced still further to the level of a leisure pastime. Here is Lord Diplock:

> If the husband likes to occupy his leisure by laying a new lawn in the

> garden or building a fitted wardrobe in the bedroom while the wife does the shopping, cooks the family dinner or bathes the children, I, for my part, find it quite impossible to impute to them as reasonable husband and wife any common intention that these domestic activities or any of them are to have any effect upon the existing proprietary rights in the family home on which they are undertaken.
>
> (At 826)

Again the parallel with women's domestic work is made, Lord Diplock seemingly unable to see that, while D-I-Y may well be a leisure activity, the same can hardly be said of shopping for household necessities, cooking, and childcare. Lord Diplock is thus able to distinguish *Jansen*, where the building works were *not* a leisure activity: 'The husband, in agreement with his wife, had abandoned his prospects of paid employment in order to work upon her property' (at 826). This justified financial compensation. Again, it seems to have escaped Lord Diplock's attention that the same could be said of all those wives who gave up paid employment to cook and clean and look after their husband's children.

So how did the shift occur from the dignifying of home improvements as valuable work by men to its dismissal as a leisure activity, as worthless (in material terms) as housework? I suggest that the case of *Button v Button* [1968] 1 WLR 457 played an important role. By claiming a share in the family home on the basis of her D-I-Y improvements, Mrs Button clearly encroached on masculine territory. Perhaps, if she had established that her work was actually as substantial as a man's, as Janet Eves in *Eves v Eves* [1975] 1 WLR 1338 was later to do, she might have won her case. Instead, she compounded her fault by asserting, in addition to the D-I-Y, a right to a proprietary interest on the basis of her 'economical' household management. This proved fatal. Association with housekeeping, when performed by the same person – a woman – reduced the value of the D-I-Y to zero. It ceased to be the masculine equivalent of housework and became *subsumed* in housework. As Lord Denning put it: 'The wife was economical in spending on the housekeeping, as most wives are. She helped with the decorating and improvements to the house, as many wives do' (at 462). When women do D-I-Y, then, it becomes something additional they are expected to do for free and without reward. As Willmer LJ had demanded rhetorically in *Pettitt v Pettitt* [1968] 1 WLR 443 at 448 in the Court of Appeal: 'is it to be said that, if, out of the goodness of her heart, she helps her husband on some occasion to redecorate a room – not an uncommon occupation for a wife these days – she thereby acquires some beneficial interest in her husband's property?' Of course not. This 'would clearly be an absurd result'.

Only one judge of the eight who gave judgment in Pettitt in the two appeal courts had any doubts about the correct approach to these co-ownership cases. While Lord Hodson in *Pettitt v Pettitt* [1970] AC 777, at 811, noted 'the imbalance which may be found to exist in property rights between husband and wife', and Lord Upjohn was sure that 'the doctrine of resulting trusts still represents the common sense of the matter' (at 816), Lord Reid found it 'entirely unsatisfactory' that payments to the purchase price should give rise to an interest in the home, whereas payments towards home improvements did not. He wondered, moreover, about the position of the wife who paid all the household bills, while her husband paid the mortgage instalments – why should she be denied a claim? 'And go a step farther still. The wife may not be able to make any financial contribution but by good management and co-operation she may make it possible for the husband to pay the instalments regularly' (at 794). Yet she had no claim. Was this fair? Lord Reid, the senior judge in the House of Lords, did not think so. But he believed that Parliament, not the courts, should make new law.

By excluding D-I-Y claims by husbands, the House of Lords in *Pettitt* appeared on the face of it to be treating the sexes equally: men's D-I-Y did not count, just as women's housework did not count; and neither did women's D-I-Y. But men's and women's situations were not the same. Housework was not simply a parallel gendered activity to D-I-Y: it was a substantively different form of labour. Whether husbands undertook D-I-Y or not, this work was never a daily expectation in the way that housework and childcare were daily expectations of women. Whether men's home improvements added capital value to the home or not, women's regular housework *maintained* the value of the property and added value in an emotional sense to the lives of those who occupied it. By incorporating women's D-I-Y activities into their everyday, taken-for-granted household tasks, the courts reinforced the notion that any labour done by women, unless directly replicating that done by a man in paid employment, is worth less *per se* than any labour done by men – indeed, is worth nothing, and can never give rise to an interest in property.

## Conclusion

In the Court of Appeal in *Pettitt v Pettitt* [1968] 1 WLR 443 at 456, Lord Justice Danckwerts observed: 'The law has favoured wives in relation to husbands, and it is too late now to reverse this process in favour of husbands.' With due respect to the learned judge, I think he was wrong on both counts. The truth is that English property law has always favoured husbands (why else would all the equitable protections – the marriage settlements, restraints upon anticipation and presumptions – have been needed?); and it has never been too late to reverse any process that appears to favour wives so that it favours husbands again.

The passing of the Married Women's Property Acts led, for example, to the weakening of the presumption of undue influence between husbands and wives. Increasing numbers of successful co-ownership claims by wives after the Second World War led to the emasculation of the presumption of advancement. Both presumptions had benefited women at the expense of men. Both protected and enhanced women's claims to property. Their disappearance was justified in both cases by reference to the equality of the sexes in marriage. The effect was to perpetuate *in*equality.

There is nothing accidental in the way that legal rules evolve. They are products of their milieu, of their time, of their creators. Many factors go into their making. Nevertheless, while it would be overstating the matter to claim that the English rules of co-ownership represent men's interests alone, what this chapter makes clear is that men's interests are never wholly absent from consideration when new principles are being evolved and old ones modified – while women's often are. Even given the peculiar parameters of English land law, the rules governing informal co-ownership claims could have developed quite differently. Lord Denning's 'family assets' crusade could have succeeded. If 'community of property' had sounded too foreign to English judicial ears, the same arrangement could have emerged out of the ancient equitable maxim, 'Equity is equality'; as we have seen, this was often raised in the case law, and would not have required Parliamentary intervention. In the wake of the successful D-I-Y claims of the 1960s, housework might have given rise to a share in the family home by according it an equivalent economic value. The typical gendered division of labour might have been represented as a bargain related to home ownership. Or unjust enrichment could have been invoked, as in other jurisdictions. But by constantly returning to rules requiring *direct financial contributions*, the courts have wilfully and deliberately discriminated against women, whose restricted access to money of their own has been well documented.

What this chapter attempts to show is that the removal of special equitable protections for women has been justified by a rhetoric of gender equality so convincing that even those destined to lose out – women – have tended to support it. This realisation suggests that we need to be particularly alert to those egalitarian gestures that ignore the wide economic gap between men and women, and helps to explain why that gap shows so few signs of narrowing.

There is a considerable volume of feminist critique on whether women should be treated in law exactly as men are, or whether their special characteristics and/or roles should receive special protection – the 'equality versus difference' debate. This chapter should not be taken to advocate the 'special treatment' approach. On the contrary, I recognise that women will never be equal unless and until gender in law becomes irrelevant. How then are women to obtain a justice that takes account of their structural disadvantage? And how are these destructive legal backlashes to be countered?

Insofar as law can heal itself, English property law contains within its own equitable jurisdiction the means to meet this challenge. Equity has a contextual jurisdiction: it claims the power to come to the rescue of any disadvantaged person where 'justice and conscience' demand it. But that power is more often honoured in the rhetoric than in the reality (Halliwell 1997: 9). The inability of the courts to develop rules that recognise women's economic inequality – a problem exacerbated by the class of personnel from whom the higher judiciary has traditionally been drawn[18] – is due to difficulties of recognition, empathy and, above all, *will*. I have argued elsewhere that the undue influence rules (at least until the House of Lords' decision in *Royal Bank of Scotland v Etridge (No 2) and other appeals* [2001] 4 All ER 449) demonstrate a disturbingly high legal tolerance of men's bad behaviour (Auchmuty 2002). I believe that the informal co-ownership rules presently embodied in *Lloyd's Bank plc v Rosset* [1991] 1 AC 107 reflect a deep-seated conviction that men deserve property and women do not – or, at any rate, that women deserve *less*. Both sets of rules reveal that the 'natural' and traditional bond between men and property requires particularly strong evidence to be weakened or displaced, and that the less common, more recent, and therefore less 'natural' claim by women must be thwarted or restricted, lest material power enable women to challenge men's dominance.

But the problem for women is not simply, or even fundamentally, the unfair shares they are allocated by the courts in property disputes. The real problem is that so many of them get themselves into a situation requiring judicial intervention in the first place. I am not here talking about divorce law, which changed in 1970 to take account of some of the difficulties experienced by the couples in the cases I have discussed.[19] I am talking about the informal co-ownership arrangements of unmarried couples and married couples in dispute with a third party, and the mortgages obtained through a man's undue influence on a woman. Women go into these arrangements out of ignorance, blind trust, fear and, above all, abdication of responsibility. It would surely make sense for them to know beforehand exactly what they are letting themselves in for when they enter into these transactions, with their unwanted and unforeseen consequences. They need to know what the alternatives are and to be able to avail themselves of them.

I was heartened to learn recently that 'Civics' has been introduced as a compulsory subject in the secondary school curriculum. 'Civics' seems to me the very place to teach young people about law, not just constitutional and administrative law so that they will exercise their vote and know their rights, but family law and property law, so that they will understand the legal significance of marriage and the importance of secure proprietary interests. Statistics and case studies should accompany the legal advice, to show just how 'normal' and common these economic disasters are for women today. This may help to avert a complacent response (how often one hears, 'That's not going to happen to *me'*; '*My* relationship will be different'!).

Research by the Centre for the Study of the Family, Law and Social Policy at Staffordshire University found recently that many cohabitees have no real understanding of their legal position. A staggering 41 per cent of interviewees believed that marriage would make no difference to their property rights, and several found the idea of obtaining legal advice on the subject repugnant and untrusting (Hibbs *et al.* 2001: 200–5, and Barlow *et al.* 2005: 38–41). It is this attitude that legal education in schools need to tackle, before the young women find themselves in situations they could have avoided simply by exercising a modicum of assertiveness.

I would go further. I would encourage teachers to confront the issue of romance itself, to encourage their students to deconstruct its myriad persuasive images and to develop their critical skills in ruthless analysis of ideals like love, trust, equality and power. Why should everyone have to learn through bitter experience? Every generation thinks the battle is won, and every generation seems to have to fight it again – or, rather, they have to fight *another*, different battle, with cunningly modified parameters, in the never-ending 'war' for equality.

For a long time, even as women gradually became equal in law, equity remembered they were not, and made allowances. But as the equitable rules themselves became gender-neutral, this knowledge was lost. Erna Reiss, writing on women's legal position in 1936, celebrated the advent (as she imagined) of legal equality. But she recognised that 'economic equality has yet to be conceded'; and she concluded her survey with a word of advice to 'younger women'. Remember, she said, that 'the price of freedom is eternal vigilance' (Reiss 1936: 115–16).

Her words still hold true. Though women's situation is perceived as having improved, the general trend in co-ownership disputes has been against women. Where Martin Dixon writes, for example, that 'there have been relatively few reported cases where a claimant in a normal domestic context has actually failed to secure an interest under the *Rosset* rules (*Rosset* was one!)' (Dixon 1992: 152), one is impelled to respond: Yes – but what was the gender of the claimant, and what was the size of the share?

A close examination of those well known cases, often presented in land law textbooks as instances of equity's generosity to women, reveals the meanness of many of the awards. Janet Eves in *Eves v Eves*, for example, received not a half-share in the property but a quarter, and the court ordered that the house could not be sold (her estranged partner was living there with his new wife) as long as he made up his child maintenance arrears. So she could not even get her hands on her £10,000-worth in the property. In *Cooke v Head* [1972] 2 All ER 38, the woman got one-third, not one-half. In *Hazell v Hazell* [1972] 1 All ER 923, the woman claimed a half, but received one-fifth, the same proportion awarded to the woman in *Hall v Hall* [1982] 3 FLR 379. Contrast these results with the husband's award in *Heseltine v Heseltine* [1971] 1 WLR 342: he had taken responsibility for a mortgage worth one-fifth of the value of the house – though Mrs Heseltine *guaranteed* the mortgage – but was given one-quarter. Megaw LJ was surprised at the discrepancy but saw no reason to alter the Registrar's decision. Or consider the recent family law case of *White v White* [2000] 2 FLR 981, widely regarded as marking a huge step forward in its recognition that 'fairness' should be the overriding goal of the court in re-allocating marital property. This is a different jurisdiction from property law, but the ideology is the same and so is the outcome. Mrs White received a 40 per cent share in the home though she had borne a dual responsibility as housewife/mother and farmer. In the Court of Appeal, Lady Justice Butler-Sloss seemed 'inclined' to offer more. But she was outnumbered. Alison Diduck (2001: 182) comments:

> That Mrs White did receive only forty per cent of the property to which she had at least equally, and perhaps exceptionally contributed, even on the House of Lords' interpretation of fairness, should leave women still wary of the broad statutory discretion to promote fairness and conscious of the ongoing hegemony of the underlying ideologies of law.

The Law Commission's Consultation Paper on Cohabitation (2006) noted critically that in *Oxley v Hiscock* [2004] 3 All ER 703 non-financial contributions were disregarded in the Court of Appeal's quantification of shares, reliance being placed instead on money spent. This resulted in a reduced share for the woman.

Young women today grow up believing that the sexes are truly equal. I would rather they were prepared for the probability of unequal treatment, even if they personally never experience it, than that they should undergo the profoundly disempowering shock of disillusionment that all these women in the case law had to suffer when, having been assured they were truly 'equal' now, they discovered the extent of their *in*equality.

## Notes

1 Especially Parts 3 and 4.
2 Section 4, subsequently incorporated in the sections 24 and 25, Matrimonial Causes Act 1973.
3 Section 37, Matrimonial Proceedings and Property Act 1970
4 Schedule 5, Civil Partnership Act 2004.
5 Lord Denning and other judges tried to use s 17, Married Women's Property Act 1882 in this way but this was firmly blocked by the House of Lord in *Pettitt v Pettitt* [1970] AC 777 and *Gissing v Gissing* [1971] AC 886.
6 First Report on Family Property: A New Approach (No 52), 1973; Third Report on Family Property: the Matrimonial Home (Co-ownership and Occupation Rights) (No 86), 1978.
7 Matrimonial Homes (Co-ownership) Bill, 1980 and 1982.
8 For instance, the Equal Pay Act 1970 and the Sex Discrimination Act 1975.
9 *Pettitt v Pettitt* above n 5, *per* Lord Morris of Borth-y-Gest, at 802, approvingly quoting Woodhouse J in the New Zealand case, *Hofman v Hofman* [1965] NZLR 795.
10 For example, the salary of Mrs Gissing (who had been in paid employment all her adult life) was one-sixth that of her husband, who worked in the same firm – *Gissing v Gissing*, above n 5.

11 The restraint upon anticipation prevented women from having access to the capital of their separate estate; they could only get an income from it, so even if they handed this over to their husbands, the capital remained inviolate. This doubtless prevented many gold-digging marriages, but effectively stopped married women from investing capital sums in enterprises that might have made them successful and wealthy businesswomen, see Auchmuty (2001).
12 Representation of the People Acts 1918 (women aged 30 and over) and 1928 (women aged 21 and over).
13 Sex Disqualification (Removal) Act 1919.
14 Law Reform (Married Women and Tortfeasors) Act 1935 (abolished the creation of new restraints); Married Women (Restraint Upon Anticipation) Act 1949 (abolished existing restraints).
15 Law Reform (Married Women and Tortfeasors) Act 1935.
16 Finally conceded in *Williams & Glyn's Bank Ltd v Boland* [1981] AC 487.
17 *Davis v Johnson* [1979] AC 264.
18 The presence of Baroness Hale in the House of Lords has clearly made a difference in the last few years.
19 Section 4, Matrimonial Property and Proceedings Act 1970, subsequently ss 24 and 25, Matrimonial Causes Act 1973.

Chapter 10

# The shared home

## A rational solution through statutory reform?

*Simone Wong*

### Introduction

In late October 2004, the Civil Partnership Act 2004 was passed by the UK Parliament and it came into force in December 2005. This new Act enables same-sex couples to register their relationship as a civil partnership, which will then impose certain rights and obligations on the parties that are analogous to those of married couples. The statute includes a property distribution regime which confers powers on the courts to make property adjustment orders at the termination of a civil partnership. More crucially, the passage of the Civil Partnership Act 2004 creates a three-tier system in the UK – with marriage at the first tier, followed by civil partnerships and then all other types of domestic relationships. Consequently, parties at the third tier will have to continue relying on the common law to resolve any property disputes that arise at the termination of the relationship. The passage of the Civil Partnership Bill through Parliament was at one point nearly derailed in the House of Lords by what was described by many as wrecking amendments. Those amendments, which were subsequently removed in the House of Commons, attempted to extend the legislation to other care-giving relationships between certain familial members, who were at least 30 years of age and have lived together for a minimum period of 12 years.

There are clearly merits to the arguments made in the Lords for extending the Bill to care-giving relationships. But as the Government rightly pointed out, the Civil Partnership Bill was intended to confer civil status to a specific category of (same-sex couple) relationships, and in many ways mimics heterosexual marriage: it was clearly not suited as the vehicle for extending protection to a wider range of relationships. As a result, the Government announced that the matter of the vulnerable (opposite-sex) cohabitant would be referred to the Law Commission for England and Wales for review.[1] The Law Commission's current project on cohabitation began in 2005 and the Consultation Paper was published by May 2006 (Law Commission 2006). A project on cohabitation, however, is not new. In July 2002, the Law Commission's long awaited Discussion Paper on Home-sharing (Law Commission

2002) was published, followed shortly by the Law Society's Report on Cohabitation (Law Society 2002). Both publications dealt with the resolution of disputes over property, including the shared family home, on the termination of a close personal relationship. To some extent, the Law Commission's remit was narrower than that of the Law Society in that it focused mainly on the property rights of those who share a home rather than on the broader subject of cohabitation. Its scope, however, was wider as the examination of the property rights of home-sharers was not confined to cohabitants and extended to a wider range of relationships. These included both familial and non-familial relationships, where the parties lived together for reasons of companionship or to provide mutual care and support to each other (Law Commission 2002: para 1.1). An interesting aspect of both publications is the very different conclusions they reached regarding legal reform. On the one hand, the Law Society concluded that legislative intervention was necessary to ensure greater protection of the rights of cohabitants and that a more adequate system had to be put in place to provide such protection on relationship breakdown, including property distribution. The Law Commission, however, made no recommendation for legislative reform. After considering a possible contributions-based scheme, the Law Commission concluded that it was not possible to devise a statutory scheme that would be sufficiently flexible to operate fairly and evenly across the diversity of home-sharing relationships.

The difference in the approaches of the Law Commission and the Law Society may be explained away by their different remits but there is nevertheless a crucial overlap. In both instances, there is a common issue, i.e. the distribution of property, real and personal, at the termination of a domestic relationship, whether because of a breakdown of the relationship or death of one of the parties to the relationship. Although the Law Commission concluded in 2002 that no recommendations could be made for a statutory regime to deal with the property rights of home-sharers (including cohabitants), it will be interesting to see, following the Consultation Paper, whether under its current project on cohabitation the Commission's views would change. Its current remit, however, focuses on only (couple) cohabitation rather than home-sharers generally – it expressly excludes consideration of the position of carers[2] in a home-sharing relationship. Consequently, the question of introducing legal reform to protect economically vulnerable carers remains open. The push to extend further protection of this category of domestic relationships may not have completely died out. As can be seen from the developments that took place in the House of Lords during the passage of the Civil Partnership Bill, vulnerable economic arguments can just as easily be hijacked by this group to push for future reform.

With respect to cohabitants, the Consultation Paper suggests that it is very likely that some legal reform will be recommended this time round by the Law Commission. The question is the form which such reform will take. In that respect, more careful thought and consideration will have to be given to the possible property distribution model to adopt within this jurisdiction, and the role that property law, as opposed to say family law, should influence the shape of reform. While the Law Commission in its current project considers a family law approach that is slightly different from that of the Law Society's, the chapter focuses instead on the property law approach taken in the Law Commission's 2002 Discussion Paper by way of contrast to the Law Society's approach. For the purposes of this chapter, the discussion will focus on relationship breakdown and its impact on disputes over the shared home. There is an ongoing debate about whether such disputes should more appropriately be dealt with under property law, trusts law or family law. Some who advocate legislative reform favour adopting a regime that is similar to the family law model.[3] Property disputes between parties to a relationship are, however, inextricably linked to property rights. When dealing with the adjustment of property on relationship breakdown, the centrality of property rights cannot be ignored, even when subsumed under family law. This is because, at a practical level, there is an underlying tension between providing rights to parties in the relationship and upholding existing property rights, even where adjustive powers are given to the courts. This is particularly the case since, under the principle of separation of property, parties to a relationship, even within marriage, are seen as autonomous property owners. Hence, the starting point of assessing what rights the parties have, or are to have, in respect of the shared home often tends to be ownership of the property, thereby placing emphasis on the evaluation of contributions – more specifically financial contributions – made towards its acquisition. Relatedly, should reform be extended to other domestic relationships in due course, the adoption of a family law model, while arguably appropriate for couple cohabitation, may not be well suited to deal with other forms of non-couple relationships which are not analogous to marriage or cohabitation. The transplantation of the existing family law model may not necessarily provide a practicable regime for the resolution of disputes over the shared home in a wider range of relationships.

Given these tensions, this chapter will firstly consider the issue of the basis upon which statutory reform should be premised. Here, the proposed legislation would need to give careful consideration to whether the basis for property adjustment should be addressed from a property law (e.g. based on contributions, etc.) or a relationship perspective (e.g. where the nature of the parties' relationship as a form of joint partnership and their needs, present and future, are, *inter alia*, considered to be relevant factors). This is important to female claimants[4] as the choice of one or the other may have significantly different consequences in terms of establishing an entitlement to the shared home. The chapter will also consider the further issue of whether, notwithstanding the Law Commission's current remit, legislative reform should only be limited to unmarried opposite and same-sex cohabitants, or be extended to a wider range of relationships such as care-giving relationships. The use of arguments based on economic vulnerability arising from interdependent relationships to promote the protection of vulnerable groups (such as cohabitants) plays into the hands of other vulnerable groups.[5] With legal protection being based on economic vulnerability rather than status, the exclusion of other economically vulnerable groups such as carers may, for example, raise issues of discrimination that will be contrary to the Human Rights Act 1998. These two issues are not necessarily mutually exclusive.

## The current law

At present, except for the Matrimonial Causes Act 1973 which applies to spouses and the Civil Partnership Act 2004 to same-sex civil partners, English law does not provide the courts with adjustive powers to deal with property disputes on relationship breakdown. Consequently, claimants have to rely on contract law, property law and/or trusts law to determine their rights to the shared home. In many cases, claimants have relied upon trusts principles, especially the common intention constructive trust as formulated in *Lloyds Bank v Rosset* [1991] 1 AC 107. Criticisms of the *Rosset* test have already been subject to extensive discussion (Bottomley 1993 and 1998, Eeekelaar 1991, Gardner 1993, Glover and Todd 1996, Halliwell 1991, Lawson 1996, Wong 1998 and 1999). This chapter will not revisit these arguments except to reiterate that the criticisms have been mainly levelled at two particular aspects of the test. The first is the requirement for a common intention, which many have argued is rarely articulated by the parties, whether orally or in writing, prior to or at the commencement of the relationship (Bottomley 1993 and 1998, Clarke 1992, Gardner 1993, Glover and Todd 1996). The second is the narrow approach taken in inferring intention from the parties' conduct. Here, the courts have confined themselves to direct financial contributions as being the only type of contribution sufficient to justify the inference of a common intention to share. Indirect financial and non-financial contributions are insufficient even when they are substantial.[6]

From a feminist perspective, it has been argued that the little significance given to indirect contributions is not only discriminatory but also forms an effective barrier to female claimants successfully establishing the existence of the requisite common intention.[7] Cases like *Midland Bank v Cooke* [1995] 4 All ER 562[8] and, more recently, *Oxley v Hiscock* [2004] EWCA Civ 546; [2004] 3 All ER 703[9] indicate the courts' willingness to take a slightly more generous approach in respect of indirect contributions, that is to survey 'the whole course of dealing' between the parties. This more generous approach is, however, taken in determining detrimental reliance and the quantification of beneficial interest, rather than common intention itself. A claimant relying on an implied common intention to share would still be required to make some direct financial contribution towards the purchase of the property in order to get the claim off the ground. Even then, the courts have not always demonstrated a tendency to be overly generous in quantifying the parties' respective shares. While Mrs Cooke was awarded a half-share in the property, the shares of claimants in other cases, for example *Oxley v Hiscock*, have to some extent been determined by their financial contributions towards the purchase of the property. This has led many commentators like Bailey-Harris (1998: 81) to argue for displacing the application of trusts principles since '[the law] continues to favour the wage-earning, property-acquiring role in a family relationship'.[10]

It is arguable that a change in judicial treatment of domestic contributions may be discerned in recent matrimonial cases such as *White v White* [2001] 1 All ER 1 *Cowan v Cowan* [2001] EWCA Civ 679 and *Lambert v Lambert* [2003] Fam 103. There appears to be a greater willingness on the part of the judges to give more weight to the indirect contributions of wives on the basis that 'fairness' dictates that spouses should be treated with substantive equality. Thus, except in the most unusual of cases, the courts are unwilling to compare the various contributions made by the spouses. As held in *Lambert* [2003] Fam 103 at 114, the wife's non-financial domestic contributions were 'intrinsically different and incommensurable'; it would not be possible to compare her contributions with those of her income-earning husband since it would be like 'comparing apples with pears'.[11] The wife's indirect contributions to the care and welfare of the family therefore should not be treated as being less significant than the financial contributions of the husband. It is tempting to argue that the approach taken in *White* and *Lambert* may finally address the gender bias and discrimination that female claimants have faced in the past in relation to the treatment of domestic contributions. However, it should be noted that these cases involved so-called 'big money' where the assets available exceeded the parties' reasonable financial needs. In most 'small money' cases, needs remain central to the determination of financial and property matters at the breakdown of marriage. Thus, the 'fairness' approach taken in these 'big money' cases may be of limited application to other cases. Nevertheless, given the difficulties of comparing the 'incommensurable', it remains to be seen how far future courts are likely, or willing, to, firstly, extend the 'fairness' approach beyond 'big money' marital cases to not only 'small money' marital cases but also non-marital ones and, secondly, to reinterpret the second limb (implied common intention) of the *Rosset* test accordingly.

## Statutory frameworks

Given the limitations of the current equitable principles, the discussion has inevitably steered towards considering alternatives and, more particularly, statutory reform. In that respect, various models of statutory reform have been considered in other jurisdictions,[12] and are now being considered in England and Wales (Barlow and Lind 1999, Law Commission 2002, Law Society 2002). This section will consider the statutory schemes proposed by the Law

Society and the Law Commission respectively, with comparisons being made to that adopted in New South Wales. The aim is to attempt to rationalise the various conditions upon which courts may exercise their statutory powers to redistribute property. In so doing, the section will further address the question of whether a property law or a relationship approach should form the basis of the proposed legislation.

### *Law Commission's property law approach*

In its Discussion Paper, the Law Commission considered a contributions-based statutory scheme, where the nature of the parties' relationship will not be relevant (Law Commission 2002: Part III). The basis for making any property adjustment in relation to the shared home is wholly premised on the contributions, financial and non-financial, made. The aim of the scheme is threefold (Law Commission 2002: para 3.4). Firstly, it removes the existing reliance on common intention and gives effect to the parties' past contributions.[13] Secondly, it replaces the existing doctrines of proprietary estoppel and implied trusts in determining beneficial entitlement to the shared home. Lastly, it creates a statutory default scheme for determining beneficial ownership of the property, which will provide greater clarity and consistency.[14]

In line with a property law approach, a key feature of the Law Commission's proposed scheme is the centrality of contributions. Although the contributions need not be directly referable to the acquisition of the shared home, contributions, whether direct or indirect, have to be made in order for a share in the equity to arise. Here, the Law Commission considers two possible 'relevant' contributions. The first is direct and indirect financial contributions towards the acquisition, improvement or retention of the property. The second is non-financial contributions to the construction or improvement of the home, or to the parties' joint lives (Law Commission 2002: para 3.5).[15] Hence, under the scheme, a claimant, who has made a relevant contribution, will acquire a proprietary interest in the shared home which is proportionate to his/her contribution. There is no discretion given to the courts in terms of adjusting property although the courts do have some discretion under the broad brush approach to assessing the economic value of contributions (Law Commission 2002: para 3.83).[16]

### *Law society's family law model*

In its Report, the Law Society recommends a two-tier system. At one level, a presumptive approach is taken, in that certain rights will accrue to both opposite-sex and same-sex cohabitants, where they have lived together for a requisite minimum period of two years or have a relevant child (Law Commission 2002: paras 15 and 16). At a second level, same-sex, but not opposite-sex, cohabitants will be permitted to register their relationships whereupon they will acquire rights that are analogous to married couples. The reform envisaged by the Law Society is undoubtedly more extensive than merely dealing with property disputes between cohabitants. It is, however, narrower since it does not apply to other types of domestic relationships. Hence a female claimant, who is in neither a heterosexual nor a same-sex relationship but is in a domestic relationship of care and support,[17] will not benefit from this particular property adjustment regime.

The Law Society's proposed registration system has since been overtaken by subsequent events, namely the passage of the Civil Partnership Act 2004. Nevertheless, its proposals for a presumptive scheme for unmarried opposite-sex and unregistered same-sex cohabitation merits closer examination. Under the presumptive model, certain rights to the redistribution of property will accrue to cohabitants at the end of the relationship. The presumptive approach, however, maintains a distinction between cohabitation and marriage, and adopts an adjustive system that differs from that taken in matrimonial cases for ancillary relief. The adjustment of property is to be made on an 'economic advantage and disadvantage' basis: 'A fair account should be taken of any economic advantage derived by either party from the contributions from the other, and of any economic disadvantages suffered by either party in the interests of the other party or of the family' (Law Society 2002: para 101).[18] The Law Society goes on to explain that 'contributions' should be defined as those in money or money's worth. This can therefore include indirect contributions made as a parent, or in maintaining or running the home or family (Law Society 2002: para 102). By focusing on a 'fair account', the Law Society's proposed scheme remains closely linked to the issue of contributions, i.e. whether the cohabitants have sustained any advantages or disadvantages from the contributions made during the relationship (Law Society 2002: para 104). Hence no adjustment shall be made where neither party has sustained any advantage or disadvantage. The approach taken therefore remains retrospective in nature and very much focused on contributions.

### *Property (Relationships) Act 1984 (New South Wales)*

The Property (Relationships) Act 1984 of New South Wales provides a presumptive system which gives courts the power to make property adjustment orders at the end of a domestic relationship. This includes not only opposite- and same-sex cohabitants but also others in a close personal relationship. A 'close personal relationship' is one between two individuals who live together, whether or not related by family, where one or each of whom provides the other with domestic support and personal care.[19] The courts may make an adjustment order where it is 'fair and just', having regard to the types of contributions referred to in s 20(1)(a) and (b) of the Act.[20] The aim of the Property (Relationships) Act 1984 is to enable the courts to overcome the kind of difficulties noted in the *Rosset* test, particularly the insufficient recognition given to indirect contributions. These contributions can be in relation to either the acquisition of assets by the defendant or to his financial resources, or the care and welfare of the family. Thus the Property (Relationships) Act 1984 specifically requires that such contributions be taken into account to determine what order may be fair and just.

Although the Property (Relationships) Act 1984 is to some extent based on the Commonwealth Family Law Act 1975 which governs marital proceedings, the approach taken in the 1984 Act is not as extensive as that provided in the 1975 Act. In determining property orders under the Family Law Act 1975, the court is entitled to consider not only the past contributions made but also other factors, which are described as the 'needs and means' factors, in s 75(2) of the Act. The Property (Relationships) Act 1984 excludes the consideration of these factors and the issue of what 'fair and just' order should be made is wholly centred on contributions (Wong 2001). The Act is therefore closely modelled on a property law contributions-based approach which operates retrospectively, by looking only at the contributions made in the past, and not to any present or future needs of the parties, to determine what adjustment order to make. Where it differs from, and is wider than, the Law Commission's model is that the New South Wales courts have greater discretion since they have powers to adjust property rights where it is 'fair and just'.

### *Property law approach versus relationship approach*

An essential aspect of all the above regimes is that the claimant must make some form of contribution, whether financial or non-financial. A key difference though is the treatment and the consequence of the contributions made. In confining the approach to property law, the Law Commission's regime proposed in 2002 is clearly the most restrictive and should rightly be rejected. In effect, the proposed regime does no more than adopt a hybrid resulting trust analysis where there is scope to take into account indirect contributions. The recognition of indirect financial and non-financial contributions is placed on a statutory footing, where such contributions would otherwise be excluded under orthodox resulting trust principles. Hence any entitlement to the shared home is measured against contributions made and in most cases the award of a share will be closely linked or proportionate to the contributions made. The nature of the judges' discretion under the Law Commission's proposed scheme is declaratory rather than adjustive. While avoiding the common intention requirement, a clear weakness of this strict property law approach is that it loses some of the flexibility that the courts have under the existing common intention approach. The courts currently have at least some discretion, albeit limited, to consider what the parties' intentions regarding their beneficial shares might possibly be in the light of 'the whole course of dealing' in their relationship. Beneficial entitlement is thus not dictated by a pure mathematical calculation of the parties' shares based on the economic value of their contributions. Given that, it is not surprising that the Law Commission rejected the scheme on the grounds of inflexibility.

By contrast, although contributions of the types listed in s 20(a) and (b) of the Property (Relationships) Act 1984 are essential to the exercise of judicial discretion, the powers of the New South Wales courts are clearly adjustive. New South Wales judges are required to make adjustment orders on the basis of what is fair and just in the light of the contributions made and are not restricted to adjusting property by awarding the claimant a share that is proportionate to her contributions. The model proposed by the Law Society, likewise, provides the courts with adjustive, and not merely declaratory, powers. There are certain similarities between the Property (Relationships) Act 1984 and the Law Society's model. Both adopt a presumptive approach to conferring certain rights on the parties to the relationship. Both also provide the courts with fairly broad discretion to consider a wider range of contributions in determining whether, on the basis of fairness, an adjustment order should be made. The conferment of adjustive rather than declaratory powers no doubt gives courts a greater level of discretion. However, there is still the intractable problem of defining the notion of 'fair and just' as well as determining whether 'a fair account' has been given to contributions made, as this seems inextricably linked, whether to a greater or lesser extent, to placing value on various types of contributions. Under the Property (Relationships) Act 1984, a 'fair and just' adjustment order may be compensatory or restitutionary in nature.[21] The Law Society's 'fair account', on the other hand, takes a predominantly compensatory approach. It requires the courts to balance the economic advantages derived by one party from the contributions made by the other with any economic disadvantages sustained by the other. An adjustment order will only be made to redress an imbalance and to compensate the claimant for any disadvantages sustained, which has not been adequately compensated for by the advantages received (Law Society 2002: paras 103–104).[22] In the absence of that, no adjustment order will be made.

Whether restitutionary or compensatory in nature, both the Property (Relationships) Act 1984 and the Law Society's model require some benefit to have been given through the making of contributions. This means that courts will inevitably have to grapple with assessing the value of the contributions made in order to determine whether a 'benefit' has in fact been derived from the contributions. Concerns were, however, expressed by the Law Commission about whether the value of non-financial contributions could be fairly and objectively assessed (Law Commission 2002: para 3.48). This consequently led the Commission to conclude that its putative contributions-based scheme would not be desirable. The Law Society, on the other hand, provides little insight as to whether these concerns are shared. The Law Commission's concerns regarding the fair and objective assessment of the value of non-financial contributions are nevertheless very real and are not necessarily confined only to the property law model. The experiences of the existing equitable principles as well as statutory schemes such as the Matrimonial Causes Act 1973 and the Property (Relationships) Act 1984 reveal similar problems of assessing the value of indirect contributions, especially those of a homemaker. The incommensurability of the different types of contributions, as noted in cases like *White* and *Lambert*, further serve to compound the problem of trying to place value on such contributions.

In addition, although contributions are not as central under the Matrimonial Causes Act 1973 as compared with the Property (Relationships) Act 1984 or the Law Society's model, the marital cases, argues Diduck, demonstrate how the notion of fairness remains imbued with certain ideologies of law about relationships. These in turn result in the formulation of certain perceptions about the roles which parties to a relationship are expected to undertake (Diduck 2001). Bailey-Harris similarly observes that the law generally makes certain stereotyped assumptions about the roles assumed in domestic relationships by women and men respectively (Bailey-Harris 1998, see also Neave 1991). These assumptions of female claimants in heterosexual relationships may equally extend to those in lesbian relationships (Flynn and Lawson 1995). Consequently, courts may perceive domestic contributions made by a female claimant as being made out of 'love and affection', and thus attach little or no value to them. Similar contributions made by a male claimant might, on the other hand, be treated as acts of detrimental reliance that are capable of giving rise to an entitlement in the shared home. This is illustrated, for example, in *Wayling v Jones* [1995] 2 FLR 1029 where the unpaid labour provided by the plaintiff was treated by the court as sufficient acts of detrimental reliance to ground a claim in proprietary estoppel (Lawson 1996). However, the provision of unpaid labour were seen as insufficient in cases like *Rosset* and *Burns v Burns* [1984] 1 All ER 244; [1984] Ch 317 since such labour was treated as being provided out of natural love and affection by the female plaintiffs in those cases (Flynn and Lawson 1995, Bailey-Harris 1998). Thus, statutory provision for the recognition of indirect contributions may be of little consequence if these stereotypes and ideologies of law are permitted to apply.

A 'broad brush' approach towards assessing the value of indirect contributions may not necessarily be problem-free either. Here, some guidance may be gleaned from the approach taken by the New South Wales courts under the Property (Relationships) Act 1984. The New South Wales cases indicate that, when assessing the value of indirect, especially non-financial, contributions made, such contributions should not be regarded as being inferior to the financial contributions made by the other party.[23] Moreover, proper and full value should be given and it would be inappropriate to assess value by reference to wages that may be payable to a domestic servant or other commercial provider of such services.[24] Although the New South Wales case law shows that indirect contributions should not be given token value, little guidance is provided on the issue of valuation of such contributions under a 'broad brush' approach. This makes the assessment of indirect contributions very arbitrary and subject to judicial beneficence. In addition, the upshot of a 'broad brush' approach and the wide discretionary powers given to judges may lead to unpredictability in ascertaining the outcome of cases and the quantum of a claimant's entitlement. It is for this very reason that the Law Commission rejected providing statutory adjustive discretion (Law Commission 2002: para 3.48).[25] There is also the added danger of undervaluing indirect contributions, especially contributions of a homemaker or parent.[26] This is particularly the case where existing ideologies of law, as discussed earlier, continue to influence judicial thinking. Thus, uncertainty about the way in which courts will in fact assess indirect contributions will correspondingly lead to uncertainty regarding the quantification of shares in the adjustment order.

One of the main problems with the Law Society's model lies in its use of a family law model without dealing headlong with the tensions that arise in the model itself as a result of retaining the principle of separate property. In focusing on contributions, the model, like the existing equitable principles, emphasises and continues to favour the property-acquiring role in relationships. On the one hand, it tries to avoid the difficulties of the current law by, firstly, providing for the legal recognition of indirect contributions and, secondly, empowering the courts to make adjustment orders on the basis of a 'fair account'. So long as the focus remains on contributions, providing statutory recognition to indirect contributions does not necessarily resolve the difficulties that arise in the first place with such contributions and if courts are not given any scope to consider 'the diversity of arrangements made in such close personal relationships, nor the subtle blending of the parties' efforts' (Bailey-Harris 1998: 83).[27]

The Law Society's adoption of the 'fair account' approach, found originally in s 9(1)(b) of the Family Law (Scotland) Act 1985 still allows tensions with property law to remain. This can lead to disputes about whether the domestic contributions of one party, when weighed against the financial contributions of the other party, would be given sufficient value in determining the existence of a disadvantage that requires redress through an adjustment order. The difficulty with the transplantation of the 'fair account' approach as *the* core principle upon which property adjustment is to be made is that it crucially omits the first principle found in the Family Law (Scotland) Act 1985. That first principle provides generally for the fair sharing in the value of assets classified as matrimonial property.[28] Matrimonial property extends to include the shared home if it was acquired before or after the marriage with the intention that it is to be used as the parties' family home. The Act further provides that 'fair sharing' should be taken to mean sharing equally or in such proportions as are justified in the circumstances.[29] Thus, the Family Law (Scotland) Act 1985 provides for community of property in relation to certain types of assets.[30] The second (fair account) principle only applies where a share in the value of the matrimonial property is insufficient to correct any imbalance that may still exist in terms of the advantages or disadvantages sustained by either of the parties to the relationship.[31] This shifts the focus away from grounding an adjustment order solely on contributions alone. It further provides greater recognition of the parties' relationship as a joint partnership and for the treatment of certain assets as relationship property. Provided that the assets were intended for the parties' joint benefit, they would be shared fairly by the parties. Hence the relationship approach taken in the Family Law (Scotland) Act 1985 moves away from the family law model found in the Matrimonial Causes Act 1973 which, by adhering to the principle of separate property, allows gender bias to continue. In that respect, notwithstanding the adoption of a 'fair account' approach, the Law Society's model does not go far enough. These cases will continue to be plagued by unpredictability due to problems linked with the valuation of indirect contributions and the quantification of entitlements.

As such, any proposed legal reform for cohabitants must take a more robust approach and move away from a property law approach which places too much emphasis on contributions, direct and indirect. On the other hand, moving towards a family law model does not necessarily resolve the kind of problems identified above if contributions remain an essential aspect of determining entitlements over the shared home. Unless the model embraces a more relational approach, it will not be capable of taking into account the true nature of the parties' relationship, the diversity of the arrangements made within the relationship especially in terms of their contributions, whether direct or indirect, towards the relationship as a joint partnership.[32] It will remain vulnerable to discrimination, where stereotyped assumptions about the parties are allowed to apply, and to unpredictability about the outcomes in cases. Notwithstanding the more generous approach that has recently been adopted in cases like *White, Cowan* and *Lambert*, it remains unclear whether the courts will be willing to take a similar approach in 'small money' marital, let alone cohabitation, cases.[33] In order to overcome these problems of discrimination and gender bias, the Law Society's model should not be confined to the adoption of the 'fair account' principle found in s 9(1)(b) of the Family Law (Scotland) Act 1985. It should go further by adopting an approach that allows for the interplay between the first and second principles found in s 9(1)(a) and (b) of the Family Law (Scotland) Act 1985.

The proposed model should therefore provide for some element of fair sharing in communal/relationship property, which will generally mean equal sharing,[34] but yet reserve to the courts the discretion to deviate from this principle if there is an imbalance that is not adequately compensated for by a share in the value of the relationship property. Parties to the relationship will then have a clearer idea of what their rights are in respect of the shared home. Contributions would only be relevant where there is evidence of an imbalance suffered, which is not adequately compensated for. This will enhance both predictability and certainty.

## Scope of the statutory framework

The introduction of legal reform raises a further issue, as to how far the net of the proposed property adjustment regime should be cast. Notwithstanding the Law Commission's current remit being limited to cohabitation, should the legal reform be confined only to opposite- and same-sex cohabitants? Or, as was debated in the House of Lords in relation to the Civil Partnership Bill, should it extend to a wider range of domestic relationships where the parties to such relationships may potentially be left economically vulnerable too? Should registration of a relationship be a prerequisite for the application of a property adjustment regime? It remains anyone's guess what the Law Commission is likely to recommend after the consultation process. However, from the Government's statements made during the passage of the Civil Partnership Bill through Parliament, it is evident that the Government intends to maintain a sharp distinction between heterosexual marriage and cohabitation, whether opposite or same sex. Consequently, the Government seems unpersuaded that a separate registration scheme providing formal recognition to opposite-sex cohabitants (or carers, for that matter) is necessary. Nevertheless, for the sake of argument, the Law Commission may after the consultation process consider the issue of a registration scheme in its current project on cohabitation. The introduction of a registration requirement can bring certain benefits and drawbacks.

As the New South Wales Law Reform Commission observes, the main advantage of a presumptive approach is that it does not require parties to the relationship to take any formal steps, for example registration, to opt in. A further advantage is that it can allow parties to opt out of the adjustment regime by making private arrangements (New South Wales law Reform Commission 2002: para 2.71). The need for registration, however, has the advantage of removing legislative conditions such as a cohabitation requirement as a prerequisite for acquiring rights.[35] In addition, a registration system provides parties, who are unable or who do not wish to get marry, with the opportunity of having their relationships legally recognised. One major drawback of a registration system, however, is that it remains status-based so that no rights will be acquired in the absence of registration.[36] This raised particular concerns for the Law Society when considering the scope of Lord Lester's Civil Partnership Bill, which required registration for rights to attach (Law Society 2002: paras 8–9). The clear disadvantage of a registration system is that it does not provide protection in cases where one party to the relationship refuses to either register the relationship or get married (Law Society 2002: paras 9, 33–34). This will leave the more vulnerable party unprotected and with no rights to property adjustment and/or financial provision at the breakdown of the relationship. Consequently, a clear advantage of a presumptive system is that it will provide cohabitants with redress on relationship breakdown, without the need for registration.

A presumptive approach applies by ascribing rights to cohabitants, opposite sex and same sex, upon satisfying certain criteria. This may include, for example, a requisite period of living together (Law Society 2002: paras 15–16)[37] or being in a relationship,[38] which can equally apply to couples as well as others in close personal relationships such as care-giving relationships. The possibility of extending legal reform to a wider range of relationships is not impossible, as can be seen from the experiences of the Property (Relationships) Act 1984. However, the key difficulties of extending the scope of any legal reform to a wider range of relationships are, firstly, the definition of such relationships and, secondly, whether there is any political will to do so. In respect of cohabitants, different definitions have been considered and adopted. Defining cohabitants may probably be less problematic. In most cases, there are certain common characteristics found in these various definitions. One commonality is the reference to some form of coupledom. What is more controversial is whether or not a cohabitation requirement is also imperative. Schemes like the Property (Relationships) Act 1984 and the Law Society' model have all adopted a definition where cohabitation is a prerequisite for the extension of protection, that is a relationship based on two adults, whether opposite sex or same sex, who are not related to each other by family and are *living together* 'as a couple',[39] or 'in a relationship analogous to that of husband and wife' (Law Society 2002: para 55).[40] Varying qualifying periods of cohabitation may also be set for the applicability of the adjustive regime.[41] A key objection to the inclusion of a cohabitation requirement is that it may render the definition under-inclusive. It fails to be sufficiently flexible to deal with myriad personal relationships of emotional and financial interdependence, and interdependence may arise without the parties living together or providing care and support (Millbank and Sant 2000).[42]

Further consideration should also be given to whether legal reform should be limited to opposite- and same-sex cohabitants. This would very much depend on what the objectives of the legal reform are. Legislation such as the Property (Relationships) Act 1984 have extended legal recognition and rights to same-sex couples since they are unable to marry and have access to the marital provisions on property adjustment.[43] The position in the UK is quite different since the passage of the Civil Partnership Act 2004. Same-sex couples who register a civil partnership may have access to rights analogous to those of married spouses. The arguments used in justifying the introduction of legal reform for same-sex couples were couched in the language of equality and non-discrimination as well as to address the economic vulnerability of a group of individuals whose relationships remained invisible in law. Raising 'economic vulnerability' as a key justification for introducing legal reform for cohabitation exposes the exclusion of other economically vulnerable groups of domestic partners, whether or not their relationships are sexual, to potential human rights challenges. Just as same-sex couples have had some measure of success in challenging their exclusion from legal protection on the grounds of sexual orientation discrimination, cohabitants might also attempt to argue that any failure to introduce some form of reform to protect their relationships might amount to martial status discrimination. However, as has been argued elsewhere, the use of marital status discrimination may be of limited mileage for cohabitants (Wong 2005). Human rights challenges by other groups of domestic partners, for example carers, may be equally problematic. It will be extremely difficult for them to piggyback on the sort of arguments made by cohabitants (sexual orientation discrimination for same-sex couples and marital status discrimination by opposite- and same-sex couples) unless a broader notion of discrimination on the basis of 'status' comes to be accepted as a ground of discrimination within the Human Rights Act 1998. The other possible route for mounting a challenge by carers is to attack the proportionality of the proposed legal reform in terms of achieving its legitimate objectives.[44] Any new legislation to be passed by Parliament will require a declaration of compatibility with the Human Rights Act 1998 from a Minister and justification will be required for the difference in treatment between cohabitants (sexual couple-based economically vulnerable parties) and carers (non-sexual and non-couple-based economically vulnerable parties).[45] Such human rights challenges may be articulated along the lines that it violates Art 8 which provides for the right to respect of private life and possibly Art 14 (prohibition of discrimination) in conjunction with Art 8 in that the measures taken (providing protection only to domestic partners who are cohabitants) are not proportionate to the aims sought (protection against economic vulnerability arising from a domestic relationship). It must, however, be said that the chances of success of such human rights challenges may be slim given that the prohibition against discrimination under the Human Rights Act 1998 is not an absolute guarantee. It also remains very unclear whether, notwithstanding economic vulnerability, carers as a group are placed in an analogous position as cohabitants for the purposes of Art 14.

The extension of any proposed legal reform to a wider range of relationships will also raise the further difficulty of formulating a sufficiently inclusive definition for all these types of interdependent relationships. Given the diversity of these relationships, the Law Society had felt that, not only would it be almost impossible to provide a single definition that would embrace such diversity, it would also be unlikely that any proposal for reform would be capable of providing a full range of remedies for each of these interdependent relationships (Law Society 2002: paras 39–42). No doubt the Law Society's concerns, which were shared by the Law Commission back in 2002, are very real and any attempt to draw up legal reform that extends to a wider range of relationships would not be a simple task. Statutory reforms such as the Property (Relationships) Act 1984, nevertheless, do offer some protection to parties in relationships involving the provision of care and support.[46] The extension of legal reform to other interdependent relationships along the lines of the Property (Relationships) Act 1984 does not, however, remove the conceptual problems that may arise. Difficulties remain at a practical level in respect of determining the meaning to be given to phrases such as 'domestic support' and 'personal care'. Notwithstanding these issues, statutes like the 1984 Act indicate that the extension of legal reform to a wider range of relationships is certainly possible. More crucially, any move to extend legal reform to a wider range of relationships will require the political will to do so before any careful consideration may be given to matters such as: the extent to which other relationships are to be included; the definition(s) to be adopted for these relationships; the criteria upon which the legal reform will be applicable; and, given the differences between cohabitation and care-giving relationships, whether it would be appropriate to allow the same legal consequences to apply.

## Conclusion

Much of the workability of a proposed statutory framework for resolution of property disputes at the end of a domestic relationship will depend on the objectives of the legislature and what means are employed to achieve these objectives. While it is clear that the pursuit of alternative methods of resolution has stemmed from the rigidity of the existing equitable principles, the policy objectives of the legislature must be carefully thought through and articulated. In the examples explored above, both legal and practical problems are likely to arise and have arisen. These models of reform reveal a common feature. In order to break away from the rigidity of the equitable principles, all have looked to providing statutory recognition of indirect financial and non-financial contributions. There is also a concerted effort to maintain a distinction between marriage and cohabitation. Thus the rights conferred on cohabitants do not and should not go as far as those available to married couples (and civil partners). This is reflected in the fact that the factors, which the courts are required to take into account for making an adjustment order, are more limited in the case of cohabitation and tend to remain focused, to a lesser or greater extent, on contributions.

The models considered generally confine the scope of the courts' adjustive powers to looking at the parties' contributions, direct and indirect, financial and non-financial. None take a more robust approach by examining more closely the nature of the parties' relationships and questioning whether the retrospective evaluation of contributions is sufficient to bring about fairness between the parties on relationship breakdown.[47] From the perspective of a female claimant, the legal recognition of non-financial contributions presupposes that the process of determining whether an adjustment order should be made would become more gender neutral and thus fairer to them. This is because the main arguments raised about discrimination are then adequately dealt with by removing the very source of that discrimination, i.e. through providing courts with adjustive, and not merely declaratory, powers and for the statutory recognition of indirect financial and non-financial contributions. This, however, misses the point. Once again, the law is responding in a way that provides protection through conferring formal rather than substantive equality to female claimants. In adopting an approach that looks to the contributions made by the parties to the relationship as the principal means of determining whether an adjustment order should be made, the law has failed to grapple with the sources of women's inequality under the law such as the various ideologies of law which act to women's disadvantage.

The adoption of a family law approach, which continues to treat all parties to intimate personal relationships, including spouses and cohabitants, as autonomous property-acquiring actors, may not necessarily alleviate the discrimination suffered by women. Family cases continue to demonstrate how problematic the assessment of contributions remain, even where other factors such as spouses' needs may be taken into account. Given the narrow context within which the courts in *White, Cowan* and *Lambert* were dealing with the issue of contributions, the concept of 'fairness' (non-discrimination and substantive justice) as applied in those cases may be of limited mileage in other cases. Furthermore, there is the potential for gender bias to persist as the notion of 'fairness' may continue to be imbued with certain ideologies of the law regarding the roles assumed by men and women in personal relationships. The more effective solution is to introduce reform that adopts a relational approach, which will allow close personal relationships to be treated as joint partnerships, and for certain assets such as the shared home to be classified as relationship/communal property. Such property will thus be shared fairly by the parties. This may be achieved by expanding the Law Society's 'fair account' approach through including the first core principle and its mode of application as contained in ss 9(1)(a) and 10(1) of the Family Law (Scotland) Act 1985. This suggests a presumption of equal sharing unless the circumstances are such that there will be undue hardship or injustice to one party, in which case the courts are given residual powers to reallocate beneficial interests in the shared home.

Finally, there is the added issue of whether reform should only be limited to one group of economically vulnerable domestic partners, namely cohabitants. Again, this raises concerns for feminists in that most domestic care-giving relationships, I suspect, involve female, rather than male, carers. A failure to extend some protection to this group of economically vulnerable individuals means that the valuable contributions made in terms of care-giving remain invisible and unrecognised by the state, which in turn reinforces the gendered dimensions of care-giving in personal relationships. But the difficulty of getting the issue of protecting economically vulnerable carers back on the agenda stems more from an absence of political will rather than the conceptual problems of framing legal reform.

## Notes

1 *Hansard*, Commons col. 179, 12 October 2004, Jacqui Smith. The Scottish Parliament has since passed the Family Law (Scotland) Act 2006 which provides certain rights to cohabitants. Briefly, these rights are not as extensive as those of married couples and civil partners. There is no property adjustment regime for cohabitants within the Family Law (Scotland) Act 2006; nor do cohabitants have any property-sharing rights over the shared home as married couples do with matrimonial property under the Family Law (Scotland) Act 1985. Sharing rights are limited to household goods, and money and assets derived from housekeeping allowances: Family Law (Scotland) Act 2006, ss 26 and 27. The courts are instead given powers to make financial orders on the basis of a fair account of the economic advantages and disadvantages of the parties: Family Law (Scotland) Act 2006, s 28.

2 The term 'carers' is taken to mean parties, whether related by family or not, who are living together in a domestic relationship involving the provision of care and support.

3 See the recommendation made in Section IV of Law Society (2002), stating that family law, rather than property law and trusts law, would deal more appropriately with the disputes between cohabitants. Yet, as will be seen in the discussion below, the model adopted by the Law Society has its limitations as it does not wholly break ties with a property law approach.

4 A female claimant can fall into one of three possible categories. She may be in an opposite-sex relationship, or a same-sex relationship, or a domestic relationship of care and support. At present, if she were in a same-sex relationship, she may protect herself by registering a civil partnership under the Civil Partnership Act 2004. However, if legislative reform is restricted to opposite- and same-sex cohabiting couples, it means that a female claimant who is in a domestic relationship of care and support will be left unprotected and will have to look to the existing common law to establish a beneficial interest in the shared home.

5 This can be seen from the developments that took place in Australia, e.g. in New South Wales and Tasmania. State legislation was initially introduced to deal with the property and financial matters of unmarried opposite-sex couples on the grounds of economic vulnerability arising from their interdependent relationships. However, unmarried same-sex couples and parties to care-giving relationships were able to 'piggyback' on the economic vulnerability argument, which led to the legislation being extended to the latter two groups. See Wong (2001) for a fuller discussion.

6 *Per* Lord Bridge in *Rosset*. See also *Burns v Burns* [1984] 2 FLR 167, which is often cited as the classic example of the harshness of the equitable principles.

7 This is mainly because the *Rosset* approach tends to ignore the continued existence of sexual division of labour in domestic relationships, which in turn impacts on the ability of many female claimants to satisfy the narrow conditions formulated. See Neave (1991); Bailey-Harris (1998) and Wong (1998).

8 See also *Drake v Whipp* [1996] 1 FLR 826.

9 The 'whole course of dealing' approach taken in *Oxley v Hiscock* is however different from that in *Midland Bank v Cooke*. In *Oxley*, the Court of Appeal held that, where there is no evidence of the parties' intentions regarding their respective shares to the property, their shares ought to be determined by what is 'fair' in the light of the parties' 'whole course of conduct'. The approach clearly brings together more closely common intention trust and proprietary estoppel.

10 Bottomley (2006) argues for caution in introducing legal reform that is more closely aligned with family law on the grounds of 'realism' and economic vulnerability.

She questions the veracity of 'realism' arguments that property (trusts) law has failed female cohabitants as well as that family law would be more robust (than property law) in dealing with and/or addressing the emotional and economic vulnerability arising from cohabitation.

11 Quoting Coleridge J in *G v G (Financial Provision: Equal Division)* [2002] 2 FLR 1143.

12 In Australia, sub-national legislation has been passed to deal with such financial and property matters of unmarried opposite- and same-sex couples and in some cases, even domestic partners in non-couple care-giving relationships. See, e.g., the Property (Relationships) Act 1984 of New South Wales; the Domestic Relationships Act 1994 of the Australian Capital Territory; and the Relationships Act 2003 of Tasmania. Because of the constraint of space, I will focus on the Property (Relationships) Act 1984 in this chapter since it is the model that is most closely aligned with a property law contributions-based approach. For a fuller discussion of these statutes in regulating property redistribution at the end of a relationship, see Wong (2004).

13 The Law Commission (2002), however, conceded (at paras 3.24 and 3.25) that it would be unrealistic and impractical to completely deny any importance to the parties' intentions. However, the approach taken in the proposed scheme is that intention is not a requirement and plays merely an evidential role for raising a rebuttable presumption of a share in the property.

14 The Law Commission (2002) stressed (at para 3.47) that the proposed scheme would not be similar to granting ancillary relief on divorce and the aim of making any adjustive order was not to accommodate the parties' present and future needs.

15 However, where non-financial contributions were being relied upon, the Law Commission (2002) considered that a minimum two-year period of sharing should be required (para 3.54).

16 But see also n 14. Notwithstanding a 'broad brush' approach being taken, the scope of the courts' discretion remains narrower than in the grant of ancillary relief since any property adjustment under the proposed scheme would not take into account the parties' present and future needs.

17 The essential aspect of the relationship in that case is care-giving rather than whether the woman has a sexual relationship with the other party or is a family member of the other party.

18 This approach to property adjustment is lifted from the second principle stated in s 9(1)(b) of the Family Law (Scotland) Act 1985, which is to be applied in determining whether an order for financial provision should be made.

19 Property (Relationships) Act 1984, s 5(1)(b).

20 *Evans v Marmont* (1997) 21 Fam LR 760. The contributions covered in para (a) cover financial and non-financial contributions that have contributed, directly or indirectly, to the acquisition, conservation and improvement of any property of the parties or either of them. The contributions in para (b), on the other hand, refer to non-financial contributions as homemaker or parent to the welfare of the other party or the family constituted by the parties.

21 *Wallace v Stanford* (1995) 19 Fam LR 430; *Evans v Marmont* (above).

22 Note the approach taken under the Family Law (Scotland) Act 1985, where s 9(1)(b) is treated as being compensatory and not necessarily restitutionary in nature. As Thomson (1987) explains, unlike in restitution, the economic disadvantage suffered by one party need not be matched by a corresponding economic advantage to the other.

23 *Black v Black* (1991) 15 Fam LR 109.

24 *Green v Robinson* (1995) 18 Fam LR 594.

25 The element of unpredictability will always exist when dealing with judicial discretion. This is equally true even of the existing equitable principles, as can be seen in cases like *Midland Bank v Cooke* and *Drake v Whipp,* where Mrs Drake, who made a greater financial contribution than Mrs Cooke, ended up with a smaller share than Mrs Cooke.

26 These concerns about the workability of the Property (Relationships) Act 1984 and, more particularly, in assessing indirect contributions have recently been noted by the New South Wales Law Reform Commission. See New South Wales Law Reform Commission (2002) at paras 5.40–5.58 and Wong (2001).

27 Although Bailey-Harris makes this criticism with respect to the existing trusts principles, I would argue that a similar criticism may be levelled at the existing marital provisions and any proposed statutory reform that attempts to model itself, whether to a lesser or greater extent, on that system.

28 Family Law (Scotland) Act 1985, s 9(1)(a) provides that there should be fair sharing of the value of the matrimonial property. Matrimonial property is defined in s 10(1)(4) as all property belonging to the parties or either of them as at the date of final separation which was acquired during the marriage.

29 See Family Law (Scotland) Act1985, s 10(1).

30 Note the approach taken in Lord Lester's Civil Partnerships Bill, which was introduced as a private Member's Bill in 2002 but was subsequently withdrawn when the Government promised to look into the matter. Clause 9(1) of that Bill provided that 'communal property' would include, *inter alia*, any dwelling house which was owned by either or both parties to the relationship and was used by them jointly as their principal or only home. Such property would be treated as held jointly by the parties in equal shares. However, Lord Lester's Bill applied only when cohabitants had registered their relationship as a civil partnership. No such provision is included in the Law Society's model; nor did the Scottish Parliament include provisions comparable to s 9(1)(a) and s 10 of the Family Law (Scotland) Act 1985 in the Family Law (Scotland) Act 2006 in relation to cohabitants. Anne Barlow and Elizabeth Smith are currently undertaking research funded by the Nuffield Foundation on 'Community of Property: A Regime for England and Wales?' My thanks to Anne Bottomley for bringing this to my attention.

31 See also cl 36 of Lord Lester's Bill (above) which provided the courts with residual discretion to make adjustment orders where it considered that financial or other hardship was likely to be sustained by one party to the relationship.

32 For a fuller discussion on the questions that the Law Commission might need to consider in order to provide for a more robust relational approach to dealing with the property matters of cohabitants see Wong (2006).

33 There may, however, be strong arguments in favour of the principles of non-discrimination and substantive equality gradually seeping into judicial thinking in non-spousal cases as a consequence of the impact of the Human Rights Act 1998 and the emerging human rights culture. The Human Rights Act 1998 may not provide cohabitants a direct cause of action for the infringement of the Convention rights but may provide developmental influence in the common law and statutes relating to private disputes. For a discussion of the possible impact of the Human Rights Act 1998 in private family property disputes, see Wong (2003) and Wong (2005).

34 For the purposes of the proposed property adjustment scheme, the relationship property shall include the shared home.

35 For example, there is no cohabitation prerequisite for the registration of a civil partnership under the Civil Partnership Act 2004; note Lord Lester's Bill, cl 2(1)(c) which provided for a cohabitation condition and that an application for the

registration of a civil partnership could be made where the parties had lived together for a period of six months ending on the date of the application.

36 Interestingly, the New South Wales Law Reform Commission (2002: para 2.74) found that the Gay and Lesbian Rights Lobby had expressed concerns about a registration system on the grounds that this would create a hierarchy of legally recognised relationships, with registered same-sex relationships being seen as a 'second best' option.

37 The Law Society proposes a two-year cohabitation period; note the Family Law (Scotland) Act 2006 does not stipulate a minimum period of cohabitation for the Act to apply to cohabitants.

38 The omission of a cohabitation requirement can be found in some of the Australian sub-national statutes, for example the Domestic Relationships Act 1994 of the Australian Capital Territory and the Relationships Act 2004 of Tasmania.

39 Property (Relationships) Act 1984, s 4(1). There is also guidance in s 4(2), by way of a list of circumstances which the courts may take into account, to determine whether a couple are in a qualifying relationship.

40 Using conjugality as a reference for defining a qualifying relationship raises concerns about the way in which the marriage model is being stretched to accommodate other intimate relationships within the law. For a fuller discussion, see Bottomley and Wong (2006).

41 For example, the Property (Relationships) Act 1984 and the Law Society both provide for a qualifying period of at least two years' cohabitation or, in that absence of that period, that there is a child of the parties. See Property (Relationships) Act 1984, s 17 and Law Society (2002: para 61).

42 See also the Family Law (Scotland) Act 2006. The Scottish Act of 2006 adopts a presumptive system for ascribing certain rights to cohabitants but does not impose any pre-requisite period of cohabitation for a relationship to qualify: see Family Law (Scotland) Act 2006, s 25.

43 This may be particularly the case where legal reform is to take the form of a registration system. In that case, policy arguments may be made that such system should not extend to opposite-sex cohabitants. As noted by the Law Society (2001), this will create a two-tier system for opposite-sex couples and one clear disadvantage is that 'unscrupulous partners in opposite-sex relationships would be given the opportunity to consider whether registration or marriage would be more financially advantageous to them on the breakdown of a relationship (para 34).

44 *Ghaidan v Mendoza* [2002] 4 All ER 1162 (CA), [2004] 3 All ER 411 (HL); *Wandsworth London Borough Council v Michalak* [2002] 4 All ER 1136; *R v Director of Public Prosecutions, ex p Kebeline* [1999] 4 All ER 801.

45 Human Rights Act 1998, s 19.

46 Property (Relationships) Act 1984, s 5(1)(b). The conditions for the applicability of the adjustment regime are: cohabitation (although the presence of a sexual relationship is not a requirement); and the provision of domestic support and personal care. Other relationships which may involve the provision of domestic care and support but not the sharing of the same household are excluded.

47 In fact, only a few models have gone beyond contributions to include, for example, present and future needs, as factors for determining whether there should be property redistribution: see, for example, the Domestic Relationships Act 1994 of the Australian Capital Territory and the Relationships Act 2003 of Tasmania.

Chapter 11

# Networking resources

## A gendered perspective on Kwena women's property rights

*Anne Griffiths*

### Introduction

This chapter explores feminist perspectives on land from an ethnographic standpoint. Derived from social actors' perceptions and experiences of daily life, it focuses on the way in which individuals form part of networks which shape their world and channel their access to resources. The position individuals occupy in their networks of kinship, family and community is a crucial factor in facilitating or constraining their access to resources such as land, as well as other forms of property. This perspective represents an anthropological approach to the study of law through its focus on local, micro-studies and the specific, concrete, lived-experiences that inform peoples' lives. It is an approach that is absent from most lawyers' analyses of law which centre on law-as-text through a rigorous exposition of doctrinal analysis founded on a specific set of sources, institutions and personnel, that form the heart of formal legal discourse. Anthropological approaches to law have challenged conventional legal theory, from the early work of Schapera (1938), Llewellyn and Hoebel (1941) and Gluckman (1965), through to more recent studies, such as those from Comaroff and Roberts (1981), Collier and Starr (1989) and Harris (1996). Feminist commentators, including Olsen (1983), Smart (1984) and Delphy and Leonard (1992) have, like the anthropologists, sought to extend the scope of what constitutes a legitimate focus for legal inquiry, drawing together the threads of 'public' and 'private' dimensions of social life to reveal the underpinning of relations between power, law, and the discourses that governs people's lives. Feminist and anthropological approaches to law have been intertwined in some explorations of the figuring of kinship, including legal interventions into its fabrication. Varley (2002: 458), in the context of her own research in urban Mexico on the benefits, or otherwise, from legalisation of land tenure, has argued against 'locating all power in the public' whilst according insufficient attention to the importance of informal networks amongst friends and family, particularly for women. Strathern (1992) too has explored the relations between kinship and law from both a feminist and an anthropological perspective.

My chapter explores how Kwena women's relationships with land are mediated through the gendered networks of family and household, in conjunction with the broader economic, political, ideological and social domains of which they form part. It highlights how these factors shape the power of individuals to negotiate with one another, the types of discourse they employ and, in particular, the difficulties that women encounter in accessing and utilising land due to the gendered dimensions of the world in which they operate. This perspective focuses on what formalist legal analysis often ignores, namely the gendered world in which women live, a world in which the reality of power and authority undercuts the prescribed status of individual equality and neutrality that that model of law upholds.

The data is taken from fieldwork carried out in Botswana (Southern Africa) among the Bakwena (which translates as 'the people of the Kwena') in Molepolole village between 1982 and 1989[1] and focuses on the life histories of persons in the Mosotho *kgotla* which document individuals' experiences, as well as the connections of these persons to the broader social polity to which they belong. The life histories I gathered, combined with those collected by Isaac Schapera in 1937, provide a picture of continuity and change across two generations that highlights the differences between and among the sexes as well as demonstrating how membership of different family networks shapes women's and men's access to resources, including land. Of course, the fieldwork, carried out nearly 20 years ago, is already outdated through rapid economic and social change. However, my purpose is to develop an analysis of the data that demonstrates ways in which a gendered perspective on property shifts the focus away from formal rights towards a much more complex pattern of identifying the issues governing women's access to the use of ownership of property. It is not an attempt to try and provide a full contemporary picture of Botswana, rather it is hoped that working from an ethnographic study of this kind, reappraising data from an earlier period, may raise questions beyond the immediate geography of place and time.

The significance of writing this chapter in this book is, of course, primarily the issues it raises for women and property within a primarily rural economy in a rapidly developing country and in the final section of my chapter I shall turn to the implications of this in terms of the programmes (encouraged by such institutions as the World Bank) to formalise property rights in African jurisdictions. However, the implications of such ethnographic work extend beyond this, offering material and a methodology that may help to think about the complex relationship between women and property in very different socio-economic frames of reference. Therefore, I hope that readers will be able to use this chapter not only to introduce them to issues relating to women and property in Botswana, but also more importantly to enable them to think about how the material and the analysis might illuminate issues relating to women and property *per se*.

My discussion of land is situated within the broader context of property and access to resources because amongst Bakwena, 'land' represents only one component, albeit an important one, in the constellation of assets that individuals and families rely on for their livelihood. Thus my analysis views property in terms of social relations between people (Gluckman 1965: 78, Hann 1998: 2, Hoebel 1966: 424, Moore, S F 1988: 33 and Middleton 1998: xx), a perspective that requires it to be situated within a wide ranging set of political, economic and socio-cultural matrices. The focus of the chapter involves local people's perceptions and experiences of law, leading to an examination of the issues depicted in a dispute involving distribution of property on divorce.

## The household and the *kgotla*: some background

As with any Tswana village, the organisation of Molepolole is structured through administrative units, known as *kgotlas* and wards, which derive from households. In Tswana ideology, a household consists of a male head with a wife and their children; if a man has more than one wife there is a separate household for each wife. This ideal has long since ceased to be realised (Schapera 1950, Comaroff and Roberts 1977, Griffiths 1997, Kalabamu 1998, Pitso and Carmichael 2003), and as early as 1989 UNICEF noted the high number of households headed by women, while a subsequent government development plan (1989: 7, 9) observed that 'women headed 40% of households in urban areas and nearly half in the rural areas'. The term 'female-headed household' which appears in the literature on government planning and policy development in Botswana (Botswana 1982), is one which is the subject of some controversy (Peters 1983 and Kerven 1984). I use the term 'female head of household' to denote those households associated with *Mosotho kgotla*, in which women are in *de facto* control of the household and lands attached to it and where no adult male of equivalent generational status, whether husband, partner, or brother was present at the time of research. I use the term 'household' to represent a physical entity or domain which is located in, or associated with, a *kgotla*.

A ward is composed of a number of households organised by the chief around a *kgotla*. In pre-colonial times, all households of a ward were at least nominally descended from an eponymous founder, but this has not been the case for several decades. It is through households that the political structure of the *morafe* (polity) maintains itself. A *kgotla* is the assembly centre (both the physical location and the body of members) of a group of households presided over by a male headman or ward-head; in the past, all household heads were related through the male line but, again, this is rarely the case today. The political community within Kwena society, like that of other *Tswana merafe* (plural of *morafe*, polities), is conceived of as a hierarchy of progressively more inclusive co-residential and administrative groupings, beginning with households, and expanding to cover extended family groups in *kgotlas*, through to wards.

Wards are therefore the major units of political organisation in a *Tswana* village and are still presided over by men. The most powerful ward is *Kgosing* ('*Kgosing*' is derived from the word *kgosi*, interpreted as 'chief') and refers both to the chief's ward, which is the most senior of all Kwena wards in the polity over which it presides, and to the chief's *kgotla* (often, loosely, called the 'chief's court') which lies at the heart of *Kgosing* ward, representing the most senior of all the *kgotlas* within the ward itself. The chief's *kgotla* in *Kgosing* is the most senior and powerful in the polity and represents the apex of the administrative and political structure through which the *kgosi* exercises his power. When I began my research in Molepolole in 1982 there were six main wards[2] and 73 *kgotlas*.[3]

## Women, households and access to resources

In material terms it is clear that those women who have access to the greatest resources are those that are married or who can draw on the support of adult males (Molebatsi 2004). According to the UNICEF report in 1989, in Botswana 'Female-headed households with no male present had an annual income less than one-half that of male-headed households, and just over half that of female-headed households with a male present' (UNICEF 1989: 58). Given the range of factors affecting women's access to resources, the report concluded that 'household structure (male- or female-headed), is . . . an important predictor of poverty patterns' (UNICEF 1989: 85). The Government (Botswana 1991: 16–17) also documented that 'households headed by women (which account for nearly half of all households) have generally lower incomes than male-headed households.'

At a local level, the 30 households associated with Mosotho *kgotla* in 1984 were on a par with the national profile, as women ran the majority of them. Eighteen were headed by women at various stages in the life cycle and of varying status, including eight widows, four wives whose husbands were engaged in migrant labour, a deserted wife (whose husband had left her years before) and five unmarried women over the age of 40. The remaining 12 households were headed by married men, who in the main had come to that stage in the life cycle when they returned to their rural home to live out their later years. Among these households the best resourced were those of married couples who had the cash income to invest in buying livestock, in sustaining agricultural production and in running small businesses in the informal sector. In considering resources, my analysis links individuals with households and family groups to take account of both intra and supra household networks of co-operation and/or disaffection (Griffiths 1988: 289–316).

Membership within these differing networks has important consequences for individuals, as it provides the contexts within which different forms of power may be negotiated. This is especially pertinent for women when it comes to negotiations over their status and rights to property. Such negotiations are predicated upon structures of ownership and control and access to resources, the most essential components of which are land, livestock, and employment. Most women have access to land (which is held under customary tenure)[4] through pre- or post-mortem inheritance, through use rights accorded to them by others (who may or may not be kin) who have land but are not working it, through Tribal Land Boards, or through their husbands or male partners' rights to land. However, it is not so much access but the capacity to utilise that access that is important. As an agricultural resource this depends on women's ability to raise cash to buy the seeds and other items necessary for its maintenance (Kerven 1982), as well as their ability to mobilise the labour necessary for its cultivation (whether through kin or by hire: Izzard 1982: 712, Cooper 1982: 14). In both respects women tend to be dependent on men (Solway 1980, Kerven 1984), especially where they form part of the 'peasantariat' (a term deployed by Parson 1981), because of the nature of the social system and their poorer prospects of employment as compared with those of men.

## Gendered domains

Authority in households is based on age, sex and status. Children defer to adults who acquire greater status with marriage and age, but women do not have authority comparable with that of men. This is underlined by the fact that although they may act as heads of households, they can never qualify for the position of head of a group of households which form a *kgotla*. At each stage of her life a woman falls within the shadow of male authority. When unmarried, it is the authority of her father and her brothers; when married, that of her husband; and when widowed or in old age (if never married) that of her sons. Material and social circumstances combine to create a situation in which it is hardly surprising that households of married men and women prove the most effective in agricultural production.

The agricultural domain is closely allied to that of livestock as many people still rely on them to plough the land. Once again, women find themselves at a disadvantage in acquiring stock. This is due, in part, to the laws of succession according to which the largest category of cattle, referred to as estate cattle, is handed down from father to sons. Although a daughter can and not infrequently does acquire some livestock (where such cattle exist), her share is never on a par with that of her brothers, especially the eldest brother, who takes over responsibility for the family group on his father's death. Given the patrilineal nature of Tswana society (where descent is traced through the male line: through the man's father where the parents are married, and through the woman's father where they are not), it is not surprising that male offspring are privileged over female offspring when it comes to inheritance under customary law. Women may inherit livestock from their mothers, but a mother's opportunities for acquiring her own stock tends to be limited, as these can only derive from certain sources of labour. Cattle owned by women are mainly produced from their own (not their husbands') inherited land, which may be exchanged for livestock; or the produce of that land may be used to make beer, which in turn may be sold to provide the cash for cattle purchases.

As there is very often little surplus produce, because most of what is grown is required for home consumption and, further, given that any livestock that may be acquired are liable to perish during drought years, it is extremely hard to acquire livestock in this way. Acquiring cash to purchase stock is difficult for women, given the low rates of pay that may of them receive even when they are fortunate enough to find employment (Datta n.d.: 3, UNFPA 1989: 13). Even where such difficulties are overcome, women still have to contend with the reality of male control over animals, as it is boys and men who run the cattleposts where the livestock are kept.

Access to waged employment is one of the most important factors affecting the social and economic position of women in contemporary Botswana (Brown 1983, Kerven 1984: 267, UNICEF 1993: 12–20). Cash, so essential for survival, is less generally available to women. In the formal sector, certain types of employment on which the majority of the male population rely (for example, mining and construction) are not open to women and other occupations, particularly those of a professional nature, require a certain degree of education which women in Botswana generally fall short of compared with men (UNFPA 1989: 13). Therefore, for the majority of women the kind of employment that is open to them tends to be at the level of domestic service (Alexander 1991: 49) or working as barmaids or shop assistants. There is competition for such work, which in any case is insecure and poorly paid, and women find it hard to negotiate or enforce their terms of service, even when these terms are laid down by law. While men also have these difficulties, they also have more options with regard to potential employment. The informal sector provides a supplemental or alternative means of raising income on which many women depend (Datta n.d., Izzard 1982: 702). It is mainly women who work in this sector and, as studies elsewhere have shown (Moore, H 1988: 90), investment in this sector does not guarantee returns, especially when it involves illegal activities such as prostitution which puts the individuals concerned at risk. Bakwena experience (author's own data and Datta n.d.: 24) indicates that the returns women receive from this sector are insufficient on their own to provide for capital accumulation or personal enrichment.

In the years since independence there has been a 'remarkable economic transformation' in Botswana (Botswana NDP 6: 13) 'unmatched by any non-oil producing country in Africa' (Botswana NDP 6: 16).[5] By 1998, according to the United Nations Development Programme (UNDP), Botswana ranked fourth among African countries in terms of its Human Development Index. However, not all have benefited equally from this development (SARPN 2001). The government recognises that there is 'real poverty' (Botswana NDP

6: 19) and, from the data available on income distribution, that there is 'considerable evidence about the unequal distribution of the assets and opportunities upon which higher incomes depend.' Poverty is more evident in rural areas than among the urban population and within the rural areas: 'the households most affected are those who do not have viable cattle herds, those without cattle at all, female-headed households, and those who do not engage in agriculture at all . . . These categories overlap, so that for example households which are both female-headed and non-livestock owning are likely to be especially impoverished' (Botswana NDP 6: 21). In contrast, a minority has clearly benefited from Botswana's economic development: Primarily, with few exceptions, descendants of nineteenth-century *dikgosana* (royal families), who control vast tracts of land, are the largest cattle owners and the higher income group of wage earners, both in the public and private sectors (Botswana NDP 6: 8).

Life histories drawn from Mosotho *kgotla* demonstrate that women's access to resources is heavily dependent upon the type of network to which they belong. Such networks embody two basic forms of existence that have emerged during the course of the encounter with colonialism and which mark the process of social differentiation that is in operation in contemporary Botswana (Griffiths 1997: 17–27, 62–105). From these life histories it is possible to chart not only the common points of reference but, more significantly, the variations that allow for different life courses. Kerven observes that 'Tswana livelihoods are made within the minimal core of the family and the maximal universe of the southern African economy.'[6] In this environment families depend on a combination of 'crops, cattle and wages' for their existence, which are combined according to 'a family's class position and its stage of life cycle' (Kerven 1982: 545). This interdependence among family groups, centered around subsistence agriculture, livestock, and intermittent employment, gives rise to what Parson (1981) has termed the 'peasantariat', a social class that incorporates the majority of families in contemporary Botswana. Within this class the focus on resources is geared to subsistence agriculture, the raising of livestock and migrant labour which is generally of an unskilled nature and entered into on a contract basis (Cooper 1979). However, there is a small but growing number of those who have been able to focus on other activities and to form part of an elite, referred to by Cooper (1982) as the 'salariat'. The education (often to university level) of this class has enabled them to acquire skilled and stable forms of employment, generally within a government-based, or affiliated, organisation which carries with it a wide range of benefits.

## Mosotho *kgotla*

My data drawn from within Mosotho *kgotla* reveals families which span both the 'peasantariat' and the 'salariat', highlighting the important consequences of membership within networks for individuals, especially women, when it comes to negotiating status and rights to property. These are, of course, not rigidly fixed categories (the salariat could not exist without the possibility of social mobility) and should be thought of as the polar regions (not end points) of an uneven continuum of socio-economic-political statuses. They do, however, reflect quite accurately the lived reality of the vast majority of Batswana (citizens of Botswana) lives, as the authors in Kerven (1982) demonstrate for the period of this study.

From the life histories culled from over two generations of those living in Mosotho *kgotla*, certain patterns of existence are foregrounded which revolve round networks of varying kinds: These networks underline the ways in which power is constituted in the world of 'everyday life' which is crucial to an individual's existence, as well as highlighting the important factors that inform people's actions before disputes arise or parties turn to the courts to settle their differences.

The different life trajectories open to individuals are exemplified by the descendants of one of Mosotho *kgotla*'s founding ancestors, Koosimile, who had two sons (Radipati and Makokwe) by different wives. Makokwe's descendants, who represent the majority of families in the *kgotla*, engage in subsistence agriculture, the raising of livestock, and migrant labour of an unskilled type associated with the peasantariat. Radipati's descendants, however, have pursued another form of existence, founded on education and skilled, secure employment, which has placed them among that elite salariat nationwide. Within these groups women find themselves differentially situated from men in terms of the kinds of claims that they can pursue with respect to status and property. Further, their position in relation to one another also varies according to their affiliation within a particular group, as we shall see with three women (Olebeng, Diane, and Goitsemang) who although of the same generation and related, have had very different lives.

For peasantariat families in Botswana, marriage still plays an important role in providing access to the broader networks of supra-household management and cooperation upon which they rely for their subsistence. In Makokwe's family women find their choices, including choices in relation to marriage, shaped by male networks and structures of authority which provide the resources and mainstay for their existence. So, for example, through male sibling support some women find themselves with a power of choice which is not available to women who lack access to this type of network. This gives rise to a situation where those with choices, such as Olebeng, may opt not to marry, while those without access to the conditions under which such choice becomes available, like Diane, want to marry but are unlikely to do so because of the position in which they find themselves.

## Life histories of three women

Life for the women in Makokwe's family revolves round the village and the lands where they engage in domestic and agricultural activities. Living in the village for much of the year they are able to attend school, unlike their brothers who are away herding cattle at distant cattleposts, which means that they are able to acquire a greater degree of formal education than their brothers. Among this group, women's work is integrated with that of their male counterparts. Makokwe's only daughter, Olebeng, for example, has been part of a family network exchanging her domestic and agricultural labour in return for her brothers' assistance with ploughing and support. She has never moved beyond this sphere of operations to undertake any form of paid employment, so that throughout life her activities have been such that they have linked her into a network where she has had to rely on male support from her father, her brothers, and her male partners for existence. Within this system, she has been fortunate because her five older brothers have been quite generous in providing support by assisting her with ploughing and upholding her welfare. They consented to her taking over the natal household, because they had all married and established their own households elsewhere in the village. Compared with other women, she is therefore in a relatively strong position in that her circumstances have permitted a certain degree of choice, including whether or not to marry. She has had several children (all of whom died at birth) with a number of male partners, but has never married. This was out of choice, according to Olebeng, who maintains that from her very first pregnancy neither she nor her family had any interest in pursuing the issue of marriage.

Olebeng's situation is unusual as in an environment where emphasis is placed on subsistence agriculture, livestock, and a cash input from migrant labour, marriage is particularly important for women. Unmarried daughters and sisters find themselves at the bottom of the social hierarchy in terms of power and access to resources. Such power derives not only from status and point in the life cycle, but also includes an individual's capacity to generate or control resources. Among women, power devolves with age linked to status, so that a young unmarried childless woman is in a less influential position compared to her older married sister who has children. Both, however, defer to their mother and even more so to their grandmother, who by virtue of her age and status is considered to be in the most powerful position of them all. It is not age alone but the incidents that mark its passage, such as childbearing, that are integral parts of the life cycle which create status; the combination of age with status fuels the dynamics of power.[7]

In these circumstances, women find themselves constrained by the gendered world in which they live, where men have a greater degree of control over access to resources, such as cash, on which all households depend for their existence. Women have fewer opportunities than men to generate the income required, because they do not have access to the most common forms of male employment (the mines or construction) and the returns they receive from participation in the informal economy are insufficient on their own to provide the resources that they require. Those who are most successful are married women whose husbands have provided the cash necessary to promote and sustain their activities. Women selling fat cakes (fried bread dough), for example, need money to buy the flour with which they are made. Although women may have access to land and own livestock, the utilisation of these resources is often mediated through men. For instance, it is the men or young boys who herd the livestock at the cattlepost and who are responsible for moving them to the lands for ploughing or to the village to sell. Not infrequently a man will report that cattle have gone missing or died and, given the distances involved, it is hard to challenge a herder's claim, even though an owner may suspect that the herder has in fact appropriated them for his own purposes. For the cultivation of land most people still rely on oxen to work the plough. Those that have a team or can contribute to one, have control over ploughing and the sequence it may follow. In Mosotho *kgotla*, these are mostly married men who plough their own fields before those of their brothers and parents, and, lastly, their unmarried sisters.

Within this kind of network, an unmarried woman finds herself at a disadvantage. While part of a group formed of her family and kin who have responsibility for her (and thus obligations to plough for her), her position is a vulnerable one in that her interests are subordinated to those of other family members. This is the case with Diane and her unmarried daughters who have found themselves greatly disadvantaged by the constraints which are inherent in a kinship network. Unlike Olebeng, Diane has had a relationship fraught with conflict with her male kin. Her brothers abandoned her after their father's death, not only leaving her to fend for herself but also having appropriated for their own use the land that she was left by her mother. Without access to her brothers' network, she has found herself in a position where she has had to rely on a series of male partners for support, in relationships of '*bonyatsi*' (concubinage) that preclude marriage. Despite, or indeed because of this, she firmly expressed the view that 'it is natural with Batswana to marry. A woman must marry.' Her own life history, however, placed her in a position where marriage was no longer a viable option, given the number of children that she had had with different men.

By 1989 Diane had had ten children by four different fathers. As one of the poorest female heads of a household in Mosotho *kgotla*, her life history fits the national profile of the vulnerable female-headed household described by Kerven (1979), Izzard (1979), Brown (1983), and others, which is so much at risk and with which the Government of Botswana is so concerned. This is not only because of the highly impoverished position in which many female heads of households find themselves in, but also because this is often perpetuated in succeeding generations (Motzafi-Haller 1986). This is the case with Diane's five eldest daughters, who all, like their mother, have had to leave school early because of pregnancy in circumstances where marriage was non-negotiable.

Other women, however, who form part of an emerging salariat find themselves with a greater degree of power and control over the choices that are open to them. Within their family group, they are less reliant on the type of male networks that peasantariat women depend on for their existence. Goitsemang is just such a woman. Despite the fact that her father Radipati was Makokwe's half brother, members of Radipati's family have experienced very different life trajectories from those of Makokwe. Radipati (who died in 1950) was an educated man who placed great emphasis on his children's education, which his wife Mhudi struggled to provide after his death. As a result, his three daughters were educated (at a time when many women only received a nominal education) and acquired formal employment. The eldest unmarried daughter, Goitsemang (aged 52 in 1989) worked as a nurse in South Africa and then in a management capacity for a construction company in Botswana, so that she has been able to build a house in the capital, Gaborone. This is something which many people in the village aspire to but are unable to achieve. Her younger unmarried sister has also acquired a plot of land in Gaborone by working for the same company. Radipati's sons were also educated and two of them, most unusually for that time, went on to acquire university degrees. Through their access to education and skilled, stable employment the family fits the kind of profile associated with the emerging salariat. Among the younger generation a number of women are employed as teachers and court clerks, and the men are similarly situated within government employ. The family's activities differ from those associated with a subsistence agricultural base and they no longer plough.

Goitsemang, like her contemporaries Diane and Olebeng, has had children and remained unmarried. However, in her case, her relationships with men display the hallmarks of a potential customary marriage which failed to materialise. Such a marriage reflects a process that takes place over many years and involves reciprocal relations between the respective families. Unlike a civil or religious marriage which is registered, marriage through customary law is not necessarily predicated upon a specific, identifiable occasion. While some features, such as the transfer of '*bogadi*' (marriage payment), may be treated as definitive markers of marriage, their absence does not rule out the social recognition of a relationship as a marriage. Although among Bakwena, a ceremony, ('*patlo*'),[8] is viewed as being central to the constitution of a customary marriage, it is not the only definitive feature, so that relationships can and do acquire the status of a marriage without it. What is important is the degree to which both families have become involved in the relationship and accorded it public recognition through the giving of gifts and attendance at significant life events, such as celebrations for the birth of a child, or funerals.

Goitsemang observed that with her first partner the families met, discussed and agreed to marriage on a number of occasions, although it never materialised. This relationship provides a typical example of the kind of marital negotiations referred to by Comaroff and Roberts (1977), where the parties start out seriously exploring the potential of the relationship but over time one withdraws, usually to pursue another relationship. In her subsequent relationship, Goitsemang found herself at odds with her family. This relationship also had the potential for a customary marriage, but was rejected by Goitsemang's family because they did not want her to enter into a polygamous union.[9] Goitsemang maintained this relationship against her family's wishes. She had the power to ignore her family, because her employment gave her access to a world in which she was beyond their control. What was crucial for Goitsemang was that she was removed from the kind of pressures that accompany dependence on domestic and agricultural labour and the networks that sustain them. Her education and training had given her access to alternative means of support and these resources had empowered her to make decisions on her own account, making her less vulnerable to demands made by kin. Indeed, Goitsemang felt able to challenge her brother David's claims to control over the natal household under customary law and received sufficient support from *kgotla* members to continue running the household (Griffiths 1998).

The problem arose between Goitsemang and David because she was not prepared to accept that, as the senior family representative, he had control over the household. This was because the investment that she had made in the property went beyond the normal kind of female labour and domestic activity associated with a household, which would be taken for granted and could not be used as a bargaining tool for control in this context. Because of this investment she was able to challenge her brother's authority and to mobilise support from the *kgotla*. This support hinged on an alliance between old and new criteria, the former based on the notion that, as an unmarried woman, she should be allowed to remain in the natal household, the latter on the basis of consistent and direct financial investment of the kind that is not usually made by women. For his part, while David appealed to tradition he was also constrained by it, for a married man of his age, with his skills, is expected to have built his own household. According to Goitsemang, it reflected poorly on him that he wished to turn her and her other unmarried sisters out in order to take over the household for his own purposes. Several *kgotla* members supported her view that 'a man of his age and standing should not be fighting over what others have made'.

This is one example of how changing conditions create the space for transforming the norms that govern social life. Goitsemang was able to challenge her brother successfully, because she was able to reconfigure aspects of customary law to her advantage, drawing on traditional practice as well as integrating a novel element into the discourse, that of direct financial investment in property. It is unlikely that either element on its own account would have been sufficient to shift the status quo in her favour. Her situation is very different from that of Diane, who is unable to contest her brothers' actions, or from that of Olebeng, who survives on the basis of a co-operative relationship with her brothers. At this stage in her life, Goitsemang has no desire to marry because, as she observes, 'marriage just brings quarrels'. This is a view shared by a number of educated and employed women, who prefer to avoid the status of 'wife,' given the ways in which gender impacts on spousal roles.

## Unequal power relations: married women

The life histories I have discussed demonstrate how land is intimately bound up with other resources that form part of a family's livelihood and how individuals, particularly women, are located within kin and social networks that control their distribution and utilisation. While some unmarried women, like Goitsemang, are able to negotiate control over their resource base, the majority of women remain dependent on their relationships with their fathers, brothers, male partners, or husbands for their existence. This poses a particular problem for unmarried women like Diane, whose male kin have abandoned her and for whom marriage is no longer an option. While marriage may enable women to improve their access to resources and enhance their status they still find themselves located in unequal power relations with their husbands, which are highlighted on divorce. These inequalities arise from the different positions men and women occupy in the family hierarchy, which impact on access to and authority over resources, the gendered division of labour within the family, and also the different social conceptions that attach to the roles of husband and wife. These social conceptions of the roles of husband and wife become crucial when negotiating a divorce settlement and distribution of property.

What is at stake in the public dissolution of a relationship and distribution of property under customary law is displacing the burden of fault onto the other spouse. Such characterisation involves a manipulation of the traits associated with a 'good' husband or wife. Thus both parties seek to escape blame for marital breakdown in order to secure their share of property. The claims that are open to them, however, are sharply gendered and it is particularly hard for a wife to displace the burden of fault, principally because a wife is expected to defer to her husband's authority as head of the household. For example, a wife is not permitted to leave home without his consent or without cause (e.g. a death in the family or domestic abuse), so if she does leave she will have to overcome the appearance of negative conduct before she can assert any claim to marital property. Men's conduct, however, is not viewed in the same way. So, for example, if a husband is having an affair with another woman it is considered inappropriate for a wife to complain, unless he is failing to support her and the children or is using their family property to support the other woman. Further, even where a wife is able to meet the criterion of good conduct, she still confronts problems posed by the structure of family property.

Under Kwena customary law,[10] it is the husband who maintains control and ownership of the family property after divorce, because he is the one who is publicly accredited as head of the household and is the person who is regarded as the children's custodian. In this context he is awarded most of the property because he is responsible for handing it on to the next generation, the children's inheritance thus being a major consideration when it comes to any division of property. On divorce, children remain affiliated with their father's family, and thus their interests often effectively restrict or subordinate women's claims to property as wives. Wives therefore find themselves doubly disadvantaged, in comparison to their husbands, when it comes to making property claims.

## The Monokgotlha's hearing: Maunatlala ward

Local wards are integral to the divorce process, which may take place over many years. Given their role in dealing with family disputes, they may elect to dissolve a marriage and to divide whatever property is available between the parties even though they lack formal legal powers to do so, which are vested in the chief's *kgotla* alone. However, when it comes to handling marital disputes there is a marked degree of continuity in what takes place in local wards and at *Kgosing* (the chief's *kgotla* sitting as a customary court).

In the dispute I am going to describe, Efitlhile (the man) and Keleisetse (the woman) had had problems for years. The headman of their local ward, Maunatlala, claimed that the husband's grievances included being 'chased away from his wife's parents home', that she would not allow him to visit her when she was sick and that she had taken all their property from Masimo (the ploughfields) to Molepolole without consulting him. For her part, Keleisetse maintained that her husband 'was too troublesome in that he was forever quarrelling with her and complaining about nothing', that he 'was not supporting the children', that he denied paternity of some of her children and that he would 'torment me by telling me that the twins are not his children but have two fathers'. Finally, when she was ill he did nothing to take care of her.

The *kgotla* tried to reconcile Keleisetse with her husband. The headman recalled asking her, 'If we would punish your husband for not having supported you and for tormenting and always quarrelling with you, would you agree to return to him and begin to live peacefully?' She refused, stating it was of 'no use', because she 'knew of her husband's behaviour even if he was punished he would never improve'. This was unacceptable to the *kgotla*: 'We told her that according to Tswana custom you are then a person who is divorcing and in that connection you are required to refund the property the man has provided for you during your marriage.' The headman explained, 'In this particular case the woman did not have reasonable grounds on the facts . . . according to Tswana custom, if her husband has been ill-treating her in any way, she should have reported the matter to her husband's parents.' Keileisetse challenged the headman's account, and he himself had stated at the beginning of my interview with him that the matter came to the *kgotla* 'after they had dealt with the matter in the family compound where they did not reach any conclusion'.

In dissolving the union the headmen noted that 'the parties hadn't much property. They had a plough and one beast, a large empty water drum, one bath and other household articles such as basins, pots and other articles'. The lands at Masimo remained Efilthile's as they belonged to his kin group and he was awarded most of the property including 'the beast, the plough, the drum and the bath'. Keileisetse only received a few household articles, 'small things, not many' such as 'basins, dishes and pots'. According to the headman this was only because 'she had to do the cooking for the little children who got some blankets and mats'. Keiletse was angry because the distribution 'was not fair'. In her view the *kgotla* had favoured Efilthile's interpretation of events over hers and she was bitter because he was the one who had abandoned the family.

Efilthile told a different story following his return to Molepolole from the cattlepost: 'I found her changed altogether. She would not speak to me when I spoke to her. At night she went away to sleep.' He implied that she had a lover and that it was he who 'reported the incident to her parents'. He also maintained he had taken her to the doctor when she was ill and that it was Keleisetse who had driven him away from home. He presented himself as the model husband, reporting to her family when things went wrong and taking her for medical treatment when she required it. He disputed her version of events, asserting that: 'when the parents called us together to try to make us settle in peace, she would not allow me to come'. He alleged she was a bad wife, because she rejected him and removed all the property from Masimo. When confronted with this, she admitted she had done so, but had argued 'that the property was hers and not mine'. He also was not satisfied with the property division: 'I told the *kgotla* men that I wanted all my property', but they drew attention 'to the fact that I was ill treating her.' He explained his behaviour on the grounds that his wife needed to be disciplined: 'I often reported to her parents but they wouldn't check her behaviour towards me.'

Both parties interpreted events differently, but ultimately it was Efitlhile who succeeded in the property stakes. One explanation for this was that the ward did not take the marriage seriously because Keleitsetse already had three children with different partners when she met Efitlhile. However, what became clear when I interviewed members of the ward was that there was some dispute as to what was the proper practice in relation to both the recognition of divorce and the distribution of property.

## Ward views on what is 'the law'

The village vehemently disagreed about women's rights to property on the breakdown of a relationship. Many people were adamant that where there was no *patlo*, the woman was a '*nyatsi*' who would be returned to her family and, in these circumstances, had no right to property but might receive something for her services. One headman at *Kgosing* observed, 'where a woman is married to a man without *patlo* but a marriage which the two of them agreed upon, the only remedy is that the woman is sent home'. Another supported this view: 'people who marry on their own without the knowledge of their parents on both sides and the *kgotla* people, are not married. She is seen only as a *nyatsi*'. However, another disagreed, 'even if *patlo* had not taken place, she has the right to remain and retain the dwelling house for the sake of the children recognised as children of the family *kgotla*'.

All agreed that the situation was problematic and even where *patlo* was carried out, views varied. A member of Ntloedibe ward opined, 'all the house property which they jointly acquired and the cattle jointly acquired would go to the woman and she would go back to her parents' but only if the man was at fault and divorcing the woman for no reason. One cynical headman commented this would never happen because 'the woman is always found to be at fault', but the deputy chief disagreed. The latter stated that where the wife is not at fault and it is the man who is divorcing without cause she may remain 'because she has kept her marriage promise'. Others at Kgosing argued that she must return to her family as 'it is considered sensible, even if the man is at fault. If the man does not love her or wish to live with her she must be returned safely to live free rather than suffer the strain of isolation.' However, she must, regardless of fault, be 'provided with carriage by her husband'. Whatever her position, any land she had been cultivating through her husband's family connections, must remain with him. Her family is responsible for allocating land to her on her return, but as a divorced woman her needs will be subordinated to those of other family members placing her in a vulnerable position.

A wife's claim to cattle was also contentious. Headmen acknowledged that she was entitled to those cattle that she had acquired from her own labour, from the proceeds of selling home-made beer or from the proceeds of agricultural produce grown on her own land, but it became clear that this did not happen in practice. Even without fault, a man from Maunatlala explained: 'if a woman divorces on reasonable grounds she gets a share of the division of property but a smaller share than the man'. In assessing what this potential share might be, a reference was made to Kgari Sechele's (1931–62) practice of awarding up to eight head of cattle. When this was introduced, it was regarded as an innovation necessitated by a sudden increase in men abandoning their wives for no reason and represented the *kgosi's* attempt to control family life during a period of intensive labour migration when his authority was in danger of declining. The figure of eight head of cattle is one that many *kgotlas* regard as setting a maximum and only occurs when 'a man has sufficient cattle'. Many were of the view that this applied only when a man had a herd of at least 50 to 100 beasts and even this view was questionable. A headman forcefully argued that 'it is only one beast that is paid out and the household property the things that the wife uses for domestic purposes goes with her'. Another stressed that cattle stay with the man and that 'if a woman divorces on reasonable grounds the cattle will remain in the original place [in] the man's *kgotla* and the children remain there'.

Many *kgotla* members agreed that on division of property 'a woman gets a lesser share than a man', largely due to consideration for the children who normally remain with the man. A Tshosa ward member, when questioned about a woman's rights to property on divorce replied: 'That is not a simple question. If you mean a woman who has children in the *kgotla*, when a division of property is undertaken much consideration is given to the children who are bona fide residents of the *kgotla*.' In other words, it is the children's interests which account for an unequal division: 'The woman will go with limited property. It depends on how much property will remain in the *kgotla* for the children's heritage.'

## Conclusion: customary rights and formal law

There have been many changes in Botswana since my Bakwena study in Molepolole was carried out. Women's organisations and NGO's such as, Emang Basadi (Stand Up Women), have generated more public awareness of women's issues and linked into international networks that have supported activism on the ground, as for example, in the case of Unity Dow where the Urban Morgan Institute for Human Rights, University Cincinnati College of Law lodged an Amicus Brief on Unity Dow's behalf. Botswana has now become a signatory to CEDAW, the UN Convention on the Elimination of All Forms of Discrimination Against Women and a woman, Mosadi Seboko has been installed among Balete of Ramotswa as a *kgosi*. The Aids epidemic has taken its toll, giving rise to further changes and a reworking of family relationships (Upton 2003). It is not possible to document all the changes that have taken place but it would be interesting to factor these changes into empirical research in the future to see in what ways, if any, these changes have contributed to shifting constellations of power and what impact this has had on gender relations.

How these social phenomena effect upon women's access to and control over land needs to be empirically investigated. For law reform, if it is to be sensitive to gender, must be formulated on an informed comprehension of the social basis upon which law operates. As of June 2003 the Government of Botswana 'is in the process of reviewing its National Land Policy and the issue of women's land rights is said to be one of those being addressed'

(Radijeng 2004: 207) with a view to removing 'all forms of discrimination against women and to make all policies and law gender neutral' (Lekula 2003 quoted by Radijeng 2004: 207). Yet, as the above discussion has shown, the introduction of gender neutral language and formal changes in law will achieve little if they do not reflect a grounded knowledge and understanding of how women and men find themselves differentially situated when it comes to access and control over resources such as land. As Ngonola has observed, 'land boards[11] claim to follow a gender neutral policy on allocations. But it would be interesting to apply your type of analysis to the actual situation on the ground. There is not much information on how women have been fairing in their dealings with land boards' (Professor of Law, University of Botswana, personal communication, 2003). In Botswana, as in many other African countries, in this context some women have been subjected to disinheritance and property grabbing following the death of male kin. The effects of family dissolution are not necessarily predictable or detrimental to women (FAO 2003: 10). However, as I said in my introduction, the purpose of this chapter has been to use the data I gathered through my ethnographic studies in Botswana to raise issues which extend beyond the immediate time and place of my study.

But before I begin to explore this dimension, I need to draw together the implications of the life stories I collected and the information they revealed of the lives of those particular women in those circumstances. What has been revealed, over and over again, is that access to land and other forms of property is dependent upon the kinship networks through which and within which women operate. Whether as daughters, sisters, wives or mothers, women's access to land and the resources to make use of land as a resource depend upon their relationships within their kin groups and with their male kin. Inheritance patterns, the division of labour within the household (which, in a rural economy, is extended to agricultural labour) and their differential access to the waged labour market, all structure their access to these commodities. Further, whereas changes in employment opportunities and, in particular, a shift of focus from rural to urban living, has an impact on their life chances, many women in developing economies such as that of Botswana, are still held within a social context which privileges male authority and operates within a set of reference points which includes the patterns and practices of customary law.

Thus the difficulties women face in gaining access to or control over property, including land, under customary law are clearly derived from the gendered position they occupy in kinship networks and from the economic, political, ideological and social domains that shape the world in which they live. This is not unique to Bakwena. Studies elsewhere have documented the problems women face in the light of these constraints (Whitehead and Tsikata 2003, Muthoni Wanyeki 2003, WLSA 2001, Diop Tine and Sy 2003, Logo and Bikie 2003, Abdullah and Hamza 2003). These studies also document how law reform may prove inadequate in addressing this problem either because of its lack of implementation or through a failure to have an impact on prevailing social attitudes that militate against it (Palmer 2002).

Customary land tenure in Africa and its effects are the subject of ongoing debate in the broader context of nation building and development, a debate which has recently been revived due to intensifying competition and conflict over land on the continent (Berry 2002, Odgaard 2003, Peters 2002). Many African countries, including Botswana, inherited a legal system from their colonial administrators that provided for Western-style law which they elected to maintain on independence. In post-independence moves towards modernisation and economic development major aid agencies, such as the World Bank, adopted a negative attitude to customary land tenure because they viewed it as standing in the way of progress. They perceived the absence of clearly defined and enforceable property rights that accompany the concept of individual, registered rights of private ownership (as opposed to group 'communal' land tenure under customary law) as lacking the necessary 'security' to ensure agricultural investment and productive use of land.[12] As a result international pressure has been put on African governments, dependent on aid, to introduce or extend the registration of land.

These assumptions have been challenged using field research which questions the hypotheses upon which the demands for land law reform have been based and the probity of framing economic development on a paradigm derived from the Western European Experience (Peters 1997, 2002, 2003: 3–15, Francis 1984, Colson 1971, Berry 1975, Bruce 1988, Guyer and Lambin 1993, Netting 1993, Linares 1992, Moore, S F 1988, Manji 2001). Scholars, such as Berry (1993, 2002), Moore, S F (1986), Payne (2002) and Durand-Lasserve and Royston (2002), far from viewing indeterminacy as a problem have stressed the inherent negotiability of African customary land tenure, as something that is integral to the system. Berry (1993: 104) observes:

> The significance of ambiguous land rights for agrarian change in Africa is not so much that land rights are insecure and that land use, therefore is inefficient, but that people's access to land depends on their participation in processes of interpretation and adjudication, as well as their ability to pay. . . . People's ability to exercise claims to land remains closely linked to membership in social networks and participation in both formal and informal political processes.

Thus the customary system provides individuals with scope for manoeuvre and social agency. Indeed, in some circumstance women may use this to improve their position: Goitsemang, for instance, was able to construct a new discourse concerning her right to control over the natal household, one that *kgotla* members were prepared to entertain. She was able to shift the local terms of reference with which she was confronted to her advantage. Bikaako and Ssenkumba (2003) note that, as a result of economic and social change in Uganda, women's customary land rights are changing in that families are increasingly granting land to their daughters. Nyamu-Musembi (2003: 133) found in her field research in Kenya, that there was a measure of support for granting land to dutiful daughters. Local customary norms, therefore, are subject to change and adaptability and provide some scope for transformation.

However, these developments must be viewed in the overall context in which women pursue claims to property and land. Although Goitsemang was able to forge a breakthrough, Diane found herself at odds with a system in which she had no power to alter her position or to influence events. Whilst Bikaako and Ssenkumba (2003) note the change in granting land to daughters, they also note that for the majority of women their land rights are fragile and transient, dependent on such factors as age and marital status, the existence (and gender) of children and a judgment of women's sexual conduct. Even more disturbingly they found that the impact of inequality in land rights has aggravated women's poor socio-economic status and has led to an increase in the numbers of women engaging in sex work, exposing them to sexual harassment, violence and contributing towards marital instability, separation and divorce. Although Nyamu-Musembi (2002) documents changes in local attitudes towards daughters, she also notes how the government policy of formalising and individualising property rights in land is likely to impact adversely on women because land is registered in the names of male heads of households as sole owners. Whilst sole ownership is not a requirement of registration, the fact that this is the practice followed has led to a situation where women account for less than 5 per cent of the registered landholders nationally. The Kenyan Registered Land Act extinguishes all other interests except those that qualify as 'overriding interests' under s 30 of the Act. Interests based on customary law are no longer recognised. Thus the interests of wives under customary law, which allows them to live on and use family land by virtue of marriage, are now ignored by formal law. While practice at the local level may mediate to strike a balance between the freedom that formal title gives the title-holder, on the one hand, and the socially recognised interests of family members on the other hand, if the issue was to be formally adjudicated such interests would be discounted.

What is clear is that law reform in relation to land needs to be based on an understanding of the social basis upon which law operates. This is especially pertinent in relation to plural legal systems (as in Africa), where there has been a tendency by Western commentators to view customary law as separate and distinct from Western-style law and to therefore represent them as dual systems of law (Hooker 1975). This perspective fails to recognise how customary law and Western-style law are mutually constitutive, being underpinned by the norms and values that operate in the social world in which people live. As the data from Botswana and elsewhere (Amanor 1999) demonstrate this is a world in which people, including women, are differentially situated. Understanding what gives rise to these differences and how they operate in facilitating or constraining women and men's access to resources and land is crucial when if comes to formulating effective policies for the creation and implementation of rights and law reform. Peters (2003) has argued for the need to find a way forward that goes beyond privileging Western-style law, with its emphasis on individual property rights, over customary land tenure or vice versa. She warns against overplaying the negotiability of customary law and the power of human agency in a world where social inequality is growing and observes that 'an overemphasis on ambiguity and open-endedness is in danger of deflecting research from the patterns of inequity in landholding and the relations between the latter and broader processes of differentiation and class formation' (Peters 2002: 61). Ethnography provides the means of redressing the balance and of exploring in greater detail how class, ethnicity, gender and age contribute to relations of inequality that impact on individuals and families, especially women's, access to and control over land. This is as true in jurisdictions of primarily urban, economically developed societies as it is of those societies which have traditionally been studied by anthropologists.

## Notes

1 For a detailed account of this research see Griffiths (1997).
2 These are Kgosing, Maunatlala, Mokgalo, Ratshosa, Ntoloedibe and Borakalalo.
3 According to the 1982 list in Tribal Administration.
4 There are three main categories of land in Botswana: customary or tribal land, state land and freehold land. Customary land is administered by the Tribal Land Boards and covers 71 per cent, state land comprises 23 per cent and freehold land constitutes 6 per cent of the total land area of the country (DTRP 1998).
5 Development is largely due to the discovery of diamonds in 1967. Botswana is now one of the world's major diamond producers. Since completion of the research a diamond sorting plant opened in Molepolole.
6 The government of Botswana itself (1991: xxi, 95, 145) has noted the ways in which the country's development is inextricably linked to decisions, process and events that take place, both at regional and international levels, beyond the country's borders.
7 The same is true for men. The young childless man who has never experienced formal employment has less status than his older married brother who has children and has worked at the mines. Both should defer to their father and grandfather who have passed beyond these stages. However, this is not always done, especially where the older generation is dependent on the younger to provide for them through the cash that they remit back to the family from their earnings as migrant labourers.
8 This ceremony involves parents, relatives and friends of the man who come to the woman's *kgotla* to perform a ritual involving a public request for marriage and acceptance of this request by the woman's family. For further details see Griffiths (1997: 54–5).
9 In Botswana, individuals may marry according to customary law or register a civil

or religious marriage under the Marriage Act 1970 [Cap. 29: 09]. Under customary law, a man may marry more than one wife, but not if he is already married to a woman under the 1970 Act. Nor can he marry a woman under the 1970 Act if he is already married to another woman under customary law.

10 In most cases where parties get divorced in the village it is customary law that is applied. This is because even where the marriage is registered, where the divorce must be processed in the High Court, the property will still devolve according to customary law under s 7 of the Married Persons Property Act 1971. This is the case unless the application of customary law is expressly or impliedly excluded on the basis of the mode of life exemption contained in s 2 of the Dissolution of African Marriages (Disposal of Property) Act [Cap. 29: 06].

11 For discussion of this see Feder and Noronha (1987). The World Bank and other aid agencies as a result of the sustained critique of their policies, now subscribe to an evolutionary property rights theory. For discussion of this see Amanor (2001) and Manji (2003).

12 Land Boards administer the allocation of customary land, see n 4.

Chapter 12

# Accidental Islamic feminism

## Dialogical approaches to Muslim women's inheritance rights

*Hilary Lim and Siraj Sait*

### Introduction

Islamic inheritance regimes in the Muslim world continue to beguile gender rights advocates and feminists, non-Muslim and Muslim alike. One single characteristic, that women inherit far less property than men under the Islamic inheritance arrangements, has for long been utilised as a marker, in the west, for a perceived lack of gender equality. Whether deployed to generate general condemnation, or avoided through a polite 'multi-culturalist' judgment that these 'internal' matters cannot be subjected to external assessment, the complexity and sensitivity of inheritance practices among Muslims has rarely been directly engaged. This chapter is concerned with developing such an engagement, for very pragmatic reasons. Within the context of global 'land reform' programmes, examining the ways in which westernised patterns of land holding impact within very differing economic, social and cultural sites has become an important countervailing force against the presumption that the imposition of western patterns will operate as a progressive tool for economic and social development.

Concerns have been expressed with the extent to which such reform programmes not only 'fit' specific sites, but also the impact they (might) have on less economically powerful groups. However, implicit within the support for such strategies is a presumption that they can, or could, be a tool for empowering groups who have been excluded or marginalised within 'traditional' land holding patterns. Thus, for some, the use of westernised land reform programmes might seem to hold the potential for emancipating women from such disadvantages as the perceived inequalities of Islamic inheritance law and practices. This chapter, however, challenges such an approach by asking two questions which have rarely been articulated. First, to what extent is it correct to use the marker of inequality in Islamic inheritance law and practices as indicative of a fundamental lack of gender equality? Second, to what extent is it correct to presume that tools for emancipation are only available through the importation of westernised jurisprudence rather than through the development of Islamic jurisprudence? These questions are crucial within an overall assessment of the potential for land reform programmes which follow a westernised model within the specific context of Muslim societies.

This chapter is, however, more than an examination of these questions. It also narrates the journey of two researchers, from diverse backgrounds, whose selective identities could be arrayed as a western, non-Muslim female working on land and an Asian, Muslim, male human rights lawyer. We were brought together through a UN-HABITAT research contract to explore the potential uses of Islamic discourses in enhancing land, property and housing rights through global strategies, particularly with regard to women's rights (Sait and Lim 2006). The experiences of UN-HABITAT, the agency mandated with protection of land, property and housing rights had led to the recognition that although these rights are generally cross-cultural, there are distinctive practices regarding their regulation and protection which require further study. Our work was predicated on the realisation that very little systematic literature existed on the use of Islamic land tools. In launching this initiative the UN-HABITAT official Clarissa Augustinus may well have knowingly cast two individuals with diverse backgrounds and contrasting experiences, but could not have anticipated the intellectual, faith, feminist and political struggles which lay ahead for us. This chapter, then, is also about our own journey as we explored the questions posed by the research, which in turn raised crucial questions as to 'how' we engaged not only with the material, but with each other and with our own preconceptions.

## Researching Islam and land

Over 20 per cent of the world's population are Muslims, of whom a significantly large proportion is known to be influenced by Islamic doctrines, to varying degrees, in their pursuit of land and property rights. However, too often global reviews of land rights are undertaken without taking Islamic laws relating to land into account or addressing the complex and distinctive forms of land tenure found in Muslim societies. This can be illustrated through a brief consideration of Hernando de Soto's influential and best-selling work, *The Mystery of Capital* (2001). The thrust of his text is to predicate universal economic development and poverty alleviation, through the conversion of 'dead capital', by which he means informally owned property, into formally recognised property rights, through the processes of surveying, mapping and title registration. His approach has received considerable political support (Clinton 2001, USAID 2002), although increasingly subject to academic critique (Home and Lim 2004, Payne 2002). De Soto presumes his programme to be automatically applicable in the Muslim world, without any examination of Islamic conceptions of property and land rights. Although Egypt is on de Soto's study list, he merely explores the symptomatic problems of bureaucratic delays in asserting property rights.

The issues faced by Muslim countries, however, are far more complex than mere problems with red tape and apathy.

Where they exist, appraisals of Islamic law in relation to land have tended to be partial and fragmented, often taking the position that Islamic law in this context is inscrutable and outdated. The objective of our research was to produce a body of material which proposed strategies to enhance the knowledge and capacity of UN HABITAT and its partners, including governments and civil society, to work more effectively in Muslim contexts. The outcome of the research[1] was the identification of distinctive Islamic conceptions of land and property rights which, although varied in practice throughout the Muslim world, offer the potential of innovative and alternative approaches for the realisation of fuller land rights for various sections of Muslim societies, including women.

The lived experience of an estimated 1.2 billion Muslims worldwide and their subscription to Islamic law obviously cannot be essentialised. Muslims are geographically distributed as different ethnic, linguistic and cultural communities in Muslim countries (over 57 so-called 'Islamic countries' are members of the Organisation of Islamic Conference, OIC), as well as significant minorities in other parts of the world. What binds them is their respect for, in varying degrees and forms, principles of Islamic law, but Islam is not a monolithic religion, and despite consensus upon certain articles of faith and practice, it remains a contested zone within Muslim communities.

However, what must be recognised is that Muslims consider Islam to be a complete way of life, and property conceptions go far beyond theorisation to impact on the lived experiences of Muslims. They also inform, to varying degrees, state policies and land rights discourse. A better understanding of, and engagement with, Islamic dimensions of land can support land rights initiatives in Muslim societies, which have implications for programmes relating to land administration, land registration, urban planning and environmental sustainability. A failure to engage with the internal Islamic dialogue risks creating land systems that are bereft of authenticity and legitimacy and thereby effectiveness and durability. Even where well intentioned donor-driven efforts to establish modern land systems appear to succeed, the obduracy of informal norms, practices and processes lead to unattended dualisms that undermine the prospect of integrated and unifying land policies (Sait 2003).

The resurgence of religious appeal in several parts of the world, particularly in the Muslim world, requires the incorporation, if not centrality, of religious discourses in development approaches. Increasingly, holistic or integrated approaches to development are sought, even where there appear to be contradictions and necessary trade-offs. The profound and pervasive influence of Islamic dogma and theory in a significant number of Muslims' lives, including those of Muslim women, is such that ideas of development, progress and access to land have to be viewed through the context of Islam. A particular difficulty arises when conservative readings of the *Shari'a* (Islamic law) are intertwined with gender discriminating customary norms and presented as God's immutable word. For Muslim women preoccupied with both *duniya* (temporal life) and *akhira* (the eternal hereafter), 'wanting to be good Muslims and having their rights as well' sets up a 'high degree of conflict and frustration' in the face of patriarchal constructions. One means by which such conflicts can be resolved is through a solid jurisprudential basis derived from an Islamic feminist approach, 'which clearly shows that Islam not only does not deprive [women] of their rights, but in fact demands these rights for them' (Al-Hibri 1997: 16). Far from being viewed as an essentially archaic institution which is the source of women's inequality, Islamic law may be an important element in enhancing women's access to land.

## Dialogic methodology

We agreed, at the outset, to heed women's claim to equal rights, as well as to seek to secure the integrity of 'authentic' Islamic discourses in our explorations. This was not to be a religious study, but rather a pragmatic exercise on empowering women in relation to, and through, property rights. Therefore, Islam, like any other religion or culture, was to be constructively probed to discern its potential benefits. Within these parameters, our often contrasting standpoints, and sometimes overlapping perspectives, provoked intense debate over sources, interpretations and implications. Interestingly, these debates over the role and importance of Islam did not take place on the basis of our religious identities, nor did the importance of gender equality depend on the sex of either author. We found was that it was far easier for a non-Muslim to non-apologetically and non-defensively appreciate Islamic positions, and for a male to push harder against patriarchal systems.

The points of tension between us in exploring the gaps within the mainstream analysis of land rights, coupled with our diverse identities and standpoints, lent themselves to the development of a practice, a methodology, which we would call 'dialogue between partners'. Thus we sought, between 'ourselves' as much as between 'us' and 'our material', to develop a practice modelled not on the production of an 'authoritative discourse', which attempts to assert one truth over another, but instead a process of 'dialogue'.

Such a process must do more than win the centre ground on behalf of those persons or ideas previously excluded. Nearly two decades ago Spivak, commenting upon the work of Derrida, asserted that: 'in every textual production, in the production of every explanation, there is the itinerary of a constantly thwarted desire to make the text explain' (1987: 105). Thus, she argued that 'the possibility of explanation carries the presupposition of an explainable . . . universe and an explaining . . . subject' (Spivak 1987: 105). Each explanation therefore acquires its centrality from margins which are excluded. So, Spivak argues that attending to marginality is therefore necessary, not because one will produce a 'true' explanation or theory, nor to win the centre for the margin, but to point out the margin in every explanation. The purpose is not to 'point [an] accusing finger at the centre', but to move from the centre to the margin and back again in order to 'narrate a displacement' (Spivak 1987: 107).

It is a methodology which enabled us also to attend closely to the internal dialogue within Islam, for such a narration urges an awareness of the possible heterogeneity in the margins and the way in which explanation centralises itself. It also underpins the premise, taken here, that the idea of contradiction is not necessarily problematic, which in turn supports the particular method of research that emerged in this project. The presentation of differing positions on a subject such as land rights and inheritance, requires a shuttle to run between the margin and the centre (which of course sometimes may be the margin and then at another point the centre). Thus, synthesis, which carries with it the possibility of merely ironing out differences, should not be the aim. If one is genuinely to accord marginal experience and understandings their proper place in the production of knowledge, difference must be recognised not as a weakness, but as a source of strength. If difference and contradiction are accommodated, it becomes clear that synthesis is neither appropriate nor a requirement.

This starting point lends itself to the particular method of dialogue. Handler argues that 'dialogue is the process of two people coming to understand each other [and a] . . . dialogue entails a common bond, mutual respect, a genuine listening, an openness to test our own opinions' (1988: 1066). Turning actual dialogue into text has on occasion been a useful means of display. One has only to read the enthralling dialogue between Paolo Freire and Ira Shor (1987) – in which they considered the applicability of a pedagogy developed in the South American literacy movement to higher education within the US – to realise the potential of this methodology. The values of dialogue which Handler describes of openness, listening and respect can be instilled into text written in a more conventional manner. This is not a specifically feminist approach, although in addition to being an appropriate method for writing which seeks to avoid essentialism, it also lends itself to a situation where a man and a woman work together on questions of gender and development. We had to confront in our dialogue our own taken for granted privileges in terms of gender (Ruxton 2002), race and place. From the outset, we sought to be sensitive to arguments over orientalism (Said 1978, Tibawi 1964, Macfie 2000) – a concern with scholarship that generates essentialising statements about 'the Orient' in its texts amounting to an exercise of power over it. Post-colonial approaches and critiques of western imperialism were incorporated and we were vigilant also against occidentalist trends in literature as reactive to Orientalism (Buruma and Margalit 2004).

This research was produced from dialogue between equal partners endeavouring to confront both the exclusion of Islamic approaches to land rights and the tensions around Muslim women's property rights, while recognising the disagreements, contradictions and differences between and within the views. At the same time, dialogue in the sense of posing questions in a form of reciprocal critique emerged as a methodology between us as a means of engaging with points of tension with respect to a western non-Muslim woman and a Muslim man working on Muslim land rights and gender. The contradictions, ambiguities and tensions are discussed here, often with no attempt to produce one final conclusion, but with the hope that, in the words of Lorde, from between this 'fund of polarities . . . creativity can spark' (1981: 99). It is, we think, a methodology which can enable feminist research beyond the realms of debates around land. In order to highlight the development of this approach within our own work, the ways in which it emerged and with what effect, in the rest of our chapter we will refer to ourselves in the third person.

## Islamic feminism and Muslim women's equal rights

The authors, at first, saw themselves neither as 'Islamic feminists', nor were they even comfortable with the label and all its pejorative implications. However, in retrospect, their focus upon women's equal rights and legitimate Islamic strategies and tools meant that the journey to, and through, Islamic feminism although 'accidental' was perhaps inevitable. A dilemma for most western feminists, whether atheist, agnostic or secular, has been how to engage with what many see as a bundle of anachronistic religious patriarchal beliefs and practices. Yet, from a pragmatic point of view, an anti-religious feminist crusade is not only alienating, but misses a wide range of practices which have positive implications for women's lives. Women of faith cannot be dismissed as acting merely out of compulsion, or self-oppressive false consciousness, as exemplified by the strong pro-faith Jewish and Christian feminist lobbies. Rather than presenting secularised human rights and religion as mutually exclusive choices, for women of faith, a religious appeal can be transposed into building gender capacity. As Judge Weeramantry argues, human rights are more effective, particularly in religious societies, when ordered on a vertical relationship in more absolute terms as to how human beings discharge their duties towards God (Weeramantry 1988).

There is extensive literature on Islamic feminism and Islamic feminists, but Karam's criteria of classifying feminists as Islamist, Muslim or secular on the basis of the extent to which they assign primacy to Islamic texts, or are open to secular forms of interpretations, will suffice here (Karam 1998). If 'Islamic feminism' were a purely ideological category for women opposed to women's equal rights and excluding 'moderate' Muslims and surely non-Muslims, then neither of the authors would qualify to make any intervention, either together or as individuals. The world of pro-faith Muslim feminism, however, exhibits considerable diversity and offers inclusiveness, with gender equality and human rights approaches espoused by a large number of those who are self-proclaimed Islamic feminists. An increasing number of women across the globe do not share the misogynist and patriarchal versions of Islam (Ali 1999), and feminist Islamic hermeneutics and interpretation strategies are emerging as a significant weapon against dominant andocentric constructions and their selective use of Islamic doctrines (Barlas 2002, Wadud 1999, Hassan 1982). The authors recognised that, by whatever name, it is the pro-faith brand of feminism, embedding gender activism in the language of Islamic authenticity, which appears to be gaining the largest number of converts and needs to be considered within the quest for enhancing women's property and land rights. For the authors, their respective identities – maleness and non-Muslim – were not seen as barring participation, together through their mutual dialogue, in an Islamic feminist debate which is concerned with substantive engagement with the development of gender empowering strategies. The dialogical approach, as well as the vitality and volatility of Islamic feminism, or perhaps more correctly Islamic feminisms, in its centre(s) and margins and in its own internal dialogue(s), enabled our journey to, and through, it. The idea of 'a journey' may seem over-used, even banal, but for the authors it expresses the concern in their exploration not to occupy a discursive space but to see and to acknowledge elements within it, as if on a path, particularly in this context with respect to rights in land.

Women's equal rights to acquisition, management, administration, enjoyment and disposal of property have been an increasing component in efforts to mainstream gender rights on the international plane. Non-discrimination against women in general, and particularly with respect to property, land and housing rights, is dealt with by the 1948 Universal Declaration of Human Rights (UDHR), 1966 International Covenant on Economic, Social and Cultural Rights (ICESCR), the 1966 International Convention on Civil and Political Rights (ICCPR) and other treaties. The 1979 Convention on the Elimination of All Forms of Discrimination against Women (CEDAW) calls for equal rights in owning and administering property without discrimination (Art 15) and 'equal treatment in land and agrarian reform' (CEDAW, Art 14(2)(g)). Article 14(2)(h) requires that women not be discriminated against in their enjoyment of 'adequate living conditions, particularly in relation to housing'. These property rights have been elaborated by various human rights bodies and specialist agencies such as the CEDAW committee and by the UN-HABITAT gender mainstreaming approach. The 2005 World Summit Outcome and the recent work of the UN Task Force in relation to the Millennium Development Goal 3, with respect to women's empowerment, reiterate the importance of equal property, housing, land and inheritance rights.

A widely discussed problem regarding the implementation of CEDAW has been the extensive 'reservations' entered into by Muslim states (Artz 1990: 218–21). Of the 30-odd OIC states which have ratified the convention (just over half the OIC members), the treaty reservations entered by a dozen states in the name of Islamic principles have severely restricted the application of CEDAW provisions. In particular, caveats have been directed against Art 16, which stipulates equality of the sexes in marriage and family matters (Khaliq 1995). Mayer (1999: 106), and others, rightly conclude that evolving political contingencies, and not Islamic beliefs, determine most Muslim states' CEDAW reservations. Islamic reservations have to be interrogated to distinguish the levels of religious imperatives, socio-cultural practices, 'folk religion' and contrived patriarchal policies that underpin them. Several NGOs in the Muslim world have called for the reservations to be lifted.

However, there has been an Islamisation of the human rights agenda, including important instruments such as the 1981 Universal Islamic Declaration of Human Rights (UIDHR), in which law is clarified as denoting Islamic law (*Shari'a*). The UIDHR's provisions on property and land rights generally support the rights of women. For example, Art 6 refers to 'everyone', clarified to include 'both the male and female sexes'. This is reiterated in the Cairo Declaration on Human Rights, Art 15. However, equal rights are not explicit and the UIDHR speaks only of 'impermissible discrimination' (Art 3) and refers to 'rights of married women' (Art 20) seemingly excluding others (Halim 1994: 416). Women activists, while appreciating some important acknowledgements in the two Islamic documents, decry the lack of gender mainstreaming of rights.

Reconciling Islamic principles and gender equality human rights standards appears to pose a problem. There are difficulties in terms of both fixed Islamic inheritance rules, and the prevalence of patriarchal or gender deprecating practices in the name of Islam, but the possibilities of working out a more gender egalitarian Islamic approach to women's property rights through *ijtihad* (independent reasoning), authenticated by Islamic jurisprudence, has emerged. If conservative Islamic readings of 'the law' resistant to gender equality cannot be countered simply by appeals to human rights, what possibilities then can be offered for, and through, Islamic feminism?

## Why inheritance law and systems?

The authors focused on Islamic inheritance laws and systems in an attempt to address a perceived 'gap': Inheritance is often treated as semi-detached from general debates and policy formation concerning security of tenure, land rights, land reform or regularisation (Lim 2004). De Soto (2001), for instance, pays little or no attention to this issue, presumably regarding it as a matter for the private sphere of the family and local relationships, which lie outside the bounds of his discussion (Varley 2002). Western feminist analyses of land law too rarely recognise the significance of inheritance for women, concentrating, rather, upon rights in the family home through purchase or occupation. In these analyses matters of inheritance are usually addressed, if at all, as a peripheral and coincidental feature. Inheritance is, however, one of the commonest ways of acquiring land or access to land, especially in parts of the Muslim world. Ferchiou (1985, quoted in Cotula 2002) found, in a study of Tunisian villages, that inheritance accounted for over 70 per cent of land acquisitions. Inheritance therefore, even in the face of considerable legal, social and cultural barriers and constraints with which this chapter is concerned, is an important source of access to land for women. Stauth, considering the position of women from all social strata of rural village communities in Egypt, went as far as to state: 'Bought land is men's land, women's land is inherited' (1990: 40).

In Muslim societies, the legal rules concerning the proper devolution of property upon death are deeply embedded in popular consciousness, being a considerable source of pride because of their particularly close association with the *Qur'an*.[2] Rosen, in the context of rural village life in Morocco, writes: 'Everyone knows the Tradition that has the Prophet saying that knowledge of the laws of inheritance constitutes half of all useful knowledge in the world. And everyone in Morocco, however, well or poorly educated, has a firm grasp of the essentials of inheritance law' (Rosen 2000: 89–90). The Divinely revealed guidance (see *Qur'an* 2: 180, 2: 240, 4: 7–9, 4: 11, 4: 12, 4: 19–33, 4: 176 and 5: 105–8) on inheritance is one of the most detailed areas of Islamic law. Whilst modern reforms and changes have influenced several fields of Islamic law, the structure determining inheritance has been one of the enduring legacies of classical Islamic law. The importance of inheritance as a key area for scrutiny may, therefore, be more readily apparent within the Islamic framework than in other legal systems. And it will be argued that when they are not implemented, or rather are avoided by various means, the system of classical rules on compulsory inheritance may provide a point of reference from which discussions and debates can move forward.

The authors recognised that it was necessary to engage with key aspects of women's relations to Islamic inheritance rules, specifically from a feminist perspective. A Muslim woman possesses an independent legal, economic and spiritual identity, and therefore independence. The legal disabilities of married women which were a feature in the past of Anglo-American law are not found in Islamic law. Muslim women throughout history, whether married or not, have enjoyed autonomous legal identity and separate property rights (Lim 2001). The *Qur'an* addresses men and women as distinct persons, different, but equal, individuals. From a legal perspective, the recognition of a woman's autonomous identity leads to equal treatment between men and women in quite fundamental ways in relation to their property rights: 'There is no doubt that a Muslim woman retains control, according to Islamic law, over her pre-marital property and finances through marriage, and where applicable beyond into divorce and widowhood' (Shatzmiller 1995: 253). There are no legal restrictions on a Muslim woman purchasing property out of her earnings, but the opportunity to gain access to land through purchase is limited by socio-economic factors and land owned by women is often inherited. However, the compulsory Islamic succession rules are such that they are generally entitled to only half of an equivalent man's inheritance share.

There appears to be little appetite for discarding the Islamic inheritance rules and an interview by celebrated Egyptian secular feminist Nawal El-Sadaawi (2001) calling for a rethink of Islamic inheritance laws, drew threats of apostasy. Further, there is a robust defence of this rule in Muslim societies, including amongst many Muslim women, who argue that the totality of property arrangements within the *Shari'a* is realistic and equitable (Wadud 1999, Hassan 1982 and Barlas 2002). Commentators who support the view that women's property rights in the Islamic framework should be approached holistically, point to the *Qur'anic* stipulation that 'men spend out of their property for the support of women' and that there are no concomitant financial obligations. Other avenues of obtaining property such as gifts, dower, maintenance, and as a beneficiary under a *waqf* (endowment), are also be deemed as 'compensatory'. Al-Faruqi (2000: 81), for instance, regards the legal system *taken as a whole* to be fair, arguing that the total scheme is supportive of the family and fosters its interdependence, whilst at the same time ensuring that women are properly taken care of by their male relatives.

The authors decided to take an 'Islamic feminist leap', and investigate the assertion that the compulsory succession rules should not be viewed in isolation, but as part of a wider set of 'compensatory' rules and practices. For instance, to what extent are a variety of legal tools deployed as a form of estate planning to avoid the succession principles? And, as women's property rights and relations take place within the context of familial and social politics, what impact does implicit and explicit bargaining and negotiation have on their claims? Attention to these aspects of the inheritance system, to the complex social practices and meanings of inheritance in relation to women's lived experiences, as opposed to simply paper rights, may hold the possibility of strategies to empower women. Engagement with the seeming contradictions, challenges and dilemmas concerning land rights may suggest less obvious tactics for social transformation than legal reform, particularly if contradiction and ambiguity are not regarded as necessarily problematic in themselves. At the same time, the particular association of inheritance with the *Qur'an* also means that this is a fertile field for exploring the extent to which Islamic law enhances and protects women's rights to access land rather than operating as an inhibition or limit upon them. The authors proceeded to consider how Muslim women's inheritance rights, and their more general rights in land, theoretically well established under Islamic law, operate in practice.

## Key features of Islamic legal rules of inheritance

Under Islamic law, specific fractional shares of a deceased person's estate are distributed (after payment of debts or legacies) to certain defined heirs, 'sharers': sons, daughters, father, mother or spouse, and, in the absence of children, siblings, according to the compulsory rules derived from *Qur'anic* verses. These rules apply to all estates, whatever their size, and whether they are comprised of residential or commercial property, liquid assets or investments, sometimes leading to minute divisions. This fragmentation of property is particularly, although not exclusively, of importance in relation to agricultural land. The system may give rise to a land parcel involving many partners in unequal or equal shares. Wahlin (1994), for instance, analysed 126 fairly recent inheritance records within Muslim families in villages of the hill country in Jordan. The number of inheritors varied widely, from a single person up to 40, with an average of 7.5.

The scheme is remarkably inclusive, since estates are distributed across a range of immediate and distant relatives (depending on the closeness of kinship in relation to the deceased) and, in some cases, a large number of family members may access property. Legal entitlements to property are not conditional on the vagaries of relationships, but rather can be asserted as rights which cannot be withdrawn. Thus, the Islamic inheritance rules are not merely a set of abstract rules, but are intended to facilitate distinctive Islamic conceptions of property and family. Taken as a whole, *Shari'a* law, with respect to inheritance, legally institutes and reinforces the extended family as opposed to the conjugal family. In the more modern context, some commentators and campaigners for reform have identified a tension or contradiction between the shift towards the social primacy of the nuclear family in many communities and the emphasis on relations with the extended family within Islamic law.

Adherence to these inheritance rules is not just symbolically important, but a serious matter of religious ethics and consequences, as exemplified by the *Qur'anic* verses which stipulate that those who appropriate the property of orphans 'face hellfire' (*Qur'an* 4: 10). The rules must also be read alongside the bequest provisions in the *Qur'an* and *awqaf* (charitable endowments), which encourage Muslims as an act of piety, to provide for needy and poor relatives. While there is no ceiling on the quantum of property an individual may acquire through legitimate means, the distributive aspect of the inheritance rules also supports another facet of property law, namely the injunction against hoarding an excessive accumulation of wealth in the hands of one individual. Thus, inheritance rules are not only a part of personal law, but also serve several purposes which are public or communitarian in nature. A wide range of actors, from politicians and legal officials, through to women and men on the street and in the home, are implicated in ensuring the integrity and dynamism of the Islamic inheritance system. The Islamic feminist question focuses on the gendered impact of these rules.

## Women's shares in inheritance and as part of a wider system

The rule that a woman will receive, generally, a half share of that which a man would receive in a similar situation, differs according to claimants and contexts. Given the wide range of beneficiaries that the Islamic inheritance system seeks to cater for, through a sophisticated balancing process, the results can turn out to be hair-splitting permutations varying according to the particular scenario. There are many combinations of surviving relations of the deceased that may arise, and not every case is dealt with directly in the *Qur'anic* verses. It is on matters where the *Qur'an* makes no direct instruction, that *Sunni* and *Shia* have established different methods for the allocation of shares.

In relatively simple cases relating to *Sunni* parties, the estate will be shared according to the compulsory rules between the deceased's parents or parent, husband or wife, and children. A surviving parent will receive one-sixth of the estate, the surviving spouse one-eighth (if a wife) or one quarter (if a husband), with the balance shared between the surviving children and the sons receiving twice the share of the daughters. If the deceased has no children, a wife will receive one-quarter of her husband's estate, while a husband will receive one-half of his wife's estate. Where the deceased dies with no descendants or siblings and the parents are the only heirs, the mother will receive one third of the estate. The father will receive the remainder of the estate as the nearest male relative. However, the mother's share is reduced to one-sixth when the deceased has no children but has siblings.

At first blush, the inheritance laws disadvantage women and need to be reviewed. However, most Muslims, including women, appear to view the inheritance regime as part of a larger social and religious issue. While Islamic jurisprudence can be flexible and *ijtihad* (independent reasoning) comes into play when there is no *nass* (explicit position) under the *Qur'an* or *Sunna* (the recommended traditions of the Prophet), Muslim women generally do not challenge their unequal proportion of shares as they are fixed and compulsory (called *faraid*, pl. *fard* or duty) by the *Qur'an*. A general refrain is that what God has ordained for shares cannot be changed. Thus, Kenyan Muslim women protested against a proposed Civil Rights Bill in 2000, which would have given equal shares in inheritance to sons and daughters, on the basis that such a change would amount to a breach of *Shari'a* law (An-Naim 2002: 50). A recent study in Morocco shows that while women generally assert their rights 'to independently own and manage property and businesses', when it comes to inheritance participants in the study stated that 'equal' is not the main concern, but rather what the religion of Islam says (Katulis 2004: 17). In the words of one respondent: 'We shouldn't change inheritance laws just so women could get an equal share, If we want to change that, we are going to change religion and doctrine; I think this should not happen' (Katulis 2004: 18).

State law reforms have had virtually no impact on inheritance rights (Minault 1997: 7). Despite legal reforms which have led to an increased secularisation of the legal systems in the majority of Islamic countries, personal status/family law, which includes inheritance, remains within the domain of *Shari'a*. There has been extensive codification of the *Shari'a* principles relating to personal status and those laws which govern the institution of the family, including inheritance rules. The *Moudawana* (Code of Personal Status) (2004) in Morocco, for instance, introduced substantial changes to the formal status of women and is to a degree supportive of the nuclear, conjugal family, with both joint ownership of property in marriage and joint decision making between marriage partners envisaged. However, as elsewhere in the Arab world, reforms in relation to inheritance are relatively modest with little interference in the compulsory rules. Daughters continue to enjoy only half as much as their brothers from the estate of a parent.

The experience of state family law reforms, whether substantive or procedural, in the Muslim world cannot be generalised (Welchman 2000) but it is clear that there are negative, as well as positive, features to such processes. Some argue that such reforms have actually caused deterioration in the status of women (Moors 1995: 143) and Sonbol argues that reforms are often not innocent and have the effect of creating new institutions and practices which deny previous freedoms, while emphasising earlier discriminations (Sonbol 1996: 7, 11). With further secularisation inconceivable in most Muslim states, and changes offering superficial reforms which do little in practice to advance women's rights, there is a call for revisiting Islamic sources that is gaining momentum. The call is not for discarding Islamic inheritance rules, but appreciating them within the broader Islamic property framework.

Not only are inheritance rules presented as a complete and divinely ordained code, but many Muslim women view the inheritance distribution rules as merely one part of a 'property flow chart'. Muslim feminists such as Wadud (1999), Hassan (1982) and Barlas (2002), argue that women are adequately compensated by other sources of support. Under the integrated Islamic approach to women's property rights, their reduced inheritance rights are expected to be compensated by other means of wealth generation. These methods include a woman's equal access to purchase through earnings, endowments and gifts, and special supplements such as savings. It is also argued that women benefit from lack of financial obligations within the family, from dower (a payment which is an important effect of marriage from the bridegroom's family to the bride) and maintenance.

## The 'compensation' argument

A woman's right to property is not just an abstract ideal, or merely a matter of legal principles, it is a crucial dimension to her identity, security and empowerment (Agarwal 1994). But this is also shaped by her social status, place in the life cycle and dynamics within her household and family. Like others, Powers (2002) has argued, persuasively, that because of the clear distinction between lifetime transfers and transactions that take effect upon death, it is important that the system of compulsory inheritance rules should not be viewed in isolation. Rather, the rules on inheritance shares should be seen as part of a wider flexible system for the transmission of property across the generations and within the family (Powers 2002: 144, Doumani 1998: 7).

In principle, a woman's access to property and land will come at various stages of life, most notably through her 'rights' to dower and maintenance. Dower (*mehr/mahr*) is a payment, in cash or in property, which the husband pays ('prompt dower'), or promises to pay ('deferred dower') to the wife as a consequence of marriage (Siddiqui 1995: 14–24, Charrad 2001: 36). Its value is generally determined by the parties' socio-economic status. Dower is particularly important with respect to dissolution of the marriage due to divorce, and may even serve to discourage divorce. Where negotiations between the families result in a marriage contract which stipulates that part of the dower is deferred, the law provides that this portion of the dower must be paid in full when the husband divorces by means of his unilateral setting aside of his wife (*talaq*).

At certain points in history dower has been regarded as an important part of a woman's wealth. Tucker (1985) indicates that estate records in Nablus, Palestine during the eighteenth and nineteenth centuries suggest that women acquired wealth through dower at the time of marriage, amounting to about 15 per cent to 20 per cent of middle and upper class women's property at death. However, Moors (1995) suggests a decline in the modern importance of dower as a social institution in Palestinian society. Rising land prices since the 1960s have meant that the main expense for the family of a new husband is the provision of housing for the couple, as opposed to a dower payment to the wife. Another effect of the upward spiral in land prices is in terms of limiting women's ability to buy land with their dower wealth.

Commentators who support the view that women's property rights in the Islamic framework should be approached holistically, point also to the *Qur'anic* stipulation that 'men spend out of their property for the support of women'. There is a legal expectation that a woman's fundamental daily requirements will be met by her husband, although in practice she may lose her right to maintenance under several circumstances including the controversial justification of lack of obedience to the husband (*nushuq*). Controversy surrounds the provision of maintenance in relation to the divorced wife. Other than a right to specified dower, conservative jurists hold that the divorced wife has no financial rights against her former husband, even in a case of his arbitrary repudiation (*talaq*), since the marriage contract is dissolved. A husband may be required to provide compensation (*mutat*) in some jurisdictions, such as Egypt and Jordan, when he has repudiated his wife without good reason. However, even under the most generous provisions the sum to be paid to the wife does not exceed the value of a few years maintenance.

Despite the many barriers to women actually receiving their property rights under the holistic regime, there could be a net material flow from men to women within the family. Other avenues of obtaining property such as gifts, dower, maintenance, and as a beneficiary under a *waqf* may be deemed, even if only in legal theory, also as compensatory for women's lesser shares in inheritance.

## From wills to estate planning

Inheritance rules as part of wider inheritance systems are shaped by the interplay of competing, alternative and overlapping legal and cultural norms. While devolution of land in a number of Muslim communities takes place exclusively through the compulsory formula, it is also the case that various legal tools have developed in different contexts to permit individuals to make arrangements for the transmission of property according to their own determination. Here, the practice of Islamic wills (*wasaya*) and estate planning and their gendered impact is considered.

Gifts can be made to take effect upon death, by means of an Islamic will, although only up to one-third of an individual's estate can devolve in this manner. Such bequests are optional and for a *Sunni* it cannot be made to anyone who is entitled to a share under the compulsory inheritance rules (Zaid 1986: 12). The relationship between bequests and inheritance is widely envisaged as forming part of an integrated system, and bequests provide an opportunity for estate planning by the individual who is able to foresee any anomalies arising out of the operation of the Islamic inheritance in his or her specific case. A debate continues as to whether a Muslim has a duty (*fard*) to make a bequest, or that it is highly recommended (*wajib*), or merely a praiseworthy (*mustahab*) act. Some modern legislation has viewed the bequest as a correctional tool, for example the Egyptian law which states: 'It is necessary for every person to make a bequest to those near relatives excluded from succession' (Zaid 1986: 13).

However, there are a variety of legal techniques that a person contemplating death may deploy as a form of 'estate planning', in order to avoid the strictures of the compulsory inheritance rules. In some contexts there is a strong determination to ensure that the management of farmland, or indeed a business, remains under the control of male members of the family. Fragmentation of land, for instance, to comply with the formula for fractional division of an estate, makes neither economic nor social sense to many social actors. From this standpoint it is appropriate to seek methods to avoid the division of family wealth, whilst at the same time being able to uphold the religious quality and validity of the rules themselves.

The most obvious tool for estate planning is the *hiba* (lifetime transfer or gift), which in some societies is regarded as a socially acceptable means of mitigating the compulsory inheritance rules. For instance, Wahlin (1994) explored patterns of land ownership from 1867 to 1980, using extensive land records in the province of *al-Balqa* in the Jordan hill country and found that, through the use of a lifetime transfer of rights in land by a father to his chosen son or sons, those males who were most active in the family received their father's land. Some commentators regard such mechanisms as 'tricks' which 'keep the land from being inherited by women' (Amawi 1996: 151) and in many contexts there is a strong social convention that land ownership is not only a male preserve but that the compulsory inheritance of women may channel land away from the paternal family to that of her husband.

However, the lifetime gift can also be used for the benefit of women and address their unequal legal status with respect to inheritance. Thus compulsory inheritance rules are accepted in principle, whilst adapting the results to perceived realities. Doumani (1998: 7) argues that 'Islamic inheritance rules governing the transmission of property after death are quite detailed and rigidly set, the application of these rules, in reality, was often the last resort for families and individuals, that is, property transmission was often a conscious strategic social act, not an automatic, passive or formulaic process'.

Feillard (1997) found, in Indonesia, that the use of estate planning tools to enhance the position of women was evidenced across a range of different social groupings and classes. Moreover, it was not only socially legitimate, but deemed wholly appropriate, and used as a means of giving women and girls 'compensation' for what is customarily regarded as their disadvantaged position under the compulsory inheritance rules. Feillard (1997: 96) quotes a preacher from an influential *ulama* (priestly) family in Indonesia explaining such processes as legally legitimate: 'Islam has ruled the question of inheritance in a complete way . . . [but] there is the possibility of sharing the inheritance while the parents are still alive. Let people do it. But after death, God proposes the best solution.'

Classification of the land also affects women's access to it. Land categorised as state, or *miri*, land is regarded as lying outside the compulsory rules, and its usufruct rights are often subject to lifetime transfer. Studies (Mundy 1979; Maher 1974 cited in Badran 1985: 15) point to rural women under greater pressure as a consequence, owing to the land holding patterns and the customary transfer of usufruct rights in *miri* land from father to son. However, there is some evidence that in both Yemen and Morocco, peasant women are compensated for their loss in terms of access to land with periodic gifts and fallback security (Badran 1985).

Inheritance rules may also have a bearing upon decisions regarding the formal registration of land. Bahaa-Eldin (1999) records that, when working for the legal department of an Egyptian bank, he encountered many customer's with significant wealth who could not provide sufficient collateral for a loan. This was not because they lacked assets, but simply that they lacked documentary evidence of their ownership of assets, particularly land. Even though Egypt has a fairly efficient institutional framework for dealing with land transfers and registration, many assets remain outside the formal registration system. He cites two reasons for this lack of engagement with the registration process. First, high rates of taxes and fees associated with registration act as a barrier to many individuals. Second, and far more importantly for the purposes of this chapter, he states that: 'in view of the strict rules governing the distribution of a deceased person's estate in Egyptian law – with its origin in *Shari'a* – the distribution is often conducted informally and remains unregistered in order to avoid those strict rules' (1999: 212–13). Further, he suggests that there is a gender dimension to this failure to register, since even a woman's lesser shares under the inheritance rules are 'resented and avoided'. He indicates that, in many cases, neither the death of an original title-holder to land nor the redistribution of his estate will be notified to the relevant authorities.

## Confronting *tanazul* (renunciation)

Within the Islamic framework the compulsory shares under the inheritance laws are *faraid* (obligations). If a woman cannot demand more than half because of the fixed shares, then neither can she be given less than half. Her share is clearly an enforceable right. However, in many Muslim societies, there are well established practices allowing women to renounce their inheritance rights. This is a result of socio-cultural practice, rather than Islam, and requires close scrutiny.

It is ironic that whilst the half inheritance share is justified on the basis that women are supported by their husbands, the rationale given for renouncing the remaining half is that they may still need the support of their brothers (Chaudhry 1997: 544). Agarwal (1994: 282–4) draws an interesting contrast between Pakistan and Bangladesh, both formally governed by *Shari'a* law and both subject to the widespread practice of renouncing women's inheritance rights. She points out that a large number of researchers have found Bangladeshi village women, particularly poor women, increasingly inclined to claim their inheritance shares, whereas no such phenomenon is observed in Pakistan. She concludes that widespread landlessness and scarce resources, alongside the breakdown in traditional support networks in Bangladesh, may explain women's willingness to stake their claim, whereas in the more prosperous agricultural areas of Pakistan there are no such 'push' factors. The motivation, therefore, is contingent on a variety of social, economic, cultural and political factors.

The voluntary renunciation of an inheritance will take place for a complex set of reasons, relating largely to familial politics and custom and although the Islamic inheritance process does not conceive of rejection by the beneficiaries of their share, this has been, over time, incorporated into the legal framework under the *Shari'a*. Consequently, there is an accepted legal process through which it takes place, after confirmation that the woman is competent and fully aware of what she is doing (Al Mahmassani 2003). It is an interesting example of 'God proposes, Man disposes' in which pragmatic or socio-cultural considerations alter the impact of *Shari'a* rules.

Of itself, neither an inheritance claim, nor renunciation of an inheritance share, should be assumed to be either empowering or an act of submission (Moors 1995: 75). A woman's kinship position is an important factor with respect to inheritance and the voluntary renunciation of inheritance rights on the part of a woman may serve to underline a woman's claims upon her brothers' social and family responsibilities. For instance, Agarwal (1994: 260–2) emphasises that women in much of South Asia, both Muslim and Hindu, will place great emphasis on the need for strong ties with their brothers: 'If I take my inheritance, my brothers will forget they have a sister. If I give to them, they will remember me and take care of me if I need them' (Hartmann and Boyce 1983: 92–3, quoted in Agarwal 1994: 249). In South Asia these needs and ties are connected also with access to the family (brother's) home, which may be a safety net at times of economic, social and physical insecurity, when a woman has married outside of her village. Agarwal (1994) argues that, in the context of Bangladesh where access to the family home is widely regarded as a right, some scholars regard the renunciation of a woman's right to inheritance of land as the 'informal' price of retaining that right.

Renunciation may preserve a woman's kin relationships, when accepting compensation for relinquishing a share in land will not. Moors (1995: 55) recounts the story of a Palestinian woman forced by her husband to claim her share of her father's land, who was given cash for the land by her brothers. Her sister, who renounced her own share, retained good relations with her brothers, whereas the woman who received money as compensation was cut-off from her brothers, and the loss of their affections led to an illness from which she did not recover. Moors concluded, on the basis of discussions with Palestinian women, that 'renouncing her inheritance rights is central to the brother-sister relation'. Cultural norms may permit a woman to make a claim upon her brother for support, protection or shelter at a difficult point in her life, but as Kabeer (1985: 88, 90) observed, the reality is that this claim is more likely to be realised if a woman has renounced her share of inheritance.[3] Moors (1995) suggests a disruption of kinship ties, specifically between a woman and her brother/s, is almost inevitable should she fail to renounce her rights and Johnson's (2004: 150) analysis of contemporary Palestinian society also indicates a 'widespread phenomenon of women renouncing their share of inheritance in order to gain their brothers', sons', or other male relatives' putative social support'. Layish (1997: 355), again with respect to

Palestine, explains that *tanazul* may take place 'upon or after the succession order by the court, sometimes even after the property has been registered in their name in the Land Register'.

Into the explicit and implicit bargaining and negotiation, must also be placed cultural notions of what is 'shameful'. To make a claim upon a brother will detract from the vision of what it is to be a 'good sister'. Pressure of various kinds, including threats of violence, may be brought to bear by brothers and other male relatives upon their female kin to forgo their inheritance shares. At its most extreme, this pressure may amount to physical violence and even murder. Sonbol (1996: 190) has argued that there is a widespread belief amongst Jordanians that 'property and inheritance are at the heart of many honour crimes', 'getting rid of a sister (as is the case in many of these crimes) becomes a means of eliminating an obstacle to a brother's inheritance'.

However, class position is influential and wealthy urban women are likely to receive all or part of their share in inheritance, and Moors (1995) suggests that, in Palestine, brothers from a prosperous urban background may enhance their own prestige by 'giving' to their sisters. Furthermore, where a woman has no brothers, she is more likely to sustain a claim upon her father's estate including a claim upon land, than where she has one or more brothers. Women in a rural setting who claim a share may find their choice of marriage partner confined to a paternal cousin, where the family seeks to ensure that possession of land does not fall into the hands of outsiders.

Moors (1995) also finds that when a widow renounces her share in favour of her sons, this will generally serve to strengthen her position in the family, rather than weaken it. If the children are young, renunciation on the part of the widow is likely to ensure that the estate remains undivided for a considerable period of time and may give her day-to-day control over her husband's house and land and may strengthen her moral and emotional claims upon her sons when they grow up. Yet, there remains the possibility of lack of full information for the woman, coercion or family/social pressure and lack of compensation in any meaningful way. The net effect could be that the woman is dispossessed of her mandatory inheritance rights.

## Problems in realising the compensatory scheme

In practice, the compensatory system fails to deliver equitable access to property, particularly land, due to several impediments. Firstly, there is no mechanism to ensure that the woman is compensated for her inheritance loss in other ways, as there are different players at various stages of the woman's life. The legal ideology may be holistic, but choices are often made in a vacuum, in the sense that they are made on the basis of current demands or needs, rather than with a 'life course' perspective. Secondly, while inheritance shares are often land rights, the others such as dower, maintenance and beneficial interests under a *waqf ahli* (family endowment), the latter now largely abolished, are at best limited to usufruct rights or wealth. Property tends to flow away from women, as opposed to towards them. In any event, under social or familial pressure women may give up that inheritance right to land, or 'exchange' it for cash or other property, which may or may not actually be paid. Finally, customary norms through family and kinship structures seem to have trumped Islamic principles by making earnings and savings difficult, the dower and maintenance rights either nominal or conditional or non-enforceable, and inheritance rights often practically ephemeral. However, Islamic principles and early practice demonstrate that it does not have to be this way and that a reappraisal of Islamic law could empower Muslim women and enhance 'real' property rights for them.

If key Islamic legal materials generally support women's rights to acquire, hold, use, administer and dispose of property, how can an Islamic feminist approach bridge the gap between principles and practice?

## Women as owners and managers of property in the Ottoman period

The authors turned to a historical review of Islamic practice to answer westerners, and Muslim patriarchs, who consider women as inferior property holders. In early Islamic history, Muslim women played a variety of public roles and exercised extensive property rights, with their scriptural rights to property finding material expression. Roded describes recent findings on the ownership and management of property by women in earlier ages as 'provocative' (1999: 142). Recent studies of Ottoman records covering different regions and time periods (Sonbol 2003: 59–60, 66–9, Fay 1998: 118–40, Shatzmiller 1995) provide outlines of women's property rights. Particularly with respect to the *waqf*, these records show that Ottoman Islamic society was not as rigidly patriarchal as commonly assumed (Powers 1999) and that women's rights were upheld by the judges, muftis and male jurists (Shatzmiller 1995).

Some commentators regard these histories as an important source of legitimacy for current strategies and processes designed to enhance contemporary women's empowerment with respect to property rights (Sonbol 1996). Marsot, in her research into eighteenth-century Egypt, concludes that 'women of all strata owned property; bought, sold and exchanged property; and endowed it at will' (1996: 37, Sonbol 1996: 68–9). We should be cautious with too much emphasis placed upon women's apparent legal status and property rights as evidenced in historical documents. However, history does show, in practice, a fundamental form of equality between men and women in terms of their treatment under the law.

Drawing from the historical records, Islamic law contains important tools that can be used to enhance the position of women and their access to property. A strategy of deploying, and in some senses reviving, these 'authentic' tools could provide a route for reform, in contrast to secular legal reforms which too easily unravel. Statutory change of a secular nature struggles for acceptance in modern Islamic societies, particularly with respect to areas like inheritance and there is widespread resistance against anything other than very limited state intervention in this area, even amongst women. Finding means by which we can materialise the embedded egalitarian and distributive aspects of Islamic law has to come, primarily, from within the community and therefore from within an Islamic framework. Islamic history can be deployed to demonstrate that there is also nothing inherent in Islamic principles to inhibit the development of gender responsive tenure systems and rights, which can serve as an important argument for Islamic feminists.

## Realising the potential of the 'compensatory' approach

The approach taken through the ideology of 'the compensatory regime' could be realised through appropriate responses at several levels. At a normative level, *ijtihad* could be facilitated to clarify rights through *usul al fiqh* (Islamic jurisprudential methodology). The State could then provide means through which to possess this, in the public interest and in accordance with Islamic principles, to reform gender discriminatory provisions and practice. This requires, through institutional reform, a rearrangement of court jurisdictions or the creation of a specialist institution to interpret Islamic property rights for women, holistically, and a means by which to enforce these rights. Thus a pooling together of Islamic resources and responses could address women's property rights.

*Ijtihad* is literally 'an effort to find' the right principle and is not confined to the jurist, but is the sacred duty (*fard kafiya*) of every competent individual. There are verses such as those relating to inheritance which are regarded as unambiguous and incapable of interpretation, but there are other matters where the *Qur'an* and *Sunna* are silent, where there is scope for rationalist approaches and recourse to the egalitarian principles of the *Qur'an* itself. Far from being the prerogative of liberals or modernists, *ijtihad* has equally been a favourite with Islamic revivalists and conservatives. It is the post-facto validation through *ijma* (consensus of opinion) that converts the fruits of personal reasoning into a discovery or finding for the benefit of society.

*Ijtihad* offers, as yet untested, interesting possibilities in interpreting aspects of Islamic land law. There is nothing to suggest that maleness is a criterion for becoming a *Mujtahid* and a new genre of *Mujtahidat* (female practising *Ijtihad*) from among theorists, lawyers, students, academicians and activists have taken on virtually every contested area of gender rights. Although aspects of the Islamic property regime such as the compulsory inheritance rules may not be subject to *ijtihad* due to explicit *Qur'anic* rules (Amawi 1996: 155), other Islamic doctrines which impact on the Muslim woman's ability to make choices and access land are being clarified. These include dower and maintenance, the right to work, travel alone, vote and stand for public office, be appointed as judges, to attend prayers in mosques, custody, reproductive choices, or the practice of polygamy, *mut'a* (temporary) marriage, *talaq* (divorce), the concepts of *qiwama* (male guardianship), *ta'a* (obedience) and *nushuq* (rebellion), domestic violence and the prerogative of the *wali* (guardian). Here the methodology is to weed out gender deprecating customary norms projected as Islamic truisms, with reference to the gender empowering *Qur'anic* stipulations.

A woman does not lose financial autonomy, or assets, by virtue of marriage and can seek court protection against interference. As argued earlier, one important aspect of a woman's property rights and of the compensatory framework is the institution of dower. The prompt dower becomes payable on marriage and is enforceable. However, one area where *ijtihad* is both possible, and necessary, is in the fixing of the minimum amount of dower – a vital part of the marriage contract – as part of public policy and inflation adjusting it where its payment is deferred. This is an opportunity for innovation and a well-established tool for developing jurisprudence in light of contemporary issues (Weiss 1978: 203).

A woman does not cede her personal property to her husband, her family or her husband's family, and further scope for *ijtihad* may be available in relation to maintenance. The woman has no obligation to maintain her husband or family, rather she can expect and demand as a right that her husband maintain her and the family, even if she possesses the resources. She continues her right to acquire property through her income (for example, paid housework or through her right to work), receiving gifts or as a *waqf* beneficiary. Abu-Odeh (2004: 205–06) argues for resistance against the 'magic and temptations' of the discourse of sameness as equality and attention in legal reform through formulations which preserve the 'legal transactional logic' of the holistic approach to property rights. She argues for expansive redefinitions of maintenance to encompass the notion that it is compensating women for housework.

Further *ijtihad* is required to confirm that the husband has an obligation to maintain his wife after marriage, particularly in cases of unilateral *talaq*. In addition, the outcome of the woman initiated *khula* (judicial divorce) proceedings, which extinguishes her access to dower merely because the husband refuses to consent to the divorce in the first place, needs to be addressed. The court in divorce proceedings could bring into consideration issues of equity, specifically in the avoidance of dependence, homelessness and destitution. On all these issues, the decision maker needs to consider the entire property flow chart of gifts, inheritance and dower before proceeding to determine the quantum of maintenance, based on the rights and needs of the wife and the capacity of the husband.

Meanwhile, since the practice of women renouncing their shares in favour of siblings or other male relatives is more a customary than an Islamic practice, by the same logic there is nothing to stop male siblings from renouncing part of their shares to their sister to ensure parity. And, as it is a significant concern as to whether a woman renouncing her share does so through fully informed consent, given the *Qur'anic* nature of inheritance rights it should be incumbent that judicial records confirm the conditions of renunciation such as exchange of other property, rights or arrangements, which should be enforceable.

## Developing Islamic tools through, and for, Islamic feminism

This chapter has indicated how the research recognised the importance of inheritance for women's property rights and attempted to address a number of challenges surrounding the practices of Islamic inheritance law as they impact upon women. The dialogic methodology enabled the incorporation of feminist, human rights, development, social, historical and legal approaches. They yielded the assessment that Islamic inheritance rules and systems, properly acknowledged, could be a strong starting point for Muslim women in their assertion of a full range of rights to property, in particular land. Indeed, Islamic inheritance shares for women, although lesser than those held by men, are superior to most of the customary practices and the modest implementation of some statutory rights. The compulsory inheritance rules are a part of an inheritance system that has the potential for enhancing fully-fledged property rights and there is nothing in the Islamic property regime, taken as a whole, to prevent the establishment of women's equal rights to property. Women's disadvantages are not, therefore, as is the widespread western view, a necessary product of Islamic law

However, the compulsory inheritance rules must be understood within the wider system of property relations, including such matters as dower and maintenance, and within the inheritance practices established through the legitimate methods of estate planning. Where these legal 'techniques' serve to achieve progressive and inclusive results, efforts to enhance their social legitimacy must be facilitated but recognise the effects of compelling pressures on women: ties of affection, notions of honour and shame, economic necessity and so on, which have a bearing on whether they will assert a claim upon a share in an inheritance, agree to sell a share, whether for cash or symbolically, or renounce a share. It is important to assert the difference between Islamic principles and socio-economic and cultural practices, which have to be tested for their utility and legitimacy in view of evolving family and community structures. This is an area, particularly with regard to renunciation, where advocacy is possible to empower women.

The dialogue between partners, enabled the authors to give attention to the marginality of Islamic law with respect to the land rights debate, to narrate its absence, whilst appreciating internal Islamic dialogue. It also enabled our 'accidental' arrival in Islamic feminist debates. A dialogic method of research, including the acknowledgement of the diversity and contradictions within margins, does not give rise to smooth synthesised strategic outcomes but can give rise to 'creative sparks'. The existence of an alternative, more gender inclusive, Islamic framework for addressing access to land has been outlined. Rather than an abstract or sterile set of theories, it offers potentially several innovative solutions, even if they may involve some trade-offs. However, Islamic law cannot be used to monopolise the development of a land rights debate, not only because, as already discussed, different forms of Islam are competing, but also because Islamic jurisprudence must, and does, intersect with international, state, customary and informal systems. There is, the authors believe, significant promise in reworking Islamic law in relation to land, which could conjure both authenticity and durability in the quest for development and human rights for Muslims through greater access to land. However, such developments must recognise the importance of a gendered perspective, and so, as the authors move forward in their work, they have come to realise that they can now, both of them, uphold the significance of an 'Islamic feminism' as central to the development of a programme for the enhancement of Muslim women's rights. But that is not, could not be, an 'end', any dialogue must continue.[4]

## Notes

1 This produced eight papers on Islamic theory, law, tenure systems, human rights, women's rights, inheritance, *awqaf* (endowments) and microfinance, see *Islamic Land and Property Research Series* (2005) http://www.unhabitat.org/list.asp?typeid=3&catid=283.

2 In this respect perhaps surpassing any other area of law.

3 The ideology and practices of purdah mean also that, for many women, male kin mediate a woman's social relations outside the family, highlighting the need for nurturing emotional ties with a brother or another close male relative. This will be particularly the case when a woman is trying to access her legal rights, as in a land dispute, perhaps as a widow trying to make a claim upon her deceased husband's relatives. A brother may be an all-important ally and a representative in any formal or informal dispute forum.

4 When our research was completed in September 2005, it was widely disseminated through the UN-HABITAT website and publications and generated debate. Its findings were presented before expert group meetings, including a workshop during the Arab Ministerial Conference in Cairo (organised by UNESCWA, UN-HABITAT and Arab League) and the Asian Regional meeting in Bangkok (organised by the World Bank, UN-HABITAT, ESCAP and the International Federation of Surveyors), both in December 2005. The Arab meeting led to the endorsement of the research through the Cairo Declaration on Islamic Tools with support from the Al Azhar, the leading Islamic institution, and governments including Egypt. It was also discussed by civil society at a meeting in Oslo in

March 2006, organised by UN-HABITAT, and supported by the governments of Sweden and Norway. The Global Land Tool Network, initiated by UN-HABITAT, and launched in Vancouver at the World Urban Forum in June 2006, has taken Islamic land tools as one of its top priorities and has developed an extensive Islamic methodology for further development of the tools.

# Bibliography


Abdullah, H J and Hamza, I, 'Women and Land in Northern Nigeria: The Need for Independent Ownership Rights', in Muthoni Wanyeki, L (ed.), *Women and Land in Africa: Culture, Religion and Realizing Women's Rights*, 2003, London and Cape Town: Zed books Ltd and David Philip Publishers, pp 133–75.

Abu-Odeh, L, 'Egyptian Feminism: Trapped in the Identity Debate', in Haddad, Y Y and Stowasser, B F (eds), *Islamic Law and the Challenge of Modernity*, 2004, Walnut Creek: AltaMira Press, pp 183–212.

Acton, T, *Gypsy politics and social change*, 1974, London: Routledge and Kegan Paul.

Acton, T, Caffrey, S, Dunn, S and Vinson, P, 'Gender issues in accounts of Gypsy health and hygiene as discourses of social control', in Acton, T and Mundy, G (eds), *Romani Culture and Gypsy Identity*, 1997, Hatfield: University of Hertfordshire Press, pp 164–79.

Agarwal, B, *A Field of One's Own: Gender and Land Rights in South Asia*, 1994, Cambridge: Cambridge University Press.

Alexander, E, Ministry of Finance and Development Planning, *Women and Men in Botswana: Facts and Figures*, 1991, Gaborone: Central Statistics Office, Government Printer.

Al-Faruqi, M, 'Women's self-identity in the Qur'an and Islamic law' in Webb, G (ed.), *Windows of faith: Muslim Women Scholar-Activists in North America*, 2000, Syracuse, NY: Syracuse University Press, pp 72–101.

Al-Hibri, A, 'Islam, Law and Custom: Redefining Muslim Women's Rights' (1997) 12:1 *American University Journal of International Law & Policy* 14.

Ali, S S, *Gender and Human Rights in Islam and International Law: Equal Before Allah, Unequal Before Man?*, 1999, The Hague: Kluwer.

Allen, I and Bourke-Dowling, S, *Teenage Mothers*, 1998, London: Policy Studies Institute.

Al-Mahmassani, S, *Al mabadii, al shariiya wal kanouniya fi al hajir, alnafakat, almawarith, wal wassiya*, 2003, Lebanon: Dar Al Elem Lilmalayin.

Alys, F, *Seven Walks, London 2004–5*, 2005, London: Artangel.

Amanor, K S, *Global Restructuring and Land Rights in Ghana: Forest Food Chains, Timber and Rural Livelihoods*, 1999, Uppsala: Nordiska Afrikainstitutet Research Report no 108.

Amanor, K S, *Land, Labour and the Family in Southern Ghana: A Critique of Land*

*Policy under Neo-Liberalisation*, 2001, Uppsala: Nordiska Afrikainstitutet Research Report no 116.

Amawi, A, 'Women and Property Rights in Islam' in Sabbagh, S (ed.), *Arab Women, Between Defiance and Restraint*, 1996, New York: Olive Branch Press.

Anderson, B, *Imagined Communities*, 1991, London: Verso.

An-Naʾim, Abdullahi A (ed.), *Islamic Family Law in a Changing World*, 2002, London & New York: Zed Books.

Arber, S, 'Unequal Partners: Inequality in Earnings and Independent Income within Marriage', in McKie, L, Bowlby, S and Gregory, S (eds), *Gender, Power and the Household*, 1999, Basingstoke: Macmillan.

Arden, A, 'Homelessness: A Step Backwards' (1995) August, *Legal Action* 22.

Arden, A and Hunter, C, *Homelessness and Allocations*, 2002, London: Legal Action Group.

Artz, D E, 'The Application of International Human Rights Law in Islamic States' (1990) 12:2 *Human Rights Quarterly* 202.

Auchmuty, R, 'The Fiction of Equity', in Scott-Hunt, S and Lim, H (eds), *Feminist Perspectives on Equity and Trusts*, 2001, London: Cavendish Publishing, pp 1–26.

Auchmuty, R, 'Men Behaving Badly: An Analysis of English Undue Influence Cases' (2002) 11 *Social and Legal Studies* 257.

Auchmuty, R, 'The Rhetoric of Equality and the Problem of Heterosexuality', in Mulcahy, L and Wheeler, S (eds), *Feminist Perspectives on Contract Law*, 2005, London: Cavendish Publishing, pp 51–74.

Auge, M, *Non-Places: Introduction to an anthropology of supermodernity*, trans. J Howe, 1995, London: Verso.

Badran, M, 'Islam, Patriarchy and Feminism in the Middle East' (1985) 4:1 *Trends in History* (Fall) 49.

Bahaa-Eldin, Z, 'Formal and Informal Finance in Egypt' in B. Dupret, M. Berger and L. al-Zwaini (eds), *Legal Pluralism in the Arab World*, 1999, The Hague, London: Kluwer, pp 205–18.

Bailey-Harris, R, *Dividing the Assets on Family Breakdown*, 1998, Bristol: Jordan Publishing Ltd.

Baker, M, 'Gender: Enabling Perspective or Politically Correct Term? An Analysis of how Gender and Material Culture are Viewed by 1990s Academia', in Donald, M and Harcombe, L (eds), *Gender in Archaeological Perspective*, 2000, Basingstoke: Macmillan, pp. 56–68.

Baker, P V, Case Notes (1968) *Law Quarterly Review* 306.

Bakhtin, M M, *The Dialogic Imagination*, 1981, Austin: University of Texas Press.

Balderson, J, *Patrol Report no. 1–69/70, Suau Census Division, Milne Bay District*, 1970, National Archives of Papua New Guinea.

Baldwin Brown, G, *The Care of Ancient Monuments*, 1905, Cambridge: Cambridge University Press.

Bancroft, A, ' "Gypsies to the Camps!": Exclusion and Marginalisation of Roma in the Czech Republic', (1999) 4:3 *Sociological Research Online*, http://www.socresonline.org.uk/socresline/4/3/bancroft.html.

Barlas, A, *Unreading Patriarchal Interpretations of the Qur'an*, 2002, Austin: University of Texas Press.

Barlow, A and Lind, C, 'A matter of trust: allocation of rights in the family home' (1999) 19 *Legal Studies* 468.

Barlow, A, Duncan, S, James, G and Park, A, *Cohabitation, Marriage and the Law: Social Change and Legal Reform in the 21st Century*, 2005, Oxford: Hart Publishing.

Barnes, J, 'African models in the New Guinea Highlands' (1962) 62 *Man* 5.

Barr, C J *et al.*, *Countryside Survey 1990*, 1993, London: Department of the Environment.

Barry, J, Herity, B and Solan, J, *The Travellers Health Status Study: Vital Statistics of Travelling People*, 1987, Dublin: Health Research Board.

Battaglia, D, ' "We feed our father": paternal nurture among the Sabarl of Papua New Guinea' (1985) 12 *American Ethnologist* 427.

Battersby, G, 'Equitable Fraud Committed by Third Parties' (1995) 15 *Legal Studies* 35.

Battersby, G, 'Case Commentary: *Oxley v Hiscock* in the Court of Appeal, the search for principle continues' (2005) 17(2) *Child and Family Law Quarterly* 259.

Bauman, Z, *The Individualized Society*, 2001, Oxford: Polity.

Beach, H, (1999) 'Injury Rates in Gypsy-Traveller Children', unpublished MSc dissertation in Community Health, University of Wales College of Medicine.

Beier, A L, 'Vagrants and the Social Order in Elizabethan England' (1974) 64 *Past and Present* 3.

Beier, A L, *Masterless Men: The Vagrancy Problem in England, 1560–1640*, 1985, London: Methuen.

Belcher, A, 'A Feminist Perspective on Contract Theories from Law and Economics', (2000) 8 *Feminist Legal Studies* 29.

Belgrave, M, 'Indigenous land rights and social well-being in New Zealand', in Home, R and Lim, H (eds), *Rethinking Ownership, Occupation and Use in Land*, 2007, Oxford: Hart Publishing (forthcoming).

Bender, B, 'Stonehenge – contested landscapes (Medieval to present day)', in Bender, B (ed.), *Landscape: Politics and Perspectives*, 1993, Providence RI and Oxford: Berg, pp 245–80.

Bender, B, *Stonehenge: Making Space*, 1998, Oxford and New York: Berg.

Bennet, G (ed.), *Cultural Landscapes: The Conservation Challenge in a Changing Europe*, 1996, London: Institute for European Environmental Policy.

Berry, S, *Cocoa, Custom and Socio-Economic Change in Rural Western Nigeria*, 1975, Oxford: Clarendon Press.

Berry, S, *No Condition is Permanent: The Social Dynamics of Agrarian Change in sub-Saharan Africa*, 1993, Madison: University of Wisconsin Press.

Berry, S, 'Debating the Land Question in Africa' (2002) *Comparative Studies in Society and History* 638.

Betterton, R, *Intimate Distance: Women, Artists and the Body*, 1996, London: Routledge.

Beuka, R, *SuburbiaNation*, 2004, New York: Palgrave.

Beveridge, Sir W, *Report of the Committee on Social Insurance and Allied Services*, Cmnd 6404, 1942, London: HMSO.

Bianchini, F and Schwengel, H, 'Reimagining the City', in Corner, J and Harvey, S (eds), *Enterprise and Heritage*, 1991, London: Routledge, pp 212–34.

Bikaako, W and Ssenkumba, J, 'Gender, Land and Rights: Contemporary Contestations in Law, Policy and Practice in Uganda', in Muthoni Wanyeki, L (ed.), *Women and Land in Africa: Culture, Religion and Realizing Women's Rights*, 2003, London and Cape Town: Zed Books Ltd and David Philip Publishers, pp 232–78.

Birks, P B H, *An Introduction to the Law of Restitution*, 1985, Oxford: Oxford University Press.
Blomley, N, *Law, Space and the Geography of Power*, 1994, New York: Guilford Press.
Blomley, N, *Unsettling the City*, 2004, London: Taylor and Francis.
Blum, A, 'The Mall Goes Under Cover: It Now Looks Like a Shopping Street', 2006, http://www.slate.com/id/2116246/.
Bohannan, P, *Justice and Judgment among the Tiv*, 1957, London: Oxford University Press for the International African Institute (2nd edn published 1968).
Bolyanatz, A, 'Musings on matriliny: understandings and social relations among the Sursurunga of New Ireland', in Maynes, M J, Waltner, A, Soland, B and Strasser, U (eds), *Gender, Kinship, Power: A Comparative and Interdisciplinary History*, 1996, New York: Routledge, pp 81–97.
Bondi, E and Domosh, M, 'Other figures in other landscapes: on feminism, post-modernism and geography' (1992) 10 *Environment and Planning D: Society and Space* 199.
Bordern, I, 'Boundaries', in Pile, S and Thrift, N (eds), *City A-Z*, 2000, London: Routledge, pp 20–2.
Borden, I, Miles, M and Hall, T, *The City Cultures Reader*, 2000, London: Routledge.
Borrow, G, *Lavengro*, 1851, republished 1944, London: Dent.
Borrow, G, *Romany Rye*, 1857, republished 1969, London: Dent.
Botswana, Government of, *Migration in Botswana: Patterns, Causes and Consequences*, 1982, Final Report of the National Migration Study, volume 3, Gaborone: Ministry of Finance and Development Planning, Central Statistics Office, Government Printer.
Botswana, Government of, *National Development Plan 1985–1991 (NDP6)*, 1985, Gaberone: MFDP and Central Statistics Office, Government Printer.
Botswana, Government of, *National Development Plan 1991–1997 (NDP7)*, 1991, Gaborone: MFDP and Central Statistics Office, Government Printer.
Botswana, Government of, *National Development Plan 2003/04–2008/09 (NDP9)*, 2003, Gaborone: MFDP, Government Printer.
Bottomley, A, 'Self and Subjectivities: Languages of Claim in Property Law' (1993) 20 *Journal of Law and Society* 56.
Bottomley, A, 'Figures in a Landscape: Feminist Perspectives on Law, Land and Landscape', in Bottomley, A (ed.), *Feminist Perspectives on the Foundational Subjects of Law*, 1996, London: Cavendish Publishing, pp 109–24.
Bottomley, A, 'Women and Trust(s): Portraying the Family in the Gallery of Law', in Bright, S and Dewar, J (eds), *Land Law: Themes and Perspectives*, 1998, Oxford University Press, pp 206–28.
Bottomley, A, 'Our Property in Trust; Things to Make and Do' in Scott-Hunt, S and Lim, H (eds), *Feminist Perspectives on Equity and Trusts*, 2001, London: Cavendish, pp 257–87.
Bottomley, A, 'From Mrs Burns to Mrs Oxley: Do women (still) need family law?' (2006) 14:2 *Feminist Legal Studies* 181.
Bottomley, A and Conaghan, J, 'Introduction In special issue: Feminist Theory and Legal Strategy' (1993) 20:1 *Journal of Law and Society* 1.
Bottomley, A and Moore, N, ' "You will never finish paying": Contract and Regulation, Globalization and Control' (2007) *Review of Law and Social Change* (forthcoming).

Bottomley, A and Roche, J, 'Conflict and Consensus: A critique of the Language of Informal Justice', in Mathews, R (ed.), *Informal Justice*, 1988, London: Sage, pp 87–101.

Bottomley, A and Wong, S, 'Shared Households: A New Paradigm for Thinking the Reform of Domestic Property Relations', in Diduck, A and O'Donovan, K (eds), *Feminist Perspectives on Family Law*, 2006, London: Glasshouse, pp 39–57.

Bright, S and Dewar, J (eds), *Land Law Themes and Perspectives*, 1998, Oxford: Oxford University Press.

Brown, B, 'The Impact of Male Labour Migration on Women in Botswana' (1983) *African Affairs* 367.

Bruce, J W, 'A Perspective on Indigenous Land Tenure Systems and Land Concentration', in Downs, R E and Reyna, S P (eds), *Land and Society in Contemporary Africa*, 1988, Hanover, New Hampshire: University Press of New England, pp 23–52.

Bryden, J and Geisler, C 'Community Based Land Reform: Lessons From Scotland', 2004, Paper Presented at the IRSA XI Congress of Rural Sociology, Trondheim, Norway http://www.caledonia.org.uk/land/what%27s.htm (site accessed 21/08/06).

Buchanan, I, 'Practical Deleuzism and Postmodern Space', in Fuglsang, M and Sorenson, B M (eds), *Deleuze and the Social*, 2006, Edinburgh: Edinburgh University, pp 135–50.

Burnett, J, *A social history of housing*, 1980, Cambridge: Cambridge University Paperbacks.

Buruma, I and Margalit, A, *Occidentalism: The West in the Eyes of Its Enemies*, 2004, New York: The Penguin Press.

Butler, J, 'Performative Acts and Gender Constitution: An Essay in Phenomenology and Feminist Theory', in Case, S-E (ed.), *Perfoming Feminisms: feminist critical theory and theatre*, 1990, Baltimore: The Johns Hopkins University Press, pp 270–82.

Butler, J, *Gender Trouble: Feminism and the Subversion of Identity*, 1999, London and New York: Routledge.

Campaign to Protect Rural England, National Trust and Heritage Link, 'Recharging the Power of Place. Valuing local significance', 2004, http://www.cpre.org.uk/resources/pub/pdfs/planning-and-development/heritage/recharging-the-power-of-place-report.pdf (site accessed 30/04/2006).

Careri, F, *Walkscapes*, trans. S. Piccolo and P. Hammond, 2002, Barcelona: Editorial Gustavo Gili, SA.

Carman, J, *Valuing Ancient Things: Law and Archaeology*, 1996, Leicester: Leicester University Press.

Carr, H and Cowan, D, 'Labelling: constructing definitions of anti-social behaviour?, in Flint, J (ed.), *Housing, urban governance and anti-social behaviour: Perspectives, policy and practice*, 2006, Bristol: Policy Press, pp 57–78.

Carroll, L, 'Life Interests and Inter-Generational Transfer of Property Avoiding the Law of Succession' (2001) 8:2 *Islamic Law and Society* 245.

Charlesworth, L, 'The Law of Settlement and Removals viewed as a model of property rights for the poor' in Home, F and Lim, H (eds), *Rethinking Ownership, Occupation and Use in Land*, 2007, Oxford: Hart Publishing (forthcoming).

Charrad, M M, *States and Women's Rights*, 2001, Berkeley, Los Angeles, London: University of California Press.

Chaudhry, Z, 'The Myth of Misogyny: A Reanalysis of Women's Inheritance in Islamic Law' (1997) 61 *Albany Law Review* 511.

Chippindale, C, 'The Making of the First Ancient Monuments Act 1882 and its Administration under General Pitt-Rivers' (1983) 2:1 *Archaeological Review from Cambridge* 1.

Chippindale, C, Devereux, P, Fowler, P, Jones, R, and Sebastian, T (eds), *Who Owns Stonehenge?*, 1990, London: Batsford.

Circular 1/94, *Planning and Gypsies*, Department of Environment.

Clark, C, ' "Severity has often enraged but never subdued a Gypsy": the history and making of European Romani stereotypes', in Saul, N and Tebbutt, S (eds), *The Role of Romanies*, 2005, Liverpool: Liverpool University Press, pp 226–46.

Clark, C and Dearling, A, 'Ethnicity, nomadism and "Traveller" identity: in pursuit of common ground' (2000) 7:1 *Social Work in Europe* 42.

Clark, C and Greenfields, M, *Here to Stay: The Gypsies and Travellers of Britain*, 2006, Hatfield: University of Hertfordshire Press.

Clarke, P, 'The Family Home: Intention and Agreement' (1992) 22 *Family Law* 72.

Clay, B, *Pinikindu: Maternal Nurture, Paternal Substance*, 1977, Chicago: University of Chicago Press.

Cleere, H (ed.), *Approaches to the Archaeological Heritage*, 1984, Cambridge: Cambridge University Press.

Clinton, W, 'The Struggle for the Soul of the 21st Century', 2001, London: Dimbleby Lecture, BBC.

Coates, I, 'Environmental concern in Britain 1919–1949: Diversity and Continuity', in Elworthy, S, Coates, I, Stroh, M, Anderson, K and Stephens, P (eds), *Perspectives on the Environment* 2, 1995, Aldershot: Avebury, pp 61–78.

Cobbe, F P, 'Criminals, Idiots, Women, and Minors' (1868), in Hamilton, S (ed.), *'Criminals, Idiots, Women, and Minors': Victorian Writing by Women on Women*, 1995, Peterborough: Broadview Press, pp 132–70.

Coffin, J N, 'The United Mall of America: Free Speech, State Constitutions, and the Growing Fortress of Private Property' (2000) 33 *Michigan Journal of Law Reform* 615.

Collier, J and Starr, J (eds), *History and Power in the Study of Law: New Directions in Legal Anthropology*, 1989, Ithaca, New York: Cornell University Press.

Colson, E, 'The Social Consequences of Resettlement: The Impact of the Kariba Resettlement upon the Gwembe Tonga', *Volume 4 Kariba Studies*, 1971, Manchester: Manchester University Press for the University of Zambia.

Colson, E, 'The resilience of matrilineality: Gwembe and Plateau Tonga adaptations', in Cordell, L and Beckerman, S (eds) *The Versatility of Kinship*, 1980, New York: Academic Press, pp 359–74.

Comaroff, J L and Roberts, S A, 'Marriage and Extra-marital Sexuality: The Dialectics of Legal Change among the Kgatla' (1977) 21 *Journal of African Law* 97.

Commission for Racial Equality, Press Release on 'Gypsy and Traveller Strategy', 2 April, 2004.

Comaroff, J L and Roberts, S A, *Rules and Processes: The Cultural Logic of Dispute in an African Context*, 1981, Chicago: University of Chicago Press.

Commission for Racial Equality, *Common Ground: Equality, good race relations and sites for Gypsies and Irish Travellers: A Report of a CRE Inquiry in England and Wales*, 2006, London: CRE.

Conkey, M, 'Making the Connections: Feminist Theory and the Archaeologies of

Gender', in du Cros, H and Smith, L (eds), *Women in Archaeology. A Feminist Critique*, 1993, Canberra: The Australian National University, pp 3–15.
Conkey, M, 'Dwelling at the Margins, Action at the Intersection? Feminist and Indigenous Archaeologies, 2005' (2005) 1:1 *Archaeologies* 9.
Conkey, M, and Spector, J, 'Archaeology and the study of gender' (1984) 7 *Archaeological Method and Theory* 1.
Connell, R, *Masculinities*, 1995, Oxford: Polity Press.
Conway, J (ed.), *Prescription for Poor Health: The Crisis for Homeless Families*, 1988, London: London Food Commission, Maternity Alliance, SHAC and Shelter.
Conway, J and Kemp, P, *Bed and Breakfast: Slum Housing of the Eighties*, 1985, London: SHAC Policy Paper No 7.
Cookson, N, *Archaeological Heritage Law*, 2000, Chichester: Barry Rose.
Cooper, D, 'Private Country? Hunting, Land and Judicial Interventions', in Holder, J and McGillivray, D (eds), *Locality and Identity: Environmental Issues in Law and Society*, 1999, Aldershot: Ashgate, pp 111–32.
Cooper, D, *Challenging Diversity*, 2004, Cambridge: Cambridge University Press.
Cooper, D M, *Economy and Society in Botswana. Some Basic National Socio-Economic Co-ordinates Relevant to an Interpretation of National Migration Statistics*, 1979, National Migration Study Working Paper no. 2. Gaborone: Government Printer.
Cooper, D M, *An Overview of the Botswana Class Structure and Its Articulation with the Rural Mode of Production: Insights from Selebi-Phikwe* (dated 1980), 1982, Cape Town: Centre for African Studies, University of Cape Town.
Cordell, L and Beckerman, S (eds), *The Versatility of Kinship*, 1980, New York: Academic Press.
Cornwell, J, *Improving health care for Travellers*, 1984, London: King's Fund.
Cotula, L, *Gender and Law – Women's Rights in Agriculture*, 2002, Rome: FAO Legislative Study.
Coulby, D, and Jones, C, *Postmodernity and European Education Systems: Cultural Diversity and Centralist Knowledge*, 1995, Stoke-on-Trent: Trentham Books.
Cowan, D and Fionda, J, 'Back to Basics: the Government's Homelessness Consultation Paper' (1994) 57 *Modern Law Review* 611.
Cowan, D and Marsh, A, 'From Need to Choice: *R (A) v Lambeth LBC; R (Lindsay) v Lambeth LBC*' (2004) 67 *Modern Law Review* 478.
Crawford, A, *Local Governance of Crime: Appeals to Community and Partnership*, 1999, Oxford: Oxford University Press.
Crawford, A, 'Joined Up but Fragmented: Contradiction, Ambiguity and Ambivalence at the Heart of New Labour's Third Way', in Mathews, R and Pitts, J (eds), *Crime, Disorder and Community Safety*, 2001, London: Routledge, pp 54–80.
Crawford, K, 'A History of the Right: The Battle for Control of National Curriculum History 1989–1994' (1995) 43(4) *British Journal of Educational Studies* 433.
Crawford, M, 'The World in a Shopping Mall', in Sorkin, M (ed.), *Variations on a Theme Park: The New American City and the Loss of Public Space*, 1992, New York: Hill and Wang, pp 3–30.
Crawford, M, 'Blurring the Boundaries: Public Space and Private Life', in Cheese, J, Crawford, M and Kaliski, J (eds), *Everyday Urbanism*, 1999, New York: Monacelli Press, pp. 22–35.
Crawley, H, *Moving Forward: the provision of accommodation for Travellers and Gypsies*, 2004, London: Institute of Public Policy Research.

Cretney, S, *Family Law in the Twentieth Century*, 2003, Harmondsworth: Penguin.
Cumberpatch, C, 'Power of Place: Critique and Response' (2001) 6 *Assemblage* http://www.shef.ac.uk/~assem/issue6/Cumberpatch_Power_web.html (site accessed) 9/3/2001.
Cunliffe, B, Davies, W and Renfrew, C (eds), *Archaeology. The Widening Debate*, 2002, Oxford: Oxford University Press for the British Academy.
Danbakli, M (ed.), *On Gypsies: Texts issues by International Institutions*, 1994, Toulouse: Centre de Recherches Tsiganes.
Daniel, G, *The Origins and Growth of Archaeology*, 1967, Harmondsworth: Penguin.
Daniel, G, *Towards a History of Archaeology*, 1981, London: Thames and Hudson.
Daniels, S, *Fields of Vision*, 1993, Brighton: Polity Press.
Darvill, T, Saunders, A and Startin, B, 'A question of national importance; approaches to the evaluation of ancient monuments for the Monuments Protection Programme in England' (1993) 61 *Antiquity* 393.
Datta, K, *Research on Women in Economy and Its Impact on Policy Making in Botswana*, n.d., Gender Research Programme, Gaborone: University of Botswana and National Institute of Development Research and Documentation.
Davidoff, L, *Worlds Between: Historical Perspectives on Gender and Class*, 1995, Cambridge: Polity Press.
Davies, E, *Gypsies and Housing*, 1987, London: Department of the Environment, HMSO.
Davies, M and Naffine, N, *Are Persons Property?*, 2001, Ashgate: Dartmouth.
Davis, J and Hoult, H, 'Travelling Families' Health Needs', in Rowbotham, A and Sheldrake, D (eds), *Health Visiting Specialist and Higher Level Practice*, 2000, London: Churchill Livingstone, pp 382–96.
Davis, M, *City of Quartz*, 1998, London: Pimlico.
DCMS, 'Protecting out historic environment: Making the system work better', 2003, http://www.culture.gov.uk/global/consultations/2003+closed+consultations/HPR_Consultation.htm (site accessed 20/04/06).
DCMS, 'Review of Heritage Protection: The Way Forward', 2004, http://www.culture.gov.uk/global/publications/archive_2004/review_heritage_protection.htm (site accessed 20/04/06).
DCMS, press release 081/04 28 June 2004 'Looking Forward To The Past: Heritage Minister Sets Out The Future For Heritage Protection', 2004b, http://www.culture.gov.uk/global/press_notices/ (site accessed 09/08/04).
DCMS, 'Better Places to Live', March 2005, http://www.culture.gov.uk/global/publications/archive_2005/better_placesto_live.htm (site accessed 14/04/2006).
DCMS, 'Better Places to Live: Government, Identity and the Public Value of Heritage', 2006, http://www.culture.gov.uk/global/publications/archive_2006/better_places_-responses.htm (site accessed 10/03/06).
de Certeau, M, *The Practice of Everyday Life*, trans. S. Rendall, 1988, Berkeley: University of California Press.
de Coppet, D, '. . . Land owns people', in Barnes, R H, de Coppet, D and Parkin, R J (eds), *Contexts and Levels: Anthropological Essays on Hierarchy*, 1985, Oxford: JASO, pp 78–90.
de Soto, H, *The Mystery of Capital: Why Capitalism Triumphs in the West and Fails Everywhere Else*, 2001, London: Black Swan.

de Souza Santos, B, 'Law: a map of misreading: towards a postmodern conception of law' (1987) 14 *Journal of Law and Society* 279.

de Souza Santos, B, *Towards a New Common Sense: Law Science and Politics in the Paradigmatic Transition*, 1995, London: Routledge.

Delaney, C, 'The meaning of paternity and the virgin birth debate' (1986) 21 *Man* (N.S.) 494.

Delaney, D, Ford, R T and Blomley, N, 'Preface: Where is Law?', in Blomley, N, Delaney, D and Ford, R T (eds), *The Legal Geographies Reader*, 2001, Oxford and Malden Mass. US: Blackwells, pp xiii–xxii.

Deleuze, G, *The Fold: Leibniz and the Baroque*, trans. D Conley, 1992, Minneapolis: Minnesota University Press.

Deleuze, G, *Negotiations*, trans. M Joughin, 1995, New York: Columbia University Press.

Deleuze, G and Guattari, F, *A Thousand Plateaus: Capitalism and Schizophrenia*, trans. B Massumi, 1987, London: Athlone Press.

Deleuze, G and Guattari, F, *What is Philosophy?*, trans. H Tomlinson and G Burchel, 1994, New York and Chichester W. Sussex: Columbia University Press.

Delle, J A, Mrozowski, S A and Paynter, R (eds), *Lines that Divide: Historical Archaeologies of Race, Class, and Gender*, 2000, Knoxville: University of Tennessee Press.

Delle, J A, Mrozowski, S A and Paynter, R, 'Introduction', in Delle, J A, Mrozowski, S A and Paynter, R (eds), *Lines that Divide: Historical Archaeologies of Race, Class, and Gender*, 2000, Knoxville: University of Tennessee Press, pp xi–xxxi.

Delphy, C and Leonard, D, *Familiar Exploitation: A New Analysis of Marriage in Contemporary Western Societies*, 1992, Cambridge: Polity Press.

Demian, M, 'Custom in the courtroom, law in the village: legal transformations in Papua New Guinea' (2003) 9 *Journal of the Royal Anthropological Institute* (N.S.) 97.

Demian, M, 'Disputing damage versus disputing ownership in Suau', in Kalinoe, L and Leach, J (eds), *Rationales of Ownership: Transactions and Claims to Ownership in Contemporary Papua New Guinea*, 2004, Oxford: Sean Kingston Publishing, pp 27–41.

Denning, Sir A, *The Changing Law*, 1953, London: Sweet & Maxwell.

Denning, Lord, *The Due Process of Law*, 1980, London: Butterworths.

Department for Education and Employment, *Pupil Mobility in Schools: Research Brief*, No 168, 2000, (Dobson, J and Henthorne, K).

Department of Environment and Science, *Education for All, the report of the Committee of Enquiry into the Education of Children from Ethnic Minorities* (The Swann Report), 1985, London: HMSO.

Department of Environment, *A report on the analysis of responses to consultation on the operation of Caravan Sites Act* (The Wibberley Report), 1968, London: HMSO.

Department of the Environment, 'Temporary Accommodation: A Survey of Homeless People', 1992, unpublished.

Department of the Environment (DoE), *Access to Local Authority and Housing Association Tenancies: A Consultation Paper*, 1994, London: DoE.

Department of the Environment and Welsh Office, *Our Future Homes: Opportunity, Choice, Responsibility*, Cm. 2901, 1995, London: HMSO.

Department of the Environment, Transport and the Regions (DETR), *Managing Unauthorised Camping: A Good Practice Guide*, 1998, London: DETR.

Department of the Environment, Transport and the Regions and Department of Social Security (DETR), *Quality and Choice: A Decent Home for All, The Housing Green Paper*, 2000, London: Stationery Office.

Derbyshire Gypsy Liaison Group (DGLG), *A better road: an information booklet for health care and other professionals*, 2003, DGLG Derbyshire: Traveller Issues Working Group.

Dewsbury, J D and Thrift, N, 'Genesis Eternal: After Paul Klee', in Buchanan, I and Lambert, G (eds), *Deleuze and Space*, 2005, Edinburgh: Edinburgh University Press, pp 89–108.

Diamond, E, 'Refusing the Romanticism of Identity', in Case, S-E (ed.), *Perfoming Feminisms: feminist critical theory and theatre*, 1990, Baltimore: The Johns Hopkins University Press, pp 92–108.

Diaz-Andreu, M, and Champion, T (eds), *Nationalism and Archaeology in Europe*, 1996, London: UCL Press.

Diduck, A and Kaganas, F, *Family Law, Gender and the State: Texts, Cases and Materials*, 2nd edn, 2006, Oxford: Hart Publishing.

Diduck, A, 'Fairness and Justice for All? The House of Lords in *White v White* [2000] 2 FLR 981' (2001) 9:2 *Feminist Legal Studies* 173.

Diop Tine, N and Sy, M, 'Women and Land in Africa: A Case Study from Senegal', in Muthoni Wanyeki, L (ed.), *Women and Land in Africa: Culture, Religion and Realizing Women's Rights*, 2003, London and Cape Town: Zed Books Ltd and David Philip Publishers, pp 207–31.

Dixon, M, *Principles of Land Law*, 4th edn, 1992, London: Cavendish Publishing.

Dixon, M, 'Resulting and Constructive Trusts of Land; The Mist Descends and Rises' (2005) *Conveyancer and Property Lawyer* Jan/Feb 79.

Dobres, M-A and Robb, J, *Agency in Archaeology*, 2000, London and New York: Routledge.

Dommasnes, L, 'Women, Kinship and the Basis of Power in the Norwegian Viking Age' in Hays-Gilpin, K and Whitley, D (eds), *Reader in Gender Archaeology*, 1998, London and New York: Routledge, pp 337–48.

Domosh, M and Seager, J, *Putting Women in Place*, 2001, New York and London: The Guilford Press.

Donald, M and Harcombe, L (eds), *Gender in Archaeological Perspective*, 2000, Basingstoke: Macmillan.

Donzelot, J, *The Policing of Families*, trans. R Hurley, 1997, Baltimore and London: The Johns Hopkins University Press.

Dorn, M L, 'Beyond nomadism: the travel narratives of a "cripple" ', in Nast, H J and Pile, S (eds), *Places through the body*, 1998, London and New York: Routledge, pp 183–206.

Doumani, B, 'Writing Family: Waqf, Property and Gender in Tripoli and Nablus, 1800–1860' (1998) 40:1 *Comparative Studies in Society and History* 3.

Drakakis-Smith, A and Mason, K, 'Out for the Count: a critical examination of the DETR bi-annual account of Gypsies/Travellers in England with special reference to Staffordshire', Radical Statistics, 2001, http://www.radstats.org.uk/noo78/drakakis-smithandmason.htm.

Duncan, J and Duncan, N, *Landscapes of Privilege*, 2004, New York: Routledge.

Duncan, N, *BodySpace*, 1996, London: Routledge.

Durrand-Lasserve, A and Royston, L, *Holding Their Ground: Secure Land Tenure for the Urban Poor in India, Brazil and South Africa*, 2002, London: Earthscan.

Eekelaar, J, 'A Woman's Place – A Conflict between Law and Social Values' (1987) *Conveyancer and Property Lawyer* 93.

El Saadawi, N, Interview Reported on Monday 9 July as Egypt Apostasy Trial Adjourned, 2001, BBC Online.

Elworthy, S and Holder, J, *Environmental Protection*, 1997, London: Butterworths.

Engelstad, E, 'Another F-word? Feminist Gender Archaeology', in Oestigaard, T, Anfinset, N and Saetersdal, T (eds), *Combining the Past and the Present, Archaeological Perspectives on Society*, 2004, BAR International Series 1210, Oxford: Archaeopress, pp 39–45

English Heritage, Government Review of Policies Relating to the Historic Environment: An Invitation to Participate, Discussion Paper 1, 2000, http://www.britarch.ac.uk/info/ehreview3.html (site accessed 21/05/2001).

English Heritage News Release 7 April, 'English Heritage Pioneers a New Approach to Heritage Protection', 2004, http://cairnworld.free.fr/guideapp4.php (site accessed 11/05/06).

FAO, 'Seeking ways out of the impasse on land reform in Southern Africa: notes from an informal "think tank" meeting', 2003, Manhattan Hotel, Pretoria, South Africa.

Fay, M A, 'From Concubines to Capitalists: Women, Property, and Power in Eighteenth-century Cairo' (1998) 10 *Journal of Women's History* 118.

Feder, G and Noronha, R, 'Land Rights Systems and Agricultural Development in Sub-Saharan Africa' (1987) 2:1 *World Bank Research Observer* 143.

Feder, G S, 'Traveller Gypsies and primary care' (1989) 39 *Journal Royal College of General Practitioners* (October) 425.

Fehlberg, B, *Sexually Transmitted Debt: Surety Experience and English Law*, 1997, Oxford: Clarendon Press.

Feillard, A, 'Indonesia's Emerging Muslim Feminism: Women Leaders on Equality, Inheritance and Other Gender Issues' (1997) 4:1 *Studia Islamika* 83.

Ferchiou, S, *Les Femmes dans l'Agriculture Tunisienne*, 1985, Aix-en-Provence: Edisud.

Fernandes, E and Varley, A (eds), *Illegal Cities: Law and Urban Change in Developing Countries*, 1998, London: Zed Books.

FFT, *Confined, Condemned and Constrained*, 1996, Friends, Families and Travellers Support Group.

Fineman, M A, 'Implementing Equality: Edeology, Contradiction and Social Change – A Study of Rhetoric and Results in the Regulation of Consequences of Divorce' (1983) 4 *Wisconsin Law Review* 789.

Fineman, M A, 'Contract, marriage and background rules', in Bix, B (ed.), *Analysing Law: New Essays in Legal Theory*, 1998, Oxford: Clarendon Press, pp 132–70.

Flynn, L and Lawson, A, 'Gender, sexuality and the doctrine of detrimental reliance' (1995) 3:1 *Feminist Legal Studies* 105.

Foucault, M, 'Texts/Contexts Of Other Spaces' (1986) *Diacritics* 22.

Foucault, M, *The Order of Things*, 2002, London: Routledge.

Foucault, M, *Power: Essential Works of Foucault 1954–1984* Volume 3, trans. R Hurley, 2002, London: Penguin.

Foucault, M, *Society must be defended*, trans. D Macey, 2003, London: Penguin.

Fox, J and Sather, C (eds), *Origins, Ancestry and Alliance*, 1996, Canberra: Australian National University.

Francis, P, 'For the Use and Common Benefit of All Nigerians: Consequences of the 1978 Land Nationalization Act' (1984) 54:3 *Africa* 5.

Franck, T, *The Empowered Self: Law and Society in the Age of Individualism*, 1999, Oxford: Oxford University Press.

Fraser, A, *The Gypsies*, 1992, Oxford: Basil Blackwell.

Fraser, N, 'Rethinking the Public Sphere; A Contribution to the Critique of Actually Existing Democracy' in Robbins, B (ed.), *The Phantom Public Sphere*, 1993, Minneapolis: University of Minnesota Press, pp 1–32.

Freire, P and Shor, I, *Pedagogy for Liberation*, 1987, New York: Macmillan Palgrave.

Frug, M J, *City Making: Building Cities without Building Walls*, 1999, Princeton: Princeton University Press.

Gardner, S, 'Rethinking Family Property' (1993) 109 *Law Quarterly Review* 263.

Gathercole, P and Lowenthal, D (eds), *The Politics of the Past*, 1994, London: Routledge.

Gero, J and Conkey, M (eds), *Engendering Archaeology: Women and Prehistory*, 1991, Oxford: Blackwell.

Gero, J M, 'Archaeological Practice and Gendered Encounters with Field Data' in Wright, R P (ed.), *Gender and Archaeology*, 1996, Philadelphia: University of Pennsylvania Press, pp 251–68.

Gero, J M and Conkey, M W, 'Tensions and Pluralities, and Engendering Archaeology: An Introduction to Women and Prehistory' in Gero, J M and Conkey, M W (eds), *Engendering Archaeology. Women and Prehistory*, 1991, Oxford: Blackwell, pp 3–30.

Gilchrist, R, *Gender and Archaeology*, 1999, London: Routledge.

Glover, N and Todd, P, 'The myth of common intention' (1996) 16 *Legal Studies* 325.

Gluckman, M, *The Ideas in Barotse Jurisprudence*, 1965, New Haven and London: Yale University Press.

Goff, R and Jones, G H, *The Law of Restitution*, 6th edn, 2002, London: Sweet & Maxwell.

Goodman, C, ' "We'll Go No More A-Roving" – Seeking a New Definition of Gypsy and Travellers' (2005) *Journal of Environment and Planning Law* 1159.

Goodrich, P, *Reading the Law: Critical Introduction to Legal Method*, 1986, Oxford: Blackwell Publishers.

Goodrich, P, *Legal Discourse: Studies in linguistics, rhetoric and legal analysis*, 1987, Oxford: Palgrave Macmillan.

Gordon, R W, 'Paradoxical Property', in Brewer, J and Staves, S (eds), *Early Modern Conceptions of Property*, 1996, London and New York: Routledge, pp 95–110.

Gough, K, 'The modern disintegration of matrilineal descent groups', in Schneider, D M and Gough, K (eds), *Matrilineal Kinship*, 1961, Berkeley: University of California Press, pp 632–52.

Graves-Brown, P, Jones, S and Gamble, C (eds), *Cultural Identity and Archaeology: The Construction of European Communities*, 1996, London: Routledge.

Gray, K, 'Property in Thin Air' (1991) 50 *Cambridge Law Journal* 252.

Gray, K and Gray, S F, 'The Idea of Property in Land', in Bright, S and Dewar, J, (eds), *Land Law: Themes and Perspectives*, 1998, Oxford: Oxford University Press, pp 15–51.

Gray, K J and Gray, S F, *Land Law*, 2005, Oxford: Oxford University Press.

Gray, S F and Gray, K, 'Civil Rights and Civil Wrongs and Quasi-Public Space' (1999a) 3 *European Human Rights Law Review* 46.

Gray, S F and Gray, K, 'Public Property and Public Propriety', in McLean, J (ed.), *Property and the Constitution*, 1999b, Oxford: Hart, pp 11–39.

Greed, C H, *Women and Planning: Creating Gendered Realities*, 1994, London: Routledge.

Green, H, *Counting Gypsies*, 1991, London: HMSO.

Green, K and Lim, H, 'Weaving Along the Borders: Public and Private, Women and Banks', in Scott-Hunt, S and Lim, H (eds), *Feminist Perspectives on Equity and Trusts*, 2001, London: Cavendish, pp 85–109.

Greenfields, M (2002) 'New Travellers and Post-Separation-Parenting Arrangements', unpublished Phd thesis, University of Bath.

Greenfields, M and Home, R, 'So What's Changed for Gypsies since 1968 then?', July 2006 Conference Paper presented at the Social Policy Association conference.

Griffin, S, *Woman and Nature: the roaring inside her*, 1978, New York: Harper and Row.

Griffiths, A, 'Support among the Bakwena', in von-Benda-Beckmann, F (ed.), *Between Kinship and the State: Social Security and Law in Developing Countries*, 1988, Dordrecht: Foris Publications, pp 289–316.

Griffiths, A, *In the Shadow of Marriage: Gender and Justice in an African Community*, 1997, Chicago: University of Chicago Press.

Griffiths, A, 'Mediation, Gender and Justice in Botswana' (1998) 154 *Mediation Quarterly* 335.

Griffiths, A, 'Gendering Culture: Towards a Plural Perspective on Kwena Women's Rights', in Cowan, J, Dembour, M B and Wilson, R A (eds), *Culture and Rights*, 2001, Cambridge and New York: Cambridge University Press, pp 102–26.

Griffiths, A, 'Doing Ethnography, Living Law, Life Histories and Narratives from Botswana', in Starr, J and Goodale, M (eds), *Practicing Ethnography in Law: New Dialogues, Enduring Methods*, 2002, New York: Palgrave/St Martin's Press, pp 160–81.

Guadagni, M, 'Trends in Customary Land Property', in Sanchez Jordan, M E and Gambero, A (eds), *Land Law in Comparative Perspective*, 2002, The Hague, Netherlands and Norwell, Mass. US: Kluwer Law International, pp 7–10.

Guyer, J and Lambin, E F, 'Land Use in an Urban Hinterland: Ethnography and Remote Sensing in the Study of African Intensification' (1993) 95:4 *American Anthropologist* 839.

Gypsy Problem, *The Gypsy Problem: Possible Further Legislation*, 1964–1967, London: Public Record Office.

Habermas, J, *The Structural Transformation of the Public Sphere: An Inquiry into a Category of Bourgeois Society*, trans. T Burger and F Lawrence, 1962, Cambridge, Mass: MIT Press.

Hajioff, S and McKee, M, 'The health of the Roma people: a review of published literature' (2000) 54 *Journal of Epidemiology and Community Health* 864.

Halfacree, K, 'The Distribution of Gypsy caravans in England, 1979–94' (1996) 81 *Geography* 37.

Halim, A, 'Challenges to Women's International Human Rights in the Sudan', in Cooke, R (ed.), *Human Rights of Women: National and International Perspectives*, 1994, Philadelphia: University of Pennsylvania Press.

Hall, P and Ward, C, *Sociable Cities*, 1998, Chichester: Wiley.

Hall, S, 'Cultural Identity and Diaspora', in Rutherford, J (ed.), *Identity, Community, Difference*, 1991, London: Lawrence & Wishart, pp 222–37.

Halliwell, M, 'Equity as injustice: the cohabitant's case' (1991) 20 *The Anglo-American Law Review* 550.

Halliwell, M, *Equity and Good Conscience in a Contemporary Context*, 1997, London: Old Bailey Press.

Handler, J F, 'Dependent People, the State and the Modern/Postmodern Search for the Dialogic Community' (1988) 35 *University of California Law Review* 999.

Hann, C M (ed.), *Property relations: Renewing the anthropological tradition*, 1998, Cambridge: Cambridge University Press.

Harris, O (ed.), *Inside and Outside the Law: Anthropological Studies of Authority and Ambiguity*, 1996, London and New York: Routledge.

Hartmann, B and Boyce, J K, *A Quiet Violence: View from a Bangladeshi Village*, 1983, Dhaka: University Press Ltd.

Hassan, R, 'On Human Rights and the Qur'anic Perspective', in Swindler, L (ed.), *Human Rights in Religious Traditions*, 1982, New York: Pilgrim Press, pp 51–65.

Hawes, D, *Gypsies, Travellers and the Health Service: A study in inequality*, 1997, Bristol: The Policy Press.

Hawes, D and Perez, B, *The Gypsy and the State: The ethnic cleansing of British society*, 1996, Bristol: Policy Press.

Hays-Gilpin, K and Whitley, D, 'Introduction: Gendering the Past' in Hays-Gilpin, K and Whitley, D (eds), *Reader in Gender Archaeology*, 1998, London and New York: Routledge, pp 3–10.

Health Visitors' Association and General Medical Services Committee, *Homeless Families and their Health*, 1988, London: General Medical Council.

Hegel, G W F, *Philosophy of Right*, 1996, Loughton: Prometheus Books.

Heller, C, 'For the Love of Nature: Ecology and the Cult of the Romantic', in Gaard, G (ed.), *Ecofeminism: Women, Animals and Nature* 1993, Philadelphia: Temple University Press, pp 219–42.

Helsinger, E, 'Land and National Representation in Britain', in Rosenthal, M, Payne, C and Wilcox, S (eds), *Prospects for the Nation: Recent Essays in British Landscape 1750–1880*, 1997, New Haven and London: Yale University Press, pp 13–35.

Hendrick, H, 'Constructions and reconstructions of British childhood: an interpretative survey, 1800 to the present' in Muncie, J, Hughes, G and McLaughlin, E (eds), *Youth Justice Critical Readings*, 2002, London: Sage, pp 22–44.

Hetherington, K, *The Badlands of Modernity*, 1997, London: Routledge.

Hewison, R, *The Heritage Industry*, 1987, London: Methuen.

Hibbs, M, Barton, C, and Beswick, J, 'Why Marry? – Perceptions of the Affianced' (2001) *Family Law* 197.

Hirst, P, *After Thatcher*, 1989, London: Collins.

Hodder, I, 'Archaeological Theory', in Cunliffe, B, Davies, W and Renfrew, C (eds), *Archaeology: The Widening Debate*, 2002, Oxford: Oxford University Press for the British Academy, pp 77–89.

Hoebel, E A, *Anthropology: The Study of Man*, 1966, New York: McGraw Hill Book Company.

Holcombe, L, 'Victorian Wives and Property: Reform of the Married Women's

Property Law, 1857–1882', in Vicinus, M (ed.), *A Widening Sphere: Changing Roles of Victorian Women*, 1980, Bloomington: Indiana University Press, pp 3–28.

Holcombe, L, *Wives and Property: Reform of the Married Women's Property Law in Nineteenth-Century England*, 1983, Toronto and Buffalo: University of Toronto Press.

Holder, J, 'Law and Landscape: The Legal Construction and Protection of Hedgerows' (1999) 62 *Modern Law Review* 100.

Holder, J, 'New Age: Rediscovering Natural Law' (2000) 53 *Current Legal Problems* 79.

Holquist, M, 'Introduction', in Bakhtin, M M and Holquist, M (eds), *The Dialogic Imagination*, 1981, Austin: University of Texas Press, pp xv–xxxiii.

Home Office, *Draft Framework Guide on Managing Unauthorised Gypsy/Traveller Encampments*, 2003, London: Home Office/ODPM.

Home, R K, 'Planning problems of self-help gypsy sites' (1982) *Journal of Planning Law* 217.

Home, R and Lim, H (eds), *Demystifying the Mystery of Capital: Land Tenure and Poverty in Africa and the Caribbean*, 2004, London: Glasshouse Press.

Home, R, 'Towards a pro-poor legal history of British colonial land settlement' in R. Home and H. Lim (eds), *Rethinking Ownership, Occupation and Use in Land*, 2007, Oxford: Hart Publishing (forthcoming).

Hooker, M, *Legal Pluralism: An Introduction to Colonial and Neo-Colonial Laws*, 1975, Oxford: Oxford University Press.

Hudson, A, *Equity and Trusts*, 4th edn, 2005, London: Cavendish.

Hunt, A, *A Survey of Women's Employment*, 1968, London: HMSO.

Hunter, C and Nixon, J, 'Taking the blame and losing the home: women and anti-social behaviour' (2001) 23:4 *Journal of Social Welfare and Family Law* 395.

Hunter, C and Miles, J, 'The Unsettling of Settled Law on "Settled Accommodation": the House of Lords and the Homelessness Legislation Old and New' (1997) 19 *Journal of Social Welfare and Family Law* 267.

Huxley, J, *Conservation of Nature in England and Wales, Report of the Wild Life Conservation Special Committee*, Cmd 7122, 1947, London: HMSO.

Institute of Housing, *Housing Allocations: Report of a Survey of Local Authorities in England and Wales*, 1990, London: Institute of Housing.

Institute of Housing, *One Parent Families – Are they Jumping the Housing Queue?*, 1993, London: Institute of Housing.

Institute for Public Policy (IPPR), *Moving Forward: a consultation paper on the provision of accommodation for Travellers and Gypsies*, 2003, London: Institute of Policy Research.

Issawi, C, 'The Adaptation of Islam to Contemporary Economic Realities', in Haddad, Y Y (ed.), *The Islamic Impact*, 1984, Syracuse: Syracuse University Press, pp 27–45.

Izzard, W, *Rural-Urban Migration of Women in Botswana, Final fieldwork report for National Migration Study Botswana*, 1979, Gaborone: Government Printer.

Izzard, W, 'The Impact of Migration on the Roles of Women', in *Migration in Botswana: Patterns, Causes and Consequences, Final report of the National Migration study* 3, 1982, Gaborone: Government Printer, pp 654–707.

Jameson, F, *Post-Modernism or the Cultural Logic of Late Capitalism*, 1991, London: Verso.

Johnson, J, 'Literary Geography: Joyce, Woolf and The City' (2000) 4:2 *City* 199.

Johnson, P, 'Agents for reform: the women's movement, social politics and family law reform', in Welchman, L (ed.), *Women's Rights and Islamic Family Law*, 2004, London: Zed Books, pp 144–63.

Jones, S, *Archaeology and Ethnicity: A theoretical Perspective*, 1996, London: Routledge.

Jordan, E, 'Exclusion of Travellers in State Schools' (2001) 43:2 *Educational Research* 117.

Jowell, T, 'From Consultation to Conversation', Capturing the Public Value of Heritage, Royal Geographical Society 26 January 2006 http://www.culture.gov.uk/global/press_notices/archive_2006 (site accessed 20/04/2006).

Kabeer, N, 'Do Women Gain from high fertility?', in Afshar, H (ed.), *Women, work and ideology in the third world*, 1985, London: Tavistock, pp 83–106.

Kahn, M, *Always Hungry, Never Greedy: Food and the Expression of Gender in a Melanesian Society*, 1986, Cambridge: Cambridge University Press.

Kalabamu, F, 'Effects of gendered land rights on urban housing by women in Botswana', *International Conference on Land Tenure in the Developing World with a Focus on Southern Africa*, 1998, University of Cape Town.

Karam, A, *Women, Islamisms and The State: Contemporary Feminisms In Egypt*, 1998, London: Macmillan.

Katulis, B, *Women's Freedom in Focus: Morocco*, 2004, Freedom House Survey.

Kaye, M, 'Equity's Treatment of Sexually Transmitted Debt' (1997) 5 *Feminist Legal Studies* 35.

Kendall, S, 'Sites of resistance on the margin – the traveller homeplace', in Acton, T (ed.), *Gypsy Politics and Traveller identity*, 1997, Hatfield: University of Hertfordshire Press, pp 70–89.

Kennett, W, *Preservation*, 1972, London: Temple Smith.

Kenrick, D and Clark, C, *Moving on: the Gypsies and Travellers of Britain*, 1999, Hatfield: University of Hertfordshire Press.

Kerven, C, *Urban and Rural Female-Headed Households' Dependence on Agriculture*, 1979, Gaberone: Central Statistics Office and Government Printer.

Kerven, C, 'The Effects of Migration on Agricultural Production', in *Migration in Botswana: Patterns, Causes and Consequences, Final report of the National Migration Study* 3, 1982, Gaborone: Government Printer, pp 526–622.

Kerven, C, 'Academic, Practitioners and all Kinds of Women in Development: A Reply to Peters' (1984) 10:2 *Journal of Southern African Studies* 259.

Khaliq, U, 'Beyond the Veil? An Analysis of the Provision of the Women's Convention in the Law as Stipulated in the Shari'a', 2 *Buffalo Law Journal* 2.

Khan, M M, *Islamic Law of Inheritance*, 1989, New Delhi: Nusrat Ali Nasri for Kitab Bhavan.

Klein, V, *Britain's Married Women Workers*, 1965, London: Routledge & Kegan Paul.

Kohl, P and Fawcett, C, *Nationalism, Politics and the Practice of Archaeology*, 1995, Cambridge: Cambridge University Press.

Küchler, S, 'Landscape as memory: the mapping of process and its representation in a Melanesian society', in Bender, B (ed.), *Landscape: Politics and Perspectives*, 1993, Oxford: Berg, pp 85–106.

Kudielka, R, *Paul Klee: The Nature of Creation*, 1992, London: Hayward Gallery.

Lackova, I, *A False Dawn: My Life as a Gypsy Woman in Slovakia* (Hubschmannov, M, ed.), 1999, Hatfield: University of Hertfordshire Press.

Lambrick, G, 'Blinkers off now' (2000) 56 *British Archaeology* 26.
Law Commission Report No 52, *First Report on Family Property: A New Approach*, 1973.
Law Commission Report No 86, *Third Report on Family Property: The Matrimonial Home (Co-ownership and Occupation Rights)*, 1978.
Law Commission, *Sharing Homes: A Discussion Paper*, Law Com. No. 278, 2002.
Law Commission Consultation Paper No 179, *Cohabitation: the Financial Consequences of Relationship Breakdown*, 2006, London. www.lawcom.gov.uk/cohabitation.htm, accessed 12/06/06.
Law Society, *Cohabitation: The case for clear law: Proposals for Reform*, 2002, London: The Law Society.
Lawrence, P, *The Garia*, 1984, Manchester: Manchester University Press.
Lawson, A, 'The Things We Do For Love: Detrimental Reliance in the Family Home' (1996) 16 *Legal Studies* 218.
Layish, A, 'The Family *Waqf* and the *Shar'ia* Law of Succession in Modern Times' (1997) 4:3 *Islamic Law and Society* 352.
Layish, A, 'The Muslim *Waqf* in Jerusalem after 1967: Beneficiaries and Management', in Bilici, F (ed.), *Waqf dans le monde musulman contemporain (XIXe-Xxe siecles)*, 1994, Istanbul: Institut francais d'etudes anatoliennes, pp 145–67.
Layton, R (ed.), *Who needs the Past? Indigenous Values and Archaeology*, 1989, London: Unwin Hyman.
Leakey, R and Lewin, R, *The Sixth Extinction*, 1998, London: Phoenix.
Lechte, J '(Not) belonging in Postmodern Space', in Watson, S and Gibson, K (eds), *Postmodern Cities and Spaces*, 1995, Oxford: Blackwell, pp 99–111.
Lee, P, 'Historical knowledge and the National Curriculum', in Bourdillon, H (ed.), *Teaching History*, 1994, London and New York: The Open University, pp 41–8.
Lefebvre, H, *Everyday Life in the Modern World*, trans. S Rabinovitch, 1971, New York: Harper and Row.
Lefebvre, H, *The Production of Space*, 1991, trans, D Nicholson-Smith, Oxford: Blackwell.
Lefebvre, H, *Rhythmanalysis: Space, Time and Everyday Life*, trans. S Edlen and G Moore, 2004, London and New York: Athlone Contemporary European Thinkers, Continuum International Publishing Group.
Lekula, G, *Efficient Land Administration as a Tool to Secure Women's Land Rights – Botswana's Experience*, 2003, Pretoria, South Africa: The Women's Land Rights Workshop 17th–19th June.
Lepowsky, M, *Fruit of the Motherland: Gender in an Egalitarian Society*, 1993, New York: Columbia University Press.
Levine, N, 'Fathers and sons: kinship value and validation in Tibetan polyandry' (1987) 22 *Man* (N.S.) 267.
Levi-Strauss, C, *The Savage Mind*, 1966, London: Weidenfeld and Nicholson.
Levinson, M P and Sparkes, A C, 'Gypsy Masculinities and the School-Home Interface: Explaining Contradictions and Tensions' (2003) 5 *British Journal of Sociology and Education* 587.
Lewis, J, 'The working-class wife and mother and state intervention, 1870–1918' in Lewis, J (ed.), *Labour and Love: Women's Experience of Home and Family 1850–1940*, 1986, Oxford: Blackwell, pp 99–122.

Liegeois, J-P, *School Provision for Ethnic Minorities: The Gypsy Paradigm*, 1998, Hatfield, University of Hertfordshire Press.

Lim, H, 'Mapping Equity's Place: Here be Dragons', in Bottomley, A (ed.), *Feminist Perspectives on the Foundational Subjects of Law*, 1996, London: Cavendish Publishing, pp 125–48.

Lim, H, 'Waqf in Trust', in Scott-Hunt, S and Lim, H (eds), *Feminist Perspectives on Equity and Trusts*, 2001, London: Cavendish Press, pp 47–64.

Lim, H, 'Inheritance, HIV/AIDS and Children's Rights to Land in Africa', in Home, R and Lim, H (eds), *Demystifying the Mystery of Capital: Land Tenure and Poverty in Africa and the Caribbean*, 2004, London, Glasshouse Press, pp 51–72.

Linares, O, F, *Power, Prayers and Production: The Jola of Casuance, Senegal*, 1992, Cambridge: Cambridge University Press.

Linthwaite, P, *The Health of Traveller Mothers and Children in East Anglia*, 1983, London: Save the Children Fund.

Lipe, W, 'Value and Meaning in Cultural Resources', in Cleere, H (ed.), *Approaches to the Archaeological Heritage*, 1984, Cambridge: Cambridge University Press, pp 1–11.

Llewellyn, K N and Hoebel, E A, *The Cheyenne Way*, 1941, Norman: University of Oklahoma Press.

Lloyd, G and Stead, J, ' "Boys and Girls Not Calling me Names, and the Teachers believing me", Name Calling and the Experiences of Travellers in School', 15 *Children and Society* 361.

Locke, J, *Second Treatise of Government*, 1964, first published 1690, Cambridge: Cambridge University Press.

Logo, P B and Bikie, E H, 'Women and Land in Cameroon: Questioning Women's Land Status and Claims for Change' in Muthoni Wanyeki, L (ed.), *Women and Land in Africa: Culture, Religion and Realizing Women's Rights*, 2003, London and Cape Town: Zed Books Ltd and David Philip Publishers, pp 31–65.

London Research Centre, *Housing Homeless Households in the Private Rented Sector*, 1996, London: London Research Centre.

Lo Picccolo, F and Thomas, H, 'Legal Discourse, the Individual and the Claim for Equality in British Planning' (2001) 2:2 *Planning Theory and Practice* 187.

Lorde, A, 'The Master's Tools Will Never Dismantle the Master's House', in Moraga, C and Anzaldua, G (eds), *This Bridge Called My Back*, 1981, New York: Kitchen Table – Women of Color Press, pp 98–101.

Lowe, P, Cox, G, McEwen, M, O'Riordan, T and Winter, M, *Countryside Conflicts*, 1986, Aldershot: Gower.

Lowenthal, D, *The Past is a Foreign Country*, 1985, Cambridge: Cambridge University Press.

Luba, J and Davies, L, *The Homelessness Act 2002: Special Bulletin*, 2nd edn, 2002, Bristol: Jordans.

Lush, M, 'Changes in the Law Affecting the Rights, Status and Liabilities of Married Women', in Council of Legal Education, *A Century of Law Reform*, 1901, London: Macmillan, pp 342–78.

Macdonald, S, 'A Suicidal Woman, Roaming Pigs and a Noisy Trampolinist: Refining the ASBO's Definition of "Anti-Social Behaviour" ' (2006) 69:2 *Modern Law Review* 183.

MacDonald, S and Porter, J, *Putting on the Style*, 1990, London: Geffrye Museum.

Macfie, A L, *Orientalism*, White Plains NY: Longman.
Macintyre, M, 'Better homes and gardens', in Jolly, M and Macintyre, M (eds), *Family and Gender in the Pacific: Domestic Contradictions and the Colonial Impact*, 1989, Cambridge: Cambridge University Press, pp 156–69.
MacKenzie, R, 'Beauty and the Beastly Bank: What Should Equity's Fairy Wand Do?', in Bottomley, A (ed.), *Feminist Perspectives on the Foundational Subjects of Law*, 1996, London: Cavendish Publishing, pp 149–71.
MacKinnon, K, 'Feminism, Marxism, Method and the State: An Agenda for Theory' (1983) 8:2 *Signs* 635.
McDowell, L, 'Introduction: Rethinking Place', in McDowell, L (ed.), *Undoing Place? A Geographical Reader*, 1997, London: Arnold, pp 1–12.
McDowell, L, *Gender, Place and Identity*, 1999, Cambridge: Polity.
McGaw, J, 'Reconceiving Technology: Why Feminine Technologies Matter' in Wright, R P (ed.), *Gender and Archaeology*, 1996, Philadelphia: University of Pennsylvania, pp 52–75.
McKinnon, S, 'The economies in kinship and the paternity of culture: origin stories in kinship theory', in Franklin, S and McKinnon, S (eds), *Relative Values: Reconfiguring Kinship Studies*, 2001, Durham: Duke University Press, pp 277–301.
Maher, E, 'Divorce and Property in the Middle East and Morocco' (1974) IX *Journal of the Royal Anthropological Institute* 103.
Manji, A, 'Land Reform in the Shadow of the State: Implementing New Land Laws in Sub-Saharan Africa' (2001) 22:3 *Third World Quarterly* 327.
Manji, A, 'Capital, Labour and Land Relations in Africa: A Gender Analysis of the World Banks' Policy Research Report on Land Institutions' (2003) 24:1 *Third World Quarterly* 97.
Mann, K and Roseneil, S, ' "Some Mothers Do 'Ave 'Em": Backlash and the Gender Politics of the Underclass Debate' (1994) 3:3 *Journal of Gender Studies* 317.
Mann, K and Roseneil, S, 'Unpalatable Choices and Inadequate Families: Lone Mothers and the Underclass Debate', in Bortolaia Silva, E (ed.), *Good Enough Mothering? Feminist Perspectives on Lone Motherhood*, 1996, London: Routledge, pp 191–210.
Marcuse, P, 'Not Chaos, but Walls: Postmodernism and the Partitioned City' in S. Watson and K. Gibson (eds), *Postmodern Cities and Spaces*, 1995, Oxford: Blackwell, pp 243–53.
Marsh, A, McKay, S, Smith, A and Stephenson, A, *Low-Income Families in Britain: Work, Welfare and Social Security in 1999*, 2001, London: Policy Studies Institute.
Marsot, A L al-S, 'Entrepreneurial Women', in Yamani, M (ed.), *Feminism in Islam, Legal and Literary Perspectives*, 1996, Reading: Ithaca, pp 33–47.
Massey, D, *Space, Place and Gender*, 1994, Cambridge: Polity Press.
Massey, D, 'Politics and space/time' (1992) 196 *New Left Review* 65.
Massumi, B, 'Translator's Foreword: Pleasures of Philosophy', in Deleuze, G and Guattari, F, *A Thousand Plateaus*, 1998, London and New York: Athlone Contemporary European Thinkers, Continuum.
Massumi, B, *A User's Guide to Capitalism and Schizophrenia – Deviations from Deleuze and Guattari*, 1992, Cambridge Mass. US: MIT Press.
Matsuda, M 'Looking to the Bottom: Critical Legal Studies and Reparations' (1987)22 *Harvard Civil Liberties-Civil Rights Review* 323.

Mayall, D, *English Gypsies and State Policies*, 1995, Hatfield: University of Hertfordshire Press.

Mayer, E A, 'Religious Reservations to the Convention on the Elimination of All Forms of Discrimination against Women: What Do they Really Mean?', in Howland, C (ed.), *Religious Fundamentalism And The Human Rights Of Women*, 1999, New York: St. Martins Press, pp 106–16.

Merriman, N. 'Archaeology, heritage and interpretation', in Cunliffe, B, Davies, W and Renfrew, C (eds), *Archaeology. The Widening Debate*, 2002, Oxford: Oxford University Press for the British Academy, pp 541–66.

Merry, S E, *Urban Danger, Life in a Neighborhood of Strangers*, 1981, Philadelphia PA: Temple University Press.

Michelman, F, 'The Common Law Baseline and Restitution of the Lost Common: A Reply to Professor Epstein' (1997) 64 *University of Chicago Law Review* 64.

Middleton, J, Foreword, in Downs, R E and Reyna, P (eds), *Land and Society in Contemporary Africa*, 1988, Hanover, NH: University Press of New England.

Millbank, J and Sant, K, 'A Bride in Her Everyday Clothes: Same Sex Relationship Recognition in New South Wales' (2000) 22 *Sydney Law Review* 181.

Miller, M, *Letchworth: The First Garden City*, 2002, Chichester: Phillimore.

Molebatsi, C, 'Botswana: "Self-Allocation"; "Accommodation" and "Zero Tolerance" in Mogoditshane and Old Naledi', in Home, R and Lim, H, *Demystifying the Mystery of Capital: Land Tenure and Poverty in Africa and the Caribbean*, 2004, London: Glasshouse Press, pp 73–97.

Moore, H L, *Feminism and Anthropology*, 1988, Minneapolis: University of Minnesota Press.

Moore, S F, *Law as Process: An Anthropological Approach*, 1978, London: Routledge and Kegan Paul.

Moore, S F, *Social Facts and Fabrications; 'Customary Law' on Kilimanjaro 1880–1980*, 1986, Cambridge: Cambridge University Press.

Moore, S F, 'Changing African Land Tenure: Reflections on the Incapacities of the State' (1998) 10:2 *The European Journal of Development Research* 33.

Moore, S F, 'Law and Social Change: The Semi-Autonomous Social Field as an Appropriate Subject of Study' (1973) 7 *Law & Society Review* 719,

Moors, A, *Women, Property and Islam: Palestinian Experience, 1920–1990*, 1995, New York: Cambridge University Press.

Morin, K and Berg, L, 'Emplacing Current Trends in Feminist Historical Geography' (1999) 6:4 *Gender, Place and Culture* 311.

Morris, M, 'Things to do with shopping centers', in During, S (ed.), *The Cultural Studies Reader*, 1993, London: Routledge, pp 295–319.

Morris, R, 'Gypsies, Travellers and the Media: Press Regulation and racism in the UK' (2000) 5:6 *Communications Law* 213.

Morris, R and Clements, L (eds), *Gaining Ground: Law Reform for Gypsies and Travellers*, 1999, Hatfield: University of Hertfordshire Press.

Morris, R and Clements, L, *At what cost? The economics of Gypsy and Traveller encampments*, 2002, Bristol: Policy Press.

Motzafi-Haller, P, 'Whither the "True Bushman": The Dynamics of Perpetual Marginality', in Rotland, F and Vossen, R (eds), *Proceeding of the International Symposium on African Hunters and Gatherers*, volume 7:1, Sprache and Geschichte in Afrika, 1986, Sankt Augustin: Monastery of Sankt Augstin, pp 259–328.

Mouffe, C, 'Democracy, Power and the Political', in Benhabib, S (ed.), *Democracy and Difference: Contesting the Limits of the Political*, 1996, Princeton: Princeton University Press, pp 245–56.

Mundy, M, 'Women's Inheritance of Land in Highland Yemen (1979) V *Arabian Studies* 161.

Murphy, W T, Roberts, S and Flessas, T, *Understanding Property Law*, 2004, London: Sweet & Maxwell.

Murray, T, 'The history, philosophy and sociology of archaeology: the case of the Ancient Monuments Protection Act (1882)', in Pinsky, V and Wylie, A (eds), *Critical Traditions in Contemporary Archaeology*, 1989, Cambridge: Cambridge University Press, pp 55–67.

Muthoni Wanyeki, L (ed.), *Women and Land in Africa: Culture, Religion and Realizing Women's Rights*, London and Cape Town: Zed Books Ltd and David Philip Publishers.

Nader, L and Yngvesson, B, 'On studying the Ethnography of Law and its Consequences', in Honigman, J (ed.), *Handbook of Social and Cultural Anthropology*, 1973, Chicago: Rand McNally, pp 883–921.

Naffine N, *Feminism and Criminology*, 1997, Cambridge: Polity Press.

Nasir, J J, *The Islamic Law of Personal Status*, 2002, The Hague, London, New York: Kluwer Law International.

Nast, H J and Pile, S (eds), *Places Through the Body*, 1998, London and New York: Routledge.

National Audit Office, *More Than A Roof: Progress in Tackling Homelessness*, HC 286 Session 2004–2005, 2005, London: The Stationery Office.

Nead, L, *Victorian Babylon: People, Streets and Images in Nineteenth-Century London*, 1993, New Haven: Yale University Press.

Neave, M, 'Living Together – Legal Effects of the Sexual Division of Labour in Four Common Law Countries' (1991) 17 *Monash University Law Review* 14.

Neligan, D, *Report of Specialist Health Visitor for Travelling Families* May 1990-November 1992, 1993, Bristol: United Bristol Healthcare NHS Trust.

Nelson, S M, *Gender Archaeology: Analyzing Power and Prestige*, 2nd edn, 2004, Walnut Creek: Altamira Press.

Neocleous, M, *The fabrication of social order: a critical theory of police power*, 2000, London: Pluto Press.

Netting, R M, *Smallholders, Householders: Farm Families and the Ecology of Intensive, Sustainable Agriculture*, 1993, Stanford: Stanford University Press.

New South Wales Law Reform Commission, Discussion Paper 44 *Review of the Property (Relationships) Act 1984 (New South Wales)*, 2002.

Niner, P, *Local Authority gypsy/Traveller Sites in England*, 2003, Birmingham: Centre for Urban and Regional Studies, University of Birmingham.

Niner, P, *Counting Gypsies and Travellers: A Review of the Gypsy Caravan Count System*, 2004, Birmingham: University of Birmingham.

Nyamu-Musembi, C, 'Are Local Norms and Practices Fences or Pathways? The Example of Women's Property Rights', in An-Naím, A A (ed.), *Cultural Transformation and Human Rights in Africa* 2002, London and New York: Zed Books Ltd, pp 126–50.

O'Donovan, K, *Sexual Divisions in Law*, 1985, London: Weidenfeld and Nicholson.

O'Dwyer, M, *Irish Travellers Health Access Project Draft Report*, 1997, London: Brent Irish Advisory Service, Irish Travellers Project.

Odgaard, R, 'Scrambling for Land in Tanzania: Processes of Formalisaiton and Legitimisation of Land Rights', in Tor, A and Lunds, C (eds), *Securing Land Rights in Africa*, 2003, London and Portland: Frank Cass, pp 71–88.

Office of the Deputy Prime Minister (ODPM), *Quality & Choice: A Decent Home for All – The Way Forward for Housing*, 13 December 2000.

Office of the Deputy Prime Minister (ODPM), *Implementing and Developing Choice-Based Lettings, A Guide to Key Issues*, March 2005.

OFSTED, *The Education of Travelling Children, A survey of educational provision for Travelling children*, 1996, London: Ofsted Publications Centre.

OFSTED, *Raising the attainment of minority ethnic pupils, School and LEA responses*, 1999, London: Ofsted Publications Centre.

Okely, J, *The Traveller-Gypsies*, 1983, Cambridge: Cambridge University Press.

Okely, J, 'Cultural ingenuity and travelling autonomy: not copying, just choosing', in Acton, T and Mundy, G (eds), *Romani Culture and Gypsy Identity*, 1997, Hatfield: University of Hertfordshire Press, pp. 188–203.

Okin, S M, *Justice, Gender and the Family*, 1989, New York: Basic Books.

Olsen, F, 'The Family and the Market: A Study of Ideology and Legal Reform' (1983) 96:7 *Harvard Law Review* 1497.

Ondaatje, M, *The English Patient*, 1993, London: Pan Books.

Oprea, A, *The Erasure of Romani Women in Statistical Data: Limits of Race versus Gender Approach*, 2003, American Romani Alliance, http://www.eumap.org.

Osborn, F J and Whittick, A, *New Towns: Their origins, achievements and progress*, 1977, London: Leonard Hill.

Parliamentary Culture, Media and Sport Committee, 'Protecting, preserving and making accessible our nation's heritage', 2006, http://www.parliament.uk/parliamentary_committees/culture__media_and_sport/cms051115.cfm (site accessed 15/02/06).

Pahl, J and Vaile, M, 'Health and Health Care among Travellers' (1998) 17:2 *Journal of Social Policy* 195.

Palmer, R, *Gendered Land Rights – Process, Struggle or Lost C(l)ause?*, 2002, http://www.Oxfam-org.uk/landrights/gendered.docu.

Parekh, B, *et al.*, *The Future of Multi-Ethnic Britain: The Report of the Commission on the future of multi-ethnic Britain, 2000, The Parekh Report*, London: The Runnymede Trust.

Parry, G, Van Cleemput, P, Peters, J, Moore, J, Walters, S, Thomas, K and Cooper, C, *The Health Status of Gypsies and Travellers in England: A report to the Department of Health*, 2004, Sheffield: University of Sheffield.

Parson, J, 'Cattle, Class, and State in Rural Botswana' (1981) 7 *Journal of Southern African Studies* 236.

Pavanello, M, 'The work of the ancestors and the profit of the living: some Nzema economic ideas' (1995) 65 *Africa* 36.

Pawson, H, Levison, D, Lawton, G, Third, H and Parker, J, *Local Authority Policy and Practice on Allocations, Transfers and Homelessness*, 2001, London: Department of Environment, Transport and the Regions.

Payne, G (ed.), *Land, Rights and Innovation: Improving Tenure Security for the Urban Poor*, 2002, London: Intermediate Technology Development Group Publishing.

Peters, P, 'Gender, Developmental Cycles and Historical Process: A Critique of Recent Research on Women in Botswana' (1983) 10:1 *Journal of Southern African Studies* 100.

Peters, P, 'Against the Odds' (1997) 17:2 *Critique of Anthropology* 189.

Peters, P, 'The Limits of Negotiability: Security, Equity and Class Formation in Africa's Land Systems', in Juul, D and Lond, C (eds), *Negotiating Property in Africa*, 2002, Portsmouth, NH: Heinemann, pp 45–66.

Peters, P, 'Paper on Beyond Embeddedness: A Challenge Raised by a Comparison of the Struggles over Land in African and Postsocialist Countries', 2003, Halle, Germany: International Conference on Changing Properties of Property, Max Planck Institute for Social Anthropology, July 2–4.

Petersen, G, 'Ponapean matriliny: production, exchange, and the ties that bind' (1982) 9 *American Ethnologist* 129.

Pinkstone, R, 'Using local government planning regulations to enhance young people's access to shopping center space', Conference Paper Australian Institute of Criminology, 2005, http://www.aic.gove.au/conferences/2005-cp/pinkstone.html.

Pitso, J W N and Carmichael, G A, 'Premarital Childbearing in Thamaga Village, Botswana' (2003) 20:2 *Journal of Population Research* 187.

Poewe, K, 'Matrilineal ideology: the economic activities of women in Luapula, Zambia', in Cordell, L and Beckerman, S (eds), *The Versatility of Kinship*, 1980, New York: Academic Press, pp 333–57.

Pollock, Sir F and Maitland, F W, *The History of English Law Before the Time of Edward I*, 2nd edn, 1898, Cambridge: Cambridge University Press.

Pospisil, L, *Kapauku Papuans and Their Law*, Yale University Publications in Anthropology, no. 54, 1958, New Haven, Conn.: Yale University Press.

Pottage, A, 'The Measure of Land' (1994) 57:3 *Modern Law Review* 361.

Pottage, A, 'The Originality of Registration' (1995) 15:3 *Oxford Journal of Legal Studies* 371.

Pottage, A, 'Instituting Property' (1998) 18 *Oxford Journal of Legal Studies* 331.

Pottage, A, 'Persons and things: an ethnographic analogy' (2001) 30:1 *Economy and Society* 112.

Pottage, A, 'Introduction: the fabrication of persons and things' in Pottage, A and Mundy, M (eds), *Law, Anthropology and the Constitution of the Social*, 2004, Cambridge: Cambridge University Press, pp 1–39.

Power, S, White, G and Youdall, D, *No Place to Learn: Homelessness and Education*, 1996, London: Shelter.

Powers, D S, 'The Islamic Inheritance System: A Socio-Historical Approach' in Mallat, C and Connors, J (eds), *Islamic Family Law*, 1993, London: Graham & Trotman, pp 27–9.

Powers, D S, 'The Islamic Family Endowment (Waqf)' (1999) 32:4 *Vanderbilt Journal of Transnational Law* 1167.

Powers, D S, *Law, Society, and Culture in the Maghrib, 1300–1500*, 2002, Cambridge: Cambridge University Press.

Prescott-Clarke, P, Clemens, S and Park, A, *Routes into Local Authority Housing: A Study of Local Authority Waiting Lists and New Tenancies*, 1994, London: HMSO.

Presdee, M, *Cultural Criminology and the Carnival of Crime*, 2000, London and New York: Routledge.

Probert, R, 'Land, Law and Ex-Loves' (2005) *Conveyancer and Property Lawyer* 168.

Public Services Ombudsman for Wales, *Housing Allocations and Homelessness: A Special Report by the Local Government Ombudsman for Wales*, 2006, Pencoed: Public Services Ombudsman for Wales.

Pugh-Smith, J and Samuels, J, *Archaeology in Law*, 1996, London: Sweet and Maxwell.

Rackham, O, *The History of the Countryside*, 1986, London: Weidenfeld and Nicholson.

Radijeng, G (2004) 'Customary Law and Equality: the Legal Status of Women in Botswana', unpublished PhD thesis, University of Oxford.

Radin, M J, *Reinterpreting Property*, 1993, Chicago: Chicago University Press.

Radin, M J, *Contested Commodities*, 1996, Cambridge: Harvard University Press.

Rappaport, E, 'The Halls of Temptation: Gender, Politics and the Construction of the Department Store in Late Victorian England' (1996) 35 *Journal of British Studies* 58.

Rappaport, E, *Shopping for Pleasure: Women in the Making of London's West End*, 2000, Princeton: Princeton University Press.

Reiss, E, 'Changes in Law', in Strachey, R (ed.), *Our Freedom and Its Results*, 1936, London: Hogarth Press, pp 77–116.

Rendell, J, 'Ramblers and Cyprians: Mobility, Visuality and the Gendering of Architectural Space', in Durning, L and Wrigley, R (eds), *Gender and Architecture*, 1996, Chichester: John Wiley & Sons Ltd, pp 135–54.

Richards, A, 'Some types of family structure amongst the Central Bantu', in Radcliffe-Brown, A R and Forde, D (eds), *African Systems of Kinship and Marriage*, 1950, London: Oxford University Press, pp 207–51.

Rickard, G, *Vagrants, Gypsies and Travellers in Kent 1572–1949*, 1995, Canterbury: the author.

Robbins, B, 'Introduction, the Public as Phantom', in Robbins, B (ed.), *The Phantom Public Sphere*, 1993, Minneapolis: University of Minnesota Press, pp vii–xxvi.

Robins, K, 'Prisoners of the City: Whatever Could a Postmodern City Be', Carter, E, Donald, J and Squires, J (eds), *Space & Place: theories of identity and location*, 1993, London: Lawrence and Wishart, pp. 303–30.

Roded, R, *Women in Islam and the Middle East*, 1995, London and New York: I. B. Tauris.

Rose, C M, *Property and Persuasion: Essays on the history, theory and rhetoric of ownership*, 1994, Boulder: Westview Press.

Rose, G, *Feminism and Geography*, 1993, Cambridge: Polity.

Rose, N, *Powers of Freedom: Reframing political thought*, 1999, Cambridge: Cambridge University Press.

Rosen, L, *The Justice of Islam*, 2000, Oxford, Oxford University Press.

Ross, A and Stockdale, A, 'Multiple environmental designations: a case study of their effectiveness for the Ythan Estuary' (1996) 14 *Environment and Planning C: Government and Policy* 89.

Rowlingson, K and MacKay, S, *Lone Parent Families: Gender, Class and State*, 2002, Upper Saddle River NJ: Prentice Hall.

Rowlingson, K and McKay, S, *The Growth of Lone Parenthood: Diversity and Dynamics*, 1998, London: Policy Studies Institute.

Ruxton, S, *Men, Masculinities and Poverty in the UK*, 2002, Oxford: Oxfam Publishing.

Sahibzada, M H, *Conceptualising an Islamic approach to poverty alleviation*, 1997, Islamabad: Institute of Policy Studies, Pakistan.

Said, E W, *Orientalism*, 1978, New York: Vintage Books.

Sait, S, 'Negotiating Customary & Islamic Land Law' (2003) 9:4 *UN HABITAT DEBATE* 7.

Sait, S and Lim, H, *Land, Law and Islam: Property and Human Rights in the Muslim World*, 2006, London: Zed Books.

Sale, K, *Dwellers in the Land: the Bioregional Vision*, 1985, San Francisco: Sierra Club Books.

Sarai Collective, *Sarai Reader 01: The Public Domain*, 2001, Delhi: The New Media Initiative.

Sarai Collective, *Sarai Reader 02: The Cities of Everyday Life*, 2002, Delhi: The New Media Initiative.

Şaul, M, 'Matrilineal inheritance and post-colonial prosperity in southern Bobo country' (1992) 27 *Man* (N.S.) 341.

Saunders, A, 'A Century of Ancient Monuments Legislation' (1983) 63 *The Antiquaries Journal* 11.

Save the Children Fund, *Denied a Future? The right to education of Roma/Gypsy and Traveller children in Europe*, 2001, volume 3: Western and Central Europe.

Schapera, I, *A Handbook of Tswana Law and Custom*, 1938, London: Oxford University Press for the International African Institute.

Schapera, I, 'Kinship and marriage among the Tswana', in Radcliffe-Brown, A R and Forde, D (eds) *African Systems of Kinship and Marriage*, 1950, London: Oxford University Press, pp 140–65.

Scott, E M (ed.), *Those of Little Note: Gender, Race, and Class in Historical Archaeology*, 1994, Tucson and London: University of Arizona Press.

Scott, Sir L, *Report of the Committee on Land Utilisation in Rural Areas 1941–2*, Cmd 6378, 1942, London: HMSO.

Sellar, D, 'Community Rights and Access to Land in Scotland', Proceedings from a Workshop on Old and New Commons, Centre for Advanced Study, Oslo, Norway 11th–13th March 2003 http://www.caledonia.org.uk/land/what%27s.htm (site accessed 21/08/06).

Sennett, R, *Flesh and Stone: The Body and the City*, 1994, London: Faber.

Shanks, M and Hodder, I, 'Processual, Postprocessual and Interpretive Archaeologies', in Hodder, I, Shanks, M, Alexandri, A, Buchil, V, Carman, J, Last, J, and Lucas, G (eds), *Interpreting Archaeology: Finding Meaning in the Past*, 1995, London: Routledge, pp 3–28.

Shatzmiller, M, 'Women and property rights in Al-Andalus and the Maghrib: social patterns and legal discourse' (1995) 2 *Islamic Law and Society* 220.

Sheilds, R, *Lifestyle Shopping*, 1992, London: Routledge.

Shelter, *Homelessness in the 1990s: Local Authority Practice*, 1994, London: Shelter.

Shelter, *Home Truths: A Response to the Consultation Paper*, 2004b, London: Shelter.

Shennan, S (ed.), *Archaeological Approaches to Cultural Identity*, 1994, London: Routledge.

Siddiqi, M, 'Mahr: Legal Obligation or Rightful Demand' (1995) 6 *Oxford Journal of Islamic Studies* 14.

Smart, C, *The Ties That Bind: Law, Marriage and Reproduction of Patriarchal Relations*, 1984, London and Boston: Routledge and Kegan Paul.

Smart, C, *Feminism and the Power of Law*, 1989, London: Routledge.
Smart, C, 'Deconstructing Motherhood', in Bortolaia Silva, E (ed.), *Good Enough Mothering? Feminist Perspectives on Lone Motherhood*, 1996, London: Routledge, pp 37–57.
Smith, L. 'Feminist issues in Cultural Resource Management', in du Cros, H and Smith, L (eds), *Women in Archaeology: A Feminist Critique*, 1993, Canberra: The Australian National University, pp 210–14.
Smith, L, 'Heritage management as postprocessual archaeology?' (1994) 68 *Antiquity* 300.
Smith, L, *Archaeological Theory and the Politics of Cultural Heritage*, 2004, London and New York: Routledge.
Smith, L, 'Heritage and its Intangibility', 7th Annual Cambridge Heritage Seminar, Intangible-Tangible Cultural Heritage. A Sustainable Dichotomy? May 2006 http:/ /www.arch.cam.ac.uk/heritage-seminar/abstracts.html (site accessed 15/05/2006).
Smout, C, *The Highlands and the Roots of Green Consciousness, 1750–1990*, 1990, Perth: Scottish Natural Heritage.
Soja, E, *Postmodern Geographies: The Reassertion of Space in Critical Social Theory*, 1989, London: Verso.
Solway, J, *People, Cattle and Drought in the Western Kweneng District*, 1980, Rural Sociology Report Series, no 16, Gaborone.
Sonbol, A El-A, *Women of Jordan*, 1996, Syracuse New York: Syracuse University Press.
Sørensen, M L S, 'Identifying or Including: Approaches to the engendering of archaeology' (1996) 21 *Kvinner i arkeologi I Norge* 51.
Sørensen, M L S, *Gender Archaeology*, 2000, Cambridge: Polity Press
SARPN, 'Africa Regional Poverty Network SARPN, Botswana Poverty Reduction Tender', *Newsletter No 4*, 2001, November.
Sparkes, P, A *New Land Law*, 2nd edn, 2003, Oxford and Portland, Oregon: Hart Publishing.
Spivak, G C, *In Other Worlds: Essays in Cultural Politics*, 1987, Oxford: Methuen.
Stauth, G, 'Women, Properties, and Migration: Access to Land and Local Conflicts in Rural Egypt' (1990) 3 *Zeitschrift Der Deutschen Morgenlandischen Gesellschaft* 32.
Steinhart, E I, 'Hunters, Poachers and Gamekeepers: Towards a Social History of Hunting in Colonial Kenya' (1998) 30 *Journal of African History* 247.
Stonewall Citizenship 21 Project, 'Profiles of Prejudice, Survey', MORI Press Release, 19 June 2001.
Strathern, M, *The Gender of the Gift*, 1988, Berkeley CA: University of California Press.
Strathern, M, *Reproducing the future: Anthropology, kinship and the new reproductive technologies*, 1992, Cambridge: Cambridge University Press.
Strathern, M, *Property, Substance and Effect: Anthropological Essays on Persons and Things*, 1999, London: Athlone Press.
Sugarman, D, 'A Hatred of Disorder': Legal Science, Liberalism and Imperalism', in Fitzpatrick, P (ed.), *Dangerous Supplements*, 1991, London: Pluto Press, pp 34–67.
Swadling, W J, 'The Law of Restitution' (1992) *All England Reports Annual Review* 254.
Sweetman, C, *Men's Involvement in Gender and Development Practice: Beyond Rhetoric*, 2001, Oxford, Oxfam Publishing.

Sykes, K, 'Paying a school fee is a father's duty: critical citizenship in central New Ireland' (2001) 28 *American Ethnologist* 5.

Take a Break, 'Down's Bride's Mother Says Why We Back Mum's Army', 16 March 2006.

Talin, E, *New Urbanism and American Planning*, 2005, London: Routledge.

*The Independent*, 7 March 2006.

Thomas, P and Campbell, S, *Housing Gypsies*, 1992, Cardiff: Cardiff Law School.

Thompson, M, *Rubbish Theory: The Creation and Destruction of Value*, 1979, Oxford: Clarendon Press.

Thompson, M, 'Constructive Trusts, Estoppel and the Family Home' (2004) *Conveyancer and Property Lawyer* 496.

Thomson, M, *Family Law in Scotland*, 1987, London: Butterworths.

Tibawi, *English Speaking Orientalists*, 1964, London: Luzac.

Tiley, J, 'The More-Than-Handy Husband' (1969) 27 *Cambridge Law Journal* 81.

Tilley, C, 'Archaeology as socio-political action in the present', in Pinsky, V and Wylie, A (eds), *Critical Traditions in Contemporary Archaeology*, 1989, Cambridge: Cambridge University Press, pp 104–16.

Tims, C and Mean, M, *People Make Places*, 2005, London: Demos.

Toft, S (ed.), *Compensation for Resource Development in Papua New Guinea*, 1997, Canberra: Law Reform Commission of Papua New Guinea/Australian National University.

Trigger, B, 'Romanticism, nationalism and archaeology' in Kohl, P and Fawcett, C (eds), *Nationalism, Politics and the Practice of Archaeology*, 1995, Cambridge: Cambridge University Press, pp 263–79.

Tucker, J, *Women in Nineteenth Century Egypt*, 1985, Cambridge: Cambridge University Press.

Ucko, P, 'Foreword', in Stone, P G and Mackenzie, R, *The Excluded Past: Archaeology in Education*, 1990, London and New York: Unwin Hyman, pp ix–xxiii.

UNICEF, *Children, Women and Development in Botswana: A Situational Analysis, A consultant's report compiled for the joint GOB/UNICEF Programme and Planning and Co-ordinating Committee*, 1989, Gaborone: UNICEF and Minstry of Finance and Development Planning.

UNICEF, *Children, Women and Development in Botswana: A Situational Analysis, Report prepared by Mandeleo (Botswana) for the Government of Botswana and UNICEF*, 1993.

United Nations Population Fund (UNFPA), *Gender Population and Development, Report on the High-Level Seminar for Chiefs and District Commissioners*, Divasse, L and Mookodi, G (eds), 1989, Gaborone: Macmillan Botswana.

Upton, R L, ' "Women have no tribe": connecting carework, gender and migration in an era of HIV/AIDS in Botswana' (2003) 17:2 *Gender and Society* 314.

Urry, J, 'Globalizing the Tourist Gaze', 2002, http://www.lancs.ac.uk/fss/sociology/research/restopic.htm.

USAID, *Promoting Effective Property Rights Systems for Sustainable Development*, 2002, Washington, DC: US Agency for International Development.

Van Cleemput, P, 'The Health Care Needs of Travellers' (2000) 82:1 *Archives of Disease in Childhood* 32.

Varley, A, 'Private or public: debating the meaning of tenure legalization' (2002) 26:3 *International Journal of Urban and Regional Research* 449.

Vostanis, P and Cumella, S, *Homeless Children: Problems and Needs*, 1999, London: Jessica Kingsley.

Voyce, M, 'Neoliberalism, Shopping Malls and the End of "Property"?', in Freeman, M (ed.), *Law and Popular Culture*, 2005, Oxford: Oxford University Press, pp 537–59.

Waddams, S, *Dimensions of Private Law*, 2003, Cambridge: Cambridge University Press.

Wadud, A, *Qur'an And Woman: Rereading The Sacred Text From A Woman's Perspective*, 1999, New York: Oxford University Press.

Wagner, R, 'Are there social groups in the New Guinea Highlands?' in Leaf, M (ed.), *Frontiers of Anthropology*, 1974, New York: D. Van Nostrand Company, pp 95–122.

Wahlin, L, 'Inheritance of land in the Jordanian Hill Country' (1994) 21:i *British Journal of Middle Eastern Studies* 57.

Walsh, K, *Representations of the Past: Museums and heritage in the post-modern world*, 1992, London and New York: Routledge.

Warner, M, *Alone of all her sex: the myth and cult of the Virgin Mary*, 1976, London: Weidenfeld and Nicholson.

Warren, K, 'A Philosophical Perspective on the Ethics and Resolution of Cultural Properties Issues', in Messenger, P (ed.), *The Ethics of Collecting: Whose Culture? Whose Property?*, 1989, Albuquerque: University of New Mexico Press, pp 1–25.

Waterson, M, ' "I want more than green leaves for my children": Some developments in Gypsy/Traveller education 1970–1996', in Acton, T and Mundy, G (eds), *Romani Culture and Gypsy Identity*, 1997, Hatfield: University of Hertfordshire Press, pp 127–49.

Waterton, E, 'We have trouble communicating: Intangible Heritage and the Dominant Heritage Discourse', 7th Annual Cambridge Heritage Seminar, *Intangible-Tangible Cultural Heritage: A Sustainable Dichotomy?*, May 2006.

Watson, S, 'The Public City', in Eade, J and Mele, C (eds), *Understanding the City*, 2002, Oxford: Blackwell, pp 49–65.

Watt, G, *Trusts and Equity*, 2003, Oxford: Oxford University Press.

Webster, L, *A Report for the Children's Society on the impact of the Criminal Justice and Public Order Act on the lives of Travellers and their children*, 1995, Bath: Children Society.

Weeramantry, C G, *Islamic Jurisprudence: An International Perspective*, 1988, London: Palgrave Macmillan.

Weiner, A, *Women of Value, Men of Renown*, 1976, Austin: University of Texas Press.

Weiss, B, 'Interpretation in Islamic Law: The Theory of Ijtihad' (1978) 38 *American Journal of Comparative Law* 203.

Welchman, L, *Beyond the Code*, 2000, The Hague: Kluwer.

Wertsch, J, 'The Multi-voicedness of Meaning', in Wetherell, M, Taylor, S and Yates, S (eds), *Discourse Theory and Practice a Reader*, 2001, London: Sage, pp 67–92.

Weyrauch, W O (ed.), *Gypsy Law: Romani Legal Traditions and Culture*, 2001, London: University of California Press.

Weyrauch, W O and Bell, M A, 'Autonomous Lawmaking: the case of "Gypsies" ', in Weyrauch, W O (ed.), *Gypsy Law: Romani Legal Traditions and Culture*, 2001, London: University of California Press, pp 11–87.

Whitehead, A and Tsikata, D, 'Policy Discourse on Women's Land Rights in Sub-

Saharan Africa: The Implications of the Re-Turn to the Customary' (2003) 3:1–2 *Journal of Agrarian Change* 67.

Whitley, D, 'New Approaches to Old Problems: Archaeology in Search of an ever elusive past', in Whitley, D (ed.), *Reader in Archaeological Theory: Postprocessual and cognitive approaches*, 1998, London and New York: Routledge, pp 1–30.

Williams, T, *Private Gypsy Site Provision*, 1999, Harlow, Essex: ACERT.

Willoughby, S, *Evaluation of London Gypsy and Traveller Unit*, 1996, London: CES.

Wilson, E, *The Sphinx in the City*, 1991, Berkeley: University of California Press.

Wilson, E, 'The Invisible *Flaneur*,' in Watson, S and Gibson, K (eds), *Postmodern Cities and Spaces*, 1995, Oxford: Blackwell, pp 59–79.

Wilson, M A, *Directory of Planning Policies for Gypsy Site Provision in England*, 1997, Bristol: Policy Press.

WLSA (Women and law in Southern Africa and Educational Trust), *A Critical Analysis of Women's Access to Land in the WLSA Countries*, 2001, Harare: WLSA Regional Office.

Wolpole, K, 'The age of leisure', in Corner, J and Gibson, K (eds), *Enterprise and Heritage*, 1991, London: Routledge, pp 137–50.

Wong, S, 'Constructive trusts over the family home: lessons to be learned from other commonwealth jurisdictions?' (1998) 18 *Legal Studies* 369.

Wong, S, 'When trust(s) is not enough: an argument for the use of unjust enrichment for home-sharers' (1999) 7:1 *Feminist Legal Studies* 47.

Wong, S, 'Property Rights for Home-sharers: Equity versus a Legislative Framework?' in Scott-Hunt, S and Lim, H (eds), *Feminist Perspectives on Equity and Trusts*, 2001, London: Cavendish, pp 133–51.

Wong, S, 'Trusting in trust(s): the family home and human rights' (2003) 11:2 *Feminist Legal Studies* 119.

Wong, S, 'Property regimes for Home-sharers: The Civil Partnership Bill and some Antipodean models' (2004) 26:4 *Journal of Social Welfare and Family Law* 361.

Wong, S, 'The Human Rights Act 1998 and the Shared Home: Issues for Cohabitants' (2005) 27:4 *Journal of Social Welfare and Family Law* 265.

Wong, S, 'Cohabitation and The Law Commission's Project' (2006) 14:2 *Feminist Legal Studies* 145.

Woolf, V, *A Room of One's Own and Three Guineas*, 2000, first published 1927, London: Penguin.

Worthington, S, *Personal Property Law Text and Materials*, 2000, Oxford: Oxford University Press.

Wright, R P (ed.), *Gender and Archaeology*, 1996, Philadelphia: University of Pennsylvania Press.

Wylie, A, 'The interplay of evidential constraints and political interests: recent archaeological research on gender', in Hays-Gilpin, K and Whitley, D (eds), *Reader in Gender Archaeology*, 1998, London and New York: Routledge, pp 15–35.

Wylie, A. 'Gender Theory and the Archaeological Record: Why Is There No Archaeology of Gender?', in Gero, J M and Conkey, M W (eds), *Engendering Archaeology. Women and Prehistory*, 1991, Oxford: Basil Blackwell, pp 31–54.

Young, A, *Imagining Crime*, 1996, London: Sage Publications.

Young, I M, *Justice and the Politics of Difference*, 1991, Princeton: Princeton University Press.
Young, I M, 'Communication and the Other: Beyond Deliberative Democracy', in Benhabib, S (ed.), *Democracy and Difference: Contesting the Limits of the Political*, 1996, Princeton: Princeton University Press, pp 120–35.
Young, M, *Oil palm for Milne Bay? A social feasibility study of a proposed oil palm project in Milne Bay Province*, 1981, Papua New Guinea Institute of Applied Social and Economic Research.
Zaid, A M, *The Islamic Law of Bequest*, 1986, London: Scorpion Publishing.
Zukin, S, *Landscapes of Power: From Detroit to Disney World*, 1991, Berkeley: University of California Press.

# Index